# THE REVOI

# THE REVOLTING SELF

## Perspectives on the Psychological, Social, and Clinical Implications of Self-Directed Disgust

*Edited by*

*Philip A. Powell, Paul G. Overton, and Jane Simpson*

KARNAC

First published in 2015 by
Karnac Books Ltd
118 Finchley Road
London NW3 5HT



British Library Cataloguing in Publication Data

A C.I.P. for this book is available from the British Library

ISBN-13: 978-1-78220-008-6

Typeset by V Publishing Solutions Pvt Ltd., Chennai, India

Printed in Great Britain

www.karnacbooks.com

*For all those who have ever felt revolting*

—Philip A. Powell

*To Kory and my four girls*

—Paul G. Overton

*For Marthy May; even though you are twelve years old,*
*we think of you …*

—Jane Simpson

# *CONTENTS*

# *ABOUT THE EDITORS AND CONTRIBUTORS*

**Thomas G. Adams**, MA, is a doctoral candidate at the University of Arkansas, USA, and is currently completing his predoctoral internship in clinical psychology at the Medical University of South Carolina and the Ralph H. Johnson VA Medical Center in Charleston, South Carolina. His research interests revolve around the unique and complementary roles of neurocognitive and emotional processes in the aetiology, maintenance, and treatment of obsessive-compulsive and related psychopathology. More recently, he has focused on the identification and manipulation of basic cognitive processes to augment and improve psychosocial interventions.

**Fahad Saeid. M. Alanazi**, MSc, is currently a doctoral candidate in clinical psychology at the University of Edinburgh, UK. He was post-graduate demonstrator then lecturer at King Abdullah College in Saudi Arabia. He holds a bachelor's degree in psychology from King Saud University and a master's degree in psychological health care from Naif Arab University. He trained as a clinical psychologist at Alamal Complex for mental health in Riyadh then Dammam.

**Christal L. Badour**, MA, is a doctoral candidate at the University of Arkansas, USA, and is currently completing her predoctoral internship in clinical psychology at the Medical University of South Carolina and the Ralph H. Johnson VA Medical Center in Charleston, South Carolina. Her research focuses on the roles of emotion and emotion regulation in the development and maintenance of psychopathology following traumatic events. She has a particular interest in the role of disgust in sexual trauma and post-traumatic stress disorder.

**Outi Benson**, MPhil, is currently an Honorary University Fellow at the University of Exeter Medical School and a freelance research consultant. Before this she was a Research Manager at the mental health charity SANE, London, UK. She is the chief investigator on three recent qualitative studies on suicide and self-harm.

**Zoë V. R. Boden**, PhD, is a Lecturer in Psychology at London South Bank University, UK. Her PhD was a hermeneutic-phenomenological exploration of men's experiences of guilt which explored the dimensions of temporality, narrative, and embodiment. Her research interests centre on feelings, emotions, and relationships in the context of mental health and wellbeing, including themes such as trust and connectedness.

**Charmaine Borg**, PhD, is a postdoctoral researcher and lecturer at the University of Groningen, the Netherlands, where she conducted her PhD studies following her MSc at the Institute of Psychiatry in London. Her main research interests are around disgust, sexual arousal, sexual pain, and sexual preferences. She uses various methods, including electromyography, fMRI, and behavioural measures, to answer her questions in this field.

**Jason A. Clark**, PhD, is a postdoctoral researcher in the Institute of Cognitive Science at Osnabrueck University, Germany. His work has centred primarily on the evolution of human emotions, including both empirical research and philosophical, conceptual, and ethical issues, with a special focus on shame, pride, and disgust. He also has ongoing interests in neuroplasticity, neuroethics, addiction, and mood disorders.

**Nathan S. Consedine**, PhD, is an Associate Professor at the University of Auckland, New Zealand, whose research concentrates on questions linking emotion/emotion regulation and health in developmentally diverse samples. He has published nearly a hundred scientific works in areas including screening, help-seeking, adherence, health behaviour, mindfulness, and compassion. He has held appointments in psychology at Long Island University, in consulting and clinical psychology at Teacher's College (Columbia), and in epidemiology at Columbia University Medical School. He returned to the University of Auckland in late 2009.

**Graham C. L. Davey**, PhD, is Professor of Psychology at the University of Sussex, UK. His research interests extend across mental health problems generally, and anxiety, disgust, and worry specifically. He has published over a hundred and forty articles in scientific and professional journals, and has written or edited sixteen books, including: *Psychopathology; Clinical Psychology; Applied Psychology; Complete Psychology; Worrying and Psychological Disorders; Managing Anxiety with CBT for Dummies*; and *Phobias: A Handbook of Theory, Research and Treatment*. He has served as President of the British Psychological Society, and is currently Editor-in-Chief of the *Journal of Experimental Psychopathology* and *Psychopathology Review*.

**Peter J. de Jong**, PhD, is Professor of Experimental Psychopathology and Chair of Clinical Psychology at the University of Groningen, the Netherlands. Following a transdiagnostic approach, his research focuses on cognitive-motivational mechanisms that may help explain the aetiology and course of various disorders, including eating disorders, depression, anxiety, and sexual dysfunctions. One of his main research lines concerns the role of disgust in psychopathology and its implications for treatment.

**John R. E. Fox**, D.Clin.Psy, PhD, is Consultant Clinical Psychologist with Barnet, Enfield, and Haringey Mental Health NHS Trust. In the past, he has worked as Senior Lecturer in Clinical Psychology at the University of Manchester, UK and as a Lecturer at Lancaster University. His research interests have focused on eating disorders, especially the role of emotions in understanding their potential aetiology and maintenance. This work has led to the development of the SPAARS-ED model (with Mick Power), and he is now looking at the application of this model to the treatment of eating disorders.

**Paul Gilbert**, PhD OBE, is head of the Mental Health Research Unit as well as Professor of Clinical Psychology at the University of Derby, UK. He has a degree in economics (Wolverhampton, 1973), masters in experimental psychology (Sussex, 1975), PhD in clinical psychology (Edinburgh, 1980), and a diploma in clinical psychology awarded by the British Psychological Society (1980). He was made a fellow of the British Psychological Society for contributions to psychological knowledge in 1993, and was president of the British Association for Cognitive and Behavioural Psychotherapy in 2003. After years of exploring the processes underpinning shame and its role in a variety of psychopathologies, his current research is exploring the neurophysiology and therapeutic effectiveness of compassion-focused therapy.

**Neesha Grange**, MSc, completed her undergraduate and postgraduate studies at the University of Manchester, UK. She undertook a study, as a part of her master's degree, that looked at eating disorder patient experiences of leaving or changing their inpatient treatment. This work left Neesha with an interest in this area, and she is hoping to gain a place on clinical psychology training in the near future.

**David Jones**, MA, MSc, is a psychoanalytic psychotherapist and therapy manager at Gartree Prison, Market Harborough, UK. He leads a new treatment facility for serious violent offenders with learning disabilities. Previously, he had worked at Millfields, a medium-secure unit and part of the DSPD (Dangerous and Severe Personality Disorder) project, and before that at HMP Grendon, the only prison in the UK to be devoted to therapy. He is the editor of two books, *Working with Dangerous People* (2004) and *Humane Prisons* (2006), and has written a number of papers, which recently have focused on disturbed dynamics within forensic organisations.

**Rebecca Lo Presti**, PhD, is a clinical psychologist working in New York. She utilises a cognitive-behavioural approach in addressing issues related to anxiety, depression, and obsessive-compulsive disorder. She has a particular interest in eating and weight disorders; much of her research has focused on body image and eating behaviours. Rebecca graduated with distinction from Boston University and earned her doctorate degree in clinical psychology from Fairleigh Dickinson University.

**Sarah A. McCambridge**, MSc, graduated from the University of Auckland, New Zealand, in 2010, after completing her BA in psychology and sociology, and went on to complete a postgraduate diploma in science (health psychology) in 2011. In 2012, Sarah achieved first-class honours for her master's thesis, which examined the effects of disgust and embarrassment on decisions related to sexual health care. She has also collaborated on other projects involving the investigation of disgust on health-related decision-making. Sarah is currently working clinically as a health psychologist with chronic pain patients at the Auckland Regional Pain Service (TARPS).

**Dean McKay**, PhD, is Professor of Psychology at Fordham University, USA, where he has been a member of the faculty for the Doctoral Training Program in Clinical Psychology for eighteen years. He is certified in cognitive-behavioural psychology from the American Board of Professional Psychology (ABPP), and currently serves on their board of directors. He is a past President of the Association for Behavioral and Cognitive Therapies (2013–2014). He is also on the Scientific Advisory Board of the International Obsessive-Compulsive Disorder Foundation (IOCDF), and is on the Scientific Council of the Anxiety and Depression Association of America (ADAA). His research primarily focuses on obsessive-compulsive disorder and related conditions, across all ages.

**Paul G. Overton**, PhD, is Professor of Neuroscience at the University of Sheffield, UK, and is currently the head of the Department of Psychology. The majority of his research focuses on the basal ganglia, a group of structures involved in action selection, cognition, and emotion. Although historically his work has been conducted using infrahuman species, his recent work has moved to include human subjects, particularly in relation to attention deficit hyperactivity disorder, Parkinson's disease, and disgust.

**Philip A. Powell**, PhD, is a research psychologist with an interest in discrete emotions and their unique effects on our psychological well-being, behaviour, and decision-making. He completed his PhD in 2013 on the topic of self-disgust and its link to depression. Philip is currently appointed as a postdoctoral Research Associate in the Institute for the Economic Analysis of Decision-Making (InstEAD) at the University of Sheffield, UK, and is an associate member of the International Society for Research on Emotion (ISRE).

**Michael J. Power**, DPhil, is a clinical psychologist who works for the NHS Lothian Trauma Service in Edinburgh, UK. In the past, he has worked at universities and hospitals in London, Tromsø, Birmingham, Lisbon, Beijing, and Milan. He is also currently an adviser to the World Health Organization on the measurement of wellbeing and quality of life. He is the founding editor of the journal *Clinical Psychology and Psychotherapy*.

**Donna Reeve**, PhD, is an honorary teaching fellow at the Centre for Disability Research (CeDR)/Division of Health Research at Lancaster University, UK. Her research and writing interrogates the phenomenon of psycho-emotional disablism and attempts to unpack the interconnections between disablism, impairment, and culture.

**Lisa M. Reynolds**, MSc, is a health psychologist whose research examines aspects of disgust, avoidance, and mindfulness, primarily in the context of colorectal cancer. She is currently completing a PhD at the Department of Psychological Medicine, University of Auckland, New Zealand, where her research includes experimental study of the moderating role of mindfulness on disgust-driven avoidance; and the investigation of a mindfulness-based intervention to address psychological distress and associated avoidant behaviour in cancer patients undergoing chemotherapy. Her research has been shaped by several years' clinical experience working with cancer patients at the Cancer Society, Auckland Division, and in private practice.

**Jane Simpson**, PhD, is a Senior Lecturer at the University of Lancaster, UK, with an interest in the relationship between cognition and emotion. Her interest in self-disgust arose from the clinical observation that addressing emotional issues in therapy was as important as trying to change cognitions. She also felt that some clients expressed such a visceral dislike of the self that it seemed different from shame, self-loathing, and other related constructs. She is currently Research Director on the Doctorate in Clinical Psychology at Lancaster University.

**Diego Vitali**, MSc, is a researcher and clinical psychologist, currently working as a freelance research consultant in London, UK. He has worked as a psychologist and researcher in psychopathology in Venice, Italy, and as a researcher in London with Barnet, Enfield, and Haringey Mental Health Trust (NHS). His interests include phenomenological psychopathology, quantitative and qualitative research applied within NHS contexts.

# FOREWORD

*Graham C. L. Davey*

Disgust is a pervasive emotion. We all probably experience some form of disgust on a daily basis, whether it be from encounters with primary disgust objects such as faeces, vomit, or mucus, which are characterised by their ability to elicit fear of oral incorporation or contamination, or with complex disgusts, consisting mainly of behaviours or activities that are considered to be socially or morally unacceptable. Unlike other common negative emotions such as fear, anxiety, and anger, disgust has had a relatively short history as a topic for intensive psychological and biological research, and it is interesting to trace the history of this research because it provides a background to why the study of self-disgust is so important at this time.

Disgust has a distinctive facial expression, distinctive behavioural manifestations (e.g., avoidance, the inhibition of oral incorporation), and a particular subjective experience (e.g., feelings of nausea and sickness), and it was these characteristics that initially drove researchers to try to understand the evolutionary significance of the emotion. The facial expression associated with disgust (i.e., wrinkled nose to prevent the intake of smells, and downturned corners of the lips to allow any contamination or poison to dribble out) was seen to be a clear manifestation of a food-rejection response; it appeared to be derived from the innate distaste reaction exhibited by newborn infants, and it was this function of disgust that was originally most widely researched. This function of "core" disgust served to prevent the spread of disease by limiting contact with potential germ-ridden stimuli, and served as an effective avoidance mechanism for the rejection of any stimuli that may act as vehicles for the spread of disease. However, the search for the contemporary functions of the disgust emotion did not end there. It became clear that the disgust emotion had also become linked to a wide variety of stimuli and events that might indirectly be related to the spread of illness and disease. One prominent example of this was the role of disgust in many animal phobias, and this gave rise to our own disease-avoidance model of animal phobias, in which we hypothesised that many common animal phobias were driven by disgust rather than fear. The reason for this was because many fear-relevant animals either were, or had in the past been, associated with the transmission of disease (e.g., rats and cockroaches), or possessed characteristics that resembled primary disgust elicitors (e.g., looked slimy, like snakes or reptiles, or resembled faeces, such as slugs and snails). This model even offered one explanation of why spider phobia was so widespread in Western cultures—because during the times of the great plagues in Europe, the spider had often been seen as a harbinger of disease.

However, disease avoidance is certainly not the sole function of the disgust emotion, and like most emotions, disgust has evolved derivative functions that have important social and communicative roles in the dissemination of cultural values. This is because strong negative emotions such as disgust provide a powerful means of transmitting negative affect and, as a consequence, influencing moral judgements. For example, the activities of groups that violate accepted social and moral values (e.g., paedophiles) are often labelled as "disgusting", and colloquialisms for faeces are used almost universally as a derogatory term. Endowing culturally unacceptable behaviours or attributes with disgust makes the event salient, helps to ensure internalisation, and therefore makes it more resistant to change. It is quite possible that a role for disgust in the defining of moral standards evolved very early on in the development of human culture, and recent research suggests that disgust increases the severity of moral judgements, harmless activities are viewed as potentially harmful if associated with disgust, morality and body comportment are mediated by disgust, and morality has close links with cleanliness and physical cleansing. A link between pathogen and moral disgust has even been identified in common neural mechanisms.

An obvious extension of the role of disgust in defining moral standards and communicating what is and is not socially acceptable is when this evaluative function of disgust is turned inward on the self. It has long been argued that disgust is an emotion that can be associated with more abstract triggers such as inferiority and debasement, physical or psychological deterioration, or turned inwards as a form of "self-disgust". In particular, the emotion of shame has historically often been associated with self-disgust—especially when the individual views themselves as possessing negative characteristics or being responsible for negative events. This latter factor may be an important one, because empirical studies have frequently found shame and disgust—especially self-disgust—to be closely related, especially in the context of anxious psychopathologies such as eating disorders and pain catastrophising.

The present book represents a much needed and detailed look at the phenomenon of self-disgust, and chapters examine the role of self-disgust in relation to physical functioning such as disability (Reeve), chronic physical health (Reynolds, McCambridge, & Consedine), and sexual dysfunction (de Jong & Borg); while other chapters are dedicated to the role of self-disgust in relation to psychological experiences and potential ensuing psychopathology, including the experience of rejection and betrayal (McKay & Lo Presti), traumatic experiences (Badour & Adams), depression (Alanazi, Powell, & Power), eating disorders (Fox, Grange, & Power), and self-harm and suicide (Benson, Boden, & Vitali). A chapter by Powell, Overton, and Simpson opens the book by providing some important theoretical insights into how self-disgust might be constructed and structured as an emotional experience, and two chapters by Jones and Gilbert explore how self-disgust might be related to other psychological characteristics such as contagion, hatred, and compassion. Finally, Powell, Overton, and Simpson provide some views on the future directions in research on self-disgust. The book offers some exciting new ideas and findings for a wide range of potential readers, including students interested in emotion, health, and psychopathology; researchers interested in new developments in the study of emotion and their application to the understanding and treatment of emotional disorders; and practitioners with professional interests in health, clinical psychology, and psychiatry.

There is no doubt that self-disgust is an important emotion that is experienced intensely by many individuals, and its effects are most likely to be negative ones in terms of both self-evaluation and the impact of this on the individual's mental health. In terms of understanding self-disgust, and as this volume attests, there is still much to be done. Some obvious empirical questions for the future include: What experiences and psychological processes lead to some people turning the evaluative function of disgust inwards onto their own physical and psychological characteristics? What is the relationship between self-disgust and other evaluative emotions such as shame and guilt? What role does self-disgust play in both the acquisition and maintenance of psychopathology symptoms? And, perhaps most importantly, what interventions can we develop that will help individuals to overcome the self-stigma inflicted by self-disgust?

# *PREFACE*

*Paul G. Overton, Philip A. Powell, and Jane Simpson*

Our capacity to acquire dysfunctional self-directed disgust reactions, or the phenomenon of "self-disgust", is a relatively novel topic for psychological enquiry, and—at least partly as a consequence of that—it is a concept that is shrouded in ambiguity. Hence, up to now, the "self-disgust" label has been used somewhat inconsistently, devoid of any real clarification. At the same time, and perhaps somewhat paradoxically, an increasingly large body of evidence now suggests that self-disgust may be critically involved in a range of health problems. As a consequence, we felt the time was right to seek to provide further clarification of what we believe to be a distinct and complex, disgust-based psychological phenomenon, and at the same time explore the psychological and clinical implications of self-directed disgust. To this end, in this volume we have assembled a series of chapters from leading experts that address certain key aspects of these issues.

## *Chapter One*

Self-disgust is attracting increasing recognition in the clinical domain, yet its theoretical grounding as a psychological construct has hitherto remained undeveloped and ambiguous. In this introductory chapter, with reference to the wider literature and our own research, we present in detail our conceptual framework of self-disgust as a unique emotional schema. Drawing on relevant evidence and prior theorising, we discuss how and when the essentially adaptive emotion of disgust can become maladaptive through acquisition as a response to particular features of the self. We illustrate how the psychological experience of self-disgust involves more than simply the felt basic emotion of disgust directed towards the self, and proceed to review explicitly some of the negative effects an enduring sense of self-disgust can have on an individual's mental health. Further, we critically consider the thorny issues of conceptual measurement, individual differences, and the relationship between self-disgust and other related constructs. In sum, our aim in this opening chapter was to introduce a developed theoretical model of self-disgust, which we hope will serve to ground further research and theoretical development on the topic.

## *Chapter Two*

Disgust towards both others and the self has been linked to negative outcomes in moral judgement and psychopathology. A growing number of authors have argued that such harmful outcomes are due to intrinsic features of the emotion itself, and that disgust has no positive role to play in morality or mental health. Here, Jason A. Clark offers an initial defence of disgust's virtues in both inter- and intra-personal (self-directed) sociomoral dynamics. He focuses on integrating work in social psychology and social neuroscience, comparing the values of cognitive and behavioural responses associated with anger and disgust, and emphasising the involvement of regions of the brain that are active both when we mentalise about others and when we mentalise about ourselves. Clark does not deny that disgust can be a highly damaging emotion, but instead argues that these instances are not characteristic of its ordinary operations. Hence, his claim is not that disgust is always morally or psychologically appropriate, but rather that (1) disgust can play a positive role in such contexts, and (secondarily) that (2) disgust is not unique in its ability to generate such negative outcomes, but rather has many unindicted emotional co-conspirators.

## *Chapter Three*

There has been little written within disability studies about the role of self-disgust in the lives of disabled people. Drawing on both psychological and sociological approaches, this chapter by Donna Reeve looks at the assumptions and realities of self-disgust in the lives of those whose "impaired" bodies and minds cause them to be labelled as "disabled" and, therefore, in the eyes of some, to be viewed as deviant and "disgusting". It has been argued that the emotion of disgust is largely responsible for maintaining the disability vs. non-disability binary and a social hierarchy whereby "normal" people are superior to those perceived to be impaired. This chapter shows how interpersonal and moral forms of disgust can be revealed in contemporary examples of psycho-emotional disablism, an attitude towards disability that has a negative impact on how a disabled person feels about themselves. In this chapter, Reeve discusses the relevance of self-disgust when considering the different ways in which disabled people manage and challenge internalised oppression. In addition, Reeve considers the experiences of disabled people who live with incontinence, an impairment that directly challenges the modernist ideal that demands bodies to be contained, clean, and free from contamination. She shows that rather than simply feeling self-disgust towards bodies that truly are unruly and leaky, over time these disabled people can develop alternative ways of being which provide more positive and healthy relationships between body and psyche than might otherwise be expected.

## *Chapter Four*

Studies of self-disgust have mostly concentrated on examining it in the context of mental health processes and outcomes; in this chapter, Lisa Reynolds and colleagues evaluate the implications self-disgust may have for physical health, specifically examining how it may be relevant as individuals adapt to chronic physical health conditions. After briefly reviewing evidence for disgust's relevance to health, the authors draw from evolutionarily inspired theories of disgust and disgust sensitivity, conceptualising self-disgust as a specific variant of disgust in which aspects of the physical or psychological self act as an elicitor. Following this characterisation, Reynolds and colleagues examine how disgust's evolved avoidance and withdrawal-promoting function(s) may lead to poor outcomes in physical health contexts, concentrating on two likely pathways. First, they evaluate the likelihood that self-disgust motivates avoidance of medical contacts, screenings, treatments, and side-effects because aspects of these processes entail being faced with undesirable aspects of the physical or psychological self. Second, and more speculatively, it is argued that because the emotional responses of the self are used when attempting to anticipate those of social others, self-disgust may increase estimations regarding the likelihood of disgust (and rejection) in others. Consequently, self-disgust may promote a psychologically self-protective dynamic in which possible or imagined social rejections are prevented by reducing engagement in medical treatment and by avoiding, delaying, and withdrawing from support networks. Using cancer as a model, Reynolds and colleagues evaluate the nature, place, and implications of self-disgust for adaptation in chronic ill health, concentrating on examining how self-disgust may promote withdrawal and avoidance in interpersonal, social, and intimate/sexual contexts.

## *Chapter Five*

Self-disgust is probably not the first thing that comes to mind when most people think about sex. In this chapter, Peter J. de Jong and Charmaine Borg argue that there might nevertheless be an important link between self-disgust and sexual experiences. Current models of sexual behaviour propose that sexual responses involve an interaction between sexual excitatory/inhibitory processes. From such a perspective, the generation of sexual responses may be compromised when sexual inhibition outbalances sexual excitation. Accordingly, relatively strong inhibitory tendencies may interfere with functional sexual behaviours and may give rise to sexual problems. The present chapter illustrates that self-disgust (and related preoccupations) might be important candidates in the inhibition of sexual responses. On the one hand, enhanced self-disgust might compromise pleasurable sexual functioning, whereas on the other (memories of) sexual behaviours of the self or of others might give rise to self-disgust. Accordingly, people may enter a self-perpetuating cycle in which enhanced self-disgust becomes an increasingly important feature of the self.

Current theories of disgust differentiate between three types of disgust: pathogen, sexual, and moral. In the first part of the chapter, de Jong and Borg discuss how each disgust subtype might give rise to particular types of sex-relevant self-disgust, outlining how self-disgust may serve as a strategy to distance the self from the desecrated, unworthy, or deplorable aspects of the self, in a way to preserve the integrity of the core self. In the second part of the chapter, the authors present an heuristic model to explain how enhanced self-disgust might contribute to the generation of sexual problems, and vice versa. Finally, the authors briefly address the potential clinical implications of the proposed interrelationships between self-disgust and sexual behaviours/experiences, and discuss some critical issues that call for further research.

## *Chapter Six*

The intersection of disgust and psychopathology has largely emphasised its role in disorders of avoidance, such as anxiety conditions. This line of inquiry has demonstrated that disgust is an important contributor to clinical phenomena. Further, research into the treatment of disgust shows it is a particularly resistant emotion to direct clinical intervention. In the experience of disgust, the primary components (core, animal reminder, and contamination) do not fully explain higher-order experiences of the emotion and how they intersect with other complex emotional states such as shame and guilt. The aim behind Dean McKay and Rebecca Lo Presti's chapter is to examine possible mechanisms that lead from basic disgust experiences to the higher-order complex emotional processes, including self-disgust. Recent findings suggest that moral disgust may unify these other emotional components, and may be critically involved in other psychopathology. The authors use specific examples to show how moral disgust (a) emerges from the basic components of disgust, and (b) may be implicated in complex psychological conditions such as body dysmorphic disorder, eating disorders, and post-traumatic stress disorder.

## *Chapter Seven*

A growing body of theoretical and empirical work suggests traumatic experiences involving feelings of violation, debasement, immorality, or impurity may be capable of eliciting a phenomenon termed "mental contamination", or the perception of internal dirtiness that persists despite repeated cleansing or washing. Traumatic events involving sexual victimisation have been specifically linked to heightened mental contamination. Within this context, it has been suggested that mental contamination may arise, at least in part, as a result of the internalisation of feelings of disgust associated with instances of sexual assault or abuse. Preliminary evidence further suggests mental contamination may relate to increased symptoms of post-traumatic stress. This chapter, by Christal L. Badour and Thomas G. Adams, provides an overview of the theory in this area, the existing empirical literature is reviewed, and several clinical implications and directions for future research are provided.

## *Chapter Eight*

This chapter, authored by Fahad S. M. Alanazi and colleagues, considers the importance of disgust as a critical emotion in depression. The available literature on disgust and depression is reviewed, and it is subsequently argued that the most important form of disgust in depression is when it comes to be focused on the self, particularly in the form of more complex emotional states such as shame and guilt, in terms of their derivation within a basic emotions approach (Power & Dalgleish, 2008). An aetiological model of depression (SPAARS) is presented that incorporates multilevel representation systems of emotion. Within this model, the authors propose that the depressive state is a direct result of the emotional coupling of sadness and self-disgust.

## *Chapter Nine*

It is, perhaps, surprising that research looking at the application of disgust to eating disorders has started only in the last ten or so years. Moreover, a number of authors have questioned the application of disgust to eating disorders, as some empirical evidence has suggested that general disgust is not specifically applicable to these particular conditions. In this chapter, written by John R. E. Fox and colleagues, it is argued that this is a conceptual shortcoming, as disgust should be thought of as being domain-specific, and disgust towards the self appears to be particularly salient for an eating disorder population. Although work in this field is very much in its infancy, this chapter includes a review of both the theoretical and the empirical literature of the application of self-disgust to eating disorders. The authors also consider some of the general models of emotion that have been applied to eating disorders and the pivotal role that disgust, including self-disgust, plays in these models (e.g., SPAARS-ED). A key feature of these models is that disgust becomes "coupled" with other emotions, such as anger and/or sadness, and this is regarded as a key emotional process in eating disorders. Fox and colleagues also consider these theories and research within the treatment of eating disorders, as it is argued that disgust is an often neglected emotion in clinical approaches to eating pathology.

## *Chapter Ten*

Self-criticism, self-punishment, and self-directed anger are known to be important in understanding acts of self-harm, but the role of self-disgust has yet to be explored in any detail. In this chapter, Outi Benson and colleagues combine analysis of first person testimonies on the experience of self-harming with a focused review of recent philosophical, psychological, and sociological literatures on disgust and self-disgust, to investigate the various ways in which these emotional experiences may be involved in self-harm.

In their chapter, Benson and colleagues distinguish three varieties of self-disgust: 1) experiences of the self as disordered, ill-fitting, or malfunctioning ("integral" self-disgust); 2) experiences of the self as worthless, hateful, or bad ("moral" self-disgust); and 3) experiences of the self as repulsive ("basic" self-disgust). They argue that integral self-disgust (i.e., a mass of emotions and thoughts experienced as "other", contaminating, and threatening to the integrity of the self) can in part acutely motivate, and be modulated by, self-harm; but moral and basic self-disgust appear to be suspended immediately prior to, and during, the act of harming. Instead, it is proposed that these two latter kinds of self-disgust may (re)surface *after* acts of self-harm—in response to other people's real or imagined negative responses—potentially contributing to an overwhelming emotional state and a vicious cycle where more self-harm follows.

## *Chapter Eleven*

While shame has rightly received attention in the psychotherapeutic literature, much less regard has been paid to disgust. Yet disgust can stimulate highly violent responses, both physical and emotional. In this chapter, David Jones argues that prejudice and violence are often linked with disgust reactions. This is examined using the concepts of splitting, projection, and introjection, which are defences concerned with the interplay between the deepest, most primitive parts of the mind (the instinctual location of disgust), and experience of and enactment within the external world. Clinical examples, some from forensic practice, are given to illustrate these processes at work. Furthermore, as disgust is a powerful force that produces unease at the very least, it is argued that the fear of contagion is as present in therapists and in the therapeutic space as elsewhere. If unnoticed, it can produce negative therapeutic effects. Jones suggests that the therapeutic stance of unbiased free association is not easy to achieve when deeply anxious parts of the self are approached, and proposes ways in which potentially damaging counter-transference effects can be moderated.

## *Chapter Twelve*

Self-criticism can take many forms and have different functions. This chapter, by Paul Gilbert, explores these with a focus on the forms and functions of self-disgust. Disgust evolved as an affect that motivates avoidance of potential disease or contaminates, often via sensory cues. It promotes the desire to expel, avoid, cleanse, and eradicate. However, disgust can also be an affect that is linked to other humans as a whole and focused primarily on out-groups and those seen as alien and a threat. Disease metaphors are often used to stimulate persecution and eradications (e.g., as in the Holocaust; "ethnic cleansing"). Contempt and hatred are then linked to disgust. Gilbert's chapter explores self-disgust from this evolutionary point of view, that individuals see parts of themselves as "alien and bad or diseased", with a wish to eradicate those aspects of self. In others words, people use the same psychology for relating to external others and internal aspects of self. The chapter also explores the roles of compassion in reducing the effects of disgust and promoting self-acceptance and integration.

## *Chapter Thirteen*

This chapter concludes the book. Selected unresolved issues are considered by the editors, with reference to certain points advanced in earlier chapters, as well as evidence contained in the wider literature. In considering the implications of the present work, an assortment of suggestions for further investigation on the topic of self-disgust is then presented, and a revised self-report measure of self-disgust is unveiled.

## *Acknowledgements*

Putting these chapters together has been a great pleasure for us, but we are aware that we owe a great debt of gratitude to the various contributors who have given their time to this work. We also owe thanks to colleagues who have been party to discussions on the issues in this book, but who are not explicitly referenced in the author list. Finally, we would like to express our thanks to Karnac Books for their faith in our ability to deliver this volume and for their understanding when our deadlines (occasionally) needed refining.

CHAPTER ONE

# An introduction to the revolting self: self-disgust as an emotion schema

*Philip A. Powell, Jane Simpson, and Paul G. Overton**

> Heaven only knows how hard I have tried to make a decent creature out of myself, but my vileness is uncontrollable … I am without medicine, a big, fat, stupid creature, without health or strength, and I am disgusted with myself.
>
> —*Talbot & Ellis*, 1896, p. 343

Boasting somewhat humbler origins as a mechanism of disease avoidance (Curtis, Aunger, & Rabie, 2004; Oaten, Stevenson, & Case, 2009), the human disgust response has matured considerably throughout biological and sociocultural evolution, into its current multifaceted and broader form. Modern theories of disgust depict a heterogeneous emotional construct, with multiple elicitors spanning the sociocultural environment and producing qualitatively diverse response patterns (Simpson, Carter, Anthony, & Overton, 2006). Anchored around a shared function of avoidance and/or rejection, contemporary disgust elicitors include a range of undesirable physical

* This work was funded by the Howard Morton Trust, Sheffield, UK. The authors would like to thank Dr. Joshua Tybur for his comments on an earlier version of this chapter.

attributes, certain animals and their secretions, decaying or spoiled organic material, unsanitary environments, atypical sexual practices, particular sociomoral violations, and immoral character traits (Rozin, Haidt, & McCauley, 1999). Although substantial cross-cultural consensus exists regarding what constitutes a repugnant entity, there is also notable sociocultural variation, particularly concerning deviations from sociomoral norms (Elwood & Olatunji, 2009). Thus, while we appear predisposed to acquire adaptive disgust reactions to a core set of stimuli (i.e., those signalling potential pathogen presence; Curtis & Biran, 2001), the acquisition of a full disgust-eliciting repertoire is advantageously flexible, readily shaped by sociocultural learning (Rozin, Haidt, & McCauley, 1999; Sawchuk, 2009). The evolutionarily adaptive implications of a malleable disgust system are clear, as the sociocultural input equips a developing organism for biological survival and social success under the conditions of the particular environment into which they emerge. Accordingly, the functional disgust response can be construed broadly as an acquired emotional gauge of that which is not acceptable within an individual's sociocultural surroundings (Power & Dalgleish, 2008).

As with all adapted systems, including the full range of human emotions (Power & Dalgleish, 2008), the existence of evolved function coincides with the potential for dysfunction, and the human disgust response represents no exception. Dysfunctional disgust reactions can arise for at least three reasons, which are not necessarily mutually exclusive. First, people may experience too much, or too little, disgust in response to particular kinds of evolutionarily adaptive and prototypical disgust stimuli (Haidt, McCauley, & Rozin, 1994). A heightened propensity to react to common disgust elicitors has been associated with a number of anxiety disorders (Olatunji & McKay, 2007), and may be particularly detrimental in certain health contexts (e.g., Reynolds, Consedine, Pizarro, & Bissett, 2013). Conversely, a muted disgust response may be associated with the poorer regulation of certain behaviours, such as food consumption (Houben & Havermans, 2012). Second, an individual may find the disgust experience itself particularly aversive, and thus evaluate it as especially negative and distressing (van Overveld, de Jong, Peters, Cavanagh, & Davey, 2006). An increased sensitivity to disgust is theoretically separable from an enhanced propensity for disgust, and the two demonstrate unique links with psychopathology (Davey, 2011). Finally, learned disgust reactions may be acquired and/or generalised to certain stimuli, which are not considered functional or adaptive (Powell, Simpson, & Overton, 2013). Of particular relevance is the idea that this can include certain features of the self (Power & Dalgleish, 2008). While most research has centred on exploring the maladaptive outcomes of an exaggerated propensity and sensitivity to disgust, it is the latter route to dysfunction that constitutes the focus of the current chapter; namely, our capacity to acquire dysfunctional self-directed disgust reactions, or the phenomenon of self-disgust.

As a relatively novel topic for psychological enquiry, the preceding literature on self-disgust has culminated in a concept that is shrouded in ambiguity. Recent publications have conceptualised self-disgust as a negative personality trait (Olatunji, David, & Ciesielski, 2012), as the basic emotional experience of disgust oriented toward the self (Overton, Markland, Taggart, Bagshaw, & Simpson, 2008), as theoretically identical to the self-conscious emotion of shame (Power & Dalgleish, 2008), and as a unique self-conscious emotion *per se* (Roberts & Goldenberg, 2007). Moreover, the term is often employed in the literature as a generic synonym for self-hatred or contempt (e.g., Green, Moll, Deakin, Hulleman, & Zahn, 2013). Hence, the "self-disgust" label has been used somewhat inconsistently, devoid of any real clarification. While the aforementioned definitions may capture some essence of the concept, we maintain that as isolated sketches they insufficiently characterise it as the distinct and complex, disgust-based psychological phenomenon that it is. Thus, in the face of increased research attention (e.g., Overton et al., 2008), it is our assertion that the theoretical grounding of self-disgust has hitherto lingered underdeveloped. With the aspiration of filling this nauseating void, in the present chapter we outline our conceptual framework for self-disgust as a unique cognitive-affective construct, or emotion schema. We begin by tackling the ultimate and more proximal origins of self-directed disgust, before advancing our schematic conceptualisation. Following this, some of the proposed theoretical links between self-disgust and other emotional and cognitive phenomena are examined. We proceed with a discussion of conceptual measurement, and the task of quantifying individual differences in self-focused revulsion. Lastly, we close with a brief review of the implications a lasting sense of self-disgust may have for mental wellbeing.

## *The origins of a repulsive self*

At the most general level, we theorise dysfunctional self-disgust as a maladaptive and persistent, self-focused generalisation (or internalisation) of the otherwise adaptive disgust response. This process is facilitated by the evolutionary emergence of a flexible disgust system and complex human self-representation. That is to say, in so much as a generalisable disgust repertoire that is amenable to sociocultural learning confers evolutionary advantage, it also allows for particular individuals (with certain characteristics, relevant learning histories, and the capacity for self-to-self appraisals) to acquire maladaptive disgust reactions towards aspects of themselves (i.e., by learning that certain self-attributes are physically and/or socially repugnant). At its core, then, self-disgust is inescapably related to a socioculturally determined index of what is repulsive, and follows when (certain aspects of) the self are perceived to feature within this (Powell, Simpson et al., 2013). Thus, parts of the self may come to elicit disgust either through being present as an individual's learned repertoire of disgust elicitors expands to encompass them, or by their acquisition (e.g., via developmental, attributional, or incidental pathways) triggering a preformed disgust response. For the present discussion, it matters not whether a person is explicitly aware of what repulses them (cf. Rusch et al., 2011), and the disgust reaction need not be consciously or appraisal-driven; the involvement of other more automatic mechanisms, including associative and conditioning routes, is acknowledged (see Power & Dalgleish, 2008). What is integral is that the elicitor is perceived as pertaining to the self, and elicits a response characteristic of disgust (i.e., involving congruent emotional, cognitive, behavioural, and physiological elements; Olatunji & Sawchuk, 2005; Rozin & Fallon, 1987).

While many features that are perceived as being a part of the self may elicit disgust and revulsion under certain conditions, it is important to emphasise that, much like externalised disgust, we do not appraise all self-directed disgust reactions as dysfunctional by their nature. For instance, the experience of disgust in response to a feature of the self that is perceived as transient or cleansable (e.g., a physically dirtied body part) may indeed be functionally adaptive (e.g., Curits, Danquah, & Aunger, 2009). Equally, disgust to a part of self that is not considered important to overall self-image is less likely to have maladaptive consequences. However, if the disgust reaction is oriented toward an attribute of the self that makes a significant contribution to an individual's enduring self-concept, and is perceived as relatively consistent, uncleansable, or difficult to alter (e.g., an individual's body weight, recurrent unwanted sexual thoughts, etc.), then the prolonged or repeated nature of that disgust response is hypothesised to be maladaptive (Powell, Simpson et al., 2013). This enduring self-disgust can be considered a dysfunctional by-product or "side effect" of the adaptive disgust system. Hence, our working conceptualisation of self-disgust, as a dysfunctional psychological phenomenon, involves an enduring (or repetitive) disgust reaction elicited by particular aspect(s) of the self, which are deemed significant to an individual's sense of self, and appraised as relatively constant and/or not easily changeable.

The potential for a persistent feature of the self to acquire any genuine disgust-provoking status is constrained by our evolved predisposition to develop disgust responses to certain types of stimuli (Curtis & Biran, 2001), and the operationalisation and transmission of disgust in relation to certain kinds of societal and moral norms (Rozin, Lowery, Imada, & Haidt, 1999). Inherent in the acquisition of a self-disgust response is an explicit and/or implicit appraisal of the self, or a feature of the self, as a repulsive object to others in the wider sociocultural group. Accordingly, people are expected to report disgust responses to particular aspects of themselves disproportionately, in a manner that reflects that which elicits disgust in their extended sociocultural environment. In particular, this includes certain physical attributes that mimic the signs of infectious disease (e.g., acne, being overweight or asymmetrical; Oaten, Stevenson, & Case, 2011), signals of poor reproductive quality (i.e., unattractiveness; Tybur, Lieberman, Kurzban, & DeScioli, 2013), and characteristics that defile certain disgust-relevant sociomoral rules, such as those associated with the moral domain of purity and divinity (e.g., promiscuity; Horberg, Oveis, Keltner, & Cohen, 2009; Rozin, Lowery et al., 1999), or those that involve some perceived violation of an idealised body border (e.g., scarification; Gutierrez & Giner-Sorolla, 2007). It is also worthy of note that the disgust system is advantageously fine-tuned to make more false alarms (i.e., type one errors) than misses (i.e., type two errors; Tybur et al., 2013), and so certain associations, generalisations, and benign attributes that appear to share the features of abhorrent stimuli can also be disgust-inducing.

As yet, two overarching categories of self-disgust have been theoretically delineated in the literature; namely, those with a physical basis and those concerned with individuals' characterological or behavioural traits (Overton et al., 2008). These two classes of elicitor appear to be highly related and can be thought of as hierarchically nested within a person's overall self-concept. Some of our recent unpublished work using the Self-Disgust Scale (SDS; Overton et al., 2008; see Quantifying Self-Disgust, this chapter) has yielded correlations of $r_s(462) = .72$, $p < .001$ and $r_s(319) = .70$, $p < .001$, between the physical and characterological domains of self-directed disgust. Therefore, although people may experience several differentiable sources of self-disgust, the strong association between physical and psychological traits as elicitors of self-oriented revulsion suggests a tendency for them to co-occur (Powell, Overton, & Simpson, 2014). The precise ways in which these different kinds of elicitor may contribute and interact within an overall sense of disgust for the self are at present unclear, but under certain circumstances physical and behavioural sources of disgust can be intimately related (e.g., visible infection and poor hygiene behaviour; Curtis & Biran, 2001). Of course, individuals may report disgust solely with their physical appearance or certain psychological traits (Powell, Overton et al., 2014), but an appraisal of the entire self as an object of repugnance is likely to be most detrimental to overall psychological wellbeing.

The actual proximal factors that may contribute to the emergence of self-disgust have not yet been systematically charted, but are likely to involve a variable combination of an individual's characteristics (e.g., specific attributes that are more or less likely to elicit disgust), temperament, and other underlying dispositional traits, the particular surrounding sociocultural environment, and personal learning (and rearing) experiences. Power and Dalgleish (2008; see also Siegal, Fadda, & Overton, 2011) have hypothesised that feelings of self-disgust may be most likely to take root in childhood. Indeed, there is preliminary qualitative data to suggest self-disgust may be particularly likely to surface throughout childhood and adolescence (Powell, Overton et al., 2014). This period corresponds with a time of stronger sociocultural influences and the emergence of a more complex, abstract, and fully ideational disgust response (Rozin & Fallon, 1987; Sawchuk, 2009). Nevertheless, we maintain that there exists a potential to develop dysfunctional self-directed disgust reactions at any age. The primary contributory factor in adulthood, though, is more likely to be a specific change in the self (e.g., due to bodily or psychological trauma, weight gain, etc.), than an explicit alteration in the repertoire of stimuli that elicits disgust.

Interestingly, we have observed small to moderate correlations between reports of self-disgust (as indexed by the SDS; Overton et al., 2008) and common measures of trait propensity to externally oriented disgust. These include: $r(109) = .25$, $p < .01$ (Overton et al., 2008) with the Disgust Sensitivity Scale (DSS; Haidt et al., 1994), and unpublished correlations of $r_s(462) = .13$, $p < .01$ with the Disgust Scale-Revised (DS-R; Olatunji, Williams, Tolin et al., 2007), and $r_s(290) = .31$, $p < .001$ with the Propensity subscale of the Disgust Propensity and Sensitivity Scale-Revised (DPSS-R; van Overveld, de Jong, Peters, Cavanagh et al., 2006). A larger coefficient was recorded when a more general, or domain-independent measure of disgust propensity (i.e., the DPSS-R; van Overveld, de Jong, Peters, Cavanagh et al., 2006) was employed, rather than a scale indexing disgust responding to a set of precise external scenarios (i.e., the DS-R; Olatunji, Williams, Tolin et al., 2007). Thus, it could be posited that an underlying non-specific tendency to experience revulsion may act as an antecedent to the acquisition of self-disgust, but such a hypothesis requires empirical testing. Irrespective of the results, a trait proneness to disgust can only be considered a contributory factor at best. A trait propensity for disgust must necessarily be combined with other proximal precipitants to produce self-disgust, the most notable of which include an individual's specific characteristics and learning history.

In conjunction with the supposed greater odds for self-disgust in those who possess characteristics likely to elicit disgust at a wider societal level (e.g., physical deformities, paedophilic tendencies), certain kinds of social learning experiences may be particularly likely to influence the emergence of self-disgust. These include: exposure to disgust-based criticism (e.g., "you smell like shit", "you make me feel sick"), particularly from valued others and family members; the internalisation of others' disgust reactions (e.g., expressions of revulsion or avoidance), which are perceived as consistent with the self as an object of abhorrence; and negative comparisons with the way others look, function, and behave (Powell, Overton et al., 2014). Furthermore, there appears to be a link between reported childhood maltreatment, including sexual and emotional abuse, and the presence of self-disgust. In unpublished work, we have observed a correlation of $r_s(462) = .42$, $p < .001$ between the SDS (Overton et al., 2008) and Child Abuse and

Trauma Scale (CATS; Sanders & Becker-Lausen, 1995). Evidently, any sociocultural factors that do contribute to the emergence of self-disgust will be influenced by certain biases in appraisal and perception caused by the existence of higher-order cognitive-affective processes. Suitably, then, the idea of self-disgust as a complex schematic construct forms our next topic for discussion.

## *Self-disgust as an emotion schema*

Given the inseparable interplay between felt emotion and higher-order cognitive processes in humans (Power & Dalgleish, 2008), it is insufficient to superficially define self-disgust as repetitive or perpetual episodes of the basic emotion of disgust elicited by the self. Instead, we advocate the concept of "emotion schema", as advanced by Carroll Izard (e.g., Izard, 2007, 2009), as the most apposite descriptive tool to characterise self-disgust. Emotion schemas represent dynamic emotion-cognition interactions, which arguably constitute the most common emotional experiences after early development (Izard, 2007, 2009). Proposed to appear typically during childhood, emotion schemas result from learned association, and represent the culmination of reciprocal, nonlinear interactions between perception, emotion, appraisals, and higher cognition (Izard, 2007). The feeling component of the emotion schema may be derived from an intrinsic pre-existing basic emotion (in this case, disgust), while the associated cognitive content is seen as fundamentally modifiable. The link between the basic feeling component and other complex cognitive processes contributes to the repetitive or perpetual duration of the schema, which could also be construed as a type of emotion trait (Izard, 2007). Consequently, as a cognitive-affective structure, emotion schemas can endure more or less indefinitely (Izard, 2009). They are theorised to have a fluctuating but continual influence on action and the way information is perceived, and can be activated by certain environmental triggers, thoughts, memories, appraisals, and other non-cognitive processes (Izard, 2007, 2009).

Utilising Izard's (e.g., 2007, 2009) theoretical framework, we propose that the maladaptive psychological phenomenon of self-disgust is best theorised as an emotion schema, involving dynamically interacting disgust-based feeling and cognitive components of which the object is (some feature of) the self. As an emotion schema, self-disgust could also be conceptualised as nested within a broader and more general disgust schema, where the cognitive and learned components have expanded (through sociocultural input) to include an enduring self-aspect as a dysfunctional element. We postulate the emotional or feeling part of the schema to be qualitatively similar to the basic emotional experience of disgust (Izard, 2007). However, as the disgust response is generally considered to be heterogeneous in adulthood (Simpson et al., 2006), self-disgust may exhibit a more elaborate profile and/or share a greater likeness to a complex disgust domain (e.g., sociomoral disgust, Simpson et al., 2010). The cognitive and higher-order content of the self-disgust schema is proposed to involve a lasting appraisal of (some feature of) the self as repulsive, which influences how further information is processed. Such an appraisal is not expected to be permanently in subjective consciousness, but when active may be evident in specific negative cognitions and beliefs (e.g., "my body is revolting", "the way I act makes me feel sick"). Indeed, some of our recent phenomenological work on self-disgust supports the idea of an enduring disgust-based orientation towards physical and behavioural aspects of the self (Powell, Overton et al., 2014). Moreover, complementary longitudinal data suggests that the trait element of self-disgust (as measured by the SDS; Overton et al., 2008), is highly stable over a twelve-month period (Powell, Simpson et al., 2013).

Our schematic model of self-disgust (Figure 1) assumes a largely reciprocal interaction between state and trait cognitive-affective elements, which ultimately result in a dysfunctional, enduring disgust-based orientation towards the self. During the early stages of an emerging self-disgust schema, initial reactionary or state-like disgust responses to (some lasting feature of) the self are hypothesised, which incorporate the cognitive, physiological, and behavioural aspects congruent with experiencing the basic emotion of disgust (e.g., Olatunji & Sawchuk, 2005). If the elicitor and disgust appraisal remain intact, then these state disgust reactions are posited to become dysfunctional, due to repeated exposure to the eliciting stimuli (which may have expanded from the original elicitor to encompass learned associations, generalisations, and other cognitive elements, such as thoughts, memories, etc.). Moreover, as a result of recurrent disgust responses, the elaborated cognitive content of the schema facilitates a more lasting, trait-like cognitive-affective orientation to the self, or some enduring and important aspect of the self, as an object of repugnance. In turn, through its top-down effect

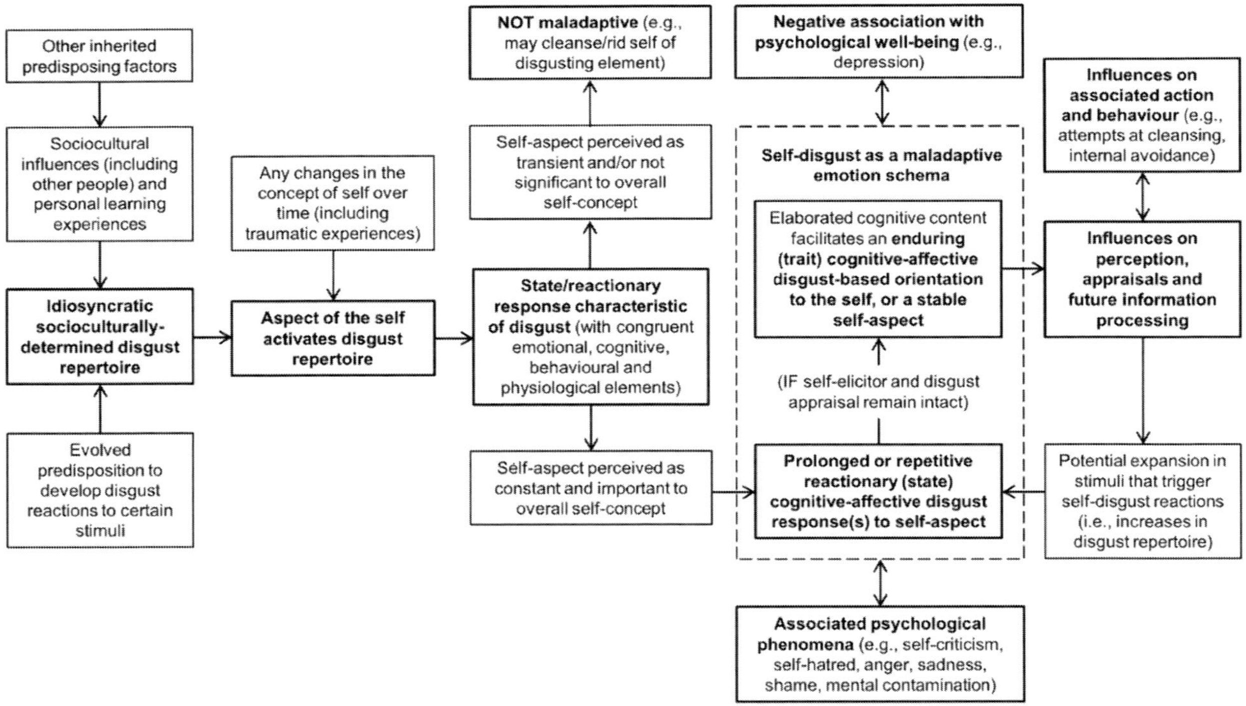


Figure 1. Illustrative diagrammatic model of self-disgust as an emotion schema.

on perception, thoughts, and appraisals, this trait sense of disgust facilitates more frequent self-focused reactionary disgust responses (i.e., in response to particular triggers that are perceived as consistent with the developing schema).

The phenomenological experience of self-disgust has been described as incorporating state and trait elements, with participants reporting a perceptual distinction between the two in terms of their subjective qualities (Powell, Overton et al., 2014). From these initial qualitative data, the state and situation-specific responses have been typically described as more emotionally intense, embodied, and engendered through identifiable sources (e.g., particular internal thoughts or appraisals, sudden bodily awareness, etc.). By contrast, participants also referred to a trait and global, more muted background sense of disgust for the self, which was ever-present, influenced their everyday lives, and was described as a "default" or "norm" (Powell, Overton et al., 2014). These data fit with the interpretation of self-disgust as a schematic construct that is enduring and influences the processing of future information. Furthermore, consistent with the idea of a modifiable self-disgust schema, participants identified some overall temporal change in their experiential sense of disgust for the self. Nevertheless, since they emerged, the cognitive-affective components of self-disgust seemed to persist, in some form, over time.

The presence of an enduring self-disgust schema has some notable ramifications, not least of which are detrimental effects on an individual's mental wellbeing, which will be discussed in more detail later in the chapter (see Psychological Implications of an Abhorrent Self, this chapter). The typical action tendency associated with disgust is one of rejection and avoidance (Rozin, Haidt, & McCauley, 1999). However, the successful execution of such behaviour is impaired when the stimulus producing disgust is internal or a part of the self; an enduring self-elicitor cannot be as easily physically and/or psychologically escaped as a typical external elicitor. That being said, individuals exhibiting self-disgust may engage in some degree of evasion, such as avoiding touching or looking at themselves (e.g., Espeset, Gulliksen, Nordbo, Skarderud, & Holte, 2012), masking aspects they perceive as abhorrent, and engaging in cognitive distraction techniques (Powell, Overton et al., 2014; Rachman, 1994). As with an externally elicited disgust response, such avoidance may inadvertently maintain the disgust reaction (or its intensity) through negative reinforcement. Moreover, once acquired, disgust responses may be particularly difficult to unlearn (Olatunji, Forsyth, & Cherian, 2007; Sawchuk, 2009), and individuals may be left with an unfulfilled desire to rid the self of the bits that they find revolting (Powell, Overton et al., 2014).

As perceived objects of disgust, individuals with an established self-disgust schema necessarily appraise themselves, or aspects of themselves, as repulsive and abhorrent to others in their sociocultural group (Powell, Overton et al., 2014; Rachman, 1994). Given the inherent sociocultural component of self-disgust (i.e., that characteristics most likely to produce self-directed disgust also elicit a disgust response at a societal level; e.g., Oaten et al., 2011), depending on the source, this may be a realistic or distorted appraisal of how an individual is in fact typically perceived by their social community. Nevertheless, the tendency for those that are self-disgusted to have a particular negative expectation of how future others will treat them may have negative consequences (i.e., leading to maladaptive behaviour), with the potential to culminate in a self-fulfilling prophecy. In some cases, self-disgust may even become associated with a perceived loss of all social belonging or an individual's very humanity (Powell, Overton et al., 2014). Reports of an enduring disgust for the self also appear to be related to acts of self-persecution and deprecation. What is more, there are a number of additional negative psychological phenomena that have hypothesised associations with the experience of self-disgust, and we proceed to consider these next.

## *Self-revulsion and concomitant psychological phenomena*

Fundamental in our treatment of self-disgust is that it defines a unique pattern of self-directed cognitive-affective responding, which, we argue, has not been as adequately characterised by any other existing psychological construct. In essence, in reaction to an enduring aspect of the self, this involves emotional responses of disgust, congruent visceral physiological reactions (e.g., repulsion and nausea), disgust-driven behavioural responses of rejection and avoidance, and a range of negative cognitions particular to disgust (e.g., "I look rotten", "my actions repulse me", "I make other people nauseous"). However, we acknowledge that self-disgust will not exist as an isolated phenomenon and is likely to exhibit varying degrees of association with other established emotional and cognitive phenomena. Of particular relevance are the constructs of self-criticism and self-hatred (Gilbert, Clarke, Hempel, Miles, & Irons, 2004); self-oriented complex variants of other basic emotions such as anger, contempt, and sadness (Powell, Overton et al., 2014); the established negative self-conscious emotions of shame, embarrassment, and guilt (Power & Dalgleish, 2008; Roberts & Goldenberg, 2007); and the fascinating psychological concept of mental pollution or contamination (Rachman, 1994).

As was alluded to previously, self-persecution has been found to co-exist with experiential self-disgust (Powell, Overton et al., 2014), and the latter is likely associated with some degree of generalised criticism for the self (Gilbert et al., 2004). Hence, while self-disgust undoubtedly incorporates some form of self-criticism, it can be theoretically demarcated based on its specific disgust-based cognitive-affective content. As has been justly argued elsewhere (Gilbert et al., 2004), it is undoubtedly feasible for someone to dislike aspects of themselves and be self-critical in the absence of any self-oriented disgust reaction. Yet, disliking aspects of the self may be a necessary (but insufficient) condition for the presence of self-disgust, and reports of self-focused hatred have been found to accompany those of self-directed revulsion (Powell, Overton et al., 2014). So, whilst they appear distinguishable, based on the supposition that self-hate can occur in the absence of self-disgust, the likelihood is that self-disgust and self-hatred may often be experienced in tandem (Gilbert et al., 2004). A more ambitious contention would be that the former cannot exist without some concurrent degree of the latter.

Hatred is thought to incorporate generalised anger as its primary emotional constituent (Ekman & Cordaro, 2011; Power & Dalgleish, 2008). Anger and disgust can be considered closely associated negative emotions, especially in the sociomoral arena (e.g., Marzillier & Davey, 2004; Nabi, 2002; Simpson et al., 2006), and thus may show a degree of overlap when applied to certain features of the self (Powell, Overton et al., 2014). However, the emotion schemas of anger and disgust can be ultimately differentiated in terms of their emotional, cognitive, physiological, and behavioural profiles (Chapman & Anderson, 2012; Ekman & Cordaro, 2011), and show discrimination even within a complex sociomoral context (Gutierrez & Giner-Sorolla, 2007; Guiterrez, Giner-Sorolla, & Vasiljevic, 2012). Likewise, despite a conjectured close relationship (Power & Dalgleish, 2008), the emotions of contempt and disgust can be separated on a range of criteria, such as their discrete physiological and neurological profiles and specific inducing events (see Simpson et al., 2010). Accordingly, based on extensive cross-cultural research, the influential emotion theorist Paul Ekman defines contempt as a distinct basic emotion (e.g., Ekman, 1999; Ekman & Cordaro, 2011; see also Izard, 2011). Another discrete emotion that may accompany self-directed disgust is sadness (Powell, Overton et al., 2014; Power & Dalgleish, 2008). Indeed, sadness appears to demonstrate a stronger relationship with more complex disgust variants (e.g., sociomoral disgust), than core disgust reactions (Simpson et al., 2006). Moreover, Power and Dalgleish (2008) postulate that self-disgust and sadness may couple (or blend) to produce the typical phenomenology of depression. Notwithstanding this proposition, there is now evidence to suggest self-disgust, as an underlying trait, can exist independently of any depressive experience (Overton et al., 2008; Powell, Simpson et al., 2013).

Self-disgust is thought to have an intimate relationship with the so-called "self-conscious" emotions, and has previously been typified as a special instance of self-conscious emotion itself (Roberts & Goldenberg, 2007; Simpson et al., 2010). As a category, the self-conscious emotions are defined by a prerequisite of self-representation, an indispensable cognitive complexity, and a later developmental emergence than other discrete emotions (Lewis, 1999; Tracy & Robins, 2004). In this sense, self-disgust can be considered a "self-conscious" emotion schema, in that it necessarily requires a self-concept and self-referential capacity. Indeed, self-representation can be considered an essential evolutionary (and developmental) ingredient in the recipe for self-disgust. Three self-conscious emotions in particular have been formerly associated with the concept of self-focused disgust, namely, embarrassment, guilt, and shame (Power & Dalgleish, 2008). It seems plausible to differentiate our proposed schematic theorisation of self-disgust from instances of embarrassment and guilt, as the former relates to core and enduring aspects of the self. Conversely, embarrassment and guilt are considered less global and embodied emotions, related to a specific, often atypical, and inconsistent action one has performed (Tangney, Miller, Flicker, & Barlow, 1996; Tracy & Robins, 2004). Therefore, the self-conscious emotion of shame presents the greatest theoretical challenge to the uniqueness of the self-disgust construct and, thus, warrants further discussion.

Shame is a fundamentally social emotion, associated with a perceived deficit in the self, which, if aired, is expected to be appraised by others as socially undesirable or impermissible (Gilbert, 2000). This broad definition hints at a degree of commonality with self-disgust, and some theorists (e.g., Power & Dalgleish, 2008) go so far as to explicitly define shame as a particular instance of disgust, where the self is the object. However, the idea that certain complex emotions are nothing more than blends or tweaks of a few "basic" emotions is controversial (e.g., Levenson, 2011). Moreover, some notable researchers classify the emotions of shame and guilt as most related to signals of sadness rather than disgust (e.g., Ekman & Cordaro, 2011, Levenson, 2011). In any case, experiences of shame and disgust are certainly separable on more grounds than simply their target objects (Ekman & Cordaro, 2011; Scherer & Wallbott, 1994), not least in terms of their unique physiological and expressive profiles (Keltner, 1995; Scherer & Wallbott, 1994; Tracy, Robins, & Schriber, 2009). In fact, shame has a long history of being classed as a discrete basic emotion by some (e.g., Ekman, 1999; Izard, 1977; Tomkins, 1984), and is typically considered "the most basic of the self-conscious emotions, fulfilling most agreed-on criteria" (Kemeny, Gruenewald, & Dickerson, 2004, p. 154; see also Ekman, 1992; Ekman & Cordaro, 2011).

While the evolutionary roots of disgust lie in disease and contamination avoidance, shame appears to have evolved as a damage-limitation strategy in social competition, signalling (to the self and others) states of submission, appeasement, and a depreciation of social rank (Fessler, 2007; Gilbert, 1997, 2007; Keltner & Harker, 1998; Martens, Tracy, & Shariff, 2012). Indeed, cruder, or more "basic", behavioural prototypes of shame (e.g., shrinking and lowered posture, gaze avoidance, etc.), can be seen in a range of non-human animals during submission in social hierarchies (Clark, 2010; Kemeny et al., 2004; Tracy & Matsumoto, 2008), and in young children following manipulated failure (e.g., Lewis, Alessandri, & Sullivan, 1992). Furthermore, innate nonverbal expressions of shame have even been observed following losses in congenitally blind human athletes (Tracy & Matsumoto, 2008). Thus, the evidence points towards two distinct basic versions of shame and disgust that evolved to serve separate functions. In turn, these primitive forms are linked to cognitively complex variants that exist as a result of humans' higher social and cognitive development, yet still retain features of their predecessors (Clark, 2010). It is the discrete emotion of disgust (and its complex self-focused variant), rather than shame, that we award primacy to in our model of self-disgust. Notwithstanding evident overlap, such as the corresponding tendencies for avoidance and rejection, there are particular features of the disgust response we do not associate with shame, but would expect to find in self-disgust. These include qualities of the physiological and expressive response specific to disgust (see Olatunji & Sawchuk, 2005; Stark, Walter, Schienle, & Vaitl, 2005), the embodied and visceral sensations of revulsion and nausea, an association with contamination and magical thinking (Rachman, 1994; see below), and specific disgust-based cognition and beliefs (e.g., "that's gross", "I feel physically sick").

The extraordinarily limited research that has utilised separate indices of self-directed disgust and shame hints at some preliminary empirical distinctiveness, grounded in the particular measures used (Penley & Tomaka, 2002; Roberts & Gettman, 2004). For example, in investigating the relations between personality variables, stress, and emotional reactions in undergraduates, Penley and Tomaka (2002) found that extraversion was significantly associated with state levels of reported self-disgust, but not shame. Openness, on the contrary, correlated negatively with state shame, but exhibited no statistically significant relationship with state self-disgust. Further, in unpublished data from a predominantly (64%) student sample of 464 participants (360 female, $M_{age} = 28.73$, $SD_{age} = 11.55$), we found that self-disgust (the SDS; Overton et al., 2008) showed a significant independent association with depressive symptoms, when controlling for state, or in-the-moment, levels of shame (using the State Shame and Guilt Scale, SSGS; Marschall, Saftner, & Tangney, 1994), $pr(461) = .33$, BCa 95% CI [.21, .43], $p < .001$.

In sum, while shame may be a common response or consequence to being the target of disgust (whether originating from others or the self; Power & Dalgleish, 2008), and thereby signifying social inferiority, we do not think it necessarily follows that shame should be considered synonymous with self-directed abhorrence. Indeed, this is a claim that remains to be proven. There exist, of course, examples of traits that may signify lower social rank or prestige, and thus elicit shame, but which we expect would fail to elicit any genuine disgust response (e.g., poor academic ability, smaller stature, unreliability, possessing fewer material resources, etc.), suggesting the two constructs are far from inextricably linked. Equally, there may be some situations that would ostensibly trigger an inherent disgust response, but not produce any shame (e.g., deformations of the body envelope sustained during honourable military service). That being said, given that appraising parts of the self as disgusting is undeniably intertwined with the possession of socially undesirable traits, a perceived lower social status or rank, and less self-esteem (Simpson et al., 2010), shame seems particularly apt as a regular counterpart of self-disgust, just not necessarily a theoretical duplicate.

A final concept that we wish to draw attention to briefly is the concept of mental contamination (Rachman, 1994). First outlined by Stanley Rachman (1994) as a "pollution of the mind", mental contamination describes a sense of internal or psychological dirtiness, associated with feelings of disgust and nausea. Seemingly driven by the laws of sympathetic magic (i.e., contagion and similarity; Rozin & Fallon, 1987), mental contamination is typically associated with internalised escape and/or avoidance, and ritualised cleansing behaviours (Rachman, 1994). Whilst initially advanced in relation to obsessive-compulsive phenomena, mental contamination can arise from a number of psychological and physical violations, including self-induced immoral thoughts, images, actions, or memories (Elliott & Radomsky, 2009, 2012; Rachman, Radomsky, Elliott, & Zysk, 2012). Indeed, recent research suggests mental contamination (and self-focused disgust) may be particularly pronounced in victims of non-consensual sexual trauma (Elliott & Radomsky, 2009, 2012; Fairbrother & Rachman, 2004; Feldner, Frala, Badour, Leen-Feldner, & Olatunji, 2010). Fascinatingly, Jung and Steil (2012) have documented the typical phenomenology of a "feeling of being contaminated" (FBC) in females following childhood sexual abuse. Described as involving uncomfortable physical sensations, victims reported a lasting awareness of remains of the perpetrator's body fluids (e.g., "a slimy, smelling mass") on or inside their body. The FBC was appraised as permanent, and more salient in certain situations, such as when attending to the body. Behavioural consequences included excessive washing and calculated care to avoid ostensibly contaminating another. Patients with a FBC reported disgust towards their body, and especially the genitals, breast, throat, and mouth regions, which resulted in both visual and tactile avoidance (Jung & Steil, 2012). Thus, this description of a contaminated self appears to incorporate significant elements of self-focused disgust, and suggests a close-knit relationship.

## *Quantifying self-disgust*

So far in this chapter, we have championed the existence of self-disgust as a unique, cognitive-affective, theoretical (or latent) psychological trait. The proven existence of such will require a convergence of evidence from multiple manifest indicators (e.g., physiological, neural, behavioural, and self-report measures), purporting to index the phenomenon. For example, relevant evidence might be sought in the facial or physiological expressions of disgust (rather than shame) in response to a self-disgust trigger (e.g., looking at the self in a mirror, or self-generated inappropriate sexual thoughts; see Neziroglu, Hickey, & McKay, 2010). Further, neurological activation of areas linked to the disgust response (e.g., the anterior insula; Calder, Lawrence, & Young, 2001; Wicker et al., 2003; Wright, He, Shapira, Goodman, & Liu, 2004), and observational evidence of congruent behavioural responses (e.g., tactile and visual avoidance, attempts at cleansing; Coughtrey, Shafran, Lee, & Rachman, 2012; Elliott & Radomsky, 2012; Powell, Overton et al., 2014) accompanying any reports of self-disgust, would strengthen such a theoretical claim. While there exist anecdotal accounts that are suggestive of some of this (e.g., behavioural and cognitive avoidance; Coughtrey et al., 2012; Powell, Overton et al., 2014), accruing formal empirical data for self-directed disgust from multiple modalities is both a useful and essential area for further work. For the present discussion, we restrict our focus to the recent attempt to quantify self-disgust by self-report.

In his psychometric work on self-criticism, Paul Gilbert differentiated two forms of self-critical responding to setbacks, one of which was described as involving hatred for the self (Gilbert et al., 2004). The concept of a "hated self" featured as a five-item self-report subscale in the Forms of Self-Criticising/Attacking and Self-Reassuring Scale (FSCRS; Gilbert et al., 2004) and was designed to assess an amalgamation of hateful, angry, and disgusted feelings towards the self. Accordingly, this subscale could be considered somewhat of a rough self-report index of levels of self-directed disgust. However, in this instance, the concepts of hate, anger, and disgust were intentionally blurred, and the "disgust" element of the subscale was utilised more as an anger synonym, rather than as a purposeful gauge of true disgust feelings (see Nabi, 2002). Consequently, the first self-report instrument actually produced with the intention of quantifying self-disgust as a distinct psychological construct is the eponymous Self-Disgust Scale (SDS; Overton et al., 2008). Incorporating items containing synonyms of "disgust" (e.g., "I find myself repulsive" and "I often do things I find revolting"), the SDS was found to have a two-factor structure assessing reported disgust towards physical self-image and behaviour (Overton et al., 2008). As touched on previously, the SDS appears to measure self-disgust as a cognitive-affective trait that persists over time, rather than a state or transient emotional reaction (Powell, Simpson et al., 2013).

The SDS is considered a reliable measure in non-clinical samples, with strong internal consistency (published $\alpha$s range from .88–.94; Overton et al., 2008; Powell, Simpson et al., 2013; Simpson et al., 2010) and high test-retest reliability (Overton et al., 2008; Powell, Simpson et al., 2013). It also displays a notable degree of concurrent validity, correlating significantly with other indices of disgust, including general trait propensity (see p. 8, this chapter), and sensitivity to experiential disgust, including unpublished correlations of $r_s(319) = .30$, $p < .001$ and $r_s(290) = .34$, $p < .001$ with the Sensitivity subscale of the DPSS-R (van Overveld, de Jong, Peters, Cavanagh et al., 2006). Furthermore, in recent, ongoing experimental work, we have found large preliminary correlations between the SDS and independent Visual Analogue Scale (VAS) ratings of "disgust" towards appearance, $r_s(24) = .71$, $p < .001$, and behaviour $r_s(24) = .81$, $p < .001$, completed two weeks later. Strong correlations have also been reported between the SDS, measures of depressive symptoms, and other self-referent constructs, such as self-esteem and dysfunctional attitudes (Overton et al., 2008; Powell, Simpson et al., 2013; Simpson et al., 2010). In spite of theory hinting at an enhanced probability for self-disgust in females (Roberts & Goldenberg, 2007), in our use of the SDS we have failed to find any significant differences in scores by gender, or reported ethnicity. These non-significant findings may be driven by the considerable positive skew in self-disgust in the non-clinical population. Nevertheless, we have consistently recorded small, significant negative effects of age on SDS responding, such as $r_s(462) = -.19$, $p < .001$ (Powell, Simpson et al., 2013).

As the first scale of its kind, the SDS appears to be a promising manifest self-report measure to tap into the latent, cognitive-affective trait of self-disgust, but the scale is not without room for improvement. Foremost, the SDS warrants further validation, particularly from other data-collection sources and the use of clinical samples, where the construct of self-disgust may be most relevant. Second, owing to their aforementioned overlap, the SDS is also likely a proxy measure for other negative self-directed phenomena, such as self-criticism, and self-directed hate or anger. Indeed, in addition to the indicative large correlation coefficients observed with separate VASs of disgust, the SDS also displayed significant (but smaller) correlations with VAS ratings of "anger" towards appearance, $r_s(24) = .46$, $p < .05$, and behaviour, $r_s(24) = .75$, $p < .001$. Moreover, the same pattern of results was also observed for ratings of "sadness" to appearance, $r_s(24) = .53$, $p < .01$, and behaviour, $r_s(24) = .75$, $p < .001$, respectively. A minority of items in the SDS actually use vocabulary such as "hate" and "dislike", which may tap into these additional constructs. While the prior theorising, and the internal consistency of the SDS, suggests these concepts may be inseparably related, the face validity of the scale could be improved by only including vocabulary associated primarily with the experience of disgust (e.g., feeling "grossed out", "repulsed", "nauseous or sick", etc.; see Nabi, 2002). Lastly, there may be aspects of self-disgust that are not adequately covered by the SDS in its present form (see Powell, Overton et al., 2014), such as certain visceral and behavioural components (e.g., "the way I look makes me feel sick to my stomach", "I try to distract myself from thoughts of disgust").

To sum up, at present we advocate the SDS as a sufficient and reliable self-report indicator, which provides the best available gauge of the cognitive-affective construct of self-disgust (as advanced in this chapter). However, as with all psychometric work, we expect the SDS (and any other self-report measures of self-disgust that should emerge) to be improved and fine-tuned over time. Accordingly, we would like to encourage further work on the quantitative assessment of self-disgust, and particularly on any measures that provide an alternative or corroboration to self-report methodology. Lately, a number of data sources, including those using the SDS, have emerged to suggest a negative link between self-disgust and psychological wellbeing, which emphasises the need to ensure the availability of valid manifest indicators of the phenomenon. It is to our succinct review of the association between self-disgust and mental wellbeing that we now turn.

## *Psychological implications of an abhorrent self*

As this is a topic that will be dealt with in much more erudite detail throughout the current volume, in this section we seek only to give the reader a brief introductory flavour for the negative bind between self-disgust and mental wellbeing. In his theorising on emotion schemas, Izard (e.g., Izard, 2007, 2009; Izard, Youngstrom, Fine, Mostow, & Trentacosta, 2006) explicitly acknowledged their potential to lead to psychopathology as a result of learned maladaptive connections between emotion feelings, cognition, and action. Moreover, he posited that a constellation of dysfunctional emotion schemas may interlink and manifest as a form of psychological distress, such as depression (Izard, 2009). Two decades of clinical research has now implicated maladaptive disgust reactions in a range of mental health problems (Davey, 2011; Olatunji & McKay, 2007; Olatunji & Sawchuk, 2005). As a consequence—and straying somewhat from its oft-quoted depiction as the forgotten emotion of psychiatry (Phillips, Senior, Fahy, & David, 1998)—disgust now appears to be well established as an emotional response that is as susceptible to dysfunction as its affective kin (Power & Dalgleish, 2008).

Emerging research hints that enduring disgust directed towards the self may be a characteristic feature of a range of mental health problems. Self-disgust is strongly associated with body dissatisfaction and stigma (Griffiths & Page, 2008), and disgust is often directed at bodily features perceived as diseased or unattractive by society in general (Oaten et al., 2011; Park, van Leeuwen, & Stephen, 2012; Shanmugarajah, Gaind, Clarke, & Butler, 2012; Smith, Loewenstein, Rozin, Sherriff, & Ubel, 2007). Individuals exhibiting eating pathology may experience elevated levels of disgust towards their own body (Coggins & Fox, 2009; Espeset et al., 2012; Fox, 2009; Troop & Baker, 2009). Experiences of self-directed disgust and associated cognitions have been well documented in anorexia nervosa, and have been reported to be linked to attempts to avoid "body awareness" (Espeset et al., 2012). Sufferers typically report feelings of self-pollution and self-disgust after eating certain food, which is in itself appraised as a toxic and contaminating stimulus (Warin, 2003). Self-focused disgust towards one's physical appearance may also play a notable role in body dysmorphic disorder (BDD; Lambrou, Veale, & Wilson, 2011; Neziroglu et al., 2010), perhaps as a consequence of a greater emotional reactivity to aesthetic deviations and imperfections (Lambrou et al., 2011).

Disgust-based feelings and cognitions for the self may feature in the aftermath of particular traumatic experiences (e.g., sexual assault, Fairbrother & Rachman, 2004; Jung & Steil, 2012), and appear to be associated with the phenomenon of mental contamination touched on earlier (Fairbrother & Rachman, 2004). Contact with a perceived contaminant, or unwanted, self-generated (particularly immoral) thoughts and images that are appraised as disgusting, may drive feelings of self-disgust in contamination-based obsessive-compulsive disorder (OCD; Rachman, 1994), particularly in the religious (Berle & Phillips, 2006). In turn, such feelings of disgust and dirtiness may promote ritualised purification or cleansing behaviours (Rachman, 1994). There is also some preliminary data indicating that people with post-traumatic stress disorder (PTSD) may implicitly associate themselves more with disgust than anxiety (Rusch et al., 2011). However, a recent study led by Christal Badour (Badour, Bown, Adams, Bunaciu, & Feldner, 2012) indicates that self-focused disgust may be more specific to obsessive-compulsive symptoms, than post-traumatic stress symptoms *per se*, after instances of physical or sexual assault. Thus, further work is needed to establish the mechanisms by which disgust (self-focused or otherwise) operates across these disorders. Nevertheless, recent research has implicated self-disgust (particularly towards the genitals and sexualised areas) in the associated domain of sexual complications (de Jong, van Lankveld, Elgersma, & Borg, 2010).

Other mental health problems that have been proposed to involve some internalisation of disgust are social phobia or anxiety (Amir et al., 2005; Amir, Najimi, Bomyea, & Burns, 2010), and borderline personality disorder (BPD; Rusch et al., 2011). We also expect self-disgust to be particularly relevant to certain conditions in which parts of the body, or bodily functions, are perceived as foreign or in some way wrong to the individual, such as in problems with gender identity (e.g., Becker & Mester, 1996; Fisher et al., 2010). While the precise cognitive and associative content of the self-disgust schema is likely to vary across (and within) mental health problems, its emotional and feeling constituents may represent a relatively underexplored area of commonality across a number of psychological issues, including the ones mentioned in this chapter. Furthermore, it could be hypothesised that this shared emotional trait may represent an underlying contributory factor to certain instances of co-morbidity between particular disorders.

To date, our own research has largely centred on the role of self-disgust in depression. Notwithstanding the restriction of using a non-clinical population, two initial publications served to demonstrate a strong cross-sectional association between measures of depressive symptoms and self-disgust (Overton et al., 2008; Simpson et al., 2010). Furthermore, these investigations hypothesised a critical role for self-disgust in the genesis of depression, with a proposed function as an affective mediator between dysfunctional thinking and depressive symptomatology. We explicitly tested this idea using a prospective research design (Powell, Simpson et al., 2013). Whilst the relationship between dysfunctional thinking and self-disgust appears to be somewhat more reciprocal than linear over time, the cognitive-affective trait of self-disgust (as measured by the SDS; Overton et al., 2008) acted as a stable predictor for future depressive experience. Our data also indicated that disgust towards physical image, which is more constant over time and place, may have more of an influence on later depression than disgust towards behavioural traits (Powell, Simpson et al., 2013).

In our most recent paper, we presented a phenomenological analysis of self-disgust in females with high levels of depressive symptoms (Powell, Overton et al., 2014). One pertinent area of commonality across the participants in that study was the difficulty they experienced in attenuating or getting rid of their sense of self-disgust, which was epitomised in reports of unsuccessful therapeutic experiences. As mentioned, there is reason to suppose that acquired disgust responses may be particularly difficult to unlearn, potentially more so than other affective reactions (Olatunji, Forsyth et al., 2007; Rozin & Fallon, 1987; Sawchuk, 2009). Furthermore, clinical distinction has been made between *rationally* and *emotionally* held beliefs, the two perhaps requiring different therapeutic approaches (e.g., Jung & Steil, 2012). Accordingly, there may be some utility in elaborating current treatments for certain mental health problems to identify and target any maladaptive self-directed disgust reactions that may exist. For example, Steil and her colleagues (Jung & Steil, 2012; Steil, Jung, & Stangier, 2011) used individualised imagery modification to augment standard cognitive restructuring techniques, when treating individuals with PTSD and persistent feelings of contamination (and disgust) following childhood sexual abuse. Thus, a therapeutic awareness and appreciation for self-disgust as a potential cognitive-affective phenomenon may prove beneficial. However, due to the heterogeneity within mental health problems, it is important to note that we do not assume self-disgust in all clinical presentations of the disorders as discussed herein. Hence, the existence and appropriate therapeutic management of self-disgust would need to be assessed on somewhat of a more idiosyncratic basis.

## Conclusion

In the present chapter, we have outlined our conceptual framework for self-disgust as a distinct maladaptive psychological phenomenon, or emotion schema, comprised of a stable pattern of disgust-based, cognitive-affective responding to (a lasting and significant aspect of) the self. Much like the object of other "basic" emotions (e.g., anger) can be internal, or some part of the self (e.g., Klonsky & Muehlenkamp, 2007; Orth & Maercker, 2009), we argue that this is also especially likely with the basic emotion of disgust (and its complex self-conscious manifestation), given its evolved sociocultural malleability. Echoing the call to arms of Roberts and Goldenberg (2007), we wish to emphasise that self-disgust (as an enduring cognitive-affective construct) represents a credible and interesting research agenda in its own right, having hitherto received relatively little attention in our field. Whilst the present volume, in which this chapter is situated, forms the first comprehensive collection of scholarly works on self-disgust as a psychological topic, there is much empirical research required. Thus, we present our theoretical model with the proviso that it is far from intended as definitive, but more as a springboard for further refinement and investigation. We hope that this chapter will go some way to meaningfully ground further research and theoretical development on the concept of self-disgust, as a distinct, detrimental, abhorrent, and pervasive psychological phenomenon.

CHAPTER TWO

# Digging disgust out of the dumpster: a neuropsychological defence of self- and other-directed disgust as a moral virtue

*Jason A. Clark*

## *Introduction*

Calls to label nearly every emotion as "toxic" have a long history, and calls to abandon emotion altogether as a guiding moral force are common. Two of the emotions that have recently been targeted as toxic are shame and disgust. While considerable evidence suggests that the biological or cultural co-optation of disgust for norm enforcement occurred because it was adaptive (Chapman, Kim, Susskind, & Anderson, 2009; Kelly, 2011; Navarrete & Fessler, 2006; Tybur, Lieberman, & Griskevicius, 2009), research has also shown potentially troubling influences of disgust on moral behaviour (Pizarro, Inbar, & Helion, 2011; Schnall, Haidt, Clore, & Jordan, 2008; Wheatley & Haidt, 2005). If disgust is not currently adaptive, there is *prima facie* reason to ask whether it was ever so and, if so, what sociomoral changes humans have undergone since then that were sufficiently radical to alter disgust's status.

Arguments concerning the malignant role of moral disgust usually contrast it unfavourably with other moral emotions. For example, Nussbaum (2004) argues that shame and disgust have no positive role to play in moral and legal judgements, while guilt and anger do. Roseman (1984) theorised that anger and guilt focus on disapproval of an act, whereas disgust and shame maladaptively focus on disapproval of the person. Ortony, Clore, and Collins (1988) construed disgust as a fixed object-focused emotion, while anger is more complex and changeable, focused on the event and agent rather than the person, and argue that situational appraisals are fundamental to anger. Similarly, Russell and Giner-Sorolla (2011a, 2013) argue that disgust is an "unreasoning" emotion, lacking the cognitive, behavioural, and situational flexibility of anger, with negative moral consequences. Kelly (2011) has also raised concerns about disgust, arguing that the features of disgust, which make it well suited for its primary pathogen-avoidance tasks, render it ill-suited for moral judgement; for example, it is proposed that it has a "hair trigger", is highly susceptible to false positives, and "the nature of the emotion itself, the slope from moralization to demonization and dehumanization is just too slippery to endorse" (Kelly, 2011, p. 178), even in the service of morally justified goals. Bloom (2013) asserts that "the intuitions associated with disgust are at best unnecessary … and at worst harmful in that they motivate irrational policies and license savage behavior" (p. 155). He argues that unlike other moral emotions which can *sometimes* go wrong (including empathy), "disgust is different" in that its verdicts at best contribute no more than a moral "coin toss", and that if the capacity for moral disgust were suddenly exterminated in humans, this would disrupt society very little, and could only have a beneficial effect.

In addition to disgust's role in enforcing sociomoral norms, if it is a toxic emotion, this has implications for the normative psychiatric standards by which we determine whether and when disgust is psychopathological, viz., norms concerning mental health, disease, and so on, which must combine both evolutionary and sociocultural norms. If disgust is a negative force in moral decision-making, then the standards by which we assess its psychiatric status should reflect this. And if disgust is damaging to its targets (or even its expressers), it is likely that self-disgust will be equally damaging to the self. On the other hand, if disgust has a positive role to play in morality, it likely has similar effects when directed onto the self.

Here, I offer an initial, admittedly partial and inconclusive defence of disgust's normative virtues in both inter- and intra-personal (self-directed) sociomoral dynamics. The claim is not that disgust is always morally appropriate, or that disgust "reveals" values in itself (Kass, 1997), but rather that disgust *can* play a positive role in normative decision-making. I will not deny that disgust should plead guilty to its role in most of the heinous crimes attributed to it, but will argue that these instances are not characteristic of its ordinary operations, and secondarily, disgust is not unique in its transgressions in such crimes, but rather has many unindicted emotional co-conspirators. I will focus on integrating work in social psychology and social neuroscience, comparing the values of cognitive and behavioural responses associated with anger and disgust, and emphasising the involvement of regions of the brain that are active both when we mentalise about others and when we mentalise about ourselves. This overlap suggests that some of the neural processes involved in externally directed disgust are also involved in self-disgust, and that conclusions about the former can be cautiously extrapolated to the latter.

Correspondingly, the "self", as I shall use the concept, should not be seen as restricted to the individual, but rather as extending outwards through a series of more abstract categories with which the individual identifies, or is identified with by others. Hence, "the self" may include possessions and personal spaces of varying degrees (e.g., homes, cities, nations), as well as in-groups of varying and ever-shifting distance from the self (e.g., family, friends, organisations, cultures). Cultures vary in the degree to which the self proper vs. the in-group is the primary source of identity (Nisbett, 2004), and we should expect such variability to be reflected in self-directed disgust as well, such that when someone commits a disgusting act, we will experience self-disgust in proportion to our identification with the actor, as has been found for shame and pride (Stipek, 1998). In addition to self-disgust at the individual level, we may also be disgusted with our own in-groups and their members. A great deal of attention has been paid to inter-group disgust (Navarrete & Fessler, 2006; Neuberg, Kenrick, & Schaller, 2011), but to my knowledge no one has proposed the concept of "intra-group disgust". Intra-group disgust, as I present it, is not simply inter-group disgust between the subcultures of an in-group—we can slice our group identities more or less finely, but at a given level of analysis, intra-group disgust consists in disgust towards those with whom we share identity.

In section two, I will discuss how to define moral disgust, adopting an inclusive definition that includes a variety of types of normative assessment. This is followed by a characterisation of the neural basis of self- and other-directed disgust. In section three, I present the case against moral disgust, which argues that disgust lacks cognitive and behavioural flexibility, and that it dehumanises those onto whom it is directed (including the self), unlike emotions such as anger. In section four, I present a defence of self- and other-directed disgust, arguing that: (i) disgust is more cognitively and behaviourally flexible than is alleged; (ii) to the extent that it less flexible than other emotions, its inflexibility can play a positive role; and (iii) dehumanisation is not always a severe or morally malignant process, and other emotions (including anger) are also likely to produce dehumanisation.

## *Moral disgust: definition and neural mechanisms*

### *Definition of moral disgust*

The disgust literature is a thicket of crosscutting taxonomies, with varying accounts of the relationships among its proposed subtypes and the processes that generated them (Clark & Fessler, 2014; Curtis, de Barra, & Aunger, 2011; Fessler & Navarrete, 2004; Kelly, 2011; Rozin, Haidt, & McCauley, 2008; Tybur et al., 2009). While attending to these distinctions is necessary to offer a full account of disgust, here I hope to bracket these issues as much as possible, in order to address questions about features of disgust that arguably cross-cut various typologies. I will also incorporate studies of the role of disgust in contexts that are often separated from moral disgust "proper", such as inter-personal disgust and inter-group disgust (Rozin et al., 2008). This is necessary to compare the results of many studies that use somewhat different disgust stimuli belonging to all of these categories. Nevertheless, all of these instances of disgust involve a strong normative element, and so can be at least provisionally united under this banner. I will concentrate on several features upon which there is near universal agreement:

1. Disgust originated as a form of pathogen avoidance.
2. In humans and only humans, disgust has come to play a role in the enforcement of sociomoral norms that is distinct from its pathogen avoidance functions, whether this occurred by biological or cultural evolution, or both.
3. Such moral disgust is a genuine emotion that involves the activation of (at least some of) the same core mechanisms involved in pathogen disgust, whether they are activated directly, or indirectly via disgust-related metaphorical cognitions.
4. Moral disgust is distinct from other moral emotions; however, it has a very close and poorly understood relationship with moral anger.

### *Neural mechanisms of moral disgust*

While disgust is widely distributed along the neuroaxis, including the brainstem, amygdala, striatum, insula and parts of the frontal cortex (Calder et al., 2007; Parker, 2003; Smith, Tindell, Aldridge, & Berridge, 2009; Toronchuk & Ellis, 2007; Wicker et al., 2003; Wright, He, Shapira, Goodman, & Liu, 2004), where moral disgust is concerned, two of the most important regions are the insula and the medial prefrontal cortex (MPFC), especially its more ventral components (VMPFC). Research on moral disgust has selectively focused on these circuits. Furthermore, it is these circuits that appear most crucial for self-directed cognition of various sorts, and are therefore likely to offer the most insight into self-disgust.

#### Insula

The insula has undergone significant transformations in humans, including uniquely human types of neurons (von Economo neurons), as well as anatomical and functional expansions, especially in the anterior insula, allowing for abstract representations of the self and others (Craig, 2003, 2009, 2011). The posterior insula generates a high-resolution first-order representation of the overall physiological state of the body, including information from all organs as well as more peripheral elements such as temperature, pain, itch, and aches. This first-order representation in the posterior insula is re-represented in the anterior insula. Craig has proposed that this higher-order representation underlies our global interoceptive sense of self, enabling multimodal awareness of the overall homeostatic condition of the self, and integration of this information with motivational, affective, and cognitive states, as well as social context. Self-related processes in the anterior insula are also active when we witness the pain or emotions of close others (Singer et al., 2004), suggesting that insular representation of the "self" may extend beyond the individual. Imaging, lesion, and electrical brain stimulation studies indicate that the insula is consistently implicated in disgust-related tasks of various sorts (Calder et al., 2007; Caruana, Jezzini, Sbriscia-Fioretti, Rizzolatti, & Gallese, 2011; Schaich Borg, Lieberman, & Kiehl, 2008; Wright et al., 2004), and Moncrieff-Boyd, Byrne, and Nunn (2013) identify the insula as a key mediator of self-disgust in anorexia nervosa. However, the insula is active in about one third of all imaging experiments (Yarkoni, Poldrack, Nichols, van Essen, & Wager, 2011), and is involved in many other processes, both affective and cognitive. Aside from its role in disgust, some of its most important additional functions for present purposes are its involvement in anger (Damasio et al., 2000), sense of knowing (Kikyo, Ohki, & Miyashita, 2002), trustworthiness (Craig, 2002; Winston, Strange, O'Doherty, & Dolan, 2002), as well as empathy and compassion (Singer, Critchley, & Preuschoff, 2009). As we shall see, in light of its multi-functionality, it can be difficult to interpret insula activity in the context of interpersonal instances of disgust.

## Medial prefrontal cortex

The medial prefrontal cortex is characterised as including: anterior cingulate cortex (ACC; Brodmann areas [BAs] 24, 25), paracingulate cortex (BA 32), temporal poles, ventromedial prefrontal cortex (BAs 9 & 10), and portions of the medial orbitofrontal cortex (MOFC; BAs 11, 14; Amodio & Frith, 2006). As a general rule, the lateral and dorsal regions of MPFC are more involved in cognitive tasks (such as attention, working memory, error monitoring, conflict management, executive control, response inhibition, and action selection and monitoring), whereas ventral and medial regions are more involved in affective processes such as reward, emotion, and outcome measurements (such as prediction errors), especially as these relate to social cognition (Bush, Luu, & Posner, 2000; Steele & Lawrie, 2004). The MPFC is a node in a broader network that supports cognition about our own and other minds, often called a "theory of mind" or "mentalising". This network includes temporoparietal junction, and posterior cingulate/precuneus (PCC; BAs 7, 23, 31), which are themselves independently associated with social cognition (Amodio & Frith, 2006; Koster-Hale & Saxe, 2013). I will call this the Theory of Mind (ToM) network.

Some of these regions mediate not merely other-directed social cognition, but rather play a general role in cognition about the attributes of people, whether of the self or others (Kelley et al., 2002; though see Schmitz, Kawahara-Baccus, & Johnson, 2004). Regions more closely associated with self-directed cognition are also more active when contemplating the minds of close others, so, as with the insula, the notion of "self" here is likely to be broader than the individual. The mental capacities attributed to MPFC include the following overlapping abilities: self-reflection (Saxe, Moran, Scholz, & Gabrieli, 2006), person perception (Harris, McClure, van den Bos, Cohen, & Fiske, 2007), making inferences about others' thoughts and mentalising (Frith & Frith, 2006; Mitchell, Banaji, & Macrae, 2005), monitoring of one's own/others' emotional state and emotion regulation (Etkin, Egner, & Kalisch, 2011; Ochsner et al., 2004).

As in the insula, representations of self and other appear to become more complex in anterior regions of MPFC. For example, posterior regions of the ACC represent objective aspects of pain and other aversive stimuli (e.g., temperature), and are only activated by self-felt pain, whereas more anterior regions of ACC subserve more abstract subjective, metacognitive awareness of aversive stimuli (Jackson, Meltzoff, & Decety, 2005). Unlike the posterior regions, these regions are also active when viewing the pain or social rejection of a close other, and track self-reported empathy for others (Singer et al., 2004). These meta-representations enable not only awareness of self, but also monitoring of the minds of others, how they evaluate us, and how this compares to our actual or desired self-image. As Amodio and Frith (2006) put it, we "close the social loop and form a second-level representation of the attributes that others apply to us" (p. 275). Such representations are essential to maintaining reputation, and associated features such as trustworthiness. Below, I will note some additional features of the VMPFC, specifically. For now, with this neuroscience background on board, I turn to evidence from social psychology, which I later integrate and illuminate with neural-level approaches.

## *The prosecution: moral disgust as a harmful emotion*

### *Don't look at me, I'm hideous: emotional responses to being the target of disgust*

Research on moral disgust has primarily focused on which types of moral violation elicit disgust and the responses of those directing it towards others (Rozin, Lowery, Imada, & Haidt, 1999), with little attention to the nature, mechanisms, and effectiveness of moral disgust responses. To understand how disgust can serve as a form of moral rebuke, it is vital to understand the effects that it has on the target, whether the self or others, In one of the few studies measuring this, Giner-Sorolla and Espinosa (2011) asked participants to view photos of anger and disgust faces, and indicate whether they would experience shame or guilt as a result of being the target of that emotion, as well as the degree to which they would feel that they had done something wrong, as opposed to feeling like a bad person in general. Anger most commonly elicited guilt, whereas the predominant response to disgust faces was shame. Correspondingly, anger led to the inference that they had committed a harm/fairness violation, whereas disgust was associated with the violation of a bodily norm. Further support for the anger/disgust opposition comes from Pond, Jr. and colleagues (2012), who found that trait disgust sensitivity is negatively associated with a variety of propensities to anger or aggression, and Fessler, Pillsworth, and Flamson (2004), who found that disgust and anger led to differential changes in risk-taking among men and women.

The mere fact that disgust may be so closely connected to shame could constitute a reason for rejecting any positive role for disgust in norm enforcement and emotional health. Shame has long gotten a bad rap, especially as compared with guilt, and some have suggested that shame is itself a maladaptive response (Tangney & Dearing, 2003). By extension, the emotions we use to generate it in ourselves or others should be considered similarly maladaptive and should be abandoned. Shame has been seen as a morally negative emotion for a variety of reasons, the most central of which are that:

1. Shame induces self-focused distress rather than other-oriented empathy.
2. Shame motivates withdrawal rather than reparation.
3. Shame is a crushingly global judgement about the worthiness of the self, rather than a judgement about our individual actions.

However, in *In Defense of Shame*, Deonna, Rodogno, and Teroni (2011) have mounted what I believe is a successful case that shame is not an intrinsically morally harmful emotion. They argue against the alleged vices of shame, and point to some of its neglected virtues. Specifically:

1. Shame is not merely about the self, narrowly construed, but also extends to close others and social or value systems with which we identify.
2. Shame motivates deeper reflection on aspects of ourselves rather than the evaluation of specific acts associated with guilt, and is involved

in more fundamental issues of character and identity. Withdrawal is often a beneficial means of promoting deeper self-reflection.

3. Shame is not a global all-encompassing emotion, but can occur with respect to some values and aspects of the self, while not affecting others.

Many of the allegedly harmful features of disgust parallel those attributed to shame, so a defence of these features of disgust will also have indirect implications for our assessment of shame. Furthermore, the match between disgust and shame in these respects partially explains why they are preferentially related. Consequently, I will not assume that disgust needs to be ashamed of its relationship with shame; it need not feel like a globally unworthy emotion, whatever its flaws.

### *Pissed off and pissed on: moral anger vs. moral disgust*

The principal reason for Russell and Giner-Sorolla's scepticism concerning disgust is that (at least compared to anger) it is an "unreasoning emotion", especially where violations of purity-based moral norms are involved. The notion of disgust's "unreasoning" nature is unpacked into multiple components, with an emphasis on disgust's lack of "flexibility" in several senses. They maintain that while anger involves appraisals of acts, disgust is associated with more rigid categorical assessments that are less likely to take into account consequences, excuses, justifications, or intentions connected to acts and are therefore more difficult to change in the face of cognitive reappraisals than anger. Correspondingly, participants in studies generally offer fewer external justifying reasons for their disgust (vs. anger) reactions, often being "dumbfounded" as to the reasons for their judgement (Schnall et al., 2008; Wheatley & Haidt, 2005).

For example, in Russell and Giner-Sorolla (2011c), participants read a scenario that described either a harm/fairness violation or a purity violation, and then reported their initial moral judgements and emotional responses toward the violation. They were then asked to list mitigating factors that might change their responses, and filled out the measures again, re-evaluating the scenario taking these factors into account. With respect to emotional responses, they found that while ratings of disgust were not altered, anger changed in differential ways for the two violation types. Anger, but not disgust, predicted revisions of moral judgements. Hence, they conclude that moral anger is a more flexible emotion than moral disgust because anger is more likely to respond to changes in circumstances.

In addition to its blindness to the circumstances in which the act was committed, disgust is held to differ from anger in its responsiveness to information about the subsequent treatment of the norm violator (e.g., cues of justice can decrease anger, whereas disgust persists despite information concerning justice; Russell & Giner-Sorolla, 2011b). They take this to indicate that anger is goal-directed, and can be "satisfied" by subsequent events, whereas contamination- and object-based associations remain impervious to such knowledge. Hence, they argue that disgust "works to track someone's fairly inflexible status as a stigmatized individual or group member, while moral anger is more responsive to momentary concerns about fairness or harm within a relationship or group" (Russell & Giner-Sorolla, 2013, p. 43). In these (and other) papers, Russell and Giner-Sorolla link these processes to disgust's ancient function in disease avoidance, holding that:

> it is functional to have a disease-bearing object or person judged automatically, in a strong negative association that is learned quickly and relatively impervious to change because an unhealthy thing should be avoided no matter where one finds it … It is impractical to have infectious things take on different values depending on the situation or one's goals. (Russell & Giner-Sorolla, 2013, p. 340)

Correspondingly, they argue that disgust can only be changed through crude and lengthy processes of habituation and the learning of new associations.

In addition to its cognitive inflexibility, Russell and Giner-Sorolla argue that disgust also lacks behavioural complexity and flexibility as compared to anger. They claim that disgust has a "straightforward behavioral outcome of avoidance" due to its insensitivity to current circumstances, while the behavioural responses for anger can vary depending on context (Russell & Giner-Sorolla, 2013). For example, they note that anger can lead to hostile approach behaviours, involving a variety of forms aggression with different behavioural profiles (Izard, 1977). They also point to research suggesting that anger can encourage persons to engage in reparative behaviours (Fischer & Roseman, 2007; Weber, 2004), and can sometimes lead to avoidance

(Barnes, Brown, & Osterman, 2009). Furthermore, they argue that one reason why anger's behaviour is more flexible is that it is responsive to strategic considerations. A reasoned and reparative approach can be less risky and more productive under some circumstances, and in conflicts with a physically or socially stronger person, avoidance or the recruitment of social support may be the better strategy. On the other hand, disgust is alleged to be a primarily defensive emotion that leads people reflexively to avoid, expel, and break off all ties from the source of their disgust. If contact is unavoidable, disgust can lead to purifying and cleansing behaviours, which Russell and Giner-Sorolla construe as another means of breaking all ties. However, they appear to construe such purification tendencies as more automatic than anger-based responses, noting that "no research has conclusively shown that situational factors can inhibit individuals from engaging in avoidance or purification behaviors once they are disgusted" (Russell & Giner-Sorolla, 2013, p. 42). Below, I will challenge this reasoning, arguing that anger responses can be just as automatic and persistent, and that purification responses can be more flexible than these authors suggest.

### *Disgust and dehumanisation*

A cornerstone of arguments against disgust is a set of studies by Harris and Fiske (2006, 2007, 2009, 2011). They examined neural activity in response to social groups perceived as exhibiting varying degrees of warmth and competence. Those groups rated as high on one or both of these traits evoked increased activity in the MPFC, however those who scored low in both warmth and competence, and who elicited the most disgust (the "low-low" condition, including the homeless and addicts), failed to recruit these responses. Strength of MPFC activation was similar in response to all but the low-low group, and they argue that responses to low-low groups are qualitatively, rather than merely quantitatively, different. Unlike other groups, low-low groups provoked increased activation within the insula and amygdala, which Harris and Fiske interpret as indicating disgust and dehumanisation (though see below for ambiguities in interpretations of insula/amygdala activity). If disgust is especially connected with the low-low quadrant, we might expect that self-disgust involves a perception of the self as low in both competence and warmth (see Gilbert, this volume).

Dehumanisation is primarily construed in terms of seeing others as animals, rather than human selves. Bastian and Haslam (2010) distinguished two types of dehumanisation: denials of characteristically human features involving animalisation, "human uniqueness" (henceforth "animalistic" dehumanisation); and a mechanistic form of dehumanisation in which people are seen as objects, "human nature". Animalisation is closer to the type of dehumanisation associated with disgust in both the perceiver and the target. Noting the lack of research on the psychological responses of targets of dehumanisation (as opposed to perceivers), Bastian and Haslam (2011) tested such responses, using minor everyday slights. Animalistic dehumanisation was associated with judgements that targets are seen as animal-like and lacking autonomy, resulting in targets feeling lowered, debased, contaminated, and disgusting, and was associated with shame, guilt, self-blame and self-directed rumination. Where self-disgust is concerned, a vital finding from Bastian and Haslam (2010) is that people view *themselves* as less human when they have been socially excluded, suggesting that disgust towards the self follows a similar pattern of appraisal and response as that associated with disgust towards others.

Its role in dehumanisation is perhaps the most egregious flaw that is attributed to disgust. The primary evidence for this derives from qualitative studies of the role of disgust in genocide, slavery, the stigmatisation of homosexuals, and other equally abhorrent scenarios (Harris & Fiske, 2011; Inbar, Pizarro, & Bloom, 2012; Nussbaum, 2004, 2010). However, surprisingly little experimental evidence links disgust to dehumanisation. In what they report as the first direct evidence that disgust can shift the human–animal boundary, Buckels and Trapnell (2013) set out to investigate disgust's causal role in dehumanisation, and whether dehumanisation occurs independently of prior negative group-based attitudes. They divided participants into two minimally meaningful, but effectively arbitrary groups (overestimators and underestimators in a guessing task), and tested the effects of disgust induction on subsequent performance on an Implicit Association Test (IAT), measuring their tendency to associate these out-group members with animals. Disgusted participants showed the greatest associations of the out-group with animals and of the in-group with humanity.

In addition, Majdandži et al. (2012) sought to determine how humanisation of an individual affected moral decisions concerning them, and the associated neural activity. They used the footbridge dilemma (Christensen & Gomila, 2012), which involves doing direct harm to an individual in order to save the lives of several people, and asked subjects to mentalise about these individuals. They found that humanised persons were sacrificed less often (i.e., participants made fewer utilitarian decisions about them), and the activation pattern during decisions about them indicated increased negative affect, emotional conflict, vicarious emotions, and behavioural control, involving ventral ACC, MOFC, anterior insula, as well as other regions in the ToM network (e.g., precuneus/PCC), including increased connectivity between ACC and anterior insula. The researchers interpreted increased insula activity as indicating *not disgust*, but rather the deployment of high-level representations of the *pain and suffering of others* that are central to *empathy* and related vicarious emotions, as well as with increased performance monitoring during situations of *uncertainty* or *conflict*.

Finally, Harris and Fiske (2011) asked participants to report on an imaginary day in the life of members of various groups, followed by tests on various human-perception dimensions. They found that participants failed to spontaneously mentalise about the thoughts of stigmatised groups (i.e., dehumanised them) when imagining a day in their life, and rated them differently on a number of human-perception dimensions. In addition to correlations with standard ToM network regions, they also found that these dimensions correlated with neural activity in regions beyond the ToM network, including areas implicated in disgust (e.g., insula), attention (occipital cortex), and cognitive control (ACC). In particular, anterior insula activity negatively correlated with "warmth perception", which they interpret as indicating less disgust. Increased posterior insula activity, however, was positively correlated with warmth perception. In addition, anterior insula activity was correlated positively with perceptions of competence. Hence, insula/amygdala activation is not always interpreted as reflecting disgust, and this interpretational ambiguity runs through many studies described here. These regions are also consistently implicated in tasks involving emotionally charged moral dilemmas, including making difficult vs. easy (Greene, Sommerville, Nystrom, Darley, & Cohen, 2001), personal vs. impersonal (Greene, Nystrom, Engell, Darley, & Cohen, 2004), or care-based vs. justice-based (Robertson et al., 2007), moral judgements.

## *The defence: rehabilitating disgust*

I begin the defence of disgust by pleading *nolo contendere* to its role in most of the atrocities to which it has been linked—disgust is indeed involved in the perpetration of genocide, violence against homosexuals, and other stigmatised groups. The question before us is not whether disgust is guilty of such crimes, but rather whether it is always and uniquely involved, and should therefore be singled out, or whether disgust also plays a positive role in morality under other circumstances. In arguing for the latter, I will address the various reasons for which disgust has been condemned.

### *Contextual/situational sensitivity*

Contrary to the idea that physically disgusting objects should always and inflexibly be treated as such, even very simple forms of disgust are sensitive to context. In animal studies, context is among the most reliably and strongly coded features of conditioned taste aversion, and context alone can sometimes make the difference between consuming or rejecting a food type (Archer, Sjoden, & Nilsson, 1985; Reilly & Schachtman, 2008). In humans, these basic responses can change relatively easily as a result of context or cognitive reappraisal. If individuals are exposed to the chemical that is the common denominator of the odours of dirty socks and parmesan cheese, their assessment of the smell's valence may vary dramatically when given contextual information about the odour's source (Ferdenzi et al., 2013; Herz, 2003).

Furthermore, even concerning items accurately appraised as disgusting, disgust is not a fixed response to particular objects or stimuli. As we have seen, whether it occurs at all can depend on situational knowledge about the stimulus. But even basic forms of disgust in other animals are flexible and sensitive in another way as well, viz., in their interactions with other motivational states and emotions. The intensity of disgust towards a given stimulus can be highly dependent on these situational features. For example, sugar, salt, fat, protein, and even water can be toxic in excessive amounts, and satiety-induced disgust is not primarily directed onto such indispensable foods as such, but rather reflects our current homeostatic state. Similar principles apply to the modulation of disgust in response to, for example, fluctuations in the reproductive cycle (Fleischman & Fessler, 2011). Furthermore, it is regulated by concurrent affective states, such as sexual desire, hunger, and thirst, which are in a continual, mutually regulatory interplay (Borg & de Jong, 2012; Fleischman, Hamilton, Fessler, & Meston, under revision; Tindell, Smith, Peciña, Berridge, & Aldridge, 2006). If one is experiencing intense desires, disgust can be down regulated. If one is experiencing intense disgust, such appetitive states can be down regulated. This is how it should be—disgust is always about trade-offs of one sort or another—most concretely, whether to starve or risk illness.

Is moral disgust similarly flexible in response to such situational factors or reappraisals? While disgust is responsive to even the most basic forms of drives, moral disgust is also in continual interaction with other more complex sociomoral emotions, including positive affects such as compassion, empathy, love, moral elevation, familial attachment, the sense of spiritual purity, and so on. As we have seen, high disgust can diminish these emotions, but importantly, this works the other way as well, and high levels of these emotions can modulate disgust reactions to the self or others. Hence, as with sexual desire and hunger, one's pre-existing situational emotional state affects the expression of disgust.

Furthermore, disgust-related processes appear to have some sensitivity to situational appraisals of blame. For example, using fMRI, Krendl, Moran, and Ambady (2013) set out to test whether impressions of homeless people, and the correlated neural activity, could be altered by perceptions of controllability vs. uncontrollability. They specifically measured brain activity not during the passive perception of social stimuli, but during the phase in which participants were actively forming their judgement. They found that perceivers engaged the MPFC in mentalising about stigmatised individuals whose status was presented as *controllable*, whereas networks including the insula, ACC, and OFC were engaged in response to those whose condition was perceived as *uncontrollable*. Again, this is somewhat unexpected given the previously discussed linkages between decreased MPFC activity and dehumanisation, and between the insula and disgust. Contrary to this, they interpreted the latter pattern of activation as indicating not disgust, but rather other insula-mediated emotions such as pity and empathy, together with emotional conflict and subsequent regulation. They suggested that impressions of uncontrollability required less attention to their intentions, and point to behavioural results indicating that uncontrollable conditions resulted in more pity and willingness to help, and less disgust compared to the controllable scenarios. In conclusion, they demonstrated that brain activity and behavioural performance in judgements of extreme out-group members are malleable in the face of additional information regarding controllability.

In addition, in the second seminal study of Harris and Fiske (2007), they asked some participants to make individuating judgements about targets, while others judged them based on their categorical membership. Decreased MPFC activity in response to categorical judgements of groups rated as low in warmth and competence (i.e., the "low-low" groups) replicated previous results. However, in the individuating condition, MPFC activity to low-low groups was increased. This suggests that our responses to low-low individuals are not fixed categorical responses, but can rather be altered by the type of information or cognition involved, not merely over time through changing associations, but in an on-line, situational manner. They argue that social cognition occurs along a continuum from more categorical to more individuated impressions. Groups are initially judged with respect to their categorical membership(s), but can be perceived as more individuated based on additional external or self-generated information. Hence, their

> … main message is that social cognition always depends on context … Even reactions as immediate as disgust to a dirty, unkempt homeless person or an IV-drug-injector can be altered if one plays the role of a soup-kitchen volunteer attempting to feed the hungry, or a social worker leading someone on the path away from drug-addiction. (Harris & Fiske, 2007, p. 50)

Such dynamics likely apply to responses of the self to self-disgust—if individuals can be led to engage in self-directed compassion (e.g., Gilbert, 2009; see Gilbert, this volume), this may assist in the treatment of pathological self-disgust. Expressing compassion towards others in stigmatised groups with which we are identified may facilitate this process (e.g., addicts helping other addicts).

### *Getting rid and getting clean: behavioural flexibility and goals*

While disgust responses are typically construed entirely in terms of avoidance, disgust does have distinctive approach-related features that have barely been investigated empirically. Indeed, it is the approach-related, exterminating aspects of disgust that are at the core of many of its most sensational crimes (see Jones, this volume). These features of disgust are quite different from those associated with anger or other approach-based emotions, though they resemble defensive aggression in some of their functional properties. In cases where a disgusting object is not on us or ours, or in our space (very broadly construed), we generally simply avoid them. On the other hand, when disgusting objects enter our space, we and other animals approach them in an effort to remove them (Curtis, 2007).

However, whereas aggression-related approach involves intense and potentially sustained contact, in disgust-related approach contact with the disgusting object is minimised as much as possible, as when we hold a contaminated object by its corner and away from the body, or when we employ contact barriers to remove it. Disgust can also lead to aggression-like behaviour when the threat is mobile, and must be exterminated or driven away. However, whereas offensive aggression ends when the object has been defeated or destroyed, destruction in disgust is just a prelude to getting rid of the remains. Essentially, it's an "approach-to-avoid" response. Such extermination responses are also likely to be directed onto parts or aspects of the extended self in self-disgust, perhaps occurring more often as a result of the fact that "mere avoidance" responses may be more difficult when the object one is trying to avoid is ever present. Examining pathologically extreme extermination responses directed onto the self is likely to illuminate disgust's role in suicide and self-harm (see Benson, Boden, & Vitali, this volume).

Nevertheless, the central response available to targets of disgust is to engage in cleansing, restoration of purity, etc. Across many taxa, such cleansing behaviours are as much a part of the standard stereotyped behavioural repertoire of disgust as are facial reactions (Hart, 1990; Steiner, Glaser, Hawilo, & Berridge, 2001). However, the advantages and complexity of this purification or cleansing response is downplayed by some authors, and so they do not put disgust on a par with anger (Russell & Giner-Sorolla, 2013). Nevertheless, in arguing that responses to disgust lack the features of anger, we may be making an unfair comparison. We must ask whether the kinds of justice and reparations that are used to establish anger's flexibility are equally applicable to disgust, or whether disgust might show its flexibility and value via other, disgust-specific routes.

Here, it again helps to look at the response features associated with more basic forms of disgust. When others react to our contact with physically disgusting objects, we remain disgusting until we have withdrawn and separated the object's traces from our body in a proper place for that activity (e.g., bathrooms). Once we have cleaned up, however, we are usually immediately suitable as dinner company. If contact with disgusting objects promoted a complete rejection of the contacted object, then we would quickly run out of people and possessions, as it's a dirty world. Sometimes, aspects of the psychological or bodily self cannot be "cleansed" because they are (or are perceived as) enduring, unchangeable features, which can be one source of pathological self-disgust. However, in general, when the object is one's own body or one's psyche, it is not a feasible general strategy to reject the entire body or self, or even the parts that have contacted disgusting things. Instead, we clean ourselves when possible.

Infectious individuals should *ceteris paribus* be avoided while infected, and those who prove to be more prone to infection in virtue of their repeated behaviours are often most safely avoided altogether. Therefore, the group-level properties of disgust in humans mean that those who commit physically disgusting acts do not merely pose threats to themselves, but endanger others, and perhaps the group as a whole. Hence, in judging the actions of such persons, we are responding not merely to the act itself or to the individual who committed it, but also to the threat of harm that they pose to us and ours. There is, therefore, a pressing demand for intra-group disgust to police the disease-relevant behaviours of their members.

Self-disgust at the level of intra-group identity can result in a variety of responses related to broader identity issues, some of which differ from those directed onto out-groups in so far as intra-group disgust reflects our identity, and requires different kinds of responses in order to preserve or renounce such group-based identities. In cases where one is in violation of the norms of a group with which one identifies, one might remove oneself from that group in order to avoid contaminating other members. In cases where other in-group members violate the norms of the group, we may feel self-disgust in virtue of our identification and association with them. This might result in an effort to reform the group by cleansing it of such members or behaviours, or the redrawing of the boundaries of the self by renouncing that group. In cases of "involuntary" identification with a group (e.g., due to race, ethnicity, gender, etc.), the result may be both an attempt to distance one's own case from that of others, including the public direction of hostility onto that group, inflicting punishment on them, and avoiding second-order punishment as a result of associating with them.

Consequently, just as we avoid contacting clean portions of our body with dirty portions before they are washed, we avoid contact with members of our in-group who have not cleansed themselves. Furthermore, we actively distance ourselves from those we care about when we are dirty, not only, or even primarily, as a result of the aversive nature of their response, but also to protect them. If you have just finished removing a rat from a trap, you do not merely avoid contact with your family because they would be disgusted if you touched them. Hence, self-disgust serves both individual and social interests, and these align insofar as we are sensitive to and care about the health of others, and consider them as part of our extended self. Correspondingly, whether and how we respond to others who have been physically contaminated depends enormously on our relationship to them. Parents approach and clean children, we care for our sick friends and relatives, and so on. Here self-disgust and intragroup disgust can lead to different responses than those directed onto out-groups.

Such dynamics also seem to characterise disgust's role in more abstract psychological domains—in short, the proper response to psychological "purity" threats is to distance and cleanse oneself before resuming contact, and we have developed all number of religious and medical rituals (e.g., therapy) to accomplish this. This is very different from the guilt-related tendency towards continued affiliative contact in an effort to offer reparations, and for good reasons—the only way to repair the situation is to withdraw and cleanse, as approach would be just be met with more disgust. Hence, disgust, too, has a goal—to cleanse the self, very broadly construed. The addict must "get clean", the chronic screw-up needs to "clean up their act", and so on, in order to be accepted into social circles again. Note that this goal is not merely that of the subject, but also often represents the goal of social expressions of disgust—people are re-accepted once, and only once they are perceived as clean, and intragroup disgust is one of the best ways to motivate this behaviour in those with whom we wish to maintain relationships. Thus, self- and intra-group disgust serve a higher-level function that is not merely about the withdrawal of the self, or others distancing themselves from us, but rather to enable re-incorporation. Such interpersonal dynamics are also likely to be reflected in intrapersonal dynamics, such that when the self is "split" and portions of the self are perceived as disgusting, they are likely to provoke avoidance, suppression, or attempted destruction of these aspects. The re-integration of rejected aspects of the self will thus depend on to what extent we can cleanse, reform, or remove them, or upon whether we can alter or correct the disgust judgements imposed on them by other parts of the self.

Are the goals of avoidance or self- or group-cleansing inferior to anger's goal of justice or retribution? As noted previously, Russell and Giner-Sorolla (2013) suggest that cleansing behaviours are motivated by fairly reflexive, associative appraisals, and are more automatic, less controllable, and less responsive to situational factors. Anger and guilt, they hold, are more complex and flexible in these respects. However, while the desire to purify may be automatic and enduring until the goal of cleanliness is achieved, anger shows a similar inflexibility with respect to justice. It is true that it can be satisfied by justice, but when justice is not served in a particular case, it can persist and spill over onto unrelated judgements or targets, as subjects have been shown to punish subsequent offenders more harshly if justice was not served in the original case (Goldberg, Lerner, & Tetlock, 1999). Furthermore, Giner-Sorolla and Russell note that the tendency to give reasons justifying our anger can go awry in so far as we feel a kind of compulsion to offer reasons for our anger, whether these are accurate or confabulations (Giner-Sorolla & Russell, 2009). Similarly, guilt can be evoked by circumstances over which we had no control (e.g., survivor's guilt), and if we are guilty for a wrong that cannot be repaired (due, e.g., to the victim's death) guilt may persist and spread. Whether this persistence can be a good or a bad thing, it pertains to both anger- and disgust-related dynamics.

While the adaptive nature of the withdrawal tendencies of sadness and fear is often recognised, the withdrawal features of shame and disgust are seen as a central part of their vices. However, it is not always a good response to approach others, even if the ultimate goal is reincorporation. Furthermore, anger is often not the best other-directed strategic response, for example, when the other has more power than we do. Here disgust can provide a strategic advantage, since disgust-based avoidance can serve the function of preserving boundaries while avoiding aggression. Whether approach-related anger or guilt is the best action depends on numerous non-situational factors. For instance, whether others accept your expressions of guilt depends in part on what your past behaviour reveals about your character. We can only express guilt about a repeated action so many times before the action is attributed to our character rather than situational factors, and in such cases what is required to mend the relationship is not merely reparation and another apology, but a more extended reformation of our character. Correspondingly, it makes sense that shame and self-disgust would be the dominant response of targets in such scenarios. Rather than simply leading to passive withdrawal, shame serves as an active signal that you recognise and aspire to the standard that you have violated. In addition, while not necessarily a global judgement, shame is about one's more permanent traits in much the same way that other-directed disgust is about their enduring features (Deonna et al., 2011). Hence, disgust serves as a signal that you must "check yourself", and search your soul in an effort to reform your character more broadly, and evokes corresponding emotions that can serve this end.

### *The virtues of cognitive inflexibility*

While I have just argued that disgust can be more flexible than its critics acknowledge, it still appears to be inflexible in ways that differ from anger. However, the inflexibility of these responses can itself provide various moral benefits, as suggested by recent work from Ciaramelli, Sperotto, Mattioli, and di Pellegrino (2013) on disgust responses in patients with damage to the VMPFC. Prior studies on the function of the VMPFC have indicated that it is a critical hub in social- and self-related cognition, and damage to it has been linked to decreased interest in, and evaluation of social stimuli, while sparing the valuation of physical objects. Such studies indicate that VMPFC patients are likely to retain knowledge of moral rules (Blair and Cipolotti, 2000; Saver & Damasio, 1991) and judge impersonal and voluntary moral transgressions at normal levels (Ciaramelli, Braghittoni, & di Pellegrino, 2012; Ciaramelli, Muccioli, Làdavas, & di Pellegrino, 2007; Koenigs et al., 2007; Young et al., 2010). Especially relevant for present purposes, VMPFC is sensitive to the status others hold in a social group (Rudebeck, 2006), and BA 10 of VMPFC responds less intensely to undesirable persons that elicit disgust than to socially desirable persons (Harris & Fiske, 2006). It also imbues affective value to other individuals (Noonan, Sallet, Rudebeck, Buckley, & Rushworth, 2010; Rudebeck, 2006), and its activity increases with the perceived similarity of others to the self (Mitchell, Macrae, & Banaji, 2006; Mobbs et al., 2009; Volz, Kessler, & von Cramon, 2009). In addition, it mediates preferences and affiliative tendencies for similar others (Mitchell et al., 2006; Moll & Schulkin, 2009; Krienen, Tu, & Buckner, 2010). With respect to disgust, work by Schaich Borg et al. (2008)

found greater VMPFC activation to sociomoral disgust elicitors, than to core disgust elicitors.

Ciaramelli et al. (2013) attempted to dissociate the neural correlates of core disgust, moral disgust and interpersonal disgust by examining the responses of patients with VMPFC damage (BA 10 & BA 32) to scenarios reflecting core, interpersonal and moral disgust, with anger as a control condition. All of the scenarios required subjects to decide whether or not to engage in behaviours that resulted in a material gain, but also elicited disgust. Core disgust scenarios involved standard basic elicitors of disgust, interpersonal disgust scenarios involved contact with strangers and socially stigmatised individuals, and moral disgust scenarios involved immoral behaviours that violated norms concerning fairness, hypocrisy, betrayal, and corruption, as well as actions indicating a lack of normal human motivation, such as incest or paedophilia (Rozin et al., 2008). Ciaramelli and colleagues found that VMPFC patients showed selective diminishments in interpersonal disgust, with heightened tendencies to accept contact with strangers and individuals from stigmatised groups. Lesion volume in BA 10 predicted the extent to which patients made contact with socially undesirable others. Nevertheless, their responses to both core disgust and moral disgust, as well as their capacities to process emotional costs and benefits, and to engage in the kind of complex social cognition and valuation associated with moral judgement were retained. This was also evident in their performance in control conditions involving anger.

What, then, differentiates such moral cognition and valuation from the similar abilities required for interpersonal disgust? Ciaramelli et al. (2013) sum up these differences by saying that "[control participants] in the present study avoided others not only on the basis of what they did (moral disgust scenarios), but also on the basis of what they were (interpersonal disgust scenarios). It is here that VMPFC patients' behavior diverged from that of controls" (p. 175). Thus, in moral conditions the target of disgust was individuals' *behaviour*, whereas in interpersonal conditions, the target was individuals' *physical presence* and *identity*, i.e., "[t]he social aversion mediated by VMPFC appears driven exclusively from the appraisal of others' identity and social status and not their behavior" (Ciaramelli et al., 2013, p. 176). Based on this and previous research, they argue that interpersonal disgust does not generally depend on the evaluation of the target's contingent behaviour. Instead, disgust-relevant concerns about interpersonal contamination may be more crucially dependent on abstract representations and perspectives removed from one's immediate experience of particular acts, than are judgements concerning isolated immoral behaviours.

The connection between disgust and character is further supported by recent work by Giner-Sorolla and colleagues. While their work has emphasised moral disgust's primary relationship with bodily norm, purity violations, and anger's ties to harm/fairness violations, their more recent work challenges this neat dichotomy. In Russell and Giner-Sorolla (2011b), they manipulated an agent's (a) desire to cause harm, (b) belief that an action would cause harm (intentionality), and (c) actual harmful consequences of an action. They found that desire to harm was selectively associated with disgust, while harmful consequences predicted only anger. Measurements of participants' inferences in such judgements indicated that perceptions of bad moral character partially mediated the link between disgust and desire to harm, the idea being that such desires in and of themselves are evidence of an attribution of wrongness to more stable features of the agent's identity. By itself, belief in harm evoked anger and disgust in equal proportions, however desire increased anger in no-belief scenarios, but desire and belief did not increase anger. Hence, it appeared that either belief in harmful consequences or desire to harm is sufficient to cause anger. This fits with the results from Ciaramelli et al. (2013) insofar as VMPFC patients' sociomoral judgements were determined exclusively by consequences, and that they were insensitive to negative intents and character. Furthermore, the fact that anger can be caused merely by the association of an actor with a harmful outcome, indicates an associative aspect to anger, or at least a relatively inflexible tendency to punish and blame independently from judgements of responsibility or intent, a topic that is also discussed at length in Giner-Sorolla and Russell (2009).

The finding of dissociation between categorical classification and judgements of acts supports Giner-Sorolla and colleagues' work as do the facts that moral disgust was preserved, directed primarily onto the acts of targets, and retained a close connection to anger. What Ciaramelli et al.'s results also illustrate, however, is that such categorical classification is a highly important capacity for navigating the inter- and intra-personal world, whatever its flaws or limitations, as indicated by the fact that its absence leads VMPFC patients into countless bad and destructive relationships (Damasio, 1994, 2005; Damasio, Grabowski, Frank, Galaburda, & Damasio, 1994; Denburg et al., 2007). Insofar as disgust selectively tracks categorical information concerned with social identity, it is directed onto one's own or the other's self, rather than their immediate actions, and we are better off relying more heavily on these categorical evaluative dimensions in some cases. This may be because we have to use whatever categorical information is available in encountering unknown people, or it may be due to the fact that a well-known individual or group has consistently exhibited negative behaviour that appears to be trait-based or characterological. In such cases, downplaying the individual's attempts to justify their actions in terms of situational variables, and developing a bias against interpreting situational factors as relevant to the individual's behaviour serves a protective function.

As noted, the case against disgust rests largely on appeals to its role in genocide, extreme sexism, etc. Our recognition of the protective function of deploying such categories may be obscured by the fact they are typically discussed in terms of such extreme stigmas, and few theorists want to endorse such effects. Nevertheless, we should not be so morally delicate as to deny the value of avoiding or remaining circumspect in our dealings with many groups. For example, if an addicted relative has repeatedly broken promises, or lied to you in order to get money, always attributing it to one short-term, unexpected, usually urgent situational factor or another, you may be "sick of" or "fed up" with their excuses, and may do well to remain sceptical of *any* reasons they offer. If you are repeatedly solicited on the street for money with false stories about, for example, needing petrol money to get a child to the hospital, and so on, you do well to question the sincerity of those who approach you in this way. And if you know that panhandlers (and telemarketers) will exploit even basic polite refusals to continue pitching you, disengaging or hanging up is appropriate.

In other words, in such contexts, you are better off becoming less flexible, employing more stable categorical associations, with a subsequent bias against sensitivity to situational factors (in no small part because in justifying or excusing our failings, we tend to skew the interpretation towards uncontrollable, situational factors). In some cases, categorical information is a better predictor of behaviour than individual identity. People generally appear to perceive themselves and others positively by default, as reflected in the fact that the MPFC has a high level of baseline activity (Gusnard, Akbudak, Shulman, & Raichle, 2001). Hence, in such cases, we often must actively resist feelings like compassion and trust, even in response to those closest to us, since we may all become so wretched that even those who would give their lives for us must (and should) distance themselves.

Even if we all agree that many groups do not deserve the stigma heaped upon them, we must still ask whether the "low-low quadrant" (see Harris & Fiske, 2006) should simply be empty in our appraisals of others, or whether it is warranted and accurate to classify some people, perhaps even ourselves, in this way. There are certainly those in the world who mean us harm, and who will exploit our positive feelings in a manner that violates some norms that we hold as basic to the human contract. Psychopaths, for example, will not respond sympathetically to the pain of their victims, or their pleas for empathy and compassion. Indeed, they seem incapable of such responses, and hence to lack abilities that are core to our conception of humanity (Decety, Chen, Harenski, & Kiehl, 2013). In such cases, I maintain, we are warranted in seeing them as falling outside the human moral circle to some degree, and we would be foolish not to take this into account in our personal interactions with them.

### *Dehumanisation*

As discussed earlier, Buckels and Trapnell (2013) presented some of the first direct empirical evidence that disgust causes dehumanisation, where disgust reactions towards experimentally created out-groups increase associations of the out-group with animals (and the in-group with humanity). Interestingly, however, they found that *all* participants showed such a shift, regardless of disgust induction, and despite the arbitrariness of the groups. This suggests that dehumanisation may be a more general and fundamental part of our group psychology, rather being disgust-specific. In addition, Buckels and Trapnell note that the IAT task they used is incapable of distinguishing between strengthened associations between out-groups and animals, and strengthened associations between the in-group and humanity, as participants showed both changes. Therefore, exclusion from our circles might be a secondary effect of heightened in-group bias rather than out-group negativity.

Given the extended nature of human selves, this raises the possibility that in some cases, dehumanisation reflects distance from the extended "self" more generally. The boundaries of our moral circles and in-groups are ever shifting, and while they do not form a neat series of concentric circles, they typically display some nested structure. Hence, rather than always involving a specific comparison with animals, distance from the self may de facto put out-groups closer to animals insofar as our "self" extends to the human-animal boundary. All of this suggests that dehumanisation comes in degrees and is not always catastrophically damaging, or even negative. While identifying Jews with rats is both morally reprehensible and predictively vacuous, other comparisons are more fruitful. For example, many addicts' behaviour is so dominated by their status as an addict, that this can be a better predictor than their intentions, values, etc., since their higher human capacities are both eroded and disconnected from their ultimate desires, rationality, and behaviour. As a result, the differences between the core addictive behaviour of humans and rats are all too small, and comparisons of them can be illuminating, even for addicts themselves.

Does this mean that we should treat addicts like rats in a global, reductive sense? Absolutely not. We must consider issues concerning responsibility and moral capability, as well as the difference between dehumanisation and inhumane treatment. Whether or not animal-like characteristics are seen as disgusting depends on the target's capacity to act otherwise, and the perception that they are responsible to act in this way. Children are child-like, but this does not disgust us because we do not expect the kind of adult-like capacities for affective or cognitive regulation. Similarly, animals are certainly stupid(er) and uncivilised, but this does not morally disgust us because they do not have a capacity or responsibility to act otherwise, and we in fact show neural responses when mentalising about dogs that are similar to those in response to humans (Mitchell et al., 2005). Similarly, while animals are certainly animalised, this does not justify inhumane treatment of them. Animal rights advocates argue that we should not even treat rats like rats, so to speak. The same principle applies to those who morally disgust us. While the psychopath is dehumanised, this does not justify treating them inhumanely.

Finally, a crucial limitation to Buckels and Trapnell's study is that they use sadness as a control negative emotion, and so cannot speak to whether anger, fear, or other negative emotions would have the same dehumanising effect as disgust. This represents a pattern seen in much of the qualitative and experimental work on disgust (e.g., Chapman et al., 2009; Schnall et al., 2008). Disgust is contrasted with sadness, but there are no controls to determine whether other emotions more relevant to dehumanisation and moral judgement would have similar effects. Indeed, anger has also been shown to cause implicit negativity toward out-groups (DeSteno, Dasgupta, Bartlett, & Cajdric, 2004), and unpublished work by Giner-Sorolla and Russell (2014) has demonstrated that anger and fear also generate dehumanisation.

Thus, if we examine the atrocities to which disgust has contributed, we find many unindicted co-conspirators. The sense of elevation, purity, and pride in Aryan blood elicited by Leni Riefenstahl's films, and the anger, fear, and solidification of in-group identity evoked by Hitler's speeches, were arguably just as potent in perpetrating genocide as disgust. Yet in recent critiques, disgust has been singled out. Furthermore, critics of disgust nearly always and solely point to its role in moral behaviours that most readers will condemn, without noting that moral disgust has also been shown to occur in responses to violations such as hypocrisy, lying, cheating, racism, sycophancy, exploitation of the weak, unfairness, betrayal, and theft, among others. Critics would argue that disgust is not suited as a response to *any* moral violations, but the case is harder to make when confronted with the potential positive contribution of disgust to values with which we unreservedly identify.

## *Conclusion*

All moral emotions can have negative effects when they are in some sense inappropriate, and disgust is no exception. However, if I am correct, then (contrary to those who see little positive role for moral disgust compared to other emotion), moral disgust is also no exception in its ability to serve a morally beneficial function for individuals or groups (including the direction of disgust onto the self or one's own in-groups). It accomplishes this function via the induction of self-disgust or shame in its targets, both of which motivate them to withdraw and cleanse or reform their character. This serves to exclude such individuals in the short term in order to protect the group or self as a whole, but can also motivate reincorporation through appropriate responses on the part of the target. Hence, while disgust can be a dangerous emotion under many circumstances, in order to understand why it sometimes goes wrong, we need to understand how it usually goes right, a question I hope I have begun to answer.

*CHAPTER THREE*

# Disgust and self-disgust: a disability studies perspective

*Donna Reeve*

## *Introduction*

There has been very little written within disability studies about the role of self-disgust in the lives of disabled people, which is probably not surprising given that there is little mention of disgust *per se* in relation to disability. In order to consider how self-disgust may occur in the lives of disabled people, it is therefore necessary to look at the role of disgust in contemporary disablism and their interconnections. In doing so, I will be adopting a sociological, rather than psychological, approach to disgust and self-disgust, arguing that both dimensions need to be considered if the impact of these cognitive schemas on disabled people are to be fully understood.

This chapter will start by briefly discussing several approaches to disgust—principally the ideas of Paul Rozin (psychology), Martha Nussbaum (philosophy), and Sarah Ahmed (sociology of emotions). After presenting an historical analysis of how disgust contributed to the exclusion of disabled people from society (Hughes, 2012), this chapter will then look at how disgust can be seen within contemporary psycho-emotional disablism, experienced by disabled people at the start of the twenty-first century. Disgust can be revealed when a stranger avoids interacting with a disabled person on the street, within newspaper reports of disabled people as workshy benefit scroungers, and as part of disablist hate crime. These acts of psycho-emotional disablism contribute to the social marginalisation of disabled people and their cultural representation as less than human.

I will next consider how self-disgust can contribute to two consequences of internalised oppression—"passing" as normal and hierarchies of impairment. It is important to note that internalised oppression is not a permanent state of mind nor is it inevitable for all disabled people. Contact with disability arts and groups of disabled people who challenge the negative cultural images of disability can help counter this unconscious form of psycho-emotional disablism. I will also show that living with a "different" body can produce ways of being that are positive and creative, free of the self-disgust that might be expected from "bodies [that] violate social norms" (Roberts & Goldenberg, 2007, p. 399). Finally I will look at the ways in which disabled people live with incontinence and stomas, showing how self-disgust changes over time. Whilst society views incontinence with horror and disgust, it will be shown that, for those who live with this condition, it is possible to "unmake" self-disgust, revealing the important role that support and information has in making this happen.

This chapter comes with an important caveat. Many of the cited examples are drawn from my doctoral research which collected narratives about experiences of "disability" in the lives of people with physical impairments (Reeve, 2008); names used in quotes are pseudonyms chosen by participants. It should be remembered that this research was not looking at disgust and self-disgust in the lives of disabled people *per se*. Hence, the analysis I present here is necessarily partial and incomplete and is meant as a starting point for further discussion. I suggest that a sociological and/or disability studies-informed analysis of disgust and self-disgust in the lives of disabled people has much to offer these important topics, which are otherwise largely in the domain of the psychological.

## *The concept of disgust*

Whilst disgust is often experienced or understood as a visceral emotion, psychologist Paul Rozin has shown that disgust also has a strong cognitive component (Rozin & Fallon, 1987). Rozin, Haidt, and

McCauley (2008) unpack the cultural evolution of disgust and break it down into five stages: distaste, core, animal nature, interpersonal, and moral. Whilst bad tastes could be seen as the starting point for the emergence of a disgust reaction—bad-tasting food could signal the presence of poison—core disgust refers to the oral rejection of "offensive objects" in order to protect the body from disease and infection. Moving away from food-related objects of disgust, animal nature disgust covers examples that focus on the body rather than just the mouth, such as inappropriate sexual acts, poor hygiene, death, and deviation from the ideal body (as seen in the presence of impairment or obesity). These forms of animal nature disgust are thought to be troubling to people because they serve as reminders of our commonality to animals, particularly that we will all sicken and die in the end. However, the philosopher Nussbaum (2004) points out that whilst disgust sheds light on "our problematic relationship with our own animality" (Nussbaum, 2004, p. 89), aspects of animals such as strength, agility, and speed are not seen as inherently disgusting. Therefore, to be more accurate, disgust is associated with an anxiety about "a type of vulnerability that we share with other animals, the propensity to decay and to become waste products ourselves" (Nussbaum, 2004, p. 92).

This avoidance of contamination does not stop with certain core objects of disgust that serve as reminders of mortality and animality. In an effort to further protect the self from contamination, a buffer zone is created to repel certain groups of people in society who act as carriers of contamination and who are often portrayed as inherently smelly, foul, or otherwise contaminated (Nussbaum, 2004). This buffer group serves to further distance the dominant group from the troubling reminder of mortality and animality:

> So powerful is the desire to cordon ourselves off from our animality that we often don't stop at feces, cockroaches, and slimy animals. We need a group of humans to bound ourselves against, who will come to exemplify the boundary line between the truly human and the basely animal. (Nussbaum, 2004, p. 107)

This form of interpersonal disgust has been used throughout history to exclude and discredit certain groups of people as well as individuals (Nussbaum, 2004). For example, the portrayal of Jewish people as disgusting in Nazi propaganda in Germany was a necessary first step to their reduction to the status of animals, a group of people set outside from the rest of society. Once Jewish people had been reduced to bare biological life in this way, then the concentration camp and the horrors committed therein became possible (Agamben, 1998).

Like interpersonal disgust, moral disgust is tied up with protecting the social order and, rather than being tied up with direct contact between strangers and undesirables, tends to relate to certain moral offences which risk violating the sanctity of the soul or the purity of the body (Rozin et al., 2008). As part of her analysis of the role that moral disgust plays in the law, Nussbaum (2004) shows how words such as "horrible" or "outrageous", indicating harm, are applied to moral phenomena such as same-sex relationships, in order to support legislation outlawing such practices (Nussbaum, 2004). The core of this moral disgust is still fear of contamination and the need to separate the self from the buffer zone of the non-human/animal, but using moral disgust as the reason for legislation is deeply problematic because of the lack of actual harm. As Nussbaum comments:

> the moral progress of society can be measured by the degree to which it *separates* disgust from danger and indignation, basing laws and social rules on substantive risk and harm, rather than on the symbolic relationship an object bears to anxieties about animality and normality. (Nussbaum, 2004, p. 116, emphasis in original)

Therefore, because of the ways in which disgust is used to maintain social hierarchies, a civilised society (Elias, 2000) will work to remove/challenge these symbolic relationships which act as a "barrier to the full equality and mutual respect of all citizens" (Nussbaum, 2004, p. 117).

Nussbaum concludes her analysis of disgust by summarising that disgust has an evolutionary role in protecting health (distaste/core disgust), protects the psyche from fears about mortality and decay (animal nature disgust) and has a complex role in managing what is considered to be disgusting vs. attractive in society (interpersonal/moral disgust). This latter role of disgust which involves the transference of disgust to other objects is socially learned, common to many cultures, and ends up contributing to social groups and hierarchies. However, rather than focusing only on the ways in which one group of people is constructed as disgusting, it is also necessary to consider those who do the naming;

in other words, to include "criticism of the disgusted rather than of the constructed cause of their disgust" (Nussbaum, 2004, p. 123).

Turning the focus onto the disgusted in this way is echoed in the work of Ahmed (2004), who considers the *performative* nature of disgust; in other words, the ways in which speech acts construct disgusting objects. When someone says "that's disgusting!", this transfers:

> the stickiness of the word "disgust" to an object, which henceforth becomes generated as the very thing that is spoken … The speech act "That's disgusting!", can work as a form of vomiting, as an attempt to expel something whose proximity is felt to be threatening and contaminating. (Ahmed, 2004, p. 94)

Because of the way in which vomiting involves the expulsion of something that has already been ingested, speech acts like this create the *disgusted* subject in addition to the *disgusting* object (Ahmed, 2004, p. 94). However, speech acts are only performative in the presence of other witnesses, who form a community on the basis of their shared judgement and pulling away from the disgusting object or event.

Interpersonal and moral disgust exerts most influence on intergroup relations. For example, feelings of disgust towards another group of people who are perceived to be dissimilar, low-status, and even animal-like, such as immigrants, foreigners, or people in receipt of welfare. As I will show in the next section, this has important implications when looking at the treatment of disabled people in society who can be seen as other, inferior, and less than human. Therefore, the role that disgust plays in transmitting cultural values is important when looking at the experiences of disabled people: "Our analysis suggests a cultural evolution of disgust that brings it to the heart of what it means to be human" (Rozin et al., 2008, p. 771).

## *The role of disgust in the project of ableism*

One of the questions raised by Nussbaum that is particularly pertinent to this chapter is why people often feel disgust towards disabled people in particular. In part, it is possible that contact with people with *impairments* (i.e., a medical condition, illness, or bodily/behavioural difference) provokes a kind of "primary disgust" (Nussbaum,

2004). Impairment can result in bodies that leak in unpredictable and uncontrolled ways; hence, it could be "explained" that disgust towards disabled people (particularly those who have visible leakage such as dribbling) is provoked by a fear of contagion from a stranger's urine or saliva. In addition, the presence of impairment serves as a reminder to everyone that "we have mental facilities that can encounter arrest; even before we die, we can lose bodily parts" (Nussbaum, 2004, p. 93). Therefore, disgust towards disabled people could be "explained away" as being rooted in anxieties about mortality or fear of contagion—forms of primary disgust which will be much less commonly directed towards other minority groups in society who are non-impaired.

However, for the purposes of this chapter, I want to explore aspects of disgust and self-disgust which are not so biologically and evolutionarily ingrained; in other words, to consider the role of interpersonal and moral disgust in the production of disablism. Disgust has a social history and, for disabled people, it has been the creation of a *civilised society* which has led to the ontological invalidation and exclusion of disabled people from that society (Hughes, 2012). Drawing on the work of Norbert Elias (2000), Hughes argues that as morals and manners became refined in the name of "civilised society", so tolerance of impairment decreased. Those people who failed to behave and move within the narrow range of "acceptable behaviour" were seen as disgusting and hence as unsuitable candidates for citizenship. In addition the civilising process required that such bodies be kept out of sight and disabled people ended up excluded from mainstream society, often in large institutions on the edges of towns. The nineteenth century was also a time when people would pay money to gawp at disabled people living in asylums or as exhibits in a freak show. Here, the dual nature of disgust can be seen—fascination coupled with contempt/revulsion. The freak show also allowed the observer, a civilised person, to compare themselves favourably with the "monster" on display. Hence, a variety of congenital and progressive impairments could, with a bit of imagination, be turned into a hybrid of the human and animal, producing freak-show acts such as: "the Turtle Boy, the Mule-Faced Woman, Serpentina, the Camel Girl, the Dog-Faced Boy, the Bear Woman, the Lobster Boy, the Lion Woman, the Alligator Man, and Sealo" (Thomson, 1996, p. 5). These public displays of impaired bodies and minds served to push the "status of disability towards the animal" (Hughes, 2012,

p. 21) and represent examples of the buffer between human and animal that is policed by the emotion of disgust.

Hughes (2012) argues that the emotion of disgust is largely responsible for maintaining the disability/non-disability binary, and the social hierarchy whereby "normal" people are superior to those perceived to be impaired. An important part of this process of "othering" is down to the role of ableism which is a "child of the civilising process" (Hughes, 2012, p. 30). Ableism is defined as: "a network of beliefs, processes and practices that produce a particular kind of self and body (the corporeal standard) that is projected as the perfect, as the species-typical, and, therefore, as essential and fully human" (Campbell, 2005, p. 127).

Disgust plays a pivotal role in ableism because the body produced by ableism is clean and hygienic, contained and invulnerable, autonomous and independent—free from contamination or reminders of mortality and decay. Even though this corporeal standard is a mirage that lies outside the messiness of real blood-and-flesh bodies, ableism still operates through disgust to separate out those who are "fully human" from those who fail to meet the mark. The failure of non-disabled people to recognise their own mortality, vulnerability, and imperfections results in these fears being projected onto disabled people, who are then identified as monstrous, chaotic, and disgusting. The consequences of ableism on the lives of disabled people are profound:

> Ableism makes the world alien to disabled bodies and, at the same time, produces impairment as an invalidating experience. It is manifest in our cultural inclination towards normalcy by way of correction, towards homogeneity by way of disparagement of difference. (Hughes, 2012, p. 24)

In other words, ableism produces a society that does not take account of the needs of people with impairments and so excludes them—producing disablism. The ontological invalidation of disability as a worthwhile status encourages rehabilitation or cure as a response to impairment; whilst this may often be helpful and desirable, being forced to walk in order to be closer to "normal" may end up damaging physical health more than becoming a wheelchair user. Hughes suggests that: "The dynamic of the disgust response—down to the removal of the aversive object—is, in a concrete way, reproduced in the practice of rehabilitation" (Hughes, 2012, p. 27).

Another concrete example of the removal of impaired bodies from society on the grounds of disgust is seen in the so-called "ugly laws", which were introduced in many parts of the USA from the late nineteenth century onwards. The last ugly law was repealed in 1974 in Chicago; this law prevented anyone from appearing in public who was "diseased, maimed, mutilated, or in any way deformed, so as to be an unsightly or disgusting object" (Schweik, 2009, p. 293). Thus, the emotion of disgust was used to justify the exclusion of disabled people from mainstream society—so as not to upset the sensitivities of the general public.

## *Psycho-emotional disableism*

Ableism is entrenched in Western culture and is therefore seen in the behaviour and attitudes of both disabled and non-disabled people. When ableism is enacted, then the person with impairments experiences disablism. The extended social relational definition of disablism (Thomas, 2007) is derived from the same roots as the more familiar social model of disability, but explicitly references two dimensions of disablism. First, there is structural disablism which operates at the public/structural level and includes familiar barriers such as inaccessible buildings and discrimination in employment. The second dimension, which is most relevant to this chapter, is called psycho-emotional disablism and includes forms of social oppression that operate at a private/personal level, impacting on psycho-emotional wellbeing. Ableist assumptions can be found at the roots of both dimensions of disablism. For example, if a wheelchair user is in a space which assumes that steps can be negotiated because able-bodiedness assumes two working legs, then they experience structural disablism. On the other hand, psycho-emotional disablism can happen if that same wheelchair user is avoided or ignored by others—actions that originate from ableist assumptions that being unable to walk also removes the ability to speak for oneself or feel hurt at being spoken over in this way.

Psycho-emotional disablism itself can be broken down into two kinds (Reeve, 2008). Indirect psycho-emotional disablism describes the emotional consequences to structural disablism, such as hurt and anger at being faced with an inaccessible building or a broken hearing loop. Direct psycho-emotional disablism emerges at the interpersonal level in the relationships that a disabled person has with other people—such as friends, family, professionals, strangers—as well as the relationship they have with themselves. Examples of direct psycho-emotional disablism would include being stared at or made fun of by strangers for walking differently, or being denied access to family-planning services because of the assumption that disabled people are asexual.

I now want to develop the previous discussion of disgust in the creation of ableism, to show how disgust might be evident in examples of direct psycho-emotional disablism between disabled people and others. Disgust is particularly pertinent to this form of disablism which occurs at the interpersonal level, compared to structural disablism arising from the interaction between an impaired body and an environmental or institutional barrier. It is also interesting to note that disgust, like psycho-emotional disablism, has received relatively little attention in disability studies; this might be because of a traditional focus on processes and barriers external to the person, rather than those operating at the personal/psychological level.

Although the experience of being stared at by others can be upsetting, being avoided by strangers or friends can be just as hurtful (Reeve, 2008). For example, Robert, aged fifty-four, a wheelchair user with invisible impairments, said: "[T]hey look at you and it's, 'Oh keep away from him'—you know, it's like we've got the plague, you know. And that really gets me, that do" (Robert). Such interactions with strangers (i.e., acts of avoidance rather than engagement) remind the disabled person that they are not part of the same social world as other people. It has been acknowledged that there is a lack of cultural rules about how to interact socially with disabled people (Keith, 1996), and all too often fear of saying or doing the wrong thing results in avoidance rather than engagement. However, Adinuf (so called because he had "ad enough"), aged forty-eight, who had reflex sympathetic dystrophy, commented that he did not feel that the public were that interested in being educated and were happy to keep disabled people in their "place":

> Never mind what the disability is—have a disabled person around them, might educate Joe Public, but Joe Public keeps putting the barrier there. "Right you've got a line there, you mustn't cross that, you've got a disability so you must stay behind that line." (Adinuf)

This reluctance to change behaviour towards disabled people may have biological as well as cultural dimensions. As discussed previously, people with impairments may evoke forms of primary disgust because of their bodily difference—although in the example above, it was simply the presence of a wheelchair, a signifier of disability, that resulted in Robert being treated as if he were contagious. Research has shown that similar disgust and avoidance behaviours are shown towards people with birthmarks, which are known not to be contagious, as towards those with influenza (Ryan, Oaten, Stevenson, & Case, 2012). This false-positive that has emerged at an evolutionary level means that it may be quite difficult for people to unlearn this reaction to bodily difference. Nonetheless, research has indicated the harmful effects of this on the self-esteem of disabled people with visible impairments, who experience this kind of social distancing on a daily basis (e.g., Hawkesworth, 2001; Keith, 1996; Murphy, 1987; Shakespeare, Gillespie-Sells, & Davies, 1996; Watson, 2003). It is to be hoped that the increasing visibility of disabled people at every level of society will make impairment part of the mundane rather than the exotic, helping to challenge this evolutionary false-positive.

Negative cultural messages about disability fuel psycho-emotional disablism and therefore have a big impact on how disabled people feel about themselves. This is well illustrated by the changes made to benefits for disabled people who are too ill to work, as part of the welfare reform agenda in the UK. Media harassment of disabled people has helped to create an image of sick and disabled claimants as being less "deserving" of support than their non-disabled peers (Piggott & Grover, 2009). These negative images of disabled people as work-shy, benefit scroungers can cause psycho-emotional disablism for those attempting to claim disability benefits because of the further devaluing of disabled people caused by "being labelled 'lazy', 'feckless' and generally an affront to the apparently decent, hard-working tax payers in society" (Garthwaite, 2011, p. 372).

Soldatic and Pini (2009) analysed the role of disgust evident within government policy for welfare reform in Australia (which has informed the direction taken by the coalition government in the UK). They showed that disgust was used to move welfare entitlement from being rights-based to entailing notions of deservingness. By constructing the disabled claimant as being morally untrustworthy, "[d]isgust was used to mark out, separate and exclude a particular class of disabled citizens to redefine them as 'undeserving'" (Soldatic & Pini, 2009, p. 89). At the same time, government policy changes were supported by media releases reporting the apparent rate of fraudulent claims and "benefit cheats". Hence, the discourse of disgust that circulated throughout government policy was reproduced within popular culture, with the key intent "to shift the public imaginary of disability, rendering some bodies as not really disabled enough to deserve disability entitlements" (Soldatic & Pini, 2009, p. 89). As in the UK, this form of moral disgust serves to separate lazy, feckless, disabled benefit-scroungers from those deemed to be more deserving of welfare support at a time of economic austerity.

Disablist hate crime is an extreme form of direct psycho-emotional disablism and occurs when a disabled person is subject to harassment, hostility, assault, and abuse based solely on their (perceived) identity as disabled. The roots of disability hate crime and harassment are prejudice and contempt for disabled people "rooted in the view that disabled people are inferior; in some cases less than human" (Quarmby, 2008, p. 8). It has been suggested that media reporting of welfare reform, with its language of skivers and scroungers, may be contributing to increased rates of disablist hate crime and harassment (Briant, Watson, & Philo, 2011). The internet, which allows anyone with an online presence to express an opinion, contains many examples of disablist hate speech, such as:

> Retards coast through life unknowing of the massive drain they put on society. These massive drains are nothing more than disgusting sub-human nuisances. The worst of these untouchables is the combination of the two, the crippled retard. These sad sacs of human refuse have serious defects and don't deserve to live. What the hell is the point to keep these crack baby, drooling retard, wheelchair-bound, disgusting fucks? There is none. ("Jesus Christ", cited in Sherry, 2010, p. 35)

It is clear that "Jesus Christ" here sees him/herself as infinitely superior to those with learning difficulties (labelled as "retards" here), and places this particular group of disabled people firmly in the "less than human" category. Sherry's research into disablist hate crime found many such pieces on the internet that described disabled people as "useless, disease-spreading and drooling vegetables" (Sherry, 2010, p. 39); in other words, disabled people as objects of disgust. If one considers the performative nature of disgust, then the repetition within these internet postings of disabled people as objects of disgust serves to construct this group "as non-human, *as beneath and below the bodies of the disgusted* .... They embody that which is lower than human or civil life" (Ahmed, 2004, p. 97, emphasis in original). This creation of a group in society—disabled people—who are less than human then paves the way for an alarmingly high number of hate-speech postings, which advocate the killing of disabled people through abortion or euthanasia (Sherry, 2010).

### *Internalised oppression and self-disgust*

So far, this chapter has discussed the ways in which disabled people can be the objects of disgust and how disgust has figured in the creation of disabling barriers in society, which serve to maintain the social hierarchy between disabled and non-disabled people. Unlike other social groups, disabled people may experience more primary disgust because of the association impairment has with perceived risks of contamination or reminders of mortality. Either way, disabled people can be the objects of disgust—so what happens if people internalise this disgust and experience self-disgust?

Internalised oppression is common to any minority group in society and refers to the ways in which members of the minority group internalise the prejudices held by the majority group about them. In the case of disabled people, the internalisation of prejudices and myths about disability has a negative impact on self-esteem and self-confidence (Marks, 1999). For example, someone may believe that now that they have become disabled they are sexually undesirable or unable to be a parent. Internalised oppression (or, more correctly, internalised ableism, as discussed by Campbell, 2009) is a form of direct psycho-emotional disablism which comes about in the relationships which disabled people have with themselves (Reeve, 2008). Internalised oppression can be very difficult to identify and challenge because of the way that it operates at the unconscious level, maintained by a lack of positive images and representations of disability in society and culture. Furthermore, unlike gender and ethnicity, disabled people are often the only members of their families with impairments, so there may be few positive role models for disabled people to be found within their immediate family and circle of friends.

Two important consequences of internalised oppression are passing and hierarchies of impairment that can reveal aspects of self-disgust. "Passing" refers to the way in which someone may choose to hide their impairment, thereby appearing non-disabled to the rest of the world. So, for example, someone might choose clothes that hide physical difference or choose not to disclose their disability status at a job interview. It could be argued that this is a pragmatic choice in order to avoid having to deal with psycho-emotional disablism, such as the thoughtless comments and actions of strangers (Reeve, 2008). However, Hughes (2012) suggests that passing involves internalising the disgust response—in the form of shame—that the disabled person assumes will be invoked if their impairment is not concealed (see also Powell, Simpson, & Overton, this volume, for a discussion of how shame and self-disgust can co-exist).

In their work looking at disgust in relation to gender, Roberts and Goldenberg (2007) suggest that disgust can be directed towards the self when one fails to meet societal norms of behavioural and bodily control. They argue that self-disgust is a self-conscious emotion because "it involves self-evaluation against internalized cultural standards" (Roberts & Goldenberg, 2007, p. 398); responses to this self-disgust can be seen in the ways that women hide natural body functions such as menstruation. Applying this logic to disability, passing as non-disabled could be seen as a response to self-disgust, rejecting and avoiding the disability part of one's identity by adopting a non-disabled identity. So, it can be seen that depending on what theoretical orientation is adopted, the *reasons* for passing vary from the internalisation of the predicted disgust response, rejecting a disabled identity as a response to self-disgust, or simply wanting to avoid the experience of psycho-emotional disablism. These reasons could be expected to vary from one disabled person to another, or by time and place, or someone could be passing for a mixture of all three. The solution will also vary depending on the theoretical orientation—therapy to help dislodge the self-disgust, or changing society to be more accepting of disabled people so that passing is not necessary to ease social interaction.

Internalised oppression not only refers to how someone feels about themselves, but also affects how they treat other people within the same social group; for example, gay men may be homophobic to lesbians, black people may be racist towards Asian people (Young, 1990).

Hierarchies of impairment circulate in society and are internalised by both disabled and non-disabled people. According to these rankings, people with congenital impairments are lower than people with acquired impairments, amputation scores higher than spinal cord injury, and physical impairment is higher up the list than learning difficulties (Deal, 2003). An important factor in these hierarchies is the relative closeness to "normality".

> There is a real hierarchy of what is acceptable appearance within the disabled community: what is beautiful, what is ugly. At the top is someone who sits in a wheelchair but looks perfect. I have a friend who has cerebral palsy; she always says cerebral palsy is the dregs. They drool and have a speech impairment, movement problems, that kind of thing. On the high end of the scale is the person with a polio disability because physically they look okay. (Ann, in Chapkis, 1988, p. 20)

It could be argued that disgust plays a role in placing bodies that drool or have uncontrolled movements at the bottom of the hierarchy, thereby creating a buffer group for those higher up the hierarchy, to protect them from being reminded of their own mortality and animality, as discussed earlier (Nussbaum, 2004). This process of placing oneself on the scale and identifying the groups to which one feels superior can increase self-esteem for the individual. However, this response to internalised oppression (or self-disgust) further isolates and oppresses those groups of disabled people perceived to be towards the bottom end of the hierarchy.

As part of their discussion about gender and disgust, Roberts and Goldenberg (2007) state that: "consistently, research shows that those whose bodies violate social norms, or those who perceive their bodies to be socially unacceptable, feel self-disgust" (Roberts & Goldenberg, 2007, p. 399). This would therefore imply that most, if not all, disabled people should feel self-disgust because the criterion for disability is the presence of an impairment which by definition is not "normal". Self-disgust *may* be common when people first acquire impairment—due to a lifetime of internalised cultural messages about disabled people as "other" and disgusting. However, it is likely that this "emotion schema" (see Powell, Simpson, & Overton, this volume) will change over time as the person re-evaluates themselves now that they have become disabled.

"Coming out" as a disabled person involves recognising and rejecting this self-disgust:

> Having come out, the disabled person no longer regards disability as a reason for self-disgust, or as something to be denied or hidden, but rather as an imposed oppressive social category to be challenged and broken down. (Swain & Cameron, 1999, p. 76)

Coming out is often associated with a political awakening and meeting other disabled people; the disabled people's movement and disability arts have been crucial in helping disabled people overcome their internalised oppression and to develop more positive ways of being. Meeting disabled people and being exposed to more positive images of disability will certainly help reduce feelings of self-disgust and other forms of internalised oppression. The reactions of close family and friends are also very important—the reaction of a lover who recoils at the sight of impairment does little to reduce self-disgust. The messages about disability discussed in the previous sections—through the rhetoric of welfare reform or the reality of disablist hate crime and speech—will also tend to fuel rather than help feelings of self-disgust. Soldatic and Meekosha (2012) concluded that the process of continually fighting to prove entitlement to disability benefits in the face of media messages about disabled claimants being fraudulent and lazy, led to "internalised feelings of self-disgust" (Soldatic & Meekosha, 2012, p. 147).

It should also be remembered that being disabled, having a body that "violates social norms", is not always negative—new ways of being and freedoms can emerge within this marginalised space. So, for example, disabled people can develop new sexual identities which are not limited by the normative assumptions about sex (Siebers, 2012). A good example of this is the way that people with paraplegia, who have lost sensation in the traditional erotic body zones, find ways of eroticising other parts of their bodies that still have sensation. Disabled women can report feeling freed from the usual gender roles assigned to women, such as caring and motherhood; disabled men may renegotiate their masculinity by seeing parenting as being about raising a child rather than siring a baby (Robertson, 2004). The rise of disability arts has provided a space where bodily difference is explored and celebrated rather than treated as deviation and lack. James Partridge was badly burnt in a car fire and set up the charity Changing Faces which supports people living with conditions, marks, or scars that affect their appearance. As he said: "I am never going to conform to society's requirements and I'm thrilled because I am blissfully released from all that crap. That's the liberation of disfigurement" (Partridge, cited in Shakespeare et al., 1996, p. 81).

## *Incontinence and leaky bodies*

Incontinence is a medical condition in which a person has little or no control over urination and/or defecation; it can cause considerable distress for those who experience incontinence as well as for family and carers (Brittain & Shaw, 2007). However, incontinence is also associated with cultural norms. Seymour (1998) points out that the managing of infant continence is a public affair, as reflected by TV advertising for nappies and the provision of baby-changing areas in public spaces. Compare this with the treatment of adult continence in the public arena: the odd, discreet Tena Lady advertisement on TV (for mild bladder weakness) and very few adult changing areas in public spaces such as shopping centres and train stations (Hanson, Bichard, & Greed, 2007). Living with incontinence is a direct challenge to the modernist subject because one is living with a body that is not reliable or contained, and which generally provokes fear and disgust in others. Bodies that fail to meet this requirement of citizenship are hidden away—incontinence is used as the primary reason to place older people in residential care, second only to dementia (Help the Aged, 2008). Incontinence is also being used as a reason to justify assisted suicide on the grounds of "dignity", which rightfully concerns some people in the disability movement:

> Just as feminists declared "the personal is political", we must assert that incontinence is just another human condition, no more worthy of the death penalty than uncontrolled body temperature. Like feminists, we need to begin attending to it among ourselves, raising our consciousnesses. Because even if we aren't talking about it, the "death with dignity" forces certainly are. (Kelly, 2002, no pagination)

As discussed earlier, bodily excretions such as urine and faeces are generally seen as potential sources of contamination and objects of disgust. Therefore, bodies that are outside the cultural norms for leakiness can be viewed as less than human, sequestered outside the mainstream in residential care and hospices, eventually to be granted a merciful release. The question I now want to consider is whether people living with incontinence necessarily view themselves with self-disgust.

Several of the participants in my doctoral research talked about incontinence as a part of their illness or impairment. Laura, aged forty-one, had multiple sclerosis and described the experience of being taught how to use catheters in order to pass urine as "mortifying. It's like, 'Oh, has it come to this?'" (Laura). However, as her story later showed, her reaction towards incontinence changed markedly as she became adjusted to this new way of life:

> I think somebody like [friend with multiple sclerosis], because I give him a lift, we're driving home, and he says, "Laura, I'm sorry about this—put your emergency flashing lights on now, I'm going to wet myself". We're laughing at this—"No, no, don't make me laugh", and then of course he can't get out of the car without assistance. So I'm having to get him out of the car, he's over six foot, prop him up against the car, and then I had to disappear so he wouldn't be embarrassed. And then he can't pee. So we're there ten minutes [hesitates] but I think that's, that in a way, we were laughing about all of that ... But it's just lovely that we can [hesitates]. There was a time when I would never have—I remember when I was diagnosed, they said to me, had I had any continence problems. "Oh my God! Certainly not!" And now to be able to talk to each other like that. (Laura)

This way in which peeing (or not, as the case may be) becomes the topic of a funny story, and the easy way in which Laura and her friend could deal with his urgent need by the side of the road, show the manner in which these different forms of bodily elimination just become part of everyday life for the pair of them. It has been suggested that laughter and disgust are often interconnected: "The sudden discharge of tension achieves in laughter, as in vomiting, an overcoming of disgust, a contact with the 'abject' that does not lead to lasting contamination or defilement" (Menninghaus, 2003, pp. 10–11). Humour allows Laura to support her friend, but also causes her to reflect on how incontinence is no longer a source of deep shame and embarrassment any more. It has simply become part of everyday life, like her difficulties with walking and fluctuating energy levels.

Whilst time has led Laura to a place where bladder incontinence is just part of life to be managed, not all people are able to make this reassessment of their situation. Rhodri was an older man, aged fifty-four, who had been born with cerebral palsy and who had been a wheelchair user all his life. He had recently started to have bladder problems which meant it was difficult for him to leave the house for any length of time. However, he was reluctant to seek medical help for these difficulties because of the humiliation he had suffered whenever he had a bladder accident whilst attending residential school as a child:

> So if I do a long journey, I'll go back to being in school again. "You're a dirty, rotten so-and-so". "He's the most filthiest boy in the world" … I was put out in front of the whole school when I was coming up to a teenager, and said, "This will happen to you, if you wet your clothes". And I had to go round in a dressing gown and pants and they were spares—so I was a spare person, wasn't I. Only by having a fragment of my life, you can see why I haven't got a lot of confidence. (Rhodri)

When Rhodri had been born, the doctors at the hospital suggested that his parents should abandon him because he would never amount to much as a person. This example of psycho-emotional disablism severely undermined his self-confidence, and being made to feel like a "spare person" at school simply reduced his self-esteem further. In Rhodri's case, it was past psycho-emotional disablism that was having a direct impact on his physical health as an older adult, because the traumatic memories of being labelled as the "most filthiest boy in the world" made it difficult for him to even consider talking to a health professional about his bladder incontinence. Therefore, previous psycho-emotional disablism maintained his self-disgust towards urinary incontinence.

The final example of leaky bodies which I want to discuss is that of managing a stoma. Adinuf had gone into hospital complaining of severe stomach pains and ended up having emergency colostomy surgery because of a perforated bowel. He woke up in the hospital's High Dependency Unit and his story continues:

> "What the hell am I doing here?" I thought, "Well, I don't know, my side feels uncomfortable, what's this sticking to me?" Started pulling—"Don't pull that", she said, "don't pull that!" "What is it?", I said. "Don't pull it", she said, "It's your colostomy bag". I said, "I don't want one of them bloody things!" and promptly ripped it off. (Adinuf)

Initially, hospital staff were concerned that Adinuf was not going to manage living with a colostomy because of his refusal to get involved in his self-care. However, once Adinuf returned home, his attitude was "Oh well, I've got this damn thing", and he started taking back control of his stoma management. Although it can be seen that things were very tough initially: "I'm quite—it's a second nature to me now. But when I come home originally, oh, Christ, I couldn't handle it—I couldn't handle it" (Adinuf).

Support and information from the stoma nurses on the ward was an important factor in helping Adinuf learn to live comfortably with his stoma. Previously, when Adinuf had developed reflex sympathetic dystrophy and had a heart attack, he felt that he had been left to deal with these medical conditions alone. The support from the stoma nurses meant that he did not feel isolated then, and this support is still ongoing; for example, when planning a recent foreign holiday, Adinuf was able to find out how to manage air travel with a colostomy bag.

It is clear the journey that Adinuf has made since the day he woke up in hospital. Disgust was not a word that was used in these interviews. Nonetheless, Adinuf's attempt to rip off the colostomy back in the HDU—"I don't want one of them bloody things"—could be viewed as a visceral disgust reaction to the colostomy, and is closely related to the act of vomiting in the way that the contaminant (colostomy bag) is removed from the body. Over time, with the continual and reliable support of trained stoma nurses who provided Adinuf with good information about stoma care, Adinuf's disgust reaction to his colostomy had pretty much disappeared: "I had to learn to cope with it and how to really be able to [hesitates] get back to a normal life and cope with that, as an everyday thing, five/six times a day or whatever" (Adinuf).

Now Adinuf and his colostomy live relatively well together and he is just getting on with a "normal life". This reduction of the disgust reaction over time was suggested as one potential explanation for the negative association between disgust sensitivity and how well some adjusted to having a colostomy (Smith, Loewenstein, Rozin, Sherriff, & Ubel, 2007). As in the case of Laura, familiarity with new ways of managing urine and faeces take time to become "normalised", and reducing the potential for self-disgust is an important part of this process. But it should also be noted that continence advisors, stoma nurses, and accessible, timely information also have an important part to play in how well someone adjusts to different ways of eliminating bodily waste, and possibly in how easily someone reduces their disgust sensitivity.

I started this section by describing the horror that is the common perception of having to deal with incontinence—a fate worse than death, literally. However, as the stories indicate here, the passage of time, support, and information, as well as often having little choice in the matter, often help reduce levels of self-disgust. This "unmaking of [self-]disgust" (Rozin & Fallon, 1987, p. 38) is similar to the ways in which other body fluids can be become detached from their disgust responses through familiarity; for example, parents dealing with soiled nappies or lovers exchanging saliva and semen during sex. Thus, living with a body which *is* messy and leaky is not necessarily revolting and disgusting to the self. This is because people evolve new understandings of body "normality", which in turn have the potential to produce new forms of embodiment and being. Whilst recognising that life does become more complicated when one has to deal with a plethora of products in order to pee, there are some creative outcomes, different ways of being, that result from being forced to find alternatives to "normal" urination. For example, urostomy bags can be emptied behind a tree, obviating the need for a toilet; catheters enable a woman to pee standing up. So, to paraphrase Iris Marion Young (1980), rather than simply being able to "throw like a girl", a woman can now "pee like a man".

## *Conclusion*

This chapter has offered a disability studies-informed analysis of how disgust and self-disgust can be manifest within the lives of disabled people, often as part of psycho-emotional disablism and internalised oppression. It is possible that *some* of the disgust reactions that disabled people experience are due to a "primary disgust" response that is unique to this particular minority group because of the association impairment has with uncomfortable reminders of vulnerability and mortality (Nussbaum, 2004). However, this chapter has discussed other forms of disgust that play an important part in the exclusion of disabled people. Interpersonal disgust is seen in disablist hate speech on the internet when disabled people are described as objects of disgust, which then serves to position "disgusting disabled people" as a buffer group between "disgusted non-disabled people" and animals. Moral disgust is being utilised by government policy in conjunction with the media to present disabled people as being unworthy of financial benefits. Hence, in this regard, disgust continues to be the "emotional fuel of ableism" (Hughes, 2012, p. 24).

The association of disgust and psycho-emotional disablism is extended if one considers how self-disgust may be found within responses to internalised oppression. Passing as non-disabled may be one way of managing self-disgust by denying a disabled identity; or this choice may be a pragmatic way of avoiding psycho-emotional disablism. Internalised hierarchies of impairment can result in disabled people ranking themselves relative to other disabled people; here, self-disgust is being managed by creating a subgroup of disabled people who are perceived as being "less human" (who often have learning difficulties or uncontrolled bodies), that act as a foil reflecting one's relative closeness to "normality". However, internalised oppression and associated self-disgust are not inevitable and many disabled people are able to resist internalising denigrating messages about disability. The process of "coming out" as disabled, and developing new forms of being, are important ways of reducing self-disgust—replacing a discourse of abnormality with a celebration of diversity, and shifting "the discourse from struggle against the self to struggle against the disabling society" (Swain & Cameron, 1999, p. 78).

Self-disgust might be relatively common when someone develops incontinence or has a stoma; this would not be surprising given the internalisation of messages given by society's refusal to include people with leaky bodies in public space and culture. However, this chapter has suggested that this self-disgust has the potential to reduce over time as someone readjusts to what is "normal" for them, a process that is helped by timely, professional support and information. Overcoming internalised oppression and self-disgust demands a degree of self-confidence and self-worth; past psycho-emotional disablism or adverse life experiences, such as abuse, could be expected to make this resistance much more difficult (Reeve, 2008). Therefore, without wishing to downplay the very real distress that incontinence can cause someone (Brittain & Shaw, 2007), it is nonetheless useful to identify factors that have the potential to reduce self-disgust and distress.

As indicated at the start, this chapter is restricted in the conclusions that it can draw about disgust and self-disgust in the lives of disabled people. However, using the data from my doctoral study, together with my own experience as a disabled woman, I have utilised a disability studies approach to unpack the ways in which disgust can be manifest at the institutional, cultural, social, and individual levels, paying attention to the *disgusted subject* as well as the *disgusting object*. It is important that ableist disgust is exposed so that disabled people do not unconsciously internalise this disgust. In addition, it should not be accepted as "natural" that disabled people stay away from "civilised society" for fear of distressing non-disabled people by reminding them of their own physical frailty and eventual death.

Finally, many disabled people feel pride rather than disgust about their bodies, as reflected by a thriving disability movement, a vibrant culture of disability art, and the active participation of disabled people at all levels of society. This challenges the suggestion that impaired bodies are inherently disgusting because of the manner in which they violate social norms (Roberts & Goldenberg, 2007). Hence, further theorising and focused research is needed—from both a psychological and sociological perspective—into the factors that make it (im)possible for disabled people to throw off the shackles imposed by disgust and self-disgust.

CHAPTER FOUR

# Self-disgust and adaptation to chronic physical health conditions: implications for avoidance and withdrawal

*Lisa M. Reynolds, Sarah A. McCambridge, and Nathan S. Consedine*

## *Introduction*

An increasingly diverse body of work is investigating how emotions such as fear, embarrassment, and disgust may impact on health behaviours in ways that are at times beneficial and, at others, detrimental (Consedine & Moscowitz, 2007). Of all emotions, disgust is the most directly relevant to health, with origins in adaptive responding to health risks and contamination threat (Curtis, Aunger, & Rabie, 2004; Davey, 2011). Until recently, however, disgust has received little attention in health research. This emerging interest in disgust, and the associated withdrawal and avoidance response in health contexts, are our foci over the following pages. We begin by outlining the function, manifestations, and established elicitors of disgust, before moving to consider the specific nature of self-disgust, evaluating the implications self-disgust may have for physical health, and examining its possible relevance as individuals adapt to chronic physical health conditions.

## *Disgust, avoidance, and physical health*

Evolutionary theorists posit that disgust is a basic, universal emotion that evolved as an adaptive response to the challenges faced by distinguishing safe foods from those that posed a survival risk (Consedine & Moscowitz, 2007; Rozin, Haidt, & McCauley, 1999; Teachman, 2006). Thus, the original purpose of disgust has been to promote the avoidance of actual and potential contaminants—that is, people or stimuli that potentially pose a threat to health (Consedine & Moscowitz, 2007; Davey & Bond, 2006; Ekman, 1992; Elfenbein & Ambady, 2002; Johnson-Laird & Oatley, 1992; Rozin, Haidt, & McCauley, 1999; Simpson, Carter, Anthony, & Overton, 2006; Teachman, 2006). Given this purpose, it is likely important in physical health contexts. Disgust is viewed as the only primary emotion that specifically evolved for health purposes (Consedine, 2008) and is increasingly seen as a "disease-avoidance" emotion (Davey, 2011; Oaten, Stevenson, & Case, 2011). When stimuli are appraised as potentially contaminating, the disgust response that follows is broadly characterised by withdrawal and rejection. Disgust manifests in typical action-tendencies, experiential and cognitive states, as well as in facial movements in which the nostrils narrow (a defence against penetration), the mouth closes (to prevent incorporation or promote ejecting contaminants), salivation is increased (to dilute pollutants), and the throat constricts (to prevent swallowing; Angyal, 1941). These movements are universally displayed and readily recognised across geopolitical and cultural groups (Ekman, 1992; Elfenbein & Ambady, 2002; Johnson-Laird & Oatley, 1992; Rozin, Haidt, & McCauley, 1999).

Disgust reliably arises in response to certain stimuli, many of which are found in physical health settings. It is seen in response to stimuli that carry a risk of pathogen transmission (Curtis et al., 2004; Rozin, Haidt, & McCauley, 2000), including poor hygiene, bodily products (e.g., faeces, urine, blood, saliva), violations of the body envelope (e.g., insertions, wounds, gore, surgery, deformity), and representations of death (Berle & Phillips, 2006). Research has also denoted what may be a derived form called sociomoral disgust—an aversion to, and avoidance of, individuals outside of one's social group or who violate social or moral codes (Haidt, Rozin, Mccauley, & Imada, 1997; Simpson et al., 2006). Thus, the disgust response has a protective role—steering us away from exposure to potentially health-deleterious or contaminating stimuli—whether these be unsafe food, people we perceive as potentially carrying disease, or more subtly by navigating us through the complexities of morality and possible social rejection. Behaviourally and motivationally, the core of the disgust response involves avoidance and withdrawal (Izard, 1993), primarily achieved through either escaping or expelling the disgusting stimulus in the *immediate* context, or avoiding *future* situations altogether when we anticipate that they might contain disgust elicitors (Curtis, de Barra, & Aunger, 2011; Verwoerd, de Jong, Wessel, & van Hout, 2013).

The disgust response is, however, a somewhat imprecise "tool", and perceptions of a contamination threat can occur (or persist) in the absence of objective threat (Nemeroff & Rozin, 1994). Identifying pathogens is inherently difficult and the disgust mechanism appears to err on the side of conservatism, perhaps to avoid missing unfamiliar signals of pathogen presence (Kollei, Brunhoeber, Rauh, de Zwaan, & Martin, 2012). Thus, disgust may promote avoidance in an array of physical health contexts simply because aspects of these contexts "map" onto the evolved classes of stimuli that disgust is activated by. Many sexual health and/or cancer-related screening tests, for example, may elicit disgust (and will thus be avoided) because of disgust's close link to "holes in the body" or bodily products (Rozin, Haidt, & McCauley, 2009).

This imprecision can promote social disgust and avoidance, as well as the stigmatisation of "out-group" persons whose characteristics activate the system with varying degrees of accuracy—from people who represent a genuine contamination threat (Curtis et al., 2011), to persons or stimuli who pose no objective threat but who may be perceived as likely to carry potential pathogens—such as strangers (Raman & Gelman, 2008), those outside of one's ethnic group (Navarrete & Fessler, 2006), or people who exhibit physical abnormalities (Oaten et al., 2011; Park, Faulkner, & Schaller, 2003). Thus, disgust-generated avoidance may be strongly evident in social contexts, potentially isolating and stigmatising those who exhibit visible cues of "disease" (whether or not they pose actual risk).

Importantly from a clinical perspective, it is also well established that there are reliable individual differences in the tendency to feel disgust—known as "disgust sensitivity" (Rozin, Haidt, McCauley, Dunlop, & Ashmore, 1999). Disgust sensitivity is a dynamic, adaptive system, able to recalibrate and adapt according to variations in the system's immune vulnerability (Curtis et al., 2011). Women, for example, are normatively more sensitive to disgust (Haidt, McCauley, & Rozin, 1994; Rohrmann, Hopp, & Quirin, 2008), in theory, because health-related threats have greater fitness costs for females (Curtis et al., 2011; Oaten, Stevenson, & Case, 2009). When vulnerability to pathogens increases, for example in the first trimester of pregnancy (Fessler, Eng, & Navarrete, 2005), when conception likelihood is high (Fessler & Navarrete, 2003), or during demanding medical regimens (Kollei et al., 2012), so too does disgust sensitivity. Similarly, individuals reporting poorer current health describe greater fear of disease-relevant animals (Prokop, Fančovičová, & Fedor, 2010) and greater prejudice against the elderly and obese (Navarrete & Fessler, 2006). Recent research has also indicated that people who are depressed are more sensitive to other people's disgust expressions (Surguladze et al., 2010). From an evolutionary perspective, fluctuations in disgust sensitivity occurring in tandem with vulnerability is logical, as it should serve to minimise exposure to health threats when the system is compromised.

Emerging work in health demonstrates how experienced disgust may be related to health behaviours, including increased hand-washing (Curtis et al., 2011), particularly in the presence of foul odours or the sight of faeces (Curtis, Danquah, & Aunger, 2009), and experimental studies indicate that disgust-sensitive individuals avoid elicitors such as a used comb or a filled bedpan (Deacon & Olatunji, 2007; Olatunji, Wolitzky-Taylor et al., 2009; Tsao & McKay, 2004). Disgust is also associated with blood-injection-injury-type fears regarding injections, blood, sharp objects, mutilation, and examinations (Olatunji, Arrindell, & Lohr, 2005). Such phobias may be common in health contexts, particularly where exposure to blood and/or injections are part of regular treatment (Carey & Harris, 2005; Harris, Jones, & Carey, 2009). Other studies suggest that treatment side effects such as hair loss may elicit disgust (Rosman, 2004) and that disgust predicts poorer adjustment to colostomy and bowel surgery (Smith, Loewenstein, Rozin, Sherriff, & Ubel, 2007).

However, it is not only the *immediate experience* of disgust and its associated withdrawal response that is relevant in health contexts, but also the *anticipation* of disgust in either the self or others that may be important. Immediate and anticipated emotions are central to decision-making (Schlosser, Dunning, & Fetchenhauer, 2013) including decisions about health (Sussner et al., 2009), and are stronger predictors of vaccination behaviour than illness risk perceptions (Chapman & Coups, 2006). A recent review of disgust in colorectal cancer identified fifteen studies related to immediate and anticipated disgust, and its likely role in avoidance of cancer screening and/or treatment

(Reynolds, Consedine, Pizarro, & Bissett, 2013). However, anticipated emotion is often much worse than the actual experience (O'Carroll, Foster, McGeechan, Sandford, & Ferguson, 2011; Sussner et al., 2009; Woody & Tolin, 2002), as highlighted by persons undergoing colorectal procedures reporting that the actual event was better than anticipated (Von Wagner et al., 2009). Thus, anticipated disgust appears to be a barrier to timely participation or uptake.

Recent experiments have provided clearer evidence of disgust's *causal* relevance to avoidant behaviour in health contexts, with one study demonstrating that manipulated disgust predicted greater future intention to use condoms (Tybur, Bryan, Magnan, & Hooper, 2011). Similarly, another experimental study demonstrated that disgust promoted both immediate avoidance of a stoma bag and anticipated avoidance of a hypothetical cancer drug with disgusting side effects, but predominantly among those with certain mindfulness characteristics (Reynolds, Consedine, & McCambridge, 2014). A second report from this same study (Reynolds, McCambridge, Bissett, & Consedine, 2014) found that state and dispositional disgust sensitivity independently predicted immediate avoidance, and also interacted to predict anticipated avoidance; delay in help-seeking for bowel symptoms was greater among dispositionally more sensitive persons, but only when they were disgusted. A subsequent study showed that disgust predicted help-seeking delays when seeking help would involve exposure to disgust elicitors (i.e., self-collecting genital discharge), with disgust causing delays and avoidance among persons reporting poorer health (McCambridge & Consedine, 2014a). Such findings are consistent with data indicating increases in disgust during periods of immune vulnerability (Fessler et al., 2005). A second report found that disgust increased preferences for health-care providers whose descriptions contained disgust-minimising terms (e.g., hygienic), although only among females who had not recently had a sexual health screen and, thus, lacked a frame of reference (McCambridge & Consedine, 2014b).

## *A characterisation of self-disgust*

To this point, our discussion has focused on disgust in general, its evolved nature and manifestations, and its relevance to health contexts. Partly, this reflects the theoretical infancy and novelty of self-disgust research, although these foci are also consonant with our belief that self-disgust is most usefully conceptualised as a specific variant of disgust. In the view we adopt here, the broader realm of disgust can inform the specific understanding of self-disgust and its relevance to physical health. Disgust theorists have typically considered disgust-generating stimuli as external threats (Haidt et al., 1994), when, in fact, many elicitors may reflect aspects of the psychological or physical self. In the section to follow, we draw from this theoretical framework, suggesting that the function and manifestations of *self-disgust* are fundamentally similar to those seen in disgust in general, and that it is primarily the specific nature of the elicitors that set self-disgust apart from other variants.

Self-disgust has been characterised as a dysfunctional, self-directed adaptation of disgust that manifests when aspects of the self are appraised as "disgusting" by sociocultural definitions (Powell, Simpson, & Overton, 2013). It has been described as a "harsher" version of shame, not unlike self-loathing or self-contempt, but distinct from low self-esteem (Simpson, Hillman, Crawford, & Overton, 2010). What distinguishes self-disgust from other aversive emotions and ties it to the primary emotion of disgust is the *disgust response* (i.e., the collection of action-tendencies, experiential, and cognitive changes characterised by attempts to withdraw and reject). However, while rejection and avoidance responses may (generally) be adaptive in protecting the organism against external stimuli, where evasion of contamination is both possible and probabilistically beneficial, such responses are potentially maladaptive when the elicitor comes from within. Where disgust arises in response to stable aspects of personality or physicality, the associated response is likely to become perpetual and dysfunctional (Powell et al., 2013). Recent empirical works have implicated self-disgust in depression (Green, Moll, Deakin, Hulleman, & Zahn, 2013; Powell et al., 2013), post-traumatic stress disorder (Espeset, Gulliksen, Nordba, Skaarderud, & Holte, 2012), obsessive-compulsive symptoms (Badour, Bown, Adams, Bunaciu, & Feldner, 2012; Deacon & Olatunji, 2007), and eating disorders (Neziroglu, Hickey, & McKay, 2010; Zeeck, Stelzer, Linster, Joos, & Hartmann, 2011).

To date, however, studies have concentrated near-exclusively on examining self-disgust in the context of mental health and psychopathology, and little attention has been focused on possible roles in physical health contexts. Physical symptoms such as rotting skin, unpleasant odours, surgical alterations to body shape or appearance, tumours that disfigure, or hair that falls out in clumps, are all aspects of the self that have the potential to generate a disgust response; yet, how does one escape or withdraw from disgusting stimuli when the elicitor comprises a part of one's own body? Clearly, the withdrawal and avoidance defensive response itself may create a very serious adaptive challenge in this context.

## *Self-disgust and physical health*

Whilst possible links between self-disgust and physical health have not been directly investigated, research in related areas suggests that self-disgust may predict poorer physical health outcomes. Recent longitudinal work indicates that feelings of self-disgust may partially mediate links between dysfunctional thoughts and depressive symptoms, and it seems that disgust towards the *physical* aspects of the self (rather than towards behaviour) may be the more important predictor (Powell et al., 2013). In turn, multiple studies have linked depression to increased mortality and poorer outcomes in physical illness, including heart failure, cancer, and diabetes (Katon et al., 2005; Kiecolt-Glaser, McGuire, Robles, & Glaser, 2002; Pinquart & Duberstein, 2010; Sullivan, Levy, Russo, & Spertus, 2004). Thus, while pathways between self-disgust, depression, and *physical* health are yet to be explored, the available evidence suggests it may prove fruitful research territory. This noted, it would be precipitant to assume that self-disgust should have only a deleterious role in physical health. Below, we evaluate the possibility that self-disgust has both beneficial and detrimental effects on physical health outcomes.

### *Could self-disgust benefit physical health?*

Conceivably, there are situations when self-generated disgust and the associated avoidance in health contexts might be beneficial. There are possible cross-contamination benefits to avoiding contact with one's own infectious wounds, and disgust regarding this aspect of the physical self may help motivate greater self-care behaviours. Equally, there may also be inclusive fitness benefits from (temporarily) withdrawing from friends and family whilst contagious (Curtis et al., 2011; Hamilton, 1964) or from social relationships more broadly. Social benefits to withdrawal are implied in qualitative work among breast cancer patients (Rosman, 2004), where participants reported feeling disgusted by their chemotherapy-induced alopecia—the experience of losing hair being visible evidence of the potentially fatal nature of the illness and, thus, possibly reminding patients of their animal nature. More to the point, patients responded with typical disgust-generated avoidance, using wigs and scarves to hide and camouflage the disgust cue. Hence, self-disgust appears to have motivated a particular form of avoidance that effectively circumvented potentially awkward or uncomfortable discussions with others. While avoidance of this kind may be deleterious to important relationships (see below), confronting others with "disgusting" physical stimuli may also be socially awkward and damage relationships. Thus, social avoidance motivated by self-disgust in the short-term *may* provide longer-term benefits if the relationship is maintained over time when it otherwise might not have been. If stimuli are acute and likely to resolve quickly (compared to chronic stimuli), short-term avoidance may be an adaptive, suitable response.

Exhibiting potentially disgust-eliciting stimuli may also act as a trigger for related emotions such as social embarrassment. Research investigating the impact of other aversive emotions on behaviour indicates that men with more severe and/or frequent urinary symptoms report greater embarrassment (Roberts et al., 1994); however, only those who are bothered by the *socially observable* symptoms (e.g., wet pants, dribbling) were more likely to visit a doctor. Similarly, dental studies have found that social embarrassment caused by poor dentition motivates care-seeking (Moore, Brodsgaard, & Rosenberg, 2004) and comparable dynamics are evident in bariatric surgery decisions among overweight patients (Libeton, Dixon, Laurie, & O'Brien, 2004). Thus, as with the embarrassment examples noted above, there may be situations in which self-disgust increases health-care utilisation. Where physical symptoms generate self-disgust or are deemed likely to elicit disgust in others, and are perceived as likely to be remedied, cured, or managed with medical treatment, patients may be motivated to seek treatment.

### *How might self-disgust impair physical health?*

More likely, however, is that there are a significant proportion of instances when the (attempted) avoidance motivated by experiences of self-disgust lead to a worsening of outcomes. Experimental work has shown that priming people to consider their animal nature (an established elicitor of disgust; Rozin, 2008) results in emotional discomfort as well as an unwillingness to perform breast self-examinations (Goldenberg, Arndt, Hart, & Routledge, 2008). Some evidence suggests people may ignore their own disgust-evoking symptoms such as "foul-smelling", discharging wounds, or unpleasant bowel symptoms, for long periods of time as a misguided avoidance response (Akute, 2000; Goode, 2004). Untreated symptoms can lead to acute illness and poorer prognosis, and, when contagious, may lead to others becoming infected (Doubeni et al., 2013; Morris et al., 2012; Thomas, 2002). Surgeries that leave the body "mutilated" (e.g., when genitals have been surgically removed) or radically change the way the body functions (e.g., creating a stoma that collects faeces external to the body) are also likely to induce self-disgust and associated avoidance in many people. Qualitative work with stoma patients, for example, describes how some react with "loathing and disgust" when initially told of the need for a stoma:

> Feelings like disgust and emotional shock after surgery were described in all interviews, particularly when the stoma was dressed for the first time. Initially it was hard to look at and to touch the stoma. Patient D said "it looks like a piece of raw meat". The worst of it was when the staff told me to change the appliance myself—to wipe and change it. (Persson & Hellström, 2002, p. 105)

Thus, in addition to the risks associated with treatment decisions motivated by the desire to avoid such elicitors, the ongoing avoidance of self-management tasks may create further compounding disgust responses in both the self and others as odours and leakage worsen. However, as intimated in our discussion of disgust above, it is not just self-disgust and avoidance in immediate contexts that is relevant, but also *anticipated* self-disgust that may be of consequence. Lessons learned from affective forecasting research indicate that people typically overestimate the affective impact of illness and disability, and underestimate their ability to adapt (Ubel, Loewenstein, Schwarz, & Smith, 2005). Disgust is likely no different, and vulnerable persons may avoid medical investigation, delay treatment, or avoid medical interventions altogether because of erroneous expectations regarding how they will feel in the future. In early qualitative work with hysterectomy patients, anticipated disgust over the possibility of having a stoma constructed was seen as a greater threat than fear of malignancy or loss in sexuality or fertility: "This scares me. I don't want a bag on my stomach. I don't care about not having any children. I'm not worried about dying. All I want is to go home without a bag on my stomach" (Drellich & Bieber, 1958, p. 329).

Decisions to proceed with radical surgeries such as mastectomy (full or partial breast removal) or orchiectomy (removal of testicle and spermatic cord) require estimating one's ability to cope with the consequences; some outcomes or decisions have the clear potential to engender anticipated self-disgust. In situations when patient beliefs are such that deforming treatment options are perceived as certain to happen, anticipated disgust may be sufficient to stop people seeking medical help for disease symptoms at all. Media attention in May 2013 regarding celebrity Angelina Jolie's decision to proceed with prophylactic mastectomy highlights the complexity of such decisions and the role of affective forecasting (Payne, 2013). Whilst established news channels lauded Jolie's "bravery" without actually specifying what made this decision "brave" (reinforcing the taboo nature of disgust elicitors), explicit reference to disgust was played out in comments on social networking sites where social boundaries were less constrained (e.g., "amputating yourself as a 'precaution' is both disturbing and disgusting"; Kluger, 2013).

A second major area in which self-disgust is likely to be relevant in physical health, is found in revisiting the processes by which people estimate the likely emotional responses of others. One of the most powerful sources informing our perception of the potential behaviour of others, is our own processing of experience (Bargh, Schwader, Hailey, Dyer, & Boothby, 2012). To an extent, we project our emotions onto others (Freud, 1938) leading to situations in which we over-perceive or anticipate similar emotions in others (Kawada, Oettingen, Gollwitzer, & Bargh, 2004; Niedenthal & Halberstadt, 2003). Eliciting emotions such as fear can lead to an increased tendency to perceive relevant emotions (e.g., anger) in others (Maner et al., 2005), and persons who are depressed may be more sensitive to disgust reactions in others (Surguladze et al., 2010). The combination of self-disgust, a tendency to use our own emotions to anticipate those of others, and depression, may thus influence our expectations regarding how others may respond. Hence, while research has not yet explored how such a dynamic might apply to disgust in physical health contexts, it makes intuitive sense that if an aspect of our self "disgusts" us, we may assume others will be likewise disgusted. Equally, because we are typically compelled to reject, withdraw, or avoid when disgusted, again, we might assume (rightly or wrongly) that others will be similarly compelled to avoid or reject us, if an aspect of our physical self is the elicitor.

Data from several areas of study imply that experienced self-disgust may increase the estimations of a disgust response (and subsequent rejection) in others. Parents of children with disfiguring facial lesions cite the anticipated disgust reaction of strangers as a reason for avoiding taking their children out in public (Tanner, Dechort, & Frieden, 1998). Such steps may not be unwarranted. Indeed, before her (suspected euthanised) death, fifty-two-year-old Chantal Sebiré, who suffered from an incurable facial tumour, described how her face had been so "grotesquely" disfigured that children ran from the sight of her (Berlins, 2008). Similarly, colostomy patients report feeling highly stigmatised, a negative experience that may promote greater utilisation of medical services, poorer health, more emotional difficulty, and social withdrawal (MacDonald & Anderson, 1984). Patients with higher disgust sensitivity report greater stigmatisation, assuming others will also be disgusted by their colostomy (Smith et al., 2007). After a vulvectomy (partial or complete removal of the vulva), patients report feeling "compelled" to protect their intimate partners from the sight of the wound as well as from further sexual involvement, likely because they fear that exposing the "mutilated" vulva will arouse feelings of disgust, distaste, and rejection (Stellman, Goodwin, Robinson, Dansak, & Hilgers, 1984). Theoretically, then, self-disgust may promote a psychologically self-protective dynamic in which social rejections are anticipatorily prevented by reducing engagement with others.

Anticipation of a disgust-triggered aversive response is not confined to support networks, caregivers, and lay people. Despite the possibility that habituation and professional training might act as a safeguard, health care workers are also susceptible to a disgust response to aversive stimuli. Persons with the disfiguring ailment neurofibromatosis 1 (commonly known as the "elephant man's disease") recount medical personnel openly showing disgust at their appearance (Ablon, 2012), and qualitative work in anal health care suggests disgust responses are common among medical staff (Hardy, 2010). Thus, the anticipation of disgust-driven stigmatisation in health contexts, particularly when overt disease cues (e.g., odours, hair loss, disfigurement, wounds) are exhibited, may promote avoidance of social networks and medical support services alike. The quality of life and health implications of social isolation, withdrawal from relationships, and reluctance to present for medical assistance are significant.

### *Clinical management of self-disgust in physical health*

Whilst benefits might sometimes be gained from self-disgust in physical health, clearly, avoidance in this context is generally likely to be problematic. Preliminary evidence suggests that disgust may promote avoidance behaviours in physical health including cancer screening (Brouse, Basch, Wolf, & Shmukler, 2004; Chapple, Ziebland, Hewitson, & McPherson, 2008; Worthley et al., 2006) and treatment (Reynolds, Consedine, Pizarro et al., 2013; Rosman, 2004). Thus, while the specific role that *self*-disgust may take in shaping outcomes in physical health is yet to be determined, our discussion thus far highlights its likely deleterious influence. Below, we explore possibilities for working clinically with those struggling with self-disgust. We begin by noting the healing nature of time itself, and then explore in greater detail the potential benefit of both exposure and/or acceptance as therapeutic approaches.

In beginning, it is worth noting that for some individuals the disgust response to physical stimuli may naturally resolve over time. Distress related to aversive experiences often resolves over time without intervention (Andersen & Anderson, 1989; Lam, Shing, Bonanno, Mancini, & Fielding, 2012). Research with bowel surgery patients who required a stoma, compared to those who did not, found early adjustment issues were no longer evident at one year (Bekkers, van Knippenberg, van Dulmen, van den Borne, & van Berge Henegouwen, 1997). Similarly, a study with medical students found reduced disgust after dissecting a cadaver for some months; interestingly, reductions were specific to handling a cold, dead body and did not translate to other disgust elicitors (Rozin, 2008). Findings such as these may suggest that when repeated exposures to "disgusting" stimuli occur over time, there will be a gradual lessening of the response (at least to that specific elicitor) and/or any associated avoidance behaviours. That such habituation occurs is evident anecdotally as well as in consideration of the fact that people are not normally troubled by the act of cleaning themselves after defecation, despite the necessary proximity to faecal matter.

However, the rapidity and ease with which people habituate to disgust-inducing stimuli will likely vary (Smith et al., 2007; Stellman et al., 1984), and clinical interventions may be required for those experiencing difficulty. Early identification of those most vulnerable to self-disgust has the potential to lessen the negative impact of diagnosis and treatment by channelling at-risk individuals to appropriate support services. Some individuals may be more vulnerable to maladaptive self-disgust responses, perhaps reflecting dispositional sensitivities (Smith et al., 2007), difficulties with emotional regulation, or being less able to cope with real or perceived social rejection.

Once identified, however, there is little data to guide clinicians in physical health contexts working with persons struggling with self-disgust; thus, we are forced to draw from research in related areas. Acknowledgement and normalisation are the cornerstones of most therapeutic work (Erskine, 2011; Leahy & Tirch, 2011) and may be similarly useful when managing clinically significant levels of self-disgust. Considering the taboos that accompany many disgust elicitors (Hardy, 2010), open, well-timed communication when patients are initially adjusting to changes in body shape, appearance, and function may be beneficial. Therapeutic conversations that acknowledge and normalise self-disgust in response to excrement, body fluids, wounds, mutilation, and so on, but also reassure patients that most people learn to live with, and adjust to, initially "disgusting" stimuli, may prevent cascading patterns of disgust and withdrawal.

However, interventions may need to extend beyond psycho-education. In particular, exposure-based therapies in conjunction with cognitive restructuring and mindfulness training appear likely to be of some use. Exposure therapy using gradual or abrupt exposure to problematic stimuli has empirical support in the treatment of anxiety disorders (Franklin & Foa, 2011) and has been used where disgust arises in response to one's own body (de Jong, van Lankveld, Elgersma, & Borg, 2010). Preliminary work investigating cognitive restructuring and imagery modification to reduce the feeling of being contaminated in adult survivors of childhood sexual abuse is promising, and may translate to aspects of the physical self that are seen as disgusting. Cognitive work whereby dysfunctional beliefs and negative automatic thoughts regarding the self are challenged and reframed may also help. Finally, therapeutic work utilising mindfulness approaches also appear promising. With a focus on present moment acceptance that is fundamentally in contrast to avoidance (Reynolds et al., 2014), mindfulness training may counter mental and behavioural avoidance by encouraging the broader acceptance of bodily sensations, thoughts, and emotions (Baer, Walsh, & Lykins, 2009). This may be well suited to physical health contexts when acceptance of current physical states and disgust-eliciting stimuli is more feasible than attempting to change them.

## *The role of self-disgust in physical health—is it really all bad?*

Our aim for this chapter has been to initiate a conversation about the possible role of self-disgust in physical health contexts. Although self-disgust has mostly been studied in the context of psychopathology, its manifestations are fundamentally rooted in the same basic disgust system and its roles in promoting immediate and anticipated avoidance. However, unlike other disgust elicitors that can be avoided, self-disgust arises when aspects of the psychological or physical self activate the system. Given the effects that health symptoms and treatment effects can have on the body, exposure to the elicitors of self-disgust is likely commonplace. As importantly, however, because it is difficult to avoid aspects of the physical self and reminders are commensurately common, self-disgust may develop into a pathologically avoidant process where aspects of the self are reviled and/or rejection responses from others are anticipated. Social functioning and intimacy are almost certainly impacted, and our suspicion is that self-disgust may have a key role to play in the social withdrawal that characterises the adaptation to many chronic physical health conditions.

To date, little is known and little available to guide clinicians working in the area. While self-disgust is likely common in physical health contexts, it is difficult to argue with recent theorists who pathologise self-disgust and suggest that it is predominantly maladaptive in mental health. Certainly, the distress the response causes, together with any avoidance generated by self-disgust in physical health contexts, can have potentially serious implications. Nevertheless, given disgust's original purpose as a protective mechanism steering us away from health threats, physical health may be one of the few contexts where self-disgust might periodically play a relatively adaptive, perhaps even beneficial, role.

CHAPTER FIVE

# Self-directed disgust: reciprocal relationships with sex and sexual dysfunction

*Peter J. de Jong and Charmaine Borg*

Contemporary models of sexual behaviour propose that sexual responses involve an interaction between sexual excitatory and sexual inhibitory processes (e.g., Bancroft & Janssen, 2000). From such a perspective, the generation of sexual responses may be compromised when sexual inhibition outbalances sexual excitation. Accordingly, relatively strong inhibitory tendencies may interfere with having pleasurable sex and may give rise to sexual problems, which in turn may set the stage for the generation of a wide range of subsequent difficulties (e.g., depression, anxiety) and negative self-evaluative processes.

Recently, we have argued that disgust and disgust-related preoccupations might be important players that fuel inhibitory tendencies in sexual contexts (de Jong & Peters, 2009). It should be acknowledged, however, that thus far disgust has received only scant attention in the "sex" literature, and it is only in the last couple of years that disgust has become a topic of more systematic empirical investigation in the context of sex research (for a recent review, see de Jong, van Overveld, & Borg, 2013). When it comes to self-disgust—the central topic of this book—the empirical work is even more limited, although it needs mention that there is some work in the context of post-traumatic stress disorder (PTSD) and obsessive-compulsive disorder (OCD) that focuses on self-disgust as a factor that may help explain the phenomenology of individuals who are victims of sexual assault (e.g., Badour, Feldner, Babson, Blumenthal, & Dutton, 2013; Olatunji, Elwood, Williams, & Lohr, 2008).

Because most aspects of the link between (self-)disgust and sexual behaviours are still awaiting empirical scrutiny, the present chapter predominantly relies on informed theoretical speculation rather than on empirical data. In this chapter, we will nevertheless argue that there might be an important link between self-disgust and sexual behaviour. On the one hand, enhanced self-disgust might compromise pleasurable sexual functioning, whereas on the other hand (memories of) sexual behaviours of the self or of others might give rise to self-disgust. Accordingly, people may enter a self-perpetuating cycle in which enhanced self-disgust may become an increasingly important feature of the self. To add flesh to the theoretical speculations, we will provide some preliminary data collected in a recent research project at the University of Groningen that focused on the relationship between self-disgust and indices of sexual functioning. Finally, we will briefly address the potential clinical implications of the proposed interrelationships between self-disgust and sexual behaviours/experiences, and discuss some critical issues that call for an answer on the basis of further research.

### *Disgust, self-disgust, and sexual behaviour*

As explained in the first chapter of this book (see Powell, Simpson, & Overton, this volume), the potential for a persistent feature of the self to acquire any real disgusting status is constrained by the evolved predisposition to develop disgust responses to particular classes of stimuli. Accordingly, people are expected to report disgust to particular aspects of themselves that can be considered as elaborations of those types of disgusting stimuli that serve important adaptive functions. Current functional accounts of disgust differentiate between three types of disgust that each are assumed to be relevant for an important adaptive problem (e.g., Tybur, Lieberman, Kurzban, & DeScioli, 2013).

In the following, we will first address each of these domains of disgust, and how each type of disgust might relate to sexual behaviours and sexual problems. In this first section, we will provide some preliminary ideas on how self-disgust might be involved. In the subsequent section, we will speculate more systematically and in more depth on how each type of disgust might give rise to particular types of self-disgust, and how these types of self-disgust might relate to (memories of) sexual behaviour and sexual experiences.

### *Functional account of the three domains of disgust in sexual behaviour*

Although there is considerable variation in the exact stimuli people find disgusting, the range of disgusting stimuli seems to cluster in three coherent domains: pathogen disgust, sexual disgust, and moral disgust (e.g., Tybur, Lieberman, & Griskevicius, 2009). Each of these three domains has been proposed to relate to a qualitatively different adaptive problem that humankind faced in its phylogenetic history (for a summary, see Table 1).

#### Pathogen disgust

The first function ascribed to disgust can be defined as disease avoidance. That is, disgust would serve the avoidance of disease-causing substances or organisms. This type of disgust has been labelled as *pathogen* disgust (e.g., Tybur et al., 2013). This disgust subtype is typically elicited by stimuli such as body products and spoiled foods that somehow share common features that are implicated in an increased

Table 1. Disgust subtype and its corresponding adaptive problem.

| *Disgust subtypes* | *Adaptive problem* | *Prototypical eliciting stimuli* |
|---|---|---|
| Pathogen | Disease avoidance | Rotten food |
| Sexual | Prevent poor mate selection | Unappealing potential sex mate |
| Moral | Avoidance of social norms infringements | Transgressions |

*Notes*: First column represents the three disgust subtypes (pathogen, sexual, moral); the second column represents the adaptive problem that is prevented by the corresponding (elicited) disgust subtypes; the third and last column represents exemplars of the stimuli that could elicit the particular disgust subtype.

risk of infectious diseases. Through eliciting the urge to withdraw from the disgusting cue, pathogen disgust would facilitate the avoidance of physical contact with and/or ingestion of pathogens (Curtis, de Barra, & Aunger, 2011; Oaten, Stevenson, & Case, 2009). The physical proximity, body apertures, and exchange of bodily fluids that are implied in sexual behaviour provide ample opportunity for the transmission of pathogens. Sexual behaviour thus represents an obvious threat for the transmission of disease. It is therefore highly conceivable that pathogen-based disgust may arise during sex.

Once elicited, disgust may exert its influence in various ways. First, the subjective experience of disgust may affect the appreciation of the pertinent stimuli involved in sex, thereby interfering with the generation of sexual arousal and sexual pleasure. Second, in line with its function to prevent contamination by pathogens, disgust will logically elicit all kinds of avoidance and escape behaviours to enhance distance from the disgusting stimuli and/or to prevent or neutralise the potential impact of physical contact with these stimuli (Woody, McLean, & Klassen, 2005). For example, people may immediately start wiping off the semen from their body, or take a shower, immediately following sexual intercourse. Pertinent to the present context, these types of "neutralising" behaviours may also affect their partner, who might, for example, interpret such cleaning behaviour as a rejection, or as evidence for being evaluated as a repulsive person, thereby setting the stage for the development of self-disgust in the partner. Third, the sudden experience of being touched by a disgusting stimulus may elicit automatic defensive reflexes (e.g., Yartz & Hawk, 2002). Accordingly, disgust may elicit retching during kissing or oral sex, and/or flinching of the pelvic floor muscles during attempts at sexual intercourse. Clearly, these types of defensive reflexes may not only interfere with pleasurable sex but may also be experienced as a sign of rejection, thereby triggering negative self-evaluative appraisals (including self-disgust) in the sex partner.

Finally, disgust is often accompanied by a distinct facial expression (e.g., Darwin, 1872/1989; Vrana, 1993). Although the signal value of the typical facial expression of disgust may generally be a very functional feature of the disgust response, in the context of intimate interpersonal (sexual) behaviour, displaying disgust may be considered highly undesirable. For example, similar to the neutralising and defensive behaviours, one's mate may interpret the facial display of disgust as a sign of disapproval or rejection. To prevent such consequences, people may try to hide their (expression of) disgust in a sexual context (cf. de Jong, van Lankveld, Elgersma, & Borg, 2010). Though people have shown to be generally well able to reduce expressions of disgust (Gross & Levenson, 1993), such emotional suppression may have ironic (rebound) effects, since suppression will probably enhance activation of disgust-related concepts in memory (e.g., Wegner, 1994). Accordingly, people may end up in a vicious cycle that will paradoxically intensify the feelings of disgust, rendering it even more difficult to hide the emotion of disgust to their partner. If people are not effective in hiding their disgust, it might logically affect the self-appreciation of the sex mate, which may ultimately result in self-disgust via internalisation of the other's expression of disgust.

## Sexual disgust

This type of disgust does not refer to any disgust that may arise during sex, but specifically refers to disgust elicited by potential sexual mates. It has been proposed that this type of disgust evolved to facilitate avoidance of sexual partners and behaviours that challenge long-term reproductive success (Tybur et al., 2009, 2013). One important factor that might jeopardise reproductive success is high genetic similarity. Accordingly, people typically respond with disgust when asked to imagine having sex with a sibling or any other genetically close relative (e.g., Lieberman, Tooby, & Cosmides, 2007). In these cases, disgust might help prevent having sex with a potential partner who is characterised by too high genetic similarity, which thus might interfere with reproducing healthy offspring.

Another dimension that is relevant for reproductive success, and which seems most relevant for the present context, is the so-called intrinsic quality of the potential sex mate. This intrinsic quality is typically expressed in physical features that are also important determinants of perceived attractiveness (e.g., Thornhill & Gangestad, 2006). People with low intrinsic quality as reflected in their physical appearance (e.g., body asymmetry) might elicit disgust when being considered as potential sex partners, thereby reducing the risk of a low-value mate choice. Unfortunately, similar sexual disgust may also emerge if important physical features of the partner change significantly over time, for example due to an accident, illness, or surgical intervention such as stoma surgery (e.g., Manderson, 2005). This may also backfire on the individual when others' disgust reactions are perceived as signalling that the self is an object of abhorrence, thus giving rise to self-disgust. At the behavioural level, sexual disgust will not so much involve cleaning and neutralising activities as in the case of pathogen disgust, but will primarily elicit avoidance and withdrawal behaviour to prevent sexual interaction with the source of disgust. Pertinent to the present context it might well be that one's rejection as a potential sex-mate may be taken as a sign that the self is repulsive, thereby contributing to the generation of self-disgust.

### Moral disgust

The defensive mechanism of disgust, originally evolved to protect the physical integrity of the individual, seems to have extended to also secure individuals' social integrity (Rozin, Haidt, & Fincher, 2009; Rozin, Haidt, & McCauley, 1999). In other words, it has been proposed that a moral type of disgust has evolved to safeguard the integrity of important social norms and to secure pertinent social structures. When elicited in observers, moral disgust would serve to communicate and coordinate condemnation of particular acts that may threaten the integrity of critical social networks and social structures (e.g., Tybur et al., 2013). When elicited in the actor, the experience of moral disgust may bolster already internalised sociomoral rules (Wheatley & Haidt, 2005), which might help the actor prevent the occurrence of future infringements; in other words, the experience of disgust may, as with shame and embarrassment, help people stay on the allotted path (cf. Ferguson & Stegge, 1995; Levenson, 1999).

This more ideational type of disgust may also be elicited by sexual behaviours that violate important and strongly ingrained sociomoral rules (Rozin, Haidt, & McCauley, 1999). Holding more restrictive sociomoral standards, one would have a higher chance that particular sexual behaviour will be experienced as a transgression (i.e., a "wrongdoing"), and will thus elicit disgust targeted at the self, the witnessed behaviour, or at the person engaging in this immoral behaviour. In line with this, it has been shown that women with relatively restrictive attitudes towards sexual behaviour experienced more disgust when they viewed erotic slides and/or videos than women with more liberal values (Koukounas & McCabe, 1997). In a similar vein, people's judgements about the abnormality of particular consensual sexual behaviours have been shown to be closely associated with their ratings of elicited disgust (Giner-Sorolla, Bosson, Caswell, & Hettinger, 2012).

Thus, adherence to strict moral rules concerning sexual behaviours may influence individuals' subsequent emotional responding towards particular sexual behaviours (e.g., Borg, de Jong, & Weijmar-Schultz, 2011). It has been speculated that elicited feelings of disgust may also further confirm the importance of adhering to certain sociomoral rules. Emotional reasoning of the type: "if I feel disgusted, then it must be inappropriate behaviour" (cf. Rachman, 2004, p. 1252) will logically act in a way to further inhibit individuals' motivation to get involved in these particular disgust-eliciting sexual behaviours. What is morally correct, and what is not, is, of course, a very subjective and sensitive issue that may differ widely across (sub)cultures and individuals, and may also alter during the life span. Therefore, it is possible that a specific sexual activity will elicit strong feelings of disgust in one person, because he or she feels that it is not "right" (e.g., homosexual behaviours, transvestism), whereas the exact same activity may elicit positive feelings in other persons (e.g., Ahmed & Bhugra, 2007; Olatunji, 2008).

## *Self-disgust*

In the previous section we already provided some examples of how the various categories of disgust elicitors (pathogen, sexual, and moral) might have extended to the self (or features of the self) as the subject of disgust. In the following section, we will discuss in more detail how each type of disgust might give rise to particular types of self-disgust, and how these types of self-disgust might relate to (memories of) sexual behaviour and sexual experiences (for a summary, see Table 2).

### Pollution of the self

Like pathogen disgust tracks invisible physical contagion, a similar mechanism may be involved in tracking "invisible" ideational contagion, thereby serving as a defence against the threat of "contamination" of the self. In the context of sexual behaviours, unwanted/non-consensual sex might thus not only elicit feelings of physical pollution, but also feelings of a more symbolic, ideational type of "mental" pollution

Table 2. Self-disgust as an extension of disgust subtype and illustrative prototypical thoughts.

| *Disgust subtypes extended to the self* | *Experiences that can lead to self-disgust* | *Prototypical thought* |
|---|---|---|
| Pathogen: *Pollution of the self* | A violation (e.g., rape) can contaminate the core self, which might cause a discrepancy between the ideal self (as being a strong person) and the actual self that could not avoid the rape/violation. | "I am a repulsive person" "I am disgusted at this *new* me'" |
| Sexual: *Low mating quality of the self* | After rejection (e.g., being sexually cheated on by the partner), a discrepancy between the core self (as being a valued sex mate) and the actual self (who has been betrayed) could develop, which can give rise to self-disgust. | "I am an unworthy sex-mate" "I am unable to satisfy my partner" |
| Moral: *Transgression of own standards* | Transgressing (e.g., a sexual affair) can cause a gap between the values that define the ideal self and the actual self that engaged in this wrong-doing, which can cause the person to feel self-repugnant. | "I am a bad person" "I am a cheater" |

*Notes*: The first column represents the three disgust subtypes; the second column illustrates how this particular type of disgust (pathogen, sexual, moral) might evolve to self-directed disgust; and the third column shows the prototypical "thought" that might be at play, with the corresponding disgust type.

(Rachman, 1994). In line with this, a study among female victims of sexual assault found that deliberate recall of the assault resulted in feelings of dirtiness and the urge to wash (Fairbrother & Rachman, 2004). Supporting further the relevance of mental pollution of the self in the aftermath of a traumatic sexual assault, a more recent study showed an association between the severity of PTSD symptoms and the intensity of feelings of disgust together with urges to wash in response to the traumatic event script (Badour, Feldner et al., 2013; see also Badour & Adams, this volume). Consistent with these cross-sectional and correlational findings, there is also experimental evidence showing that the controlled experience of a non-volitional violation of the intimate border of the self may give rise to ideational feelings of dirtiness and disgust. For example, Fairbrother and colleagues showed that undergraduates who were asked to imagine experiencing a non-consensual kiss at a party reported enhanced and marked feelings of mental pollution together with an urge to wash (Fairbrother, Newth, & Rachman, 2005).

Although we started this section emphasising that mental/ideational contamination shares several features with physical contamination, there are also some critical differences between both types of contamination that are highly relevant for the present context. First, there is a difference in source. In ideational pollution, the contaminant is not an invisible trace or substance but rather a person, an act, or a thought. Second, there is a difference with regard to the target of contamination between both types of contamination. Physical "pathogen" contamination threatens the integrity/health of one's physical body, whereas the more ideational type of contamination seems generated by perceived violations of the embodied self and threatens the integrity ("health") of the core self, instead of one's mere physical constitution. Third, and perhaps most important, the more ideational pollution may set the stage for developing self-disgust. That is, to the extent that a particular violation damages parts of the core self, it may give rise to self-directed disgust as a way to distance one part of one's self from the damaged parts of the self, and to safeguard the integrity of the self in spite of its current suboptimal status.

Sexual assault may perhaps be the ultimate violation to oneself, which might help explain the clinical impression that self-disgust is a common symptom following sexual misuse. At least two different pathways may give rise to self-disgust following sexual assaults. First, being sexually molested might elicit a discrepancy between the ideal self and the actual self because a critical part of the embodied self has been damaged/desecrated by the sexual assault. Second, a discrepancy between the ideal self and the actual self may arise when the victim starts thinking that she or he should, and could, have done more to prevent the incident, and was thus somehow partly responsible for the assault. Clearly, both pathways are not mutually exclusive and may well act in concert.

The following case that was adopted from Rachman (2010) may be taken as a clinical illustration of how sexual misuse may give rise to beliefs about pollution of the self:

## Case one: sexual abuse

> A thirty-two-year-old woman sought treatment for severe compulsive washing. Her hands and arms up to the elbow were red raw from repeated washing. The problem had developed eighteen months earlier when she had to prepare evidence in the criminal prosecution of a former priest who had sexually abused the patient and some other girls when they were between eight and twelve years of age. Prior to the court case, the patient had kept the abuse secret and was extremely distressed by having to recall the upsetting events and make them public. She became depressed and tried to ease her feelings of pollution by repeated hot washes. The patient was extremely angry and felt that the priest, who was also a family friend, had doubly betrayed her—as a family friend and as her religious guide and protector. The patient's feelings of dirtiness were diffuse, internal, unresponsive to ordinary washing, had a human source, were idiosyncratic, and easily evocable by memories or images. She felt that the priest had polluted her and felt not only self-directed disgust but also felt she was repulsive to others, which might further contribute to her feelings of self-disgust, especially since the cognition of being repulsive to others is considered fundamental to self-disgust. The probable discrepancy between ideal self and actual self was illustrated by her self-evaluative thoughts such as: "I am worthless", "I totally lack judgement", "people can see that I have a weak character", "I am fated to be a lonely unhappy person".

The urge to wash following traumatic sexual assaults, which was also evident in the case description, may be driven by both pathogen disgust (because of the physical contamination associated with rape) and self-disgust (because of the ideational contamination associated with rape). Clearly, washing may be highly effective in reducing concrete traces of physical pollution. However, it is very doubtful whether it would be a similarly helpful strategy to undo the more ideational form of mental pollution. The more ideational feelings of dirtiness may thus remain and may continue to elicit the urge to wash. This may also explain why victims of sexual abuse often engage in elaborate washing rituals or may even get stuck in persistent cleaning compulsions, as was also evident in the case described above. Perhaps, then, persistent washing might be best conceptualised as avoidance behaviour, and it seems plausible to assume that washing will therefore counteract the recovery of the damaged core self (e.g., via preventing the re-evaluation of the core self in light of the dreadful incident). The association between the severity of current PTSD symptoms and the strength of the urge to wash when exposed to the script of the traumatic event in women with a history of a traumatic sexual assault (e.g., Badour, Feldner et al., 2013) is also in line with this suggestion. Clearly, it requires experimental control over the actual washing behaviours (e.g., in the context of a clinical trial) to arrive at more final conclusions in this respect.

Although we have thus far focused on sexual assault, there may be many other ways in which pathogen disgust might have extended to (sex-relevant) self-disgust. For example, self-disgust may arise if a body part that is very central to the sexual self (e.g., vagina, breasts, penis, scrotum, etc.) is somehow damaged following disease or surgical interventions. Similarly, self-directed disgust may also arise when critical body parts are otherwise not in line with the ideal/core self. For example, when having male genitals (a penis), yet actually experiencing the core self as being a woman, or when having the strong conviction (either intrinsically or through societal signalling) that one's critical sex organs, or other sex-relevant body parts, are not acceptable/congruent with one's self-concept.

## Low mating quality attributed to self

A person's physical appearance (e.g., extreme obesity, physical deformation due to accident or surgery) may not only elicit disgust in potential sex partners (see "Sexual disgust", this chapter) but may also give rise to self-disgust, fuelled by the implied low mating quality attributed to the self. This might either reflect a projection of other's views of the self or a result of an internalisation of others' disgust responses. No matter what the trigger of disgust is, as far as the person appraises him/herself as repulsive to others in their sociocultural group, which can be a realistic or distorted appraisal, both can lead to negative expectancies which may influence their behaviour in a way to confirm their expectancies (i.e., self-fulfilling prophecy). Here, self-disgust helps with distancing one part of oneself from this other, undesirable persistent feature of the self.

This type of self-disgust does not necessarily follow from concrete, explicitly definable physical features, but may also develop on the basis of more implicit social signals. For example, if a person finds out that his/her partner has systematically cheated on him/her with another person, this may be taken as a signal that the person is no longer considered as someone with sufficient mating quality. To the extent that one's mating quality is an important feature of the core self, this may give rise to self-disgust in a way to distance oneself from this damaged/shattered part of the ideal self. Consistent with this, Rachman (2010) argued that feelings of dirtiness are a common feature in victims of betrayal. The following case, also described in Rachman's (2010) psychological analysis of betrayal, may be taken as a clinical illustration of how being betrayed may (also) give rise to self-disgust.

## Case two: being betrayed

> A patient complained of persisting feelings of dirtiness that led him to wash and shower repeatedly. He was puzzled and annoyed by his inability to use many items of his clothing because they felt dirty. They remained dirty even after dry-cleaning—a classic example of "looking clean but feeling dirty". The feelings of dirtiness and associated washing and avoidance developed within a few weeks after he discovered that his fiancée had repeatedly been intimate with her former boyfriend while the patient was away on a business trip. On discovering this betrayal, the patient was shocked and distressed, and ended the engagement. He ordered his fiancée to move out of his apartment immediately and to refrain from ever speaking to him again. Directly after she had left with her belongings, he carried out a complete and vigorous cleaning of the entire apartment and took several hot showers. He flinched when talking about her, which he avoided whenever possible, and was incapable

> of speaking her name out loud. He reported feelings of internal dirtiness that were diffuse and unresponsive to ordinary washing.

Clearly, being betrayed may elicit a complex of different feelings and emotions. Most relevant for the current context, thinking back to the betrayal (also) elicited intense feelings of internal dirtiness together with a strong urge to wash. These self-directed feelings of disgust may have originated from the feeling that a critical part of the ideal self was jeopardised by his fiancée's betrayal, resulting in a discrepancy between his ideal self (implying being a superior sex mate) and the actual self (not being a preferred sex mate). The feelings of dirtiness (self-disgust) were typically elicited by cues that reminded him of this undesirable discrepancy. Thus also here, the self-directed disgust might motivate the person to distance himself from the damaged part of his ideal self in an attempt to safeguard the integrity of his core self.

A special case that might be relevant for this type of self-disgust is the persistent inability to have sexual intercourse, which is the central symptom of a sexual dysfunction known as vaginismus. In this case, the woman might have the strong feeling of being a suboptimal sex mate, which in turn may set the stage for developing self-disgust. This condition may fuel disgust directed at the self, especially when a person has the strong conviction that one can only be a proper sex mate when one is able to get involved in sexual intercourse and when being an optimal sex mate is a critical feature of one's ideal self. The following excerpt of a woman suffering from vaginismus taken from Borg (2013, p. 2) may be considered as a clinical illustration of this proposed pathway:

> I had a partner who tried to insert a finger during foreplay and was unable. I also was unable to ever insert anything myself. I thought I would never be able to have children because of it … this seriously affected me … it was embarrassing to not be able to experience every part of sex. I had to tell when I dated that I did not like insertion so they did not try it unexpectedly on me … I figured I would never be able to use my vagina as normal women did. I had low self-esteem when it came to vaginismus because I felt I was not normal … I avoided sex.

Although she did not explicitly refer to self-disgust or the urge to wash, the feeling of being "abnormal" that she reported seems a common feature of individuals who view themselves as impure, base, disgusting objects.

## Unacceptable thoughts or behaviours

Just as transgressions by other people may give rise to (moral) disgust directed at these "transgressors", transgressions of one's own norms may elicit disgust directed at the self. In these contexts, self-disgust may be taken to signal a gap between the values that define the ideal self and the actual self that engaged in this wrong-doing. Thus, if the transgression concerns a core value, it can cause the person to feel self-repugnant and may elicit the urge to wash (e.g., Rachman, Radomsky, Elliott, & Zysk, 2012).

Betraying your partner might be one of the behaviours that may generate feelings of self-disgust. This is well portrayed in a scene from a recent film *A Late Quartet* (directed by Yaron Zilberman, 2012) about the dynamics of four people drawn together by a lasting contract to rehearse and perform. At a particular scene, the second violinist of this string quartet, Robert, who is in a marriage at risk (because of the tatters of time and perhaps negligence from his wife), has a one-night stand with a beautiful woman (Liraz Charhi). The morning after, Robert is woken up by his wife, who has prepared his favourite breakfast as an apologetic sign of her negligence; he is immediately stunned at the realisation of what he has done the night before, and he goes instantly to have an intense shower, to wash off his feelings of self-disgust. This engagement in the cleaning behaviour closely resembles the ritual behaviour described in the previous examples. In this scene, Robert's behaviour could be perceived as if he were washing off his "dirt", or the (self-)disgust he felt towards his own behaviour (cf. Zhong & Liljenquist, 2006).

Complementing this type of anecdotal evidence, there is also evidence from experimental research showing that "wrong-doing" might indeed give rise to feelings of dirtiness and urges to wash. Using the "non-consensual-kiss" paradigm, Rachman and colleagues (2012) not only showed that being the victim of such a kiss might elicits feelings of pollution and the urge to wash, but also that being the actor might elicit feelings of dirtiness directed at the self. This so-called "perpetrator effect" thus supports the view that violating important values (e.g., "intimate behaviour is only acceptable if it is consensual") may give rise to disgust directed at the self.

The moral type of self-disgust does not necessarily follow from actual behaviours but may also be the result of repeated/persistent thoughts or fantasies that are in strong conflict with one's own core values. For example, self-disgust may arise when having repeated fantasies about having sex with children. In a similar vein, persistent fantasies about homosexual contacts might give rise to self-disgust in people for whom homosexuality is fully unacceptable (e.g., because of religious reasons; see also Jones, this volume). Also, here self-disgust might help retain the integrity of the core self via distancing the core self from this unacceptable persistent feature of the self.

Because the norms/standards that people may consider critical for their core self are highly idiosyncratic, the type of norm-violations that will give rise to self-disgust may also be expected to be highly variable. In the following clinical case (again taken with permission from Rachman, 2010), self-disgust seems, at least partly, fuelled by the person's violation of her rule that one should marry for love. This case also illustrates that in real life the various types of disgust often present themselves in a blended form; here, a combination of pathogen and moral-based feelings of dirtiness. The pathogen-based self-disgust seems elicited because her parents violated a critical border of the core self by pushing her into an intimate relationship in spite of her reluctance to get married with the proposed person. Yet, the clinically relevant intensity of self-disgust symptoms only became evident when she eventually realised that she not only got involved in a marriage against her will, but also that this marriage had nothing to do with love but more with improving the financial position of her parents. In other words, it seems that the feelings of disgust became especially prominent when she realised that this undesired marriage violated the core value that one should marry for love not money.

## Case three: violating one's rule that one should marry for love not money

> A patient who was overcome by intense feelings of dirtiness had become disabled by her irresistible need to wash and scrub herself for hours and hours on end. She used such abrasive cleaning

> substances and strong chemicals that her skin had become disfigured. She complained of feeling disgustingly dirty and her life was hellish. The feelings of dirtiness were pervasive and persisting, and could be exacerbated by any physical or non-physical contact with her family. A telephone call, or a letter from her family, or even talking about them, triggered bursts of intensive washing. Images or memories of the family were also triggers. It gradually emerged that she felt totally betrayed by her parents and former husband. Her parents were impoverished and living under hard conditions in South America when they introduced the patient, then nineteen years old, to a distant relation who was visiting them. He was a wealthy man of fifty-four who had been twice married and divorced, and in a triumph of hope over experience, was seeking a fulfilling marriage. The parents colluded with him in persuading the most reluctant young woman to marry the newcomer. Some time after the marriage, the patient learned that her parents had benefited financially from their role in the arrangement, and it seemed that is was then that the symptoms started to appear.

## *Self-disgust as a pathway to sexual problems*

The previous section focused on how self-disgust may arise in the context of sex-related experiences. The current section briefly addresses the potential influence of enhanced self-disgust on the generation of sexual problems. The case illustrations presented in this chapter already indicated that sex-relevant self-directed disgust may give rise to all kinds of neutralising and avoidance tendencies, such as excessive cleaning behaviours, which in turn may interfere with common functioning. Yet, self-disgust might also more directly compromise people's sexual functioning and give rise to sex-related problems.

Figure 1 presents a heuristic model/diagram that illustrates the proposed inter-relationships between disgust and sexual arousal. If people encounter a sex-relevant stimulus, this may elicit both sexual arousal and (self-)disgust. The experience of disgust will motivate avoidance of the sexual stimulus and inhibit sexual arousal. The elicited sexual arousal, on the other hand, facilitates approach behaviour and may inhibit the tendency to experience disgust. If disgust somehow outbalances sexual arousal, people may enter a negative loop that interferes

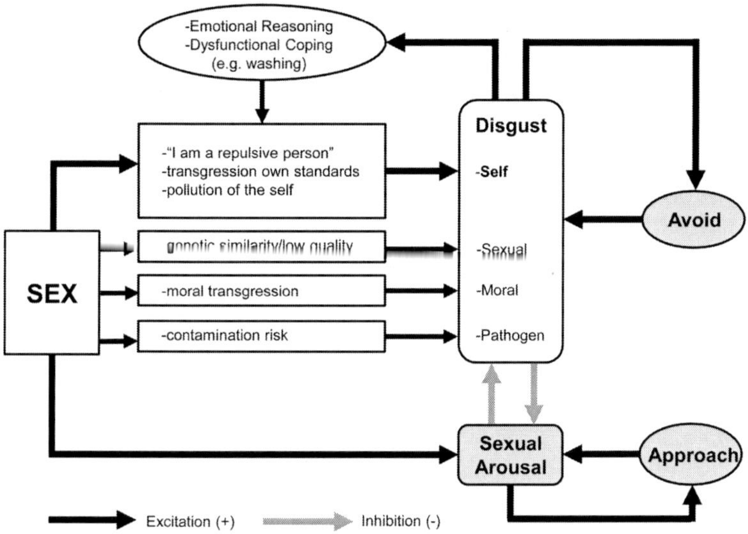


Figure 1. This model illustrates how the various types of (self-)disgust may counteract the generation of sexual arousal and may enter self-perpetuating loops (upper part), and how sexual arousal may counteract the temporary activation of (self-)disgust facilitating sex-relevant approach behaviours (lower part).

with the generation of sexual responses, whereas people will enter a positive feedback loop if sexual arousal outbalances disgust.

In addition, the experience of disgust may elicit emotional reasoning that may act in a way to confirm the cognitions associated with (self-)disgust (e.g., "if I feel disgusted, I must be an inferior sex mate"). Furthermore, the emotion of disgust may elicit all kinds of neutralising behaviours such as the urge to wash or take a shower, which can be conceptualised as attempts to escape the sources of (self-)disgust or to close the gap between the ideal and the actual self. Self-disgust-induced avoidance/neutralising behaviours will logically interfere with the functional reappraisal of the disgust-eliciting stimuli. Accordingly, persistent ritualistic washing and other avoidance strategies might not be helpful to undo the more ideational feelings of dirtiness that are directed at the self, and may therefore contribute to the persistence of sexual dysfunction.

In line with the proposed illustration, in a functional loop, sexual arousal inhibits the tendency to experience disgust, thereby temporarily allowing sexual engagement. In support of this, it has been shown that experimentally induced sexual arousal temporarily reduces both the feelings of disgust (Borg & de Jong, 2012; Stevenson, Case, & Oaten, 2011), and individuals' reluctance to get involved in disgust-relevant behavioural approach tasks (Borg & de Jong, 2012). Based on these and other findings, it has been argued that sexual arousal may counteract all kinds of mechanisms that otherwise promote avoidance of particular sexual behaviours or stimuli—be it general repulsion, moral borders (e.g., having sex with a twelve-year-old), or contamination risk (e.g., condom use). Thus, sexual arousal may undermine mechanisms that *normally* help people avoid certain (disgusting) stimuli (including aspects of the self).

Accordingly, particular sexual behaviours that in fact violate important values of the self may feel quite acceptable when being sexually aroused. Yet, the very same behaviours may retrospectively be experienced as totally unacceptable (disgusting) when sexual arousal has subsided. Thus, (self-directed) disgust may emerge following sexual engagement when sexual arousal is reduced or has disappeared (e.g., "how could I have done that, I am a dirty person/disgusting person"). Post-arousal, people may therefore experience that, for example, the goal of keeping away from contamination of the self might have been compromised. In turn, this might lead to neutralising-compensatory behaviour to minimise the intrinsic feeling of dirtiness (e.g., brushing teeth after oral sex, showering, etc.). As these avoidance tendencies will probably contribute to the persistence of these self-disgust-inducing concerns/preoccupations, people may enter a downward spiral in which disgust becomes an increasingly persistent feature of the self. Consequently, the person continues to feel dirty (and perhaps also shameful/guilty); this probably becomes even more intense if the person has either a strong moral code or a highly religious devotion that frames specific sexual behaviours as less appropriate or even sinful (Berle & Philips, 2006). This attitude/behaviour can also install the feeling of self-repugnance in the partner: "if the person I just had sex with is so disgusted of the contact we just shared, then I must be really disgusting". Similarly, the experience of disgust might strengthen further the feeling that important goals (e.g., keeping uncontaminated, feeling a highly valued sex mate) have been thwarted. Consequently, the feeling of disgust might be used as input to conclude, for example, that one is unworthy as a sex mate and should be avoided, which may further contribute to the generation of sexual problems.

Disgust directed towards bodily features that are highly relevant to one's core self (e.g., penis, vagina) might also be implicated in sexual dysfunctions such as vaginismus or dyspareunia. In an earlier publication (de Jong et al., 2010), we described a case illustration that was used to show how disgust directed towards a sexualised area, in this instance towards the woman's own vagina, could disrupt sexual engagement. This patient persistently avoided completing the homework assignment which involved a close inspection of her own genitals. To examine what made her avoid the homework assignment, the therapist asked her what would pop into her mind if she had to imagine starting this assignment during the session. Although very hesitant, she eventually started to describe her vagina as being: "a tangle of folds, slime, and secretions; it is ugly and cannot be kept clean … it stinks although I am too far off to actually smell it myself … when I had this infection, it also smelled very badly" (de Jong et al., 2010, p. 30). Clearly, then, it appeared that the pervasive avoidance tendencies originated from self-disgust. This repugnance directed towards an important feature of the self (her genitals) strongly interfered with the normal process of mental and genital sexual arousal, which in turn hindered the normal preparatory processes for intercourse to occur (e.g., lack of vaginal lubrication). Penetration became, therefore, a painful and a negative experience, to the level that this person started avoiding sexual initiation or sexual contact altogether. A series of prolonged exposure exercises with response prevention (to counteract these strong avoidance tendencies), appeared highly successful in breaking the downward cycle and to alleviate the symptoms of sexual pain (de Jong et al., 2010).

## *Self-disgust and sexual functioning: preliminary data*

As a first attempt to empirically test if indeed self-disgust has any relevance for sexual behaviour, we recently set out a study among undergraduate male ($n$ = 147), and female ($n$ = 140) students to explore the relationship between self-directed disgust and indices of sexual functioning and sexual satisfaction. To index self-directed disgust, we used a Dutch translation of the Self-Disgust Scale (SDS; Overton, Markland, Taggart, Bagshaw, & Simpson, 2008), which is a brief scale with twelve statements (e.g., "I find myself repulsive"). The self-disgust total is the cumulative score of its proposed three underlying constructs: appearance, general self-concept, and behaviour. As a measure of sexual functioning, we included the Female Sexual Functioning Index (FSFI; Rosen et al., 2000; ter Kuile, Brauer, & Laan, 2006). An exemplar item of the FSFI would be: "Over the past four weeks, how satisfied were you with your ability to reach orgasm (climax) during sexual activity or intercourse?" The FSFI scale consists of nineteen items and covers different domains of sexual functioning; namely, desire, arousal, lubrication, orgasm, satisfaction, and pain. To cover sexual behaviour (also) in men, we asked participants to complete the Golombok Rust Inventory of Sexual Satisfaction (GRISS; Rust & Golombok, 1986; van Lankveld & ter Kuile, 1999), which contains twenty-eight items and covers the most frequently occurring sexual complaints of heterosexual persons with a steady partner; a typical item is: "Are there three weeks in which you did not have sex at all?" The subscales for the female version of the GRISS include: Vaginismus, Female Avoidance and Female Dissatisfaction, whereas for the male version, the subscales include: Impotency, Premature Ejaculation, and Dissatisfaction, among others.

In line with previous literature on trait-disgust (e.g., disgust propensity, sexual disgust; Olatunji & Sawchuk, 2005; van Overveld et al., 2013), our unpublished data indicate that self-disgust is generally higher in women than in men (cf. Roberts & Goldenberg, 2007), so that self-disgust in relation to sexual behaviour may be generally more important for women than for men, which in fact also seems to be the case for sexual disgust (van Overveld et al., 2013). However, future studies are necessary to see whether this represents a stable finding, and whether this gender difference is consistent across different types of samples and across different cultures.

In line with the illustration/model suggesting that self-disgust seems to tap into the processes surrounding sexual problems, the unpublished preliminary data showed that this indeed might be the case, and could thus offer promising leads for further research in this field. In support of this proposition, when computing Pearson's correlations with a validated measure of sexual satisfaction (GRISS) in men, this relationship (self-disgust and sexual satisfaction in men) reached significance ($r = .17$), and was mainly driven by the premature ejaculation subscale ($r = .18$). Although it should be acknowledged that the effect size of this relationship was small, it seems nevertheless consistent with the view that for a man who has premature ejaculation, it is more difficult to feel valued/worthy as a sex mate. Also this disgust directed towards the self can contribute further to the insecurities surrounding the man's erection, and be in itself a risk factor for premature ejaculation, which further increases the gap between the desired self (of being a good sex mate) and the actual self (with premature ejaculation, inadequacy, etc.). Moreover, the partner can further imply a sense of lower enjoyment and frustration, which might emphasise the feeling of self-repugnance in the person suffering from premature ejaculation. In our undergraduate student sample, this relationship (of self-disgust and GRISS) in women did not reach the conventional level of significance, yet a similar tendency was observed for avoidance ($r$ = .15) and appearance ($r$ = .19). Since the absence of a significant relationship between self-disgust and sexual functioning in women may simply reflect a lack of power, it would be important to replicate this study in a larger sample.

If a person finds herself repulsive in terms of appearance (both in the way she perceives herself, but also in the way she is viewed in society), it is hard to appreciate that she is a valued sex mate and worthy of pleasure. In extreme cases, the person might feel inclined to avoid any sexual contact altogether (e.g., in women with genito-pelvic pain/penetration disorders). This avoidance could also be expressed in compensatory behaviour such as low desire (e.g., low mental sexual arousal, no strong wish to have sex). It could be expected that once self-disgust is generated (as an extension of sexual disgust), it maintains the negative cognitions about the self, causing problems with pleasurable sex, less satisfaction, and thus further hesitation to approach or engage in (future) sexual activities.

Attesting to the validity of the above argument, a significant negative relationship between the FSFI and self-disgust was observed ($r$ = –.17), which was mainly driven by the self-disgust appearance subscale ($r$ = –.24). When looking at the subscales of the FSFI, this was mainly driven by *satisfaction* ($r$ = –.24) and *desire* ($r$ = –.20). Moreover, if, for instance, a woman who experiences penetration disorders (e.g., vaginismus) feels shameful or guilty that she cannot fulfil the role of a married woman (especially in extreme religious cultures), self-disgust might become even more emphasised (as an extension of moral and or sexual disgust).

It should be noted, however, that these preliminary data concerned non-selected volunteers who showed restricted variance in their sexual functioning. Therefore, it is important to have the results replicated in groups of women and men with sexual dysfunctions. Nonetheless, the present findings are in line with the view that self-disgust might be a relevant feature to consider in sexual behaviour. Thus, these data may be taken as an important empirical demonstration of our theoretical speculations, and also serve to identify gaps in this field that need further empirical examination.

## *Recapitulation, clinical implications, and remaining issues*

Self-disgust will probably not be the first thing that pops into people's mind when thinking about sex. However, in this chapter we have illustrated that there might nevertheless be an important link between self-disgust and sexual behaviour/experiences. We have argued that there might be various ways how sex and sexual experiences may give rise to disgust directed at the self. Self-disgust may either arise from: (1) being polluted by other people's violations of the self (e.g., being sexually misused); (2) internalisation of (assumed) social evaluative appraisals of key aspects of the self (e.g., "I can never be a proper sex mate"); and (3) own behaviours/thoughts that violate important values of the self (e.g., "it cannot be me who had sex with this child"). Although there may thus be very different sources of sex-relevant self-disgust, there seems also a common feature: for all pathways, self-disgust seems to arise when a stimulus brings a critical discrepancy to the front between the ideal self and the actual self. Under these conditions, self-disgust has been argued to serve as a strategy to distance the self from the desecrated, unworthy, or deplorable aspects of the self, in a way to preserve the integrity of the core self.

To the extent that self-disgust may indeed be taken to signal a critical discrepancy in the patient's self that somehow requires a resolution, self-disgust also seems a highly relevant symptom for being considered in clinical contexts. Knowledge about the different types of self-disgust that are each assumed to be relevant for another type of self-discrepancy may then also be helpful in providing more specific guidance for therapists when searching for relevant starting points for a clinical intervention. Most relevant for the current context, considering self-disgust may also be helpful in improving the understanding of people's sexual problems, as the features that underlie the generation of disgust may be very distant from the concrete sexual dysfunction that might have motivated the patient to seek help. If, for example, persistent dyspareunia is not so much driven by a phobic fear of pain, but is essentially due to sex-triggered self-disgust, this has of course a pervasive impact on the intervention of choice and may also help in the understanding of how/why a common intervention that focuses on fear of pain is not effective in some cases.

It thus seems that considering self-disgust might be relevant for both improving patients' case conceptualisations and in designing tailored interventions (see, e.g., Coughtrey, Shafran, Lee, & Rachman, 2013). However, although self-disgust has the promise to be a highly relevant feature in sexual dysfunction, this promise is almost exclusively based on theoretical speculation and clinical impressions. A critical next step would be to actually test whether indeed self-disgust is a relevant feature in sexual dysfunctions. Event-contingent experience sampling may be a helpful tool in this, as it allows the examination of the order of events and to get a more detailed insight into the triggers of self-disgust (e.g., aan het Rot, Hogenelst, & Schoevers, 2012). In addition, by tailoring the actual questions it could also be used to examine the short- and long-term consequences of experiencing self-disgust, and the alleged impact of neutralising behaviours in the persistence of self-directed disgust.

In addition, it seems critical to examine the validity of the proposed categories of self-disgust, and to test whether the proposed types of experiences can indeed be seen as category-specific triggers. The "non-consensual-kiss" paradigm (Rachman et al., 2012) may be a helpful starting point in this. By systematically varying the type of experiences/behaviours that are assumed to give rise to the various types of (sex-relevant) self-disgust, it can be investigated to what extent these category-specific experiences indeed give rise to feelings of dirtiness/urges to wash, and it can be tested to what extent the generation of these symptoms of self-disgust can be attributed to the category-specific types of thoughts (as summarised in Table 2). It might also be relevant to test the moderating influence of individual differences in this respect. It might be, for example, that in people with relatively high trait disgust sensitivity (i.e., those who are liable to appraise feelings of disgust as a relatively negative experience), self-disgust might have a relatively strong impact on sexual functioning (cf. van Overveld et al., 2013).

Furthermore, it would be important to test whether induced sexual arousal may indeed attenuate self-directed disgust, as we proposed in the model presented in Figure 1. There is already some experimental evidence that participants indicate they are more willing to get involved in initially avoided behaviours when they are sexually aroused (e.g., Ariely & Loewenstein, 2006). However, if this would also work via lowering self-disgust, and whether having actually carried out these tasks when being sexually aroused would also lead to increased levels of self-directed disgust post-arousal, are questions which remain to be tested.

To conclude, it is still far from being clear how exactly self-disgust could be involved in common sexual behaviours and in sexual dysfunctions, and most aspects of the link between sex and self-disgust are still waiting empirical scrutiny. Accordingly, the proposed interrelationships between sex and self-disgust presented here have relied predominantly on theoretical speculations instead of empirical data. We hope that the present speculations are nevertheless helpful in illustrating that self-disgust may be a highly relevant feature in sexual (avoidance) behaviours, and may provide inspiration for future research to investigate further the proposed role of self-disgust in sexual behaviour and sexual dysfunctions.

CHAPTER SIX

# Disgust and interpersonal experiences: the complex emotional experience of rejection

*Dean McKay and Rebecca Lo Presti*

Recent research has supported a role for disgust in a wide range of psychological conditions (Phillips, Senior, Fahy, & David, 1998). This is a fairly recent development, with most studies conducted over the past twenty years and beginning with the disease-avoidance conceptualisation of phobias (Matchett & Davey, 1991). One potential explanation for the lack of consideration given to disgust is the general under-reporting of disgust experiences by clients. Further, attributing psychological distress to disgust, as opposed to fear or dysphoria, is a less common attribution, and our existing taxonomies emphasise these emotional experiences over disgust (Olatunji & McKay, 2009). In addition to this, most assessment instruments overlook disgust as a contributory emotional state for psychopathology (Olatunji, Williams, Tolin et al., 2007). This suggests that models of psychopathology do not take into consideration the role of disgust, and that until recently most clinical researchers did not even assess for the presence of this emotional state.

While much of the research on disgust has focused on its role in disorders of avoidance (such as phobias or contamination fear), there is an emerging line of inquiry showing that it is also involved in interpersonal experiences. The aim of this chapter is to highlight how interpersonal disgust, and more specifically moral disgust, has broad implications in psychopathology. However, in order to appreciate fully the implications of moral disgust, we provide a brief overview of the disease-avoidance model. The importance of this model of disgust in psychopathology sets the stage for moral disgust, which is a higher level feature of the emotion. Indeed, recent research suggests that moral disgust emerges from the basic emotional experience of disgust (Chapman & Anderson, 2013).

## *Disease avoidance and psychopathology*

The "disease-avoidance model" posits that disgust developed as a form of protection from disease (Curtis, Aunger, & Rabie, 2004; Fessler & Haley, 2006; Matchett & Davey, 1991). In their classic paper, Rozin and Fallon (1987) describe the emotion of disgust as "revulsion at the prospect of (oral) incorporation of an offensive object" (p. 23). They assert that disgust is related to three motivations for rejection: sensory-affective; anticipation of harm following ingestion; and ideation (Rozin & Fallon, 1987; Rozin, Haidt, & McCauley, 2009). Sensory-affective is the attribution of the physical experience to an emotional state. Anticipation of harm following ingestion involves the disgust experienced shortly after consuming something of questionable status (i.e., drinking milk that is near its expiration date). Finally, ideational disgust is related to the origin or nature of the stimuli and is believed to be linked to cultural standards, which are so pervasive that disgust can be evoked by an object simply associated with a disgusting item (Rozin & Fallon, 1987). Ideational disgust is closely related to the laws of sympathetic magic, whereby an object that resembles a disgusting item (law of similarity) or has been in contact with a disgusting item (law of contagion) takes on the same properties. This is a powerful aspect of the means for spreading disgust. Through the years, the dynamics of disgust have expanded beyond simple oral contaminants, such as food, into more interpersonal contexts. Disgust is believed to affect the way that people interact, specifically by limiting contact with individuals who are unknown, ill, or perceived to be tainted by disease, misfortune, or immorality (Olatunji, Cisler, McKay, & Phillips, 2010).

Disgust, and by association disgust sensitivity, has wide implication for anxiety problems. Research has suggested that disgust sensitivity increases one's propensity for experiencing anxiety, finding stress anxiety-inducing (such as through trait anxiety), and may even increase the ease of conditioning for other phobic states (Muris, 2006). Central to this is the experience of contamination concerns and excessive avoidance due to potential contact with contaminants. Typically, when considering the world around us, we accept the presence of trace contaminants to complete simple acts of living, such as breathing air (Rozin & Fallon, 1987). While most of us are aware that the world is filled with contaminants, we have become skilled at cordoning off that recognition. In the case of contamination-based fear and avoidance, and by extension disgust sensitivity, the ability to cordon off this recognition breaks down. Here, disgust sensitivity may lead the individual to attach a more catastrophic meaning to the experience of disgust, opening the door to more severe avoidance reactions. Simply put, the more sensitive one is to the experience of disgust, the more likely one is to engage in avoidance reactions (McNally, 2002).

The problem of avoidance due to disgust and the spreading of contaminants is also relevant in phobias. One of the most common phobias is for insects and animals (Davey & Marzillier, 2009). In considering the biological predisposition of humans' basic defence towards physical harm, broadly defined, these fears might seem adaptive. In fact, researchers have found that spider phobia easily fits into the disease-avoidance model (de Jong & Muris, 2002), with individuals consistently endorsing the emotion of disgust in reaction to spiders. Further, over the last several years, researchers have found that there is a high disgust sensitivity associated with small animal phobias (Davey, 1994a; Ware, Jain, Burgess, & Davey, 1994) as well as spider phobias (Mulkens, de Jong, & Merckelbach, 1996; Tolin, Lohr, Sawchuk, & Lee, 1997), which are typically classified as low predatory threats to humans (Davey & Marzillier, 2009). Indeed, as McNally (2002) noted, the dangerousness of spiders is generally low compared to the number and diversity of arachnids, and that "in almost all lethal encounters between a spider and a human being, the spider loses" (McNally, 2002, p. 562). This would strongly suggest that disgust is a more potent factor in determining the avoidance associated with spiders and insects. In fact, Tucker and Bond (1997) found that scores on the General Disgust Scale (DS; Haidt, McCauley, & Rozin, 1994) correlated with fears to stimuli classified as "repulsive invertebrates" and "fear-relevant animals," but did not correlate with larger predatory animals. Likewise, research has shown that individuals in both clinical and non-clinical populations with spider phobia, as well as blood-injury-injection (BII) phobia, indicate significantly higher disgust sensitivity than non-phobic individuals, even when neuroticism, introversion, and trait anxiety have been partialled out (Davey & Bond, 2006; Mulkens et al., 1996).

BII phobia, which is also frequently linked to disgust responses, is commonly described as persistent, excessive fear and avoidance that is triggered by the anticipation or presence of blood, injury, or injections, or related stimuli (American Psychiatric Association (APA), 2013). It is suggested that, in part, blood and injury induce feelings of disgust because they remind humans of their relatedness to animals (Page & Tan, 2009). Self-reported disgust has been positively correlated with BII phobia assessed through questionnaires (de Jong & Merckelback, 1998; Olatunji, Sawchuk, de Jong, & Lohr, 2006; Olatunji, Williams, Lohr et al., 2007). Sawchuk and his colleagues (1999) suggest there is a significant cognitive component of this phobia and note an implicit memory bias towards BII disgust stimuli. This bias is suggested to relate to the observations that BII phobics demonstrate an increased tendency to complete blood and general disgust-related word stems than non-phobics. Researchers have found that when exposed to BII stimuli, such as surgery pictures, BII-fearful individuals reported higher disgust than non-fearful or otherwise anxious control individuals (Sawchuk, Lohr, Westendorf, Meunier, & Tolin, 2002; Tolin et al., 1997). Specifically, Sawchuk and colleagues (2002) found that BII fearful individuals' self-reported emotion of disgust was greater than their self-reported fear emotion. In accordance with the traditional definition of phobia, when behavioural avoidance of BII stimuli occurs there is a positive relation to self-reported disgust. This can be seen in Olatunji, Connolly, and David's (2008) study in which individuals were asked to react to a severed deer leg. Here, high BII-fearful individuals endorsed greater avoidance than the non-fearful group, and individuals reporting disgust demonstrated stronger avoidance than BII fear.

The feeling of disgust in relation to these types of stimuli appears so pervasive that there is a predisposition to associate disgust even when the stimulus is not present (van Overveld, de Jong, & Peters, 2006). For example, spider phobics will refuse to eat a cookie they are told was touched by a spider, regardless of whether or not they witnessed the spider touching the cookie, or have evidence that this event occurred. This type of avoidance is related to the concept of the "law of contagion" that Rozin and Fallon (1987) suggest is the belief that once something is in contact, it is always contaminated.

The centrality of contamination is expressed most clearly in obsessive-compulsive disorder (OCD; McKay et al., 2004). Fear of contamination is commonly reported by individuals with OCD symptoms and is often accompanied by avoidance of contaminants or complex cleaning rituals (Foa & Kozak, 1995; Foa et al., 1995). In fact, clinical observation data suggests that OCD patients with contamination concerns who are treated through exposure therapy experience a reduction in feelings of disgust when they are permitted to engage in hand-washing compulsions (Sieg & Scholz, 2001). Thus, disgust may contribute to OCD symptoms because it causes phobic avoidance in the individual, which is relieved through compulsions and sustained through negative reinforcement. The reaction of disgust to perceived contaminants is related to Rozin and Fallon's (1987) construct of "sympathetic magic", in which items can become disgusting either by coming into brief contact with a core disgust item or by taking on the physical shape of a core disgust item. This presents significant issues for individuals with severe contamination fear, since disgust properties can be transferred to neutral objects, potentially creating the need for more compulsions.

The research examining contamination-based OCD has produced inconsistent research findings. In one study, disgust sensitivity levels in adult OCD patients did not appear significantly higher than patients suffering from social phobia (Woody & Tolin, 2002). Other studies have also demonstrated inconsistent associations between disgust sensitivity and OCD symptoms (Muris, Merckelbach, Schmidt, & Tierney, 1999; Rozin, Taylor, Ross, Bennett, & Hejmadi, 2005). Olatunji, Williams, Tolin, and their colleagues (2007) have suggested that this may be due to limitations within the available assessment measures, with some measures primarily focusing on food and others underestimating the overlap between measured constructs (Olatunji, Moretz, Wolitzky-Taylor, McGrath, & Ciesielski, 2010). Though there may be limitations with the measures, it is still important to consider the findings of some notable studies. Specifically, Muris and colleagues (2000) found that obsessive-compulsive symptoms, such as cleaning concerns, were related to disgust. Indeed, self-report measures assessing for the tendency to respond with disgust have significantly predicted obsessive-compulsive washing even when controlling for anxiety and depression (Mancini, Gragnani, & D'Olimipio, 2001; Moretz & McKay, 2008; Olatunji, Williams, Lohr et al., 2007; Thorpe, Patel, & Simonds, 2003). Further, disgust sensitivity has been significantly positively associated (Scheinle, Stark, Walter, & Vaitl, 2003) with all of the subscales of the Maudsley Obsessional Compulsive Inventory (Hodgson & Rachman, 1977), and correlated with (Thorpe et al., 2003) the Obsessive Compulsive Inventory (Foa, Kozak, Salkovskis, Coles, & Amir, 1998). Olatunji, Sawchuk, Lohr, and de Jong (2004) found that participants high on contamination fear also scored higher on the disgust sensitivity on both the DS (Haidt et al., 1994) and the Disgust Emotion Scale (Walls & Kleinknecht, 1996). Thus, though there may still be some room for improvement in the way disgust is assessed, it continues to emerge as an important factor in the development of pathological responses to perceived contaminants.

## *Higher-order disgust experiences*

The material described to this point highlights the role of disgust in a wide range of disorders associated with avoidance. The transferability of disgust is the focus of this section, as it leads ultimately to the potential for interpersonal-based disgust. Specifically, given the laws of sympathetic magic—namely, the law of contagion and the law of similarity—disgust has shown great potential in being transferred not only to objects but to other individuals, and, in some instances, toward the self.

The laws of contagion and similarity can readily apply to self-referent disgust. The law of similarity would be operative, for example, if one experiences disgust towards themselves and then encounters someone who engages in behaviour similar to their own. Such an individual may experience revulsion towards that other individual in light of the comparative aspects to their own behaviour. As for the law of contagion, this could emerge after someone no longer experiences self-referent disgust, but comes in contact with memorabilia from the time that person was disgusted with themselves. This past-tense self-referent disgust would then activate feelings of disgust again in a manner similar to ruminative experiences.

### *Moral disgust*

Disgust in its higher order forms extends to concerns over contact with, or being contaminated in some way by, ideas or individuals whose shared beliefs or ideology are deemed strongly aversive. To illustrate in the most graphic manner, Rozin and Nemeroff (1990) described an experiment whereby participants were asked if they would be willing to wear a sweater that once belonged to Hitler. In general, participants declined under all potential circumstances, including: being thoroughly washed, being torn and only small pieces being worn, or having been worn immediately prior by Mother Theresa. This impressive persistence of morally based concerns was expressed by participants as disgust, with the prevailing concept of "once in contact, always in contact" setting the stage for the sweater retaining its general "Hitlerness"

Moral disgust and associated contamination has been examined experimentally, whereby exposure to information associated with violations of cultural norms provokes greater hand-washing (Zhong & Liljenquist, 2006). Dubbed "the Macbeth effect", this suggests that there is an implicit connection between the experience of being in contact with morally compromised material and the urge to cleanse oneself afterwards. One hypothesis unexamined by the authors, but entirely possible, is that the washing is designed to alleviate self-directed disgust. Given the higher-order disgust experiences, this encompasses self-directed moral disgust (i.e., "I must have condoned this action since I did not even wash my hands after contact with the morally corrupt information"). This mediational hypothesis warrants additional empirical scrutiny. The problem of potentially compromised morality has more recently been shown to be associated with OCD. Specifically, moral concerns were alleviated after opportunities to wash in individuals with OCD to a greater extent than that of matched controls, although all participants felt moral relief after washing (Reuven, Liberman, & Dar, 2013).

It appears from the limited literature thus far that moral disgust and the other basic aspects of disgust are bi-directionally related. That is, provoking moral disgust leads to responses that would alleviate the basic aspects of disgust; alternatively, moral disgust appears also to operate based on the laws of sympathetic magic (contagion and similarity). However, the connection of moral transgressions and disgust is tenuous, since there is little risk of physical ingestion and, even if there were, less reason still to see an increased risk of harm.

## The assessment of moral disgust

At the present time, assessment instruments for moral disgust are limited. One measure, the Three Domains of Disgust Scale (TDDS; Tybur,

Lieberman, & Griskevicius, 2009), is a twenty-one-item measure with subscales for moral as well as pathogen and sexual disgust. The measure has good internal consistency, with Cronbach's alphas reported between .84 and .87 for the three scales. The moral disgust subscale is comprised of seven items. Additional recent findings suggest that the scale forms the predicted three factors, but the moral subscale has limited validity (Olatunji, Adams et al., 2012). We (Arocho, McKay, Adams, & Lohr, 2014) have developed a stand-alone moral disgust scale. Comprised of twenty four items, the scale has two factor-analytically derived subscales named proximal and distal moral disgust. Initial findings suggest the subscales are internally consistent, and are significantly correlated with measures of obsessive-compulsive symptoms, post-traumatic symptoms, and eating disorder symptoms. Additional research is currently underway examining its potential as a trans-diagnostic indicator of trauma and obsessive-compulsive symptoms.

## Terror management theory and moral disgust

Disgust, as with fear, is designed to protect individuals from death. This protection is ground in a basic avoidance of harmful substances or situations. It is the latter for which moral disgust operates. Consider for a moment that moral standards are culturally determined. Further, adherence to cultural standards procures greater protection from conspecifics through conformity and in-group identification, which in turn leads to greater survival (Vugt & Kameda, 2014). That is, by maintaining additional in-group conformity, the group is more likely to serve a protective function. Being a member of the group typically leads to the group shielding members from harm. Accordingly, conformity is a powerful behavioural motivator given the protection is provides.

Conforming to group norms, particularly for moral codes, allows for one to keep at bay the awareness of one's mortality. This is the basis of terror-management theory (TMT; Pyszczynski, Greenberg, & Solomon, 1999). There are two kinds of threats to mortality—proximal and distal. Proximal threats rapidly activate mortality fears through direct contact with dangerous stimuli. In this way, the primary disgust items (such as known contaminants) are proximal mortality threats and elicit fear reactions. On the other hand, distal mortality threats are more subtle. For example, agreeing to wear Hitler's sweater in the experiment described earlier is a violation of in-group standards, and puts one at risk of being shunned by the community. This in turn has survival implications. The development of moral disgust as a justification against participation in moral transgressions, in turn, provides protection from mortality ideas.

There is a growing body of research supporting TMT as an explanatory model for moral disgust. To illustrate, Cox, Goldenberg, Pyszczynski, & Weise (2007) conducted two experiments involving disgust eliciting stimuli. Study one included extremely disgusting stimuli (i.e., photos of faeces or people urinating), which in turn led to greater accessibility of death thoughts, based on completion of word fragments that could be completed to form either death- or neutral-themed words. In the second study, disgust stimuli were subtle (questionnaire items from a disgust scale). After priming with these more subtle stimuli, mortality cognitions were again more readily accessible to consciousness by virtue of a higher proportion of words completed to form death themes than neutral themes. This outcome is predicted by TMT, where exposure to stimuli that are not socially condoned (i.e., disgust-stimuli) increases mortality-salience. Accordingly, during periods where mortality-salience is increased, so too are concerns over death.

The research on how TMT and moral disgust play a role in psychological wellbeing has also recently been evaluated in the context of self-esteem. When esteem is lowered, TMT has suggested that it is due, in part, to a loss of the ability to keep at bay mortality thoughts. Alternatively, research on TMT shows that when external situations challenge one's belief in specific worldviews, self-esteem strivings increase, as does adherence to one's cultural, religious, and self-identified environmental milieu (Vail et al., 2012). The maintenance of self-esteem is considered, according to terror-management theorists, to be central to keep mortality thoughts inaccessible (Hayes, Schimel, Arndt, & Faucher, 2010). Next, we consider the possibility that, with the breakdown of this process, specific psychological conditions that are associated with interpersonal functioning are more likely.

## *Moral disgust, terror management, and psychological conditions*

Within a terror-management framework, self-disgust may be activated when one is faced with situations that provoke increased mortality-salience, but without the means for alleviation. Consider embarrassment as an example. In embarrassment, individuals are consumed by a feeling that their actions violated a social norm. When this occurs, since the individual committed the act, self-disgust would be activated. TMT would suggest that under such conditions there would likewise be an increase in mortality-salience. The aforementioned research suggests that esteem (a negative correlate of self-disgust; Simpson, Hillman, Crawford, & Overton, 2010) is associated with efforts to alleviate death-thought accessibility (DTA; Hayes et al., 2010). Given that self-esteem is also associated with mood (i.e., Roberts & Monroe, 1994), it would follow that as DTA increased so too would the risk for psychological disorders. The following are several interpersonally relevant psychological conditions or problems that may be marked by increased moral disgust (to the others and the self).

### *Post-traumatic stress*

One psychological condition marked by proximal mortality threats is the experience of post-traumatic reactions. Based on TMT, individuals with a trauma history should in turn have greater accessibility to mortality thoughts, lower self-esteem, and accordingly find a wider range of moral disgust elicitors in the general environment. This latter aspect is a result of the violations experienced, without warning, from the otherwise ordinary physical environment. When the entire environment, or most of it, poses a potential threat, there is increased mortality-salience. This could be an extension of the disgust experienced towards stimuli associated with predation (Prokop & Fan ovi ová, 2013). Research in our lab (i.e., Arocho, Brand, Weiner, & McKay, 2011) has shown that moral disgust is a significant predictor of trauma reactions, mediated by negative emotional experiences. However, this finding is complicated by additional research in our lab (Ojserkis, Arocho, & McKay, 2012) that showed that observing a traumatic event (i.e., witnessing a crime with a victim) was associated with a higher relationship between moral disgust and trauma experiences than actually being a trauma survivor. In a recent evaluation with sexual trauma survivors, disgust was experienced to a greater extent, as was the cognitive experience of dirtiness (referred to as mental contamination) and self-oriented disgust (Badour, Ojserkis, McKay, & Feldner, 2014; see Badour & Adams, this volume). Collectively, these studies suggest that disgust, specifically moral disgust, is an important contributor to post-traumatic reactions.

This promising line of research suggests that moral disgust is an important distal emotional experience that increases mortality-salience in trauma survivors. Further, TMT posits that the experience of moral disgust is a normative reaction that serves to prevent the accessibility of mortality cognitions. In trauma, this process breaks down, leading to potentially persistent moral disgust reactions that erode esteem, which is also adversely impacted by increased access to mortality thoughts (i.e., Hayes et al., 2010). Future experimental research is warranted to evaluate the degree that death-thought accessibility (DTA) is enhanced in individuals with post-traumatic reactions, and whether DTA is reduced with successful treatment.

### *Body dysmorphic disorder*

Body dysmorphic disorder (BDD) is now classified as a member of the obsessive-compulsive related disorders (OCRDs; DSM-5, APA, 2013). The condition is marked by excessive concern with one or a subset of body areas, where the sufferer believes the body area(s) are malformed or unattractive, and the sufferer also does not have an eating disorder or global body image disturbance. A major component of the disorder is a marked bodily obsession, including extensive mirror checking and ritualistic efforts to conceal the affected areas (McKay, Gosselin, & Gupta, 2008). Recent experimental research further suggests a role for disgust in BDD. Using a sample of thirty-one individuals with BDD and a group of matched controls, Hickey, Neziroglu, and McKay (2013) found that individuals with BDD exhibited greater avoidance of disgust-oriented stimuli. Further, individuals with BDD reported greater levels of disgust in general, and this was correlated with depression levels. Finally, Hickey, Neziroglu, and McKay (2010) showed that physiological indicators of (self-)disgust were elevated in individuals with BDD, compared to matched non-psychiatric controls.

Individuals with BDD also show preferential bias towards disgust-relevant body stimuli. In one recent study, there was a positive relationship between dysmorphic concerns and disgust, in a non-clinical sample (Onden-Lim, Wu, & Grisham, 2012). In another investigation, individuals with BDD showed no difference in perceptual processing of images of other individuals, but showed higher negative aesthetic appraisals of images of themselves (Lambrou, Veale, & Wilson, 2011).

What is less well known in BDD is the quantified level of self-directed disgust. Anecdotally, individuals with BDD report high levels of self-oriented disgust (reported in McKay et al., 2008). Given the role of self-esteem in TMT, when individuals suffer declines in self-esteem, it may be hypothesised that increases in DTA may be present. As with many psychological conditions, BDD is marked by low self-esteem, which in turn is moderated by depression (i.e., Biby, 1998; Phillips, Pinto, & Jain, 2004). At the present time, this association is non-specific in nature. Future investigations should evaluate specific factors of DTA that may give rise to reductions in self-esteem. For example, as severity of BDD symptoms increase, or for body areas that are the source of BDD symptoms and also more visible (i.e., the face) as DTA should also be higher.

### *Eating disorders*

Eating disorders, particularly bulimia and anorexia nervosa, represent a more general level model of self-oriented disgust (see also Fox, Grange, & Power, this volume), and more global psychological disturbance, compared to BDD. To illustrate, in a direct comparison between individuals with BDD and those with eating disorders, those with eating disorders showed lower self-esteem and higher depression, although both groups scored in the clinical elevated range (Rosen & Ramirez, 1998).

Interestingly, basic-level disgust stimuli seem to be less relevant in eating disorders compared to other disorders considered here. The research in this domain is still preliminary, and early findings suggest that other aversive emotional experiences are moderators of the relationship between eating disorders and disgust reactions. For example, Davey and Chapman (2009) found that the relation between eating-disorder symptoms and disgust was moderated by trait anxiety, and residual variance between eating-disorder symptoms and disgust was non-significant. A further study, comprised of a correlational and experimental investigation, showed that: (a) there were limited associations between eating-disorder symptoms and a measure of disgust; and (b) in an experimental task, women with elevated eating-disorder scores showed no difference in avoidance of disgust-related stimuli (Mayer, Muris, Bos, & Sujkerbuijk, 2008).

Of note in the research conducted thus far with people with eating disorders is the absence of moral disgust evaluations. This is a recent development, but warrants additional evaluation. In light of the aforementioned TMT considerations, moral disgust may be a potent variable in understanding and treating eating disorders. The literature is replete with instances showing that individuals with eating disorders hold very high moral standards, which in turn could also be associated with elevated moral disgust when others violate norms, or when they themselves face situations when their own moral standards are unwittingly violated. Theoretical and conceptual reviews have suggested as much, including an extreme and rigid interpretation of moral and cultural codes (Nemeroff & Cavanaugh, 1999). The state of the research at this juncture is limited to evaluations of basic-level disgust reactions and sensitivity, and has not yet considered higher-order disgust appraisals.

### *Future directions in evaluating moral disgust and interpersonal psychopathological states*

The available evidence suggests that moral disgust (to others and the self) may play a role in complex psychological conditions, particularly ones marked by interpersonal conflict. However, there is also evidence, albeit mixed, that suggests fundamental aspects of disgust also play a role in complex interpersonal psychological states. Nevertheless, the relationship is not linear, and there are other factors involved, notably aversive emotional states (such as trait anxiety or depression).

Given the recent surge of interest in disgust and its role in psychiatric conditions, it is also important to identify the limits of how this emotional state emerges in psychopathology. Indeed, it is the hallmark of any good model that the boundaries of its prediction be determined as well as the ways it describes and predicts conditions. This includes specifying mechanisms of action, identifying treatment relevance, and the potential to be falsifiable (see Taylor, McKay, & Abramowitz, 2004). At the moment, the way in which disgust contributes to psychopathology is not clearly delineated. Some models have been proposed, but have not yet been tested (Olatunji & McKay, 2009). Any putative model of disgust, including higher-order disgust experiences such as moral disgust, will necessarily require a theory to house these constructs. Terror management holds promise, and additional empirical investigations will reveal the adequacy and limitations of this model in depicting clinical states. Of particular promise is the role of TMT in understanding self-referent disgust. In this chapter, we reviewed several potential ways in which self-disgust, as determined by moral disgust and TMT, could lead to exacerbated adverse psychological reactions. An expanded understanding of this model, clarifying self-disgust as a function of mortality-salience, requires increased empirical research, focusing on the enduring traits and responsiveness to treatment.

CHAPTER SEVEN

# Contaminated by trauma: understanding links between self-disgust, mental contamination, and post-traumatic stress disorder

*Christal L. Badour and Thomas G. Adams*

A traumatic event is defined as an experience in which an individual directly encounters, witnesses, or is presented with details regarding a situation involving actual or threatened death, serious injury/harm, or sexual violation (American Psychiatric Association, 2013). Frequently studied traumatic events include exposure to interpersonal victimisation (e.g., rape, childhood sexual abuse, physical assault); combat; natural or manmade disasters; accidents or serious illnesses/injuries. Evidence suggests traumatic event exposure is relatively ubiquitous, with the majority of adults encountering at least one traumatic event during their lifetime (Kessler Sonnega, Bromet, Hughes, & Nelson, 1995; Norris, 1992; Resnick, Kilpatrick, Dansky, Saunders, & Best, 1993). Immediately following a trauma, nearly all individuals exhibit a characteristic pattern of symptoms that includes intrusive recollections of the event, heightened emotional or physiological arousal, and attempts to avoid reminders of the event (Blanchard & Hickling, 2004; Riggs, Rothbaum, & Foa 1995; Rothbaum, Foa, Riggs, & Murdock, 1992). While these symptoms generally remit within approximately three months for the majority of traumatised individuals (APA, 2013), a substantial minority continues to experience these reactions well beyond the occurrence of the traumatic event and report distress and impairment as a result (e.g., Kessler et al., 2005; Pietrzak, Goldstein, Southwick, & Grant, 2011). This pattern of symptom non-remittance is characteristic of post-traumatic stress disorder (PTSD), a condition conceptualised as failing to recover from the effects of a traumatic event (Foa & Rothbaum, 1998; Gilboa-Schechtman & Foa, 2001; Yehuda & Ledoux, 2007).

Research on affective responding within the context of traumatic events and PTSD has historically emphasised the emotions of fear and anxiety. Indeed, leading theoretical models, which have long driven research in the area of PTSD intervention, focus on fear conditioning and extinction (Foa & Kozak, 1986; Keane, Zimering, & Caddell, 1985) as well as threat-based appraisals (Ehlers & Clark, 2000). Researchers have consistently called for the expansion of this relatively narrow focus to incorporate decades of research outlining the importance of a range of negative emotions into conceptual models of PTSD (Bovin & Marx, 2011; Brewin, Andrews, & Rose, 2000; Dalgleish & Power, 2004; Davidson et al., 1996; Resick & Miller, 2009; Resick & Schnicke, 1992). Indeed, with the release of the recently revised Diagnostic and Statistical Manual of Mental Disorders (DSM-5; APA, 2013), PTSD has been moved from the anxiety disorders to a category entitled "Trauma- and Stressor-Related Disorders", to better reflect the broad array of symptoms associated with maladaptive responding to traumatic events, including the persistence of several negative emotions other than fear and anxiety. For the purposes of this discussion, we will turn our attention to the emotion of disgust.

## *Disgust*

Disgust is a negatively valenced emotion that facilitates a rejection or revulsion response aimed at distancing an organism from a potential contaminant in order to prevent disease (Davey, 1994b; Olatunji & Sawchuk, 2005; Rozin, Haidt, & McCauley, 2000). Disgust has been conceptualised as a basic emotion with characteristics that uniquely distinguish it from other negative emotions such as anger and fear (Ekman, 1992; Izard, 2007; Olatunji & Sawchuk, 2005). At its most basic level, disgust—meaning literally "bad taste"—functions through gustatory reactions, such as nausea and vomiting, to prevent the ingestion of harmful substances (Rozin et al., 2000; Woody & Teachman, 2000).

While disgust emerged as a protective mechanism related to food-rejection, it has since evolved to shield organisms from other types of stimuli. The predominant model offered by Rozin and colleagues (2000) suggests that these stimuli fall into four distinct domains: core, animal-nature, interpersonal, and moral disgust (Olatunji & Sawchuk, 2005; Rozin et al., 2000). Core disgust elicitors must be broadly conceptualised as orally ingestible, offensive in nature, and capable of contamination. These stimuli may include potentially harmful or offensive foods, biological waste products, and certain animals. Animal-nature disgust elicitors include stimuli that serve as reminders of our mortality and blur the line that differentiates us as humans from other animals. These can include unconventional or inappropriate sexual acts, body-envelope violations (e.g., gory injuries), poor hygiene, and material related to death or decay (Haidt, Rozin, McCauley, & Imada, 1997; Olatunji & Sawchuck, 2005; Rozin et al., 2000). Interpersonal disgust reactions are thought to function as means of separating an individual from contamination that might result from the "strangeness, disease, misfortune, and moral taint" of other humans (Rozin et al., 2000; Rozin, Markwith, & McCauley, 1994). This type of disgust involves a concern regarding the potential transmission of undesirable or polluting features of others, rather than distress associated with specific physical contaminants. Interpersonal disgust can be elicited through close proximity to an undesirable individual or object (e.g., wearing the sweater of a murderer; Olatunji & Sawchuck, 2005; Rozin et al., 2000) or even indirect exposure to moral transgressions (Eskine, Novreske, & Richards, 2013). Finally, the category of moral, or sociomoral, disgust, as it is often termed, is defined as a reaction to violations of culturally influenced and subjective beliefs about morality. Examples of common moral/sociomoral disgust concerns include rape, genocide, hypocrisy, racism, and exploitation (Rozin et al., 2000; Simpson, Carter, Anthony, & Overton, 2006). It has been suggested that other emotions such as anger and contempt may be involved in emotional responses to sociomoral disgust-related material (Olatunji, Forsyth, & Cherian, 2007).

Another emerging model proposed by Tybur, Lieberman, & Griskevicius (2009) is couched within an evolutionary framework. Tybur and colleagues have proposed three distinct evolutionarily adaptive domains of disgust sensitivity, including: 1) pathogen disgust (e.g., aversions towards pathogens and contaminants that increase chance of illness); 2) sexual disgust (e.g., aversions towards sexual acts that increase illness probability and/or fail to increase progeny); and 3) moral disgust (e.g., aversions towards moral transgressions that decrease cultural vitality). Conceptually, Tybur and colleagues' pathogen disgust is highly similar to Rozin et al.'s (2000) core disgust. As would be expected, there is also little difference between Tybur and colleagues' moral disgust and the moral disgust outlined prior to (Haidt, McCauley, & Rozin, 1994; Moll et al., 2005; Schnall, Haidt, Clore, & Jordan, 2008; Wheatley & Haidt, 2005) and after (David & Olatunji, 2011) their model. While Rozin and colleagues did not identify sexual disgust as a unique factor in their 2000 paper, Haidt and colleagues (1994) did show that sex and sexuality can serve as major elicitors of disgust reactions (see also de Jong & Borg, this volume).

### *Disgust as a response to trauma*

In one of the earliest observations of trauma-related disgust, Rivers (1920) described the case of a World War One officer who experienced intense and persistent re-experiencing symptoms, including intrusive images and thoughts of vomiting as well as avoidance of eating, after an explosion forced his face into the decomposing corpse of a German soldier. As detailed in this case example, the persistence of disgust following traumatic events may result in nausea or vomiting in response to intrusive images or memories of the experience. Individuals may avoid certain behaviours that serve as reminders of disgust experienced during the event (e.g., eating, sexual contact). They may also resort to the use of explicit behaviours (e.g., compulsive washing or cleaning; Fairbrother & Rachman, 2004) or internal strategies (e.g., distraction, thought suppression; Espeset, Guilliksen, Nordbo, Skarderud, & Holte, 2012; Rachman, 1994) to reduce feelings of disgust and/or contamination resulting from the event. There is some evidence to suggest that these behaviours may generalise over time; for example, individuals may begin to scan themselves, others, and their environment for signs of potential contaminants that are unrelated to the original traumatic experience (Fostick, Nacasch, & Zohar, 2012).

Theoretical models suggest traumatic event-related disgust likely emerges in two ways (Badour, Feldner, Blumenthal, & Knapp, 2013; Dalgleish & Power, 2004; Steil, Jung, & Stangier, 2011). First, contact with some traumatic stimuli such as certain smells, death, decay, or bodily products (e.g., blood, vomit, semen) may evoke strong peritraumatic (i.e., during the trauma) disgust reactions. This experience may result in the conditioning of disgust responses in a manner consistent with established models of fear and anxiety in PTSD (e.g., Foa & Kozak, 1986; Keane et al., 1985). Traumatic event-related disgust may also arise via a more cognitively mediated pathway. Specifically, post-traumatic appraisals regarding the meaning or consequences of the traumatic event (e.g., I have been contaminated/ruined), the individual's response to the event (e.g., experiencing sexual arousal during a rape, experiencing excitement when killing during combat), or the perceived immorality of one's own behaviour (e.g., I violated my own moral code) or the behaviour of others (e.g., someone betrayed/violated my trust; Rachman, 2010) may also elicit feelings of disgust. Both forms of disgust may persist well beyond the traumatic experience in response to either cued or spontaneous re-experiencing of the traumatic memory.

### *Self-disgust*

Self-disgust has been defined elsewhere in this volume as an internalised form of disgust in which the self, or aspects of the self (e.g., certain physical characteristics, personality traits, behaviours) serve as an object of disgust (see Powell, Simpson, & Overton, this volume). The same patterns of behavioural, cognitive, and physiological responses underlying disgust elicited in response to external stimuli (Cisler, Olatunji, & Lohr, 2009) are thought to characterise self-disgust responses. While transient feelings of self-disgust are likely adaptive in many instances (e.g., motivating improved personal hygiene or modification of behaviour to fit societal norms), persistent feelings of self-disgust may be conceptualised as maladaptive and potentially harmful (e.g., Espeset et al., 2012; Griffiths & Page, 2008; Lambrou, Veale, & Wilson, 2011; Neziroglu, Hickey, & McKay, 2010; Overton, Markland, Taggart, Bagshaw, & Simpson, 2008; Powell, Simpson, & Overton, 2013; Simpson, Hillman, Crawford, & Overton, 2010).

It is not difficult to imagine that self-disgust may be involved in the response to a variety of traumatic experiences. For example, the killing of another human being in war may result in feelings of self-disgust for a man who perceives this behaviour to be a violation of his own moral code or that of society. Over time, he may further come to adopt the belief that his ability to engage in such morally reprehensible behaviour is reflective of a deeper character flaw that renders not only his behaviour, but also his person, revolting. Similarly, while a rape victim may experience disgust in response to external stimuli, such as contact with bodily fluids or perceptions regarding violation or immorality associated with the perpetrator or perpetrator's behaviour, she may also experience self-focused disgust during and after the experience. For example, she may feel disgusted by her body's sexual arousal response during the rape (Levin & van Berlo, 2004), or may feel that she has been contaminated, morally tainted, or rendered unclean by the experience (Badour, Feldner, Babson, Blumenthal, & Dutton, 2013; Fairbrother & Rachman, 2004; Olatunji, Elwood, Williams & Lohr, 2008). These types of self-focused post-traumatic cognitive appraisals have been shown to predict both the development and maintenance of PTSD (Dunmore, Clark, & Ehlers, 2001; Foa & Rauch, 2004; O'Donnell, Elliott, Wolfgang, & Creamer, 2007).

### *Empirical evidence regarding the role of disgust in post-traumatic stress disorder*

Consistent with theory, researchers have documented disgust (including self-disgust; Badour, Bown, Adams, Bunaciu, & Feldner, 2012; Petrak, Doyle, Williams, Buchan, & Forster, 1997), in response to a range of traumatic events such as combat (Engelhard, Olatunji, & de Jong, 2011; Foy, Sipprelle, Rueger, & Carrol, 1984), interpersonal trauma (e.g., rape, assaultive violence, childhood sexual/physical abuse; Badour et al., 2011, 2012; Badour, Feldner, Babson et al., 2013; Badour, Feldner, Blumenthal et al., 2013; Feldner, Frala, Badour, Leen-Feldner, & Olatunjui, 2010), natural disasters (Fredman et al., 2010; McMillen, North, & Smith, 2000), and industrial accidents (Grunert et al., 1992; Grunert, Smucker, Weis, & Rusch, 2003). Growing evidence further supports a link between disgust and PTSD. For example, disgust vulnerabilities, including disgust propensity (i.e., the ease/frequency with which disgust is experienced) and disgust sensitivity (i.e., the degree to which the experience of disgust is perceived as negative or potentially harmful; van Overveld, de Jong, Peters, Cavanagh, & Davey, 2006; Olatunji & Cisler, 2009), are associated with increased post-traumatic stress symptoms following exposure to a range of traumatic events (Badour et al., 2012; Badour, Feldner, Blumenthal, & Bujarski, 2013; Engelhard et al., 2011; Rüsch et al., 2011; Olatunji, Armstrong, Fan, & Zhao, 2014). Elevated PTSD symptoms are also noted among individuals reporting greater intensity of peritraumatic disgust (Badour et al., 2012, Badour, Feldner, Blumenthal et al., 2013; Engelhard et al., 2011) and persons demonstrating increased disgust in response to reminders of traumatic events (Badour, Feldner, Babson et al., 2013; Badour, Feldner, Blumenthal et al., 2013; Olatunji, Babson, Smith, Feldner, & Connolly, 2009; Shin et al., 1999). Finally, persistent feelings of disgust serve to distinguish between individuals with and without PTSD (Finucane, Dima, Ferreira, & Halvorsen, 2012; Foy et al., 1984), and as many as ten percent of patients with PTSD report disgust as their primary experienced emotion (Power & Fyvie, 2013). Much of this research suggests that associations between disgust and PTSD symptomatology are significant even after accounting for the emotions of fear and anxiety.

Although the frequency of guilt and shame in PTSD (Andrews, Brewin, Rose, & Kirk, 2000; Feiring, Taska, & Lewis, 1996, 1998; Lee, Scragg, & Turner, 2001; Leskela, Dieperink & Thuras, 2002; Stone, 1992; Wong & Cook, 1992) has been cited as evidencing that self-disgust is likely involved (Dalgleish & Power, 2004), empirical research directly examining the role of self-disgust in PTSD is surprisingly underdeveloped and includes only two studies. First, Rüsch and colleagues (2011) employed the Implicit Association Test (IAT) to assess the automaticity (i.e., below conscious awareness) of associations between the self and the emotions of either disgust or anxiety among women with PTSD resulting from childhood sexual abuse. As compared to healthy women, those with PTSD evidenced stronger associations between the self and disgust relative to associations between the self and anxiety, while the opposite pattern emerged among controls. These results suggest that disgust may be more central to the self-concept among individuals with PTSD as compared to healthy individuals. Although severity of childhood sexual abuse was not found to relate to the scores on the IAT among individuals with PTSD, trauma history was unavailable for the healthy control group. As such, it is unclear whether these findings may be related to differential exposure to trauma between the two groups.

In the second study, Badour and colleagues (2012) examined how intensity of fear, self-focused disgust, and perpetrator-focused disgust experienced during a traumatic event, involving either sexual or physical victimisation, were related to both post-traumatic stress symptoms and contamination-based obsessive-compulsive (OC) symptoms among a sample of adult women. After accounting for overlap between these two symptom domains, which have each been independently linked to both disgust and anxiety, intensity of peritraumatic fear and perpetrator-focused disgust were associated with PTSD symptom severity, while self-focused disgust predicted increased contamination-based OC symptoms. These findings underscore the importance of examining the intersection between disgust and contamination concerns among individuals with PTSD as well as those exposed to traumatic events generally. Indeed, a number of case studies of individuals with PTSD have documented clinically significant contamination obsessions and washing compulsions resulting from memories of sexual abuse or assault, combat, witnessing the violent death of others, contact with dead bodies, and exposure to toxic chemicals (Fostick et al., 2012; Gershuny, Baer, Radomsky, Wilson, & Jenike, 2003; Jung & Steil, 2012, 2013; Sasson et al., 2005; Steil et al., 2011). We will now focus on outlining this issue in more detail.

## *Contamination fear and aversion*

The phenomenon of perceived contamination has been defined as "an intense and persisting feeling of having been polluted, dirtied, or infected, or endangered as a result of contact, direct or indirect, with an item/place/person perceived to be soiled, impure, dirty, infections, or harmful" (Rachman, 2006, p. 9). Contamination has been a topic of empirical inquiry for decades, due largely to the role of contamination obsessions and washing compulsions commonly observed and reported in obsessive-compulsive disorder (OCD). Early research suggested that, like other anxiety disorders, contamination-based OC symptoms were largely motived by fear and anxiety (Hodgson & Rachman, 1972; Hornsveld, Kraaimaat, & Van Dam-Baggen, 1979). As such, contamination-based obsessions, compulsions, and avoidance were referred to as contamination fears or contamination phobias. Recent research, however, suggests that in many instances, contamination-based obsessions, compulsions, and avoidance behaviours are motivated by disgust (Adams, Cisler, Brady, & Lohr, 2012; Adams, Cisler, Brady, Lohr, & Olatunji, 2013; Adams, Willems, & Bridges, 2011; Cisler et al., 2011; Olatunji & Broman-Fulks, 2009; Olatunji & McKay, 2007; Olatunji & Sawchuk, 2005).

The term *rejection* is a behavioural response associated with the emotion of disgust that is a unique relative to *escape* (i.e., fear) and *avoidance* (i.e., anxiety). Rejection involves distancing, removing, or repelling a stimulus in order to decrease the proximity between the stimulus and the self (e.g., spitting out rotten food). Escape and avoidance are also behaviours aimed at minimising contact with a potentially harmful stimulus. Escape involves removing the self from the proximity of an existing stimulus (e.g., jumping out of the way of an oncoming car), while avoidance functions to prevent contact between the self and the stimulus entirely (e.g., walking on the pavement instead of in the road). Within the context of contamination, washing behaviour—from normal to abnormal (compulsive) washing—may involve all three of these behavioural response systems. At the most basic level, washing is intended to remove contaminants from the skin (i.e., rejection). This rejection is functionally akin to the spitting out of food that is usually seen in gustatory aversions (Parker, Limebeer, & Rana, 2009). Washing is also done to escape unwanted negative emotions (e.g., disgust, anxiety, "feeling dirty"). Washing behaviour is also functionally related to avoidance as this behaviour is often carried out to mitigate future-oriented risk (e.g., washing to prevent transmission of disease). Avoidance (lack of approach) of stimuli and contexts that would otherwise provoke washing behaviours is also observed.

In reality, avoidance, rejection, and escape from contaminants are likely motivated by a combination of disgust, fear, and anxiety. Moreover, contamination fears and aversions are not restricted to contamination-based OCD. For example, research has shown that avoidance of contact contamination (e.g., touching a toilet seat) among non-selected participants is common and motivated by a mixture of anxiety and disgust (Adams & Lohr, 2012; Rozin, Haidt, McCauley, Dunlop, & Ashmore, 1999), although at least one study has shown that disgust was the primary mediator of avoidance (Adams & Lohr, 2012). To date, we are unaware of any research testing specific affective mediators (e.g., disgust, fear, or anxiety) of washing behaviours. It is likely that the power and covariance of these three affective systems depends on stimulus characteristics, context, and the individual's learning history.

### *Laws of sympathetic magic*

In describing bizarre but widespread cultural beliefs, Sir James George Frazer outlined the laws of sympathetic magic almost a century ago (1922). His focus had less to do with the types of contamination fears and aversions that are the focus of this chapter, but the principles outlined by Frazer, nonetheless, are germane to the topics covered herein. Frazer identified two lower-order sympathetic magical beliefs: 1) the law of similarity; and 2) the law of contact. Simply put, the laws of similarity and contact were defined as the beliefs that "like equals like" and "once in contact always in contact", respectively. The voodoo doll and the beliefs it carries—that sticking needles into it can cause harm to a target individual—serves as a useful example of the law of similarity. In his text, Frazer made reference to the example of homeopathic magic—he used the terms "homeopathic magic", "contagious magic", and "law of contact" interchangeably—that "a person can influence vegetation either for good or evil according to the good or bad character of his acts or states: for example, a fruitful woman makes plants fruitful, a barren woman makes them barren" (Frazer, 1922, p. 29).

Informed by Frazer's descriptions of magical cultural beliefs, Rozin and Fallon (1987) used the laws of sympathetic magic to describe beliefs about disgust and the spread of contaminants. They retained the label and definition of the law of similarity but changed the law of contact to the law of contagion. For all intents and purposes, however, Rozin and Fallon's definitions were nearly identical to Frazer's, but simply applied to describe phenomena associated with contamination fears and aversions.

### *Law of similarity*

Rozin, Millman, and Nemeroff (1986) developed several laboratory-based behavioural approach tasks (BAT) to assess the effects of the laws of sympathetic magic on behaviour and their relations with disgust. To test the law of similarity, Rozin and colleagues presented participants with a piece of faeces-shaped fudge and measured how close participants would come to said fudge or if they were willing to eat it. Very few participants were willing to place the fudge in their mouths, despite knowledge regarding the innocuous nature of the treat. Not surprisingly, this avoidance was strongly predicted by both contamination and disgust sensitivity (Rozin et al., 1986). This serves as a convincing example of the power and pervasiveness of the law of similarity within the context of contamination fears and aversions.

As compared Rozin and Fallon's second law, there has been considerably less work linking the law of similarity to specific pathological contamination concerns. However, one can extrapolate from learning models in PTSD (Foa & Kozak, 1986; Keane et al., 1985) to see the potential role of the law of similarity in the context of responses to traumatic events. Traumatic experiences frequently result in problematic associative learning, whereby stimuli and contexts that seemingly share little in common with the features of a traumatic event become capable of evoking pathological affective and behavioural responses. For example, following a sexual assault, an individual may evidence fear and disgust in response to bald men due to the fact that her assailant was bald. The post-traumatic appraisal that all bald men (or even all men) are dangerous or repulsive (and perhaps the concomitant affective responses) may serve as examples of "like equals like". Sexual assault may also result in learned associations between the self and the traumatic event that lead to changes in the self-concept. Specifically, links between the self and the disgusting act may result in the perception that the self or the body has taken on the disgusting properties of the experience (i.e., self-disgust).

### *Law of contagion*

Rachman (2004) aptly described the law of contagion as the belief regarding the ability of a contaminated object to permanently overwhelm and negate the properties of a clean object. He provided the descriptive example of how a teaspoon of contaminated liquid could render an entire barrel of clean water contaminated, but yet a teaspoon of clean water would have no ability to cleanse a barrel of contaminated water. Indeed, Rozin, Haidt, McCauley, Dunlop, and colleagues (1999) demonstrated experimentally that participants were unwilling to drink from a barrel of water that had one drop of urine, and were significantly less willing to drink apple juice that had been stirred with a comb that had never been used (Rozin, Haidt, McCauley, Dunlop et al., 1999). Similarly, participants were shown to avoid articles of clothing previously worn by disliked (Rozin et al., 1986) or chronically ill (Rozin, Markwith, & Nemeroff, 1992) persons, despite knowledge that the clothing had been recently washed. Importantly, the research of Rozin and his colleagues revealed disgust sensitivity and/or state disgust as strong predictors of avoidance of the aforementioned contaminants. Recent research has extended the applicability of the law of contagion to the moral and interpersonal domains. Eskine and colleagues (2013) showed that both direct and indirect contact with morally questionable individuals and acts led to increased feelings of contagion and, in the former example, increased feelings of guilt.

The majority of research regarding how the law of contagion applies to clinical populations relates to cognitive-behavioural models of OCD. To our knowledge, Tolin, Worhunsky, and Maltby (2004) were the first to explicitly examine the law of contagion in a clinical population. Using what they labelled the *chain of contagion task*, these authors compared beliefs regarding the indefinite spread of contagion among individuals with OCD to those of anxious and non-anxious controls. This was accomplished by first asking each participant to identify what they perceived as the most contaminated object in the hospital. The experimenter then took a new pencil and rubbed it on this object. A second new pencil was then rubbed on the first, a third on the second, and so forth for twelve pencils, while participants provided contamination appraisals at each step. In keeping with predictions, Tolin and colleagues showed that OCD patients with contamination/washing symptoms reported very little change across the twelve pencils, while anxious and non-anxious controls showed drastic decreases, rating pencils four to twelve as being minimally contaminated on average. Results of this, and other studies using this task (Adams et al., 2012; Cisler et al., 2011), suggest that beliefs and appraisals related to the law of contagion can be so strong in some cases, that the source stimulus is thought to fully transfer its contagious properties to a novel object despite minimal (or zero) contact, many degrees of removal, or long lapses in time.

More recently, the second author's laboratory has utilised the chain of contagion task to experimentally analyse the basic psychological mechanisms underlying the law of contagion. A clear pattern of findings has emerged to suggest cognitive and affective mechanisms may differentially mediate contamination aversion. In our first study, we showed that disgust propensity, but not trait anxiety, robustly predicted proximal contamination appraisals (e.g., pencils one to three) but had little to do with distal contamination appraisals (e.g., pencils four to twelve; Cisler et al., 2011). This same study found that distal contamination appraisals were predicted by a specific form of attention; namely, strategic (not automatic) disengagement (not orientation) of attention from disgusting (not fearful) information. A recent follow-up study provided tepid support for the effects of disgust on proximal contamination appraisals, but showed that experimentally primed threat/harm appraisals causally affected distal contamination appraisals (Adams et al., 2012; see also Riskind, 1997, and his work on the looming vulnerability cognitive style). Taken together, these results offer evidence that affective factors (i.e., state disgust, disgust propensity, disgust sensitivity) serve as robust predictors of direct contamination appraisals, while cognitive factors (e.g., appraisals, attention, beliefs) appear to increase their predictive ability in relation to contamination appraisals as the contaminated object becomes further removed from the source contaminant (i.e., indirect contamination).

Motivated by the findings outlined in the previous paragraph, we sought to develop a pen-and-paper measure of contamination aversion, the Contamination Aversion Scale (CAS; Adams et al., 2013), to test if: 1) aversions fell along a direct/indirect continuum; and 2) if cognitive and affective factors differentially predicted types of aversions. Factor analyses with multiple samples revealed a two-factor solution that was clearly split by distance of time and space of the appraised contaminant to a source contaminant. We labelled the first factor "direct contamination aversion" (e.g., "touching someone else's saliva"), although it could have just as easily been labelled proximal, contact, or normative contamination aversion. We labelled the second factor "indirect contamination aversion" (e.g., "touching an object that has been touched by strangers"). Similarly, this factor could have just as easily been labelled distal or non-normative contamination aversion. As would be predicted by our previous research, disgust propensity and disgust sensitivity were associated with direct contamination-aversion factor scores, while cognitive factors such as obsessive beliefs and emotion-regulation difficulties were linked to indirect contamination-aversion factor scores.

Consistent with the findings of Tolin and colleagues (2004) in OCD, we would expect this newly identified form of indirect contamination aversion to be particularly strong among clinical populations where contamination fears and aversions are common. As a first test of this hypothesis, we recently administered the CAS to a community-recruited sample of fifty adult women with a history of traumatic interpersonal victimisation (i.e., sexual, physical), and regressed both CAS factor scores simultaneously onto an interview-based measure of PTSD symptom severity (Adams, Badour, Cisler, & Feldner, 2014). We found indirect contamination aversion ($\beta = .47$, $t = 2.57$, $p = .01$, $R^{2\Delta} = .12$), but not direct contamination aversion ($\beta = -.09$, $t = -.51$, $p = .61$, $R^{2\Delta} = .01$), to be a robust predictor of PTSD symptom severity. We further examined links in this study between direct/indirect contamination aversion and *mental contamination*, a form of contamination that is being increasingly linked to traumatic events and PTSD (Badour, Feldner, & Babson, 2013; Fairbrother & Rachman, 2004; Olatunji, Elwood et al., 2008). We found indirect contamination to be a strong predictor of scores on our measure of mental contamination (Rachman, 2005; $\beta = .62$, $t = 4.06$, $p < .01$, $R^{2\Delta} = .001$), while direct contamination was not significantly related ($\beta = .04$, $t = .23$, $p = .82$, $R^{2\Delta} = .21$). It is likely that the unique properties associated with the law of contagion apply to both indirect contamination aversion and the related construct of mental contamination. As we review the literature on mental contamination within the context of traumatic events and PTSD, we believe that conceptual and functional similarities between indirect contamination aversion and mental contamination will become clear.

## *Mental contamination*

In observing a number of patients with contamination-based OCD who reported an inability to feel clean despite repeated and intense washing rituals, Stanley Rachman (1994, 2004, 2006) coined the term "mental pollution" to describe a subtype of perceived contamination characterised by an internal sensation of dirtiness that is capable of emerging, and persisting, in the absence of contact with an actual physical contaminant. Although mental pollution was articulated by Rachman (2006) to be a type of mental contamination (cf., contact contamination), these two terms have been used interchangeably in the empirical literature. As such, we will refer to the broader term "mental contamination" throughout this chapter. According to Rachman's theory, direct or indirect contact with a perceived contaminant of human origin (e.g., persons perceived to be immoral, impure, harmful, or contaminated) may be involved in the initial development of mental contamination concerns. However, evidence supports the author's assertion that this type of contamination can also be either initiated (Elliott & Radomsky, 2009; Fairbrother, Newth, & Rachman, 2005; Herba & Rachman, 2007; Radomsky & Elliott, 2009) or re-evoked (Badour, Feldner, Babson et al., 2013; Fairbrother & Rachman, 2004) by mental images, memories, or immoral/repugnant thoughts, as well as specific associations or interactions with others (e.g., accusations, insults, criticisms, betrayals; Coughtrey, Shafran, Lee, & Rachman, 2012; Rachman, 2010).

Sensations of internal dirtiness associated with mental contamination are typically portrayed as being diffuse and difficult to locate, with some individuals describing feeling contaminated "inside their bodies" or feeling dirty "under their skin" (Coughtrey et al., 2012). Mental contamination typically involves elements or judgements regarding morality/immorality (Coughtrey et al., 2012; Elliott & Radomsky, 2009) and persists despite washing or cleansing rituals (Coughtrey et al., 2012; Fairbrother & Rachman, 2004). Moreover, unlike traditional contamination, elicitors are typically unique to the individual (e.g., memories, repugnant thoughts), and contaminating properties are believed to be contained within the self, and thus not easily transmitted to others. Finally, while the emotion of disgust is hypothesised to be central to the experience of mental contamination, Rachman (2004, 2006) theorised that a number of other emotions including fear/anxiety, anger, shame, and guilt are likely to be involved as well.

### *Mental contamination following trauma*

Research on the emergence of mental contamination following trauma has been constrained almost exclusively to the study of responses to sexual victimisation. Rachman (2004, 2006) argued that sexual victimisation is particularly likely to result in mental contamination, and basic research consistently links sexuality and sexual behaviour to appraisals of morality/immorality, disgust (including self-disgust), and contamination (see de Jong & Borg, this volume; de Jong, Peters, Olatunji, & McKay, 2009; Inbar & Pizarro, 2014; for reviews). Sexual victimisation has indeed been associated with increased mental contamination relative to other traumatic events (Badour, Feldner, Babson et al., 2013).

In an effort to validate the theoretical tenants outlined by Rachman (1994, 2004, 2006), Fairbrother and Rachman (2004) conducted the first empirical investigation of mental contamination following sexual trauma in a sample of fifty adult women. These authors found that seventy per cent of participants reported urges to wash following their assault, with twenty-five per cent of these women continuing to experience urges for several months to more than a year after the experience. Taking longer, hotter, showers or engaging in increased scrubbing while in the shower were the most commonly endorsed washing behaviours. Seventy-seven per cent of women reported that internal feelings of dirtiness led to their washing urges. The majority of participants (sixty-six per cent) described these feelings as emotional in nature (as opposed to physical), and capable of being evoked by memories, information, or images (sixty per cent). Many participants reported that feelings of dirtiness were not fully ameliorated by washing or cleansing (forty-nine per cent), persisted in the absence of contact with any physical contaminant (thirty-seven per cent), and involved a moral element (twenty per cent). These authors found that generating a memory or image of the worst part of the assault resulted in significantly greater feelings of anxiety, distress, dirtiness, and urges to wash as compared to when generating a pleasant memory or image. Furthermore, eighteen per cent of participants reported washing their hands in response to the memory of the assault. The persistence of washing behaviours despite a significant lapse in time since contact with the original contaminant (i.e., the perpetrator of the assault) in this study could be interpreted as evidence for the law of contagion (once in contact always in contact), akin to the indirect contamination aversion discussed earlier.

In a related study, Herba and Rachman (2007) utilised what has been termed the "dirty kiss paradigm" (Rachman, Radomsky, Elliott, & Zysk, 2012), to examine differences in elicited mental contamination as a function of past unwanted sexual contact (defined by any non-consensual sexual activity ranging from undesired touching/kissing/fondling to forced intercourse). Female undergraduates in this study were presented with standardised imagery involving either a consensual or non-consensual kiss at a party. Significantly greater feelings of dirtiness and urges to wash were reported in the non-consensual condition regardless of sexual history, and twenty-seven per cent of those in the non-consensual condition reported drinking water to reduce physical sensations in their mouth or washing to reduce feelings of dirtiness. In addition, this behaviour occurred more frequently among participants with a prior history of unwanted sexual contact. There were no participants in the consensual kiss group who engaged in washing or cleansing behaviours following the imagery.

Subsequent research has bolstered support for these findings, suggesting that mental contamination is likely a frequent, and highly understudied, correlate of sexual trauma. Indeed, mental contamination concerns have been observed following instances of both childhood sexual abuse as well as sexual assault occurring during adulthood (Badour, Feldner, Babson et al., 2013; Badour, Feldner, Blumenthal, & Bujarski, 2013; Berman, Wheaton, Fabricant, & Abramowitz, 2012; Jung & Steil, 2012, 2013; Olatunji, Elwood et al., 2008; Steil et al., 2011).

*Mental contamination and post-traumatic stress disorder*

Preliminary evidence suggests that mental contamination may be involved in the development and/or maintenance of PTSD subsequent to sexual trauma. Several studies document positive correlations between questionnaire-based measures of mental contamination and both questionnaire- and interview-based measures of PTSD symptomatology, even after accounting for relevant factors such as disgust sensitivity (i.e., the degree to which the experience of disgust is perceived as negative or potentially harmful; van Overveld, de Jong, Peters, Cavanagh et al., 2006), and symptoms of anxiety and depression (Badour, Feldner, Blumenthal, & Bujarski, 2013; Fairbrother & Rachman, 2004; Olatunji, Elwood et al., 2008). Badour, Feldner, Babson, and colleagues (2013) expanded upon these descriptive studies by demonstrating that in response to individualised imagery of a past sexual trauma, PTSD symptom severity was associated with greater increases in feelings of dirtiness, urges to wash, disgust, and anxiety. While PTSD symptoms also predicted greater increases in disgust and anxiety in response to individualised trauma imagery among a group of women with a history physical trauma, PTSD symptoms were not associated with increased feelings of dirtiness or urges to wash in this group, highlighting the apparent specificity of mental contamination to PTSD resulting from sexual trauma.

*Identifying mechanisms of mental contamination*

Despite the growing link between PTSD symptomatology and mental contamination, very little research, to date, has explored specific mechanisms underlying this association. That being said, theoretical models suggest self-disgust is likely an important predictor of perceived contamination in PTSD resulting from childhood sexual abuse (Jung & Steil, 2012; Steil et al., 2011). Specifically, Steil and colleagues argue that self-disgust and additional self-focused emotions (e.g., shame, self-contempt) emerge via negative post-traumatic self-appraisals related to the traumatic experience, as well as via conditioned associations between trauma-related feelings of disgust and the individual's own body (Jung & Steil, 2012; Steil et al., 2011). Consistent with this model, Olatunji, Elwood, and colleagues (2008) found that negative post-traumatic cognitive appraisals mediated the association between mental contamination and PTSD symptomatology among a sample of undergraduate students with a history of sexual assault. Post-traumatic cognitions in this study were comprised of negative cognitions about the self and the world, as well as self-blame. Confident conclusions regarding self-focused appraisals in this study are precluded by the fact that these authors did not specifically distinguish between the different types of appraisals in their analysis. Another study found that increased mental contamination (associated with sexual victimisation) mediated the association between disgust sensitivity and PTSD symptomatology (Badour, Feldner, Blumenthal, & Bujarski, 2013). These results were interpreted as preliminary evidence that individuals high in disgust sensitivity may be more likely to interpret feelings of disgust associated with sexual trauma to mean that they have been fundamentally contaminated or permanently sullied by the experience (i.e., law of contagion). The law of similarity likely also informs this model, such that disgust sensitivity increases the likelihood that an individual will internalise or incorporate the disgusting properties of the trauma into their self-schema, possibly resulting in subsequent appraisals of the self as disgusting and contaminated following the traumatic event. Additionally, while self-disgust may result from negative post-traumatic appraisals, it is also possible that this association is bi-directional, with feelings of self-disgust increasing negative self-focused post-traumatic appraisals, which serve to maintain elevations in PTSD symptoms (see Powell, Simpson et al., 2013).

While not directly examining links with self-disgust or PTSD, a number of additional experimental studies have utilised mental imagery involving themes of sexual violation, among unselected samples, in an effort to identify specific predictors of mental contamination (Elliott & Radomsky, 2009, 2012; Fairbrother et al., 2005). For example, Fairbrother and Rachman (2005) used the dirty kiss paradigm described previously to compare responses to imagery involving either a consensual or non-consensual kiss at a party. Participants exposed to the non-consensual imagery reported increased feelings of both internal and external dirtiness, dirtiness that was non-physical in nature, and urges to wash. Increased shame, anger, sadness, anxiety, and perceptions of immorality and cheapness/sleaziness were also reported (disgust was not assessed). Participants in the non-consensual condition were more likely to avoid objects that were indirectly associated with the perpetrator (e.g., refused to accept a drink from the female host of the party that was similar to the type of drink the perpetrator brought to the party), and several reported drinking water or washing their hands to rid themselves of mental contamination induced by the experiment. This study was the first to empirically demonstrate that phenomena associated with mental contamination, documented in relation to sexual trauma, could be approximated in the laboratory in the absence of any history of contact with the actual physical contaminant (i.e., the perpetrator).

Additional research utilising this procedure has identified a number of factors that may serve as predictors of mental contamination, including individual difference variables and features of the violating experience. Given the conceptual overlap between contact contamination and mental contamination, it is not surprising that traditional OCD contamination symptoms, as well as other trait-like vulnerability factors such as anxiety sensitivity (i.e., fear of the consequences of anxiety; Reiss, Peterson, Gursky, & McNally, 1986), disgust propensity (i.e., the ease/frequency with which disgust is experienced; van Overveld, de Jong, Peters, Cavanagh et al., 2006), and neuroticism, have been associated with both feelings of dirtiness and urges to wash following the non-consensual kiss imagery (Herba & Rachman, 2007; Radomsky & Elliott, 2009). Importantly, however, after accounting for overlap with contact contamination concerns, cognitive appraisals regarding the details of the non-consensual experience appear to be most strongly linked to the emergence of feelings of mental contamination (Elliott & Radomsky, 2013; Radomsky & Elliott, 2009). Specifically, the degree to which the kiss is perceived as a violation has been shown to predict feelings of dirtiness, while perceived personal responsibility for the kiss has been associated with both feelings of dirtiness and urges to wash (Radomsky & Elliott, 2009).

Appraisals regarding characteristics of the perpetrator also appear to be linked to the elicitation of mental contamination in response to a violating experience. For example, urges to wash have been significantly correlated with ratings of perceived perpetrator immorality following imagery involving a non-consensual kiss (Radomsky & Elliott, 2009). Moreover, imagining a consensual kiss from a person deemed to be immoral in character appears to be sufficient in evoking mental contamination (Elliott & Radomsky, 2009). These findings are consistent with Rachman's (1994, 2004, 2006) assertion that mental contamination frequently involves a moral element. Interestingly, though, Elliott and Radomsky (2009) documented similar levels of heightened mental contamination in response to the non-consensual scenario, regardless of previous knowledge concerning the morality of the perpetrator. This finding suggests an act of violation may potentially override previous appraisals regarding the morality of others. In addition to perceptions of morality/immorality, other findings implicate perceived physical cleanliness in mental contamination as well. For example, results of a study conducted by Elliott and Radomsky (2012) suggest the combination of a violating experience with a perpetrator deemed to be physically dirty may result in the highest levels of mental contamination. Although lesser in magnitude, these authors further documented similar feelings of dirtiness and urges to wash among individuals imagining a consensual kiss with a physically dirty individual (contact with a potential physical contaminant in a non-violating experience) or a non-consensual kiss with a physically clean individual (violating experience without contact with a potential physical contaminant).

In an interesting spin on this procedure, Rachman and colleagues (2012) examined whether mental contamination resulting from the dirty kiss was unique to victims of sexual violation, or if perpetrators may experience this as well. Indeed, previous studies have documented urges to wash following the execution of behaviours deemed by an individual to be immoral or sinful (Coughtrey et al., 2012). Rachman and colleagues (2012) found that male undergraduate participants reported greater feelings of dirtiness and greater increases in feelings of disgust, anxiety, and shame when imagining themselves as a perpetrator of a non-consensual kiss (as compared to a consensual kiss). Increased feelings of guilt and anger were also reported when the procedure was manipulated to have participants imagine receiving criticism from a male friend following the non-consensual kiss. Furthermore, urges to wash were greater when the manipulation was changed such that the victim of the non-consensual kiss was the sister of the participant's best friend.

Although these findings will need to be replicated among individuals with a history of traumatic events, including those diagnosed with PTSD, these basic experimental findings offer significant insight into the nature of mental contamination and potential mechanisms underlying its development. In sum, these results suggest mental imagery involving a number of themes including sexual violation, contact with others perceived to be immoral or physically unclean, and the perpetration of immoral acts may be capable of eliciting feelings of mental contamination (and self-disgust). This hearkens back to Rozin's law of contagion. Minimal contact with a contaminated individual—as minimal as imagined contact in this scenario—can result in pervasive feelings of being contaminated. Moreover, cognitive appraisals regarding perceived violations of morality and personal responsibility for the occurrence of a violating experience (e.g., self-blame) appear to be particularly strong predictors of mental contamination. This is consistent with other studies suggesting that mental contamination, like the previously discussed indirect contamination aversion and sympathetic magic appraisals, may be cognitively mediated (e.g., Cougle, Lee, Horowitz, Wolitzky-Taylor, & Telch, 2008).

## *Self-disgust, general disgust, and mental contamination: implications for the treatment of individuals with post-traumatic stress disorder*

To date, there has been no systematic examination of how persistent post-traumatic disgust or mental contamination responds to existing treatments for PTSD; however, findings from initial case studies suggest that successful treatment of PTSD may not always result in the amelioration of co-occurring contamination concerns (de Silva & Marks, 1999). In addition, both basic research (Olatunji, Forsyth et al., 2007; Mason & Richardson, 2010) and evidence drawn from other types of psychopathology (Adams et al., 2011; McKay, 2006; Olatunji, Smits, Connolly, Willems, & Lohr, 2007; Smits, Telch, & Randall, 2002) indicate that, when compared to either fear or anxiety, the emotion of disgust appears to be less amenable to extinction. This may also be true of self-disgust, although this idea is clearly in need of research.

Jung and colleagues (2011) have recently developed a brief, standalone, intervention entitled "cognitive restructuring and imagery modification" (CRIM), which is designed to specifically target persistent contamination concerns among individuals with PTSD resulting from childhood sexual abuse. This intervention, comprised of a single treatment session and a booster session one week later, involves: 1) having the patient research information regarding how many times contaminated dermal skin cells have regenerated since the trauma, 2) discussion with the patient about what this new information means to him/her, 3) engagement in guided imagery related to the regeneration of skin cells, and 4) completion of exposure exercises involving the generation of distressing images of feeling contaminated. These exercises continue until the patient reports that his/her feelings of being contaminated have reduced by at least 50%, and the session ends by asking the patient to employ imagery related to the regeneration of new skin cells. Homework includes listening to an audio recording of the modified imagery once per day for a week, before returning to discuss the effects of treatment and difficulties with implementation during the booster session.

Building upon promising initial findings (Jung et al., 2011; Jung & Steil, 2012), results of a recent randomised controlled trial found large effects for improvement in the intensity, vividness, uncontrollability, and distress associated with feelings of contamination in the CRIM group as compared to a wait list control group (Jung & Steil, 2013). A large effect size was also noted for a reduction in PTSD symptom severity, with 50% of patients in the CRIM group demonstrating reliable change in PTSD symptoms, and 35.7% no longer meeting criteria for PTSD after this brief treatment. Additional studies have documented successful reduction of mental contamination concerns following similar cognitive and cognitive-behavioural interventions adapted to address mental contamination within the context of OCD (Coughtrey et al., 2012; Warnock-Parkes, Salkovskis, & Rachman, 2012). It will be important for future research to explore the mechanisms through which this type of treatment functions to reduce contamination concerns. For example, information about the regeneration of skin cells may potentially alter self-disgust-related appraisals regarding the belief that the individual has been permanently contaminated by the traumatic experience (once in contact always in contact). Future work should also consider whether incorporating this type of focused intervention into existing treatments for PTSD might offer any added benefit to individuals presenting to the clinic with the types of concerns discussed throughout this chapter.

## *Conclusion*

The focus of this chapter has been to review the mounting body of theoretical and empirical literature regarding the role of disgust (in particular self-disgust) and mental contamination in responses to traumatic events and PTSD. As a whole, extant findings converge to suggest that both disgust and mental contamination frequently emerge following a range of traumatic events, and that these phenomena are associated with a pattern of increased post-traumatic stress symptom responding. While additional research is needed to specifically elucidate the role of self-disgust in this domain, preliminary evidence suggests this construct may hold promise as a potential risk and/or maintenance factor, which could serve to enhance our understanding of traditional post-traumatic stress reactions, as well as accompanying contamination-related difficulties, following exposure to certain traumatic events.

CHAPTER EIGHT

# Depression as a disorder of disgust

*Fahad S. M. Alanazi, Philip A. Powell, and Michael J. Power*

This chapter will consider the importance of disgust as a critical emotion in depression. The available literature on disgust and depression will be reviewed, and it will be argued that the most important form of disgust in depression is when it comes to be focused on the self, particularly in the form of more complex emotional states (e.g., shame and guilt), in terms of their derivation within a basic emotions approach (Power & Dalgleish, 2008). An aetiological model of depression (SPAARS) will be presented which incorporates multilevel representation systems of emotion. Within this model, it will be proposed that the depressive state is a direct result of the emotional coupling of sadness and self-disgust.

## *Introduction*

Disgust is argued to be one of several basic human emotions (Darwin, 1872/1989; Ekman, 1992; Phillips, Senior, Fahy, & David, 1998), and it plays a significant role in our daily emotional life (Rozin, Haidt, & McCauley, 1999). Although for some time disgust was a neglected and "forgotten" emotion in psychiatry (Phillips et al., 1998), it is now enjoying increased prominence as a research topic in its own right (McNally,

2002). Multiple operational definitions of "disgust" exist. The emotion was originally researched and operationalised psychologically in the context of its oral origins, defined as "revulsion at the prospect of (oral) incorporation of offensive objects" (Rozin & Fallon, 1987, p. 23). Since then, psychological definitions have broadened to acknowledge wider elicitors of disgust, including those from core, animal-reminder, interpersonal, and sociomoral domains (Rozin, Haidt, & McCauley, 1999). Whilst the physiological expression of disgust (or "distaste" as it may be more accurately described) is observable from birth (Rosenstein & Oster, 1988), the actual range of stimuli that comes to elicit disgust in an individual is determined socioculturally and, as is argued in the current volume, may extend to incorporate the self (Power & Dalgleish, 1997).

A relationship between disgust and several other negative basic emotions, such as anger (Marzillier & Davey, 2004; Simpson, Carter, Anthony, & Overton, 2006) and fear (Cisler, Olatunji, & Lohr, 2009; Davey, MacDonald, & Brierley, 2008; Olatunji, Sawchuk, Lohr, & de Jong, 2004), has been demonstrated in previous research. For example, evidence suggests that the disgust response may be as important to the process of contamination avoidance as fear (Cisler, Olatunji, Feldner, & Forsyth, 2010), and may combine with anger in the construction of moral outrage (Salerno & Peter-Hagene, 2013). Hence, disgust is acknowledged to have a potentially coupled role with other basic emotional states across a range of psychological phenomena, including a number of mental health problems (Power & Dalgleish, 2008). In depression, it has been previously theorised that disgust (oriented towards the self) comes to be coupled (i.e., experienced simultaneously) with the basic emotion of sadness (Power & Dalgleish, 1997). Moreover, Power and Dalgleish (1997) have conceptualised self-directed disgust as being experienced in the form of complex emotion derivatives, such as shame, guilt, and embarrassment, otherwise known as "self-conscious" emotions (Lewis, 1993). However, disgust towards the self (as a complex psychological phenomenon) has not yet been extensively studied. This chapter outlines our current perspective on the relations that self-disgust may have with depression.

## *Depression*

Depression is most commonly understood as a mood disorder that can vary in severity and fluctuate from normal mood to extreme feelings of sadness, pessimism, and despondency (American Psychological Association (APA), 2013). The diagnostic profile of major depression is marked by dysphoric mood and a profound loss of interest or pleasure, typically accompanied by a variable set of additional symptoms (i.e., fluctuations in appetite, weight, sleep, and/or motor activity; fatigue or loss of energy; feelings of worthlessness or guilt; diminished ability to think, concentrate, or make decisions; and recurrent thoughts of death or suicidal ideation, plans, or attempts; APA, 2013). Increasingly recognised as a considerable health problem (National Institute for Health and Clinical Excellence (NICE), 2010), depression is predicted to become the second leading contributor to universal disease burden by 2020 (after heart disease; Hyman, Chisholm, Kessler, Patel, & Whiteford, 2006; Murray & Lopez, 1997). This pervasive mood disorder is responsible for significant reductions in quality of life and wellbeing (Moussavi et al., 2007), impaired economic and social functioning (Thomas & Morris, 2003), and may contribute directly to avoidable mortality through suicide (Goldsmith, Pellmar, Kleinman, & Bunney, 2002).

Major depression is the most common mental health problem encountered in community settings (NICE, 2010). According to the APA's Diagnostic and Statistical Manual, fifth edition (DSM-5; APA, 2013), the one-year prevalence of major depressive disorder in the United States is approximately 7%. A fairly recent systematic review of the wider literature reported a pooled one-year prevalence rate of 4.1%, and an estimated lifetime prevalence of 6.7% (Waraich, Goldner, Somers, & Hsu, 2004). There are marked differences in incidence and prevalence as a function of certain demographic factors. In particular, incidences of depression appear to be lower in the elderly (i.e., aged ≥ 65 years; Kessler et al., 2010); females are 1.5 to 3 times more likely to receive a diagnosis than males (APA, 2013); furthermore, those diagnosed depressed are typically more likely to be unemployed, of a lower socioeconomic position, and have a lower education level than those who are not depressed (e.g., Rait et al., 2009; Singleton, Bumpstead, O'Brien, Lee, & Meltzer, 2001). The typical prognosis of major depression is relatively heterogeneous. In a large prospective epidemiological survey of Danish adults, the median duration of major depressive disorder was three months, with only 20% of the cohort failing to recover after two years (Spijker et al., 2002). In this study, severity of depressive symptoms was a significant predictor of persistence.

Untreated depression has been associated with a longer duration of illness and a greater number of recurrences than treated depression (Altamura, Dell'Osso, Mundo, & Dell'Osso, 2007). The typical prognosis of depression may too vary as a function of particular demographic variables, such as age at first episode (Altamura et al., 2007; Pettit, Lewinsohn, Roberts, Seeley, & Monteith, 2009), and gender (Altamura et al., 2007).

The average age for a first episode of depression is in the second decade of life (APA, 2013). As a heterogeneous disorder, depression has a complex and multifaceted aetiology, which is likely to involve biological and genetic (e.g., Kendler & Prescott, 1999), social (e.g., Brown & Harris, 1978), and psychological (e.g., Beck, 1967; Power & Dalgleish, 2008) antecedents. In psychology, the cognitive model of depression (e.g., Beck, 1967, 1976) has been largely dominant over the last forty years, and many of its claims have been substantiated empirically (see Clark & Beck, 2010). In brief, Beck's diathesis-stress model proposes that individuals with negative self-schemata, manifested in certain dysfunctional attitudes, have a heightened vulnerability to depression when triggered by a negative life event or stressor, due to an increased tendency to experience negatively biased views of the self, world, and future (Alloy, Abramson, Keyser, Gerstein, & Sylvia, 2008). Whilst influential, it is becoming increasingly clear that cognitive factors alone are insufficient to account for all instances of depressive experience (Simpson, Hillman, Crawford, & Overton, 2010) and the link between maladaptive cognition and depression is often inconsistent (e.g., Abela & D'Alessandro, 2002; LaGrange et al., 2011; Otto et al., 2007). Consequently, more effort is now being made to consider emotional factors, which include disgust, in the aetiology and maintenance of depression, and other mental health problems (Greenberg, 2008; Power & Dalgleish, 2008).

## *The relationship between disgust and depression*

### *Depression and disgust* per se

Power and Dalgleish (1997) are credited as the first psychologists to sketch out a critical role for the disgust emotion in depression, but research evidence on this score has since been inconsistent. A number of studies have reported relatively small, or non-existent, correlations between an individual's self-reported disgust propensity to specific external elicitors and depressive symptoms (Fox & Harrison, 2008; Muris et al., 2000; Olatunji, Unoka, Beran, David, & Armstrong, 2009; Rozin, Fallon, & Mandell, 1984; Tolin, Woods, & Abramowitz, 2006). Moreover, there seems to be no heightened proneness to (externally elicited) disgust stimuli in clinically depressed groups (Schienle, Schäfer et al., 2003). However, a stronger association may be evident between depression and more general, stimulus-independent measures of proneness to disgust (e.g., Power & Tarsia, 2007; van Overveld, de Jong, & Peters, 2010). For example, a recent study reported a strong correlation between implicit indices of disgust propensity and sensitivity and explicit depressive symptoms, in the absence of a link with explicit, stimulus-dependent measures of disgust propensity (Nicholson & Barnes-Holmes, 2012).

Evidence concerning the recognition of disgusted facial expressions in depression is also unclear, with evidence of enhanced recognition (Merens, Booij, Haffmans, & van der Does, 2008), impaired recognition (Douglas & Porter, 2010), and no difference (Bediou et al., 2005; Surguladze et al., 2010). Some of these discrepant results can be attributed to certain methodological differences, such as the use of unipolar and bipolar depressives (e.g., Douglas & Porter, 2010), but any genuine effect between depression and the recognition of disgust requires further clarification.

Some more positive evidence for the link between disgust and depression exists too. There is recent fMRI data that suggests facial expressions of disgust may be appraised differently in individuals with depression, independent of any significant differences in actual recognition performance (Surguladze et al., 2010). Surguladze and colleagues (2010) presented nine medicated participants with major depressive disorder, and nine matched healthy controls, with disgusted, neutral, and fearful facial expressions of 50% and 100% morphed intensities. The depressed participants showed greater activity than the controls in the left fronto-temporal and right middle/inferior temporal regions (e.g., insula, orbito-frontal cortex) to the 100% disgust expressions. There is also independent evidence that clinically depressed patients report being more sensitive to disgust (i.e., finding the experience of disgust itself as more negative and distressing), than a comparison group of healthy controls (Ille, Schony, Kapfhammer, & Schienle, 2010).

### *Depression and self-disgust*

In the face of this inconsistent evidence between disgust and depression, it is worthy of emphasis that Power and Dalgleish's (1997) argument was that *self-disgust* may be particularly related to depression rather than disgust *per se*. This calibration in focus can be reconciled with the evidence reviewed previously. In particular, depressed individuals may display a slightly to no heightened propensity to stimulus-dependent external elicitors of disgust (e.g., Muris et al., 2000; Olatunji, Unoka et al., 2009), or recognition of others' disgust expressions (e.g., Bediou et al., 2005). However, they may experience a greater amount of disgust to internal elicitors (Power & Tarsia, 2007); find the experiential state of disgust as more distressing due to its self-focus (Ille et al., 2010), and potentially be more sensitive in response to the disgusted facial expression of others (Surguladze et al., 2010). Indeed, Power (1999) hypothesised that expressions of disgust from a significant other may contribute to depressive relapse, and this evidence is suggestive of such a mechanism.

In his literary treatise on disgust, Miller (1997) defined the melancholic self as one that is infected or contaminated by its very nature (see also Power & Dalgleish, 2008). The conviction that one is ugly or repulsive is common during states of depressed mood, and some form of dysmorphic concern is often present (Castle & Phillips, 2002). Fox and Harrison (2008) have previously speculated that disgust may be used to inhibit the more difficult emotion of anger in people with co-morbid eating disorders and depression. What is more, it has been proposed that the frequent co-morbidity between eating pathology and depression may be due to a shared emotional component, such as self-disgust (Fox & Power, 2009). Power and Dalgleish (2008) have also presented anecdotal evidence of a personal case of depression, in which an individual appraised herself as disgusting and unacceptable. Here, there was motivation for the repulsive aspects of the self to be eliminated or rejected, as per the action tendency linked to the disgust emotion. In sum, there is a strong theoretical underpinning to the idea that depression involves self-oriented disgust, in some form.

In a series of studies directly investigating the link between self-disgust and depression, Paul Overton, Jane Simpson, and their colleagues have provided some of the first explicit evidence of the hypothesised relationship (Overton, Markland, Taggart, Bagshaw, & Simpson, 2008; Powell, Overton, & Simpson, 2014; Powell, Simpson, & Overton, 2013; Simpson et al., 2010). In the initial of these investigations, Overton et al. (2008) tested the idea that self-disgust may act as a negative emotional mediator in the relationship between dysfunctional cognitions and depressive symptoms. A novel self-report scale was designed to quantify levels of self-disgust (the Self-Disgust Scale (SDS); Overton et al., 2008), and then administered to a sample of 111 undergraduates. The researchers found that self-disgust was significantly positively correlated with two measures of depression, and provided initial cross-sectional support for a partial mediation model in the theorised direction (i.e., dysfunctional cognitions leading to self-disgust leading to depression). In a second study, Simpson et al. (2010) extended this work to indicate independent roles for both self-disgust and self-esteem in mediating the path from dysfunctional thoughts to depression.

More recently, Powell et al. (2013) carried out a prospective investigation in order to assess the temporal validity of the abovementioned hypothesised model. The researchers collected self-report data on levels of self-disgust, dysfunctional cognitions, and depressive symptoms online from a non-clinical sample. Longitudinal follow-ups were conducted at six months ($n$ = 152) and twelve months ($n$ = 110) after baseline. The main study findings were that: 1) depressive symptoms were significantly predicted by trait levels of self-disgust over time, but not the reverse; 2) the mediation role of self-disgust was too simplistic, with dysfunctional thoughts and self-disgust interacting over time; and 3) physical self-disgust was a stronger predictor of later depressive symptoms, than behavioural self-disgust over six months. In a related qualitative study, Powell et al. (2014) have explored the phenomenological experience of self-disgust in females with high levels of depressive symptoms. In this paper, self-disgust was elucidated as a unique (schematic) experience state, associated with a consuming and visceral subjective experience, particular antecedent factors (e.g., disgust-based criticism from others), and negative consequences (e.g., avoiding looking at the self). Furthermore, self-disgust was described by many of the participants as being experienced alongside some other negative emotional states, including shame, anger, sadness, and depression.

In sum, based on the evidence reviewed and the theorising of Power and Dalgleish (1997), we assert that in depression dysfunctional disgust responding tends to be concentrated mainly on the self, rather than on alternative, external disgust-inducing objects. A negative orientation to the self is highlighted in Beck's influential cognitive theory of depression, in which he actually described depression as involving a "feeling of disgust" for the self (Beck, 1967). Thus, although depression has sadness as an important component emotion, we maintain that it is the self-disgust element that is responsible for turning mere sadness into a depressive disorder (Power, 2010; Power & Dalgleish, 1997). It is this self-disgust that has been theorised by Power and Dalgleish (2008) to manifest itself in the form of certain complex emotions; most notably, shame, guilt, and embarrassment.

### *Shame, guilt, and embarrassment as complex emotions of disgust*

While the authors of this chapter agree that shame, guilt, and embarrassment may be associated with self-oriented disgust in some form (see Powell, Simpson, & Overton, this volume), there is a place for debate over whether disgust experienced in response to (certain aspects of) the self represents a complex emotional phenomenon in its own right, that can be meaningfully distinguished from certain instances of shame and guilt (e.g., Powell et al., 2014; Roberts & Goldenberg, 2007; Simpson et al., 2010). In their particular theorisation, building on the earlier work of Keith Oatley and Philip Johnson-Laird (e.g., Johnson-Laird & Oatley, 1989; Oatley & Johnson-Laird, 1987), Power and Dalgleish (2008) have argued that shame, guilt, and some types of embarrassment (and, to a lesser degree, contempt) inherently involve the basic emotional experience of disgust focused on the self (or an aspect of the self). However, there are limited studies that have actually examined this hypothesised relationship (e.g., Power, 2006a).

Shame, guilt, and embarrassment can be reliably distinguished from each other on criteria such as their phenomenological features, differential elicitors, and specific action tendencies (Tangney, Miller, Flicker, & Barlow, 1996). A key distinction is that shame typically involves the global self, whilst embarrassment and guilt, on the other hand, are considered less global and embodied emotions related to a particular action that one has performed (e.g., Tangney et al., 1996; Tangney, Stuewig, & Mashek, 2007). Thus, shame represents a core and enduring aspect of the self that is being, or could be, judged negatively (Grozier, 1998). Shame has also been classed as the more maladaptive emotion, typically motivating "a desire to deny, hide, or escape" (Tangney, 1999, p. 546), in contrast to guilt's reparative and adaptive action tendency, often leading to "confessing, apologizing and the need to undo the wrong doing" (Tangney, 1999, p. 546). Indeed, a proneness to guilt has been found to be inversely related to certain negative social outcomes (i.e., antisocial and risky behaviour; see Tangney et al., 2007). Moreover, Tangney, Wagner, and Gramzow (1992) found that shame-proneness had the stronger relationship with psychopathological symptoms than did guilt-proneness. Nevertheless, as with all emotion, it is likely that both shame and guilt have the potential to become pathological if they are experienced to an excessive or diminished extent (e.g., Gilbert, 1992, 1998a, 1998b).

Given its association with core and global self-attributes, Power and Dalgleish (2008) have argued that it is self-disgust manifested as shame that is most important in depression. This is in contrast to certain prior diagnostic systems, such as APA's DSM-IV (APA, 1994), and the World Health Organization (WHO)'s International Statistical Classification of Diseases and Related Health Problems, Tenth Revision (ICD-10; WHO, 1992), which have emphasised the importance of guilt rather than shame in major depression. Evidence is amassing to support the significance of shame in depression (e.g., Orth, Berking, & Burkhardt, 2006; Power & Tarsia, 2007). For example, Power and Tarsia (2007) recorded elevated levels of a number of complex emotions (e.g., shame and guilt), theorised to be linked to disgust, in depressed and mixed depressed and anxious groups. Moreover, when controlling for an index of sadness, shame, but not guilt, was found to be a significant predictor of depressive symptoms across all participants.

Shame itself has been empirically implicated in depression for at least two decades (e.g., Allan, Gilbert, & Goss, 1994; Tangney, Burggraf, & Wagner, 1995; Tangney et al., 1992). Measures of state shame (e.g., Allan et al., 1994; Rusch et al., 2007) and trait shame proneness (e.g., Allan et al., 1994; Tangney et al., 1992), have been observed to consistently correlate with measures of depressive symptoms. Clinically depressed individuals constantly score higher than healthy controls on a range of measures of state (e.g., Andrews & Hunter, 1997; Ghatavi, Nicolson,

MacDonald, Osher, & Levitt, 2002; Thompson & Berenbaum, 2006) and trait shame (e.g., Gilbert, 2000; Guimon, Las Hayas, Guillen, Boyra, & Gonzalez-Pinto, 2007; Highfield, Markham, Skinner, & Neal, 2010). Individuals with major depression have also been shown to score higher on measures of shame than those with bipolar disorder (Guimon et al., 2007; Highfield et al., 2010; but see Power & Tarsia, 2007) and schizophrenia (Guimon et al., 2007). Furthermore, longitudinal evidence also exists demonstrating that the predictive power of shame for depressive symptoms persists over time (e.g., Andrews, Qian, & Valentine, 2002; Stuewig & McCloskey, 2005).

In sum, Power and Dalgleish (2008) have theorised shame, guilt, and embarrassment as complex (and self-conscious) emotions that may derive from the basic emotion of disgust, focused on the self. Of these, shame in particular has been evidenced by a substantial literature to have particular importance in relation to depressive experience. Whilst there is still room for debate over whether shame actually represents a direct derivative of disgust, which is simply turned on the self (i.e., Power & Dalgleish, 2008), it seems likely that shame is at least a common associate of self-disgust (Powell et al., 2014; see Powell, Simpson, & Overton, this volume), and, thus, its association with depression is noteworthy.

## *The SPAARS approach*

Power and Dalgleish (1997) developed the Schematic Propositional Analogical and Associative Representation Systems (SPAARS) multilevel model of emotion generation, detailing two possible

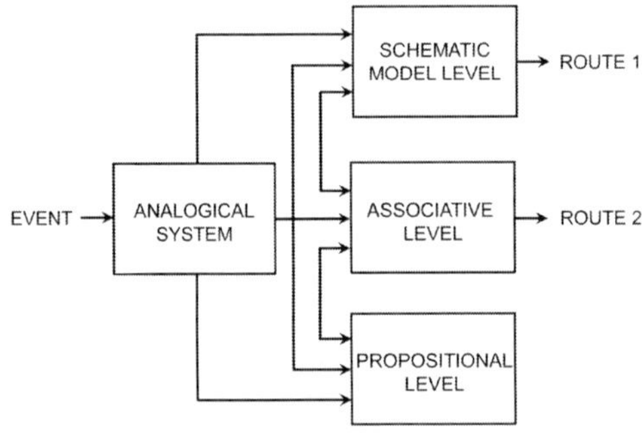


Figure 1. The SPAARS model with two routes to emotion (Power & Dalgleish, 2008).

routes to emotion experience, as illustrated in Figure 1. In brief, the first route to emotion is considered to be "effortful", as a result of higher-order cognitive interpretation and appraisals of an external and/or internal eliciting event, within a schematic framework. The second route is the more automatic, or associative, pathway, where an input can trigger an emotion in the absence of the need for any conscious appraisal. This is achieved through a combination of innate and learned associations. The SPAARS model consists of four levels of representation:

1. *The analogical system.* This system represents the initial processing of stimuli through various sensory inputs (i.e., olfactory, auditory, gustatory, visual, proprioceptive, and tactile). These external events are often emotion-inducing, and may become integrated in the memory of emotional events. The output from this system feeds into three higher representational levels (described below) that are theorised to operate in parallel.
2. *The associative level.* This system works outside of conscious awareness in the form of automatic processing. Emotions that become associated with external or internal events, certain interpretations at the schematic or propositional level, and/or propositional events may be triggered through the associative level in the absence of higher schematic processing. These associations are thought to arise as a function of repeated event-emotion interactions, and may be innately prepared.
3. *The propositional level.* This level is considered intermediate with regards to semantic representation, and can be thought of as the most language-like (e.g., propositional automatic thoughts; Beck, 1976). The propositional level is theorised to have no direct route to emotion, but generates emotion via either the associative level (i.e., language linked to emotion) or additional appraisals at the schematic model level.
4. *The schematic model level.* This is the highest level of semantic representation. This route to emotion involves the interpretation and appraisal of any relevant (internal or external) input. Here, representational/schematic models are contained, such as those about the self, world and others.

* * *

Table 1. Basic emotions and links to emotional disorders (Power & Dalgleish, 2008).

| *Basic emotion* | *Coupled emotion* | *Emotional disorder* |
|---|---|---|
| Fear | Disgust | Panic<br>Phobias<br>OCD<br>GAD<br>PTSD |
| Sadness | Anger<br>Disgust (directed at the self) | Pathological grief<br>Traumatic grief<br>PTSD<br>Depression |
| Anger | Anger/Fear | Anger disorders |
| Disgust | Fear | OCD<br>Suicide<br>Eating disorders<br>PTSD |
| Happiness | Anger/fear | Polyannaism/ pathological optimism<br>Hypomania<br>Mania<br>Love sickness/ De Clerambault's syndrome |

Within their SPAARS framework, Power and Dalgleish (1997), hypothesised that basic emotions can become coupled, either reciprocally (i.e., one emotion triggering another emotion, which may activate the previous emotion, and so on), or with a particular stimulus or event eliciting two or more basic emotions in tandem. Moreover, any complex emotions within SPAARS (e.g., shame) are seen as a direct product of basic emotions, either through coupling, further appraisals (i.e., about the emotion object), and the integration of specific appraisals relative to others' goals. Like the generation of complex emotions, in SPAARS a number of emotional disorders are also hypothesised to be ultimately derivable from the coupling of some of five basic emotional states (Power & Dalgleish, 1997; Table 1). For example, the combination of sadness and anger in reaction to a loss that is hypothesised as antecedent to states of grief, and the coupling of disgust and fear in certain instances of phobias and post-traumatic stress.

## *Major depression within the SPAARS model*

As shown in Table 1, certain instances of problematic depression have been hypothesised as a consequence of the emotional coupling of disgust (focused on the self) and sadness (Power & Dalgleish, 2008). In their social-cognitive model of depression, Champion and Power (1995; see Figure 2) argued that people with a vulnerability to depression have a tendency to overinvest in one role or goal, and neglect other areas of their lives. When the individual's (overinvested) role or goal is threatened or lost through a congruent negative event, the defensive processes that normally exist (through actively pursuing the goal) are theorised to break down. Consequently, the agent may develop feelings of negativity towards the self (i.e., self-disgust), and become dominated by perceived negative aspects of the self, which is then proposed to lead to a state of depression. Hence, in this theoretical model, the loss of an overinvested role or goal is associated with the subsequent combined emotional experience of sadness and self-negativity, predominantly in the form of self-directed disgust (theorised to be manifest in complex self-conscious emotions like shame; Power & Dalgleish, 2008). Conversely, non-vulnerable individuals are thought to be less likely to experience this maladaptive emotional coupling of sadness and self-disgust in response to a negative event, and more likely to repair their self-esteem by appealing to other valued roles/goals.

Applying the above model to the SPAARS framework, the coupling of sadness and disgust that occurs in depression is proposed to occur across all three (interacting) higher levels of representation detailed earlier (i.e., the propositional, associative, and schematic model levels; Power & Dalgleish, 1997). If we take, for example, depression as a consequence of the breakdown of a personal relationship an individual is overinvested in. Sadness may be elicited through the automatic (associative level) emotion pathway as a direct result of the loss of a loved one, whilst self-disgust (i.e., shame and low self-esteem) may be generated at the same time due to the individual's perceived inadequacy in maintaining the relationship, or associations with his inability to maintain important relations in the past. Furthermore, both sadness and

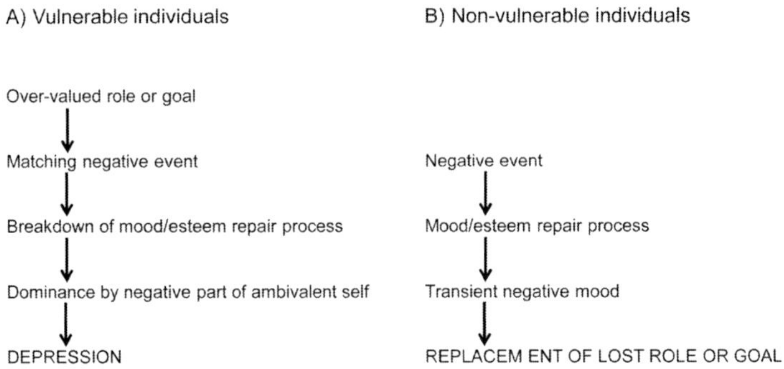


Figure 2. Champion and Power's (1995) model of depression.

self-disgust may be elicited through the effortful emotion route, by the consequent activation of a schematic model of the self as alone, unloved, inadequate, guilty, shameful, disgusting, and so on. This combination of sadness and self-disgust may be evidenced also at the propositional level of representation, in the form of congruent negative thoughts, such as "I am sad and alone", "I am shit", "I loathe myself". Between each of these different levels of representation, positive feedback loops (or "emotion cycles") are hypothesised to maintain and enhance the active emotional state (Power & Dalgleish, 2008). Thus, sadness and disgust can be considered coupled at all three levels of the SPAARS model (i.e., the associative, propositional, and schematic model).

Whilst a fully detailed SPAARS model of depression has yet to be sketched, at least in the same way that it has been for eating disorders (Fox & Power, 2009; see Fox, Grange, & Power, this volume), certainly the idea that some instances of depression are characterised by a combination of the emotions of sadness and self-disgust has acquired some support. For example, in early diary-based studies, Oatley and Duncan (1992) reported that sadness was the basic emotion most likely to occur in combination with others, including disgust. In their qualitative study, Powell and colleagues (2014) noted a number of links between experienced self-disgust and instances of sadness and depression. Quantitative measurements of self-disgust have all shown strong positive associations with measures of depression (e.g., Overton et al., 2008; Simpson et al., 2010), including in clinically depressed groups (Ille et al., 2014), and when measured over time (Powell et al., 2013).

Furthermore, complex emotional states that have been hypothesised to be derived from self-disgust (i.e., shame, guilt, and humiliation), have been shown to be important in the context of both unipolar (Power & Tarsia, 2007) and bipolar depression (Carolan & Power, 2009). So, whilst initial evidence is positive, further work is required to elucidate and validate precisely how, and under what circumstances, sadness and disgust (towards the self) come to be coupled, especially within the wider context of the SPAARS model (Carolan & Power, 2009).

## *Conclusion*

In this chapter, and based on the available literature, we have argued that the most important form of disgust in depression is when it comes to be focused on the self (i.e., self-disgust). We have explored the idea that shame, which has been shown to be a significant emotion in depression, may be a derivative of self-disgust. The SPAARS model of emotion (Power & Dalgleish, 1997) was outlined, as was a theoretical model of depression, in which it is viewed as the direct consequence of the maladaptive emotional coupling (i.e., experiential combination) of sadness and self-disgust. Initial evidence suggests that self-disgust does play a critical role in depression, but further work to delineate this role is encouraged.

CHAPTER NINE

# Self-disgust in eating disorders: a review of the literature and clinical implications

*John R. E. Fox, Neesha Grange, and Michael J. Power*

## *Introduction*

Eating disorders (EDs) are rare, but life-threatening, mental health problems that often have their onset during childhood or adolescence and most commonly affect females (Hoek, 2006; Hoek & van Hoeken, 2003). They are characterised by an over-evaluation of shape, weight, and the control of eating (Fairburn, Cooper, & Shafran, 2003). More specifically, anorexia nervosa (AN) is characterised by a preoccupation with maintaining a low body weight (body mass index (BMI) $\leq 17.5$ kg/m$^2$), a disturbance in the way one's body weight and shape are perceived, and an extreme restriction of food due to an intense fear of gaining weight (American Psychiatric Association (APA), 2013). Individuals with AN may attempt to maintain a low body weight by restricting their diet (restricting type), or by regularly engaging in self-induced vomiting or the misuse of diuretics, laxatives, and enemas (binge-eating/purging type; APA, 2013). Bulimia nervosa (BN) involves recurrent episodes of binge-eating and compensatory behaviours that occur at least twice weekly for a period of three months and a marked dissatisfaction with body shape/weight (APA, 2013).

Evidence now suggests that disgust may play a central role in the cause and maintenance of EDs. A person with an ED's reaction to food can be one of disgust, especially in AN, whilst in BN, the disgust often appears to be directed at the self (e.g., after vomiting). However, research looking at the potential role of disgust in EDs has been slow to get off the ground (Fox & Power, 2009). Indeed, research into emotions and emotion regulation within EDs has only been gathering pace over the last few years. It was Hilde Bruch who discussed the significance of understanding emotion regulation in EDs back in the 1970s, but therapeutic approaches and research have taken almost thirty years to catch up (Bruch, 1978).

Although work in this field is still very much in its infancy, this chapter will undertake a review of both the theoretical and the empirical literature of the application of disgust to EDs. It will also consider some of the general models of emotion that have been applied to EDs and the pivotal role that disgust (including self-disgust) plays in these models (e.g., the Schematic Propositional Analogical Associative Representation System applied to eating disorders (SPAARS-ED); Fox, Federici, & Power, 2012; Fox & Power, 2009). A key feature of these models is that disgust can become "coupled" with other emotions, such as anger and/ or sadness, and this is regarded as a key emotional process in EDs. This chapter will also consider the implications of these theories and research for treatment, where it will be argued that disgust is a neglected emotion in clinical approaches to EDs.

## *Research on disgust in eating disorders*

Although interest in the role of emotions in EDs has grown significantly over recent years, there are still disagreements about whether trait-like approaches (e.g., negative affect; Fairburn et al., 2003) or a basic emotion perspective (e.g., Fox & Power, 2009) are important in understanding EDs. From a basic emotion perspective, disgust is one emotion that is considered to be basic by many authors (e.g., Ekman, Friesen, & Ellsworth, 1982; Izard, 1971; McDougall, 1926; Oatley & Johnson-Laird, 1987; Plutchik, 1980; Tomkins, 1984) and has been defined by Rozin and Fallon (1987) as "revulsion at the prospect of (oral) incorporation of an offensive object. The offensive objects are contaminants; that is, if they even briefly contact unacceptable food, they tend to render that food unacceptable" (p. 23). This classic definition highlights how disgust is considered as a food rejection response; however, disgust is not simply restricted to distancing oneself from the ingestion of contaminating substances. Indeed, research has demonstrated that both primary and secondary disgusts exist, whereby primary disgust focuses on food avoidance and is defined as the ability of an item to elicit revulsion towards oral incorporation, whilst secondary disgust is comprised of behaviours and acts that are socially and morally unacceptable (Chapman, Kim, Susskind, & Anderson, 2009; Marzillier & Davey, 2004). Similarly, it has been argued that shame is very similar to secondary disgust and may therefore be considered as a complex secondary emotion derived from the basic emotion of disgust (Fox, Federici et al., 2012). According to this view, disgust, shame, and self-disgust are all emotions that involve pushing away or feeling pushed away (e.g., social rejection), and are all about the avoidance of noxious substances, situations, and so on. They all share very similar phenomenological qualities and lead the person to withdraw very quickly from aversive situations.

Due to a growing interest in disgust over recent decades, numerous measures have been developed to understand this particular emotion further. The Disgust Sensitivity Questionnaire (DSQ; Rozin, Fallon, & Mandell, 1984) focuses on food contamination, and has been extended to create the Disgust Scale (DS; Haidt, McCauley, & Rozin, 1994). The DS covers the following domains of disgust elicitors: food, animals, body products, sex, body envelope violations, death, hygiene, and magical thinking. Another measure of disgust is the Disgust Questionnaire (DQ) developed by Barker and Davey (1997), which covers five domains of disgust: foodstuffs of animal origin, human body and body products, invertebrate animals, gastro-enteric products, and sexual practices.

Davey, Buckland, Tantow, and Dallos (1998) were among the first to investigate the relationship between disgust and EDs, by examining whether or not a relationship existed between self-reported levels of disgust (using the DSQ; Rozin et al., 1984, and the DQ; Barker & Davey, 1997) and standardised measures of EDs amongst a student sample. Strong correlations were found between ED measures and reported levels of disgust, but only among females, and this relationship remained after anxiety and depression were controlled for. Although the researchers expected to find an overall global elevated disgust sensitivity, results demonstrated that elevated disgust levels were limited to the specific domains of food items and sexual practices, and no significant correlations were found between any measures of ED and the general human body (i.e., not their own body) or body products domains of disgust. A second study was conducted using a sample of ten female adolescents diagnosed with AN and BN (Davey et al., 1998). Compared to matched controls, those diagnosed with an ED had significantly higher scores on three domains of disgust from the DQ (Barker & Davey, 1997), which were foodstuffs of animal origin, the human body and body products, and gastro-enteric products. Although different heightened domains of disgust sensitivity were found among the two samples (non-clinical and clinical samples), the findings were taken to suggest that measures of EDs are not associated with a general heightened propensity to disgust, rather that disgust amongst this group is confined to the specific domains of food and the body.

Troop, Murphy, Bramon, and Treasure (2000) later failed to replicate Davey et al.'s (1998) findings, reporting no significant relationships between levels of disgust sensitivity amongst females diagnosed with an ED and matched controls. However, a re-analysis of the findings was later conducted because the researchers suggested that the failure to find any significant relationships may have been due to the separation of the sample into ED subgroups (AN restricting type, AN binge/purge type, BN, eating disorder not otherwise specified (EDNOS), and obese binge-eaters; Troop, Treasure, & Serpell, 2002). The re-analysis of the findings (using the sample as one combined ED group) demonstrated that those with an ED did in fact report significantly higher levels of disgust sensitivity compared to matched controls, and were specifically more sensitive to the disgust domains of food, animals, and body products (on the DS; Haidt et al., 1994). Troop et al. (2002) extended these findings by comparing levels of disgust sensitivity amongst women currently diagnosed with an ED and those in remission. It was found that the women in remission were significantly less likely to be disgusted by the human body or body products when compared to those currently diagnosed with an ED; however, no other significant differences were found between the two groups. When compared to non-clinical samples, those in remission demonstrated heightened levels of disgust sensitivity on the domains of foodstuffs of animal origin, the human body and body products, and invertebrate animals (Troop et al., 2002), again reflecting specified disgust towards food and the body rather than global disgust.

In contrast to the findings of Troop and colleagues, Muris and colleagues (2000) failed to find any significant relationships between disgust and EDs amongst a non-clinical sample of adults. This apparent discrepancy was suggested to be a result of using the DSQ (Rozin et al., 1984), which measures only one domain of disgust: the contamination of highly desirable food items (Muris et al., 2000). On the other hand, when examining the relationship between disgust sensitivity and ED symptoms amongst a non-clinical sample of children and adolescents (aged nine to thirteen years), Muris, van der Heiden, and Rassin (2008) found a positive association. Correlations were modest, however, which may have been due to the use of a non-clinical sample, or the low levels of symptoms found among this age group (Muris et al., 2008). The failure to find strong correlations between measures of EDs and disgust may therefore be in part a result of methodological shortcomings, rather than the lack of a real relationship.

More recently, Aharoni and Hertz (2012) investigated the relationship between disgust sensitivity and AN in particular—rather than a global sample of mixtures of ED categories—using a larger clinical sample than used in previous studies ($N = 62$). Using the DS (Haidt et al., 1994), strong correlations were found between disgust sensitivity and ED measures when compared to matched controls. More specifically, the AN group scored highly on the domains of food, body products, and magical thinking. Although the category of magical thinking has not previously been found to be related to EDs in other research, the findings serve to evidence the trend that EDs involve a heightened level of disgust in specific domains (i.e., towards particular stimuli, such as food, the body, etc.) rather than globalised elevated disgust sensitivity.

Research adopting the use of more experimental designs has, however, been less conclusive and less supportive of previous research suggesting a relationship between the emotion of disgust and EDs. Mayer, Muris, Busser, and Bergamin (2009) manipulated various mood states (disgust, anxious, happy, and neutral) and then asked participants to report general threat interpretations, negative body-related interpretations, and neutral or positive interpretations. It was hypothesised that those in the anxious and disgust-induced experimental groups would be more likely to show negative body-related interpretations than those in the happy or neutral mood states, and that this cognitive bias would be elevated in those with high levels of ED symptoms. Results, however, failed to demonstrate a correlation between the disgust mood state and higher levels of negative body-related interpretations (Mayer et al., 2009). Similarly, in another experimental manipulation, Mayer and colleagues (Mayer, Bos, Muris, & Vlielander, 2008) aimed to induce feelings of disgust using a bad smell among a non-clinical sample, by using "four nasty-smelling Limburger cheeses". Within this study, they sought to examine the relationship between ED-related concepts and explicit/implicit preferences for high-calorie foods. Those in the experimental condition did not report significantly lower levels of body esteem, higher levels of restraint eating, or body-change strategies, and failed to demonstrate decreased explicit or implicit preferences for high-calorie foods. From this research, it therefore seems that there is no causal relationship from experienced disgust to ED symptoms. However, as will be discussed below, it does not rule out whether disgust may be induced by specific eating-disorder symptoms (e.g., bingeing and vomiting). Furthermore, it is questionable whether the mood-induction procedures did in fact induce the required moods. For example, it could be questioned whether using "four nasty-smelling Limburger cheeses" did in fact induce feelings of disgust among the sample, and this may perhaps be a reason for the failure to find any significant relationships (Mayer, Bos et al., 2008). Alternatively, the results may have been different if the olfactory induction method was implicit rather than explicit (cf. Schnall, Haidt, Clore, & Jordan, 2008). In addition to this, a further reason for the lack of effect may be the exclusive use of non-clinical samples.

Research has also started to look at the relationship between disgust and other emotions within EDs. For example, Espeset, Gulliksen, Nordbø, Skårderud, and Holte (2012) interviewed women diagnosed with AN to explore how they manage negative emotions and how they link this to their ED behaviours. Findings demonstrated that the negative emotion of disgust was often linked to eating food and the feeling of being full. In order to overcome the feeling of disgust, the women adopted avoidance strategies linked to their ED behaviours, such as eating food, body awareness, restrictive eating, and purging. Interestingly, Espeset and colleagues (2012) also reported data that showed close connections between disgust and the emotions of fear and sadness. For example, the women in the study reported that when they felt sad or depressed, they would often experience their body as fat and disgusting. Furthermore, the feeling of fear led the participants to imagine their bodies as expanding, which brought feelings of disgust and body dissatisfaction.

Other research has also highlighted the role that other emotions play alongside disgust in EDs. For example, Harvey and colleagues (Harvey, Troop, Treasure, & Murphy, 2002) investigated not only the emotion of disgust but also the emotion of fear when responding to ED-relevant stimuli (i.e., images of body shapes, food and drink), among non-clinical women with high and low eating-attitude problems, as measured by the Eating Attitudes Test 26 (EAT-26; Garner, Olmsted, Bohr, & Garfinkel, 1982). Results demonstrated that the emotions of fear and disgust were significantly higher when the women in the high EAT group responded to images of high-calorie foods and overweight body shapes, when compared to the women in the low EAT group. Disgust reactions were as strong as the fear reactions for those women in the high EAT group when responding to images of high-calorie food and overweight body shapes. The authors concluded that the findings may be due to the idea that both fear and disgust are equally salient emotions involved in the process of avoiding high-calorie foods and undesirable body shapes among women with abnormal eating attitudes (Harvey et al., 2002).

Similarly, Griffiths and Troop (2006) extended Harvey et al.'s (2002) findings by examining emotional reactions to ED-relevant stimuli, in particular the relationship between disgust and eating behaviours and attitudes among a non-clinical sample. Again, both fear and disgust of high-energy foods and overweight body shapes were significantly correlated with eating attitudes; however, no relationship was demonstrated between emotional responses, eating attitudes, and actual eating behaviours. One reason why disordered eating attitudes and emotional responses to high-energy foods, weight, and body shape did not actually influence the avoidance of such foods may be that the participants involved in this research were a non-clinical sample, and perhaps the disordered attitudes would extend to disordered behaviours among a clinical sample. Nevertheless, more recent research has indeed demonstrated correlations between disgust sensitivity and external eating behaviours among a non-clinical sample of females (Mayer, Muris, Bos, & Suijkerbuijk, 2008). Mayer, Muris, and colleagues (2008) extended the findings of Harvey and colleagues (2002) by examining the differences in viewing times of disgusting images amongst participants scoring high and low in disordered eating. It was predicted that those with high eating-disorder symptoms would display shorter viewing times than those scoring low on eating-disorder symptoms; however, the results failed to support this hypothesis, because no significant differences were found between viewing times for each group.

More recent research has also demonstrated an association between images of obese bodies and the emotion of disgust, although this relationship was not due to levels of ED symptoms (Mayer, Muris, & Wilschut, 2011). In this non-clinical sample, it was found that those with higher levels of ED symptoms actually associated obese bodies with fear and anxiety, and associated slim bodies with disgust. Davey and Chapman (2009) also investigated the relationship between disgust, anxiety, and ED symptoms. Significant, but modest, correlations were found between disgust sensitivity/propensity and symptoms of ED, including body shape concerns, drive for thinness, and bulimia. However, these relationships was no longer significant when trait anxiety or anxiety sensitivity were controlled for (Davey & Chapman, 2009). The authors concluded that rather than disgust playing an independent role in EDs, it may be linked to other emotions such as anxiety (Davey & Chapman, 2009).

### *Summary of the review of research on disgust in eating disorders*

As can be seen from the prior discussion, there is a lack of conclusive evidence that links general disgust to EDs. Rather, there appears to be a specific food/body disgust sensitivity that is present in people with EDs. Moreover, there is a distinct lack of evidence that these increased levels of food/body disgust play a causal role in the development of EDs, and it could be that increased levels of disgust are a product rather than a cause of developing an ED. For example, the findings that people in remission from an ED showed significantly lower scores on disgust measures, and that there was no evidence that disgust influenced disordered eating patterns in a non-clinical group, potentially show the specificity of elevated food/body disgust within currently ill ED people. As we shall see later in the chapter, it is interesting that there is evidence that disgust may be working in conjunction with other emotions. It is important to note the problems in measuring related emotions. For example, correlations between anxiety and fear are typically very high, and it is likely that there is a significant amount of shared variance between the two constructs. Equally, the challenges in discriminately measuring disgust and fear are also likely to be high, and it remains an empirical question to what extent the aforementioned disgust measures would correlate with fear measures. However, putting aside some of these measurement issues, there are some interesting theoretical reasons why these emotions may co-occur and these will be discussed below.

What is interesting about our review of the potential role of disgust in EDs is the complete lack of research that has looked specifically at the role of self-disgust. According to Power and Dalgleish (2008), there has been an over-focus in the literature on how disgust is related to external objects, such as food, insects, and so on, and this has meant that self-disgust has tended to be overlooked. They also argue that disgust (including self-disgust) is a basic emotion, and certain complex derivatives are drawn from this emotion, such as shame and guilt. Many cognitive theorists have argued that self-disgust lies at the heart of psychological distress, and this self-disgust tends to occur following a series of negative evaluations/self-criticism of the self (i.e., "I am useless" and "a failure" leads to self-disgust; e.g., Beck, Rush, Shaw, & Emery, 1979).

However, other authors have argued that self-disgust is not just the product of cognition; rather, it is the introject of interactions as a child that gave an "emotional tone of contempt and criticism" that is internalised during the social development of the child (e.g., Greenberg, Watson, & Goldman, 1998). It is via this introject that the child starts to take forward the "internalised critical" voice, thus leaving the person with an overall sense of failure, being criticised, and self-disgust (Greenberg et al., 1998). Theoretically, these authors argue that these internalised relationships shape the "emotion scheme" that leaves the child not being able to defend against self-criticism/self-disgust in the future.

## *Self-disgust in eating disorders*

### *Social factors: objectification of the female body*

Research into self-disgust within the EDs is very much in its infancy, and there is a paucity of specific data available. However, there is growing evidence looking at the role of shame in EDs (Allan & Goss, 2012). These authors conclude that there is sufficient research to show that people with EDs have significantly higher levels of shame than other clinical groups (e.g., Frank, 1991), and that these levels of shame are present even in remission (Gee & Troop, 2003; Troop, Serpell, Allan, & Treasure, 2008). In a very revealing study by Cooper, Todd, and Wells (1998), they found that eating-disordered women differed from non-eating-disordered women in their levels of negative belief, which were "without exception, negative and unconditional". What is interesting about the work looking at shame in EDs is that it is unclear whether the proxies that have been used to demonstrate shame (e.g., unconditional negative beliefs) are appropriate. Moreover, empirically, the exact relationship between shame, self-disgust, and disgust is still unclear (see Powell, Simpson, & Overton, this volume). Roberts and Goldenberg (2007) discuss this debate by pointing out it is uncertain whether self-disgust is just a more severe form of shame, or whether shame and self-disgust are specific variants of disgust. These authors also propose that disgust is directed at the self when one fails to maintain certain societal standards in cultural normed behaviours that are designed to conceal our physical, animal nature, although these authors are unclear about which transgressions of cultural normed behaviours are important. In Western societies (where rates of EDs are highest), women are often caught in a double bind of being the providers of care and "required" to be attractive and slim. Furthermore, care is often translated into the provision of food and the facilitation of eating. Even in the twenty-first century, women are still the main providers of care in the home (often for children and elderly parents), but are now also pursuing careers and an external life away from the home (Orbach, 2006). It is within this context that young girls are being raised, and it is argued that these young girls are being subjected to higher expectations and increased objectification of their bodies. Disgust is very much the emotion of physical bodies, or at least that is where its roots are.

Objectification models, rooted in feminist theory, are conceptual frameworks that propose that women's bodies become objectified as "sexual objects" and this leads to an internalisation of these external viewpoints, so that women start to self-objectify. Fredrickson and Roberts (1997), using an experimental design, found evidence of a marked gender difference in levels of objectification, and also levels of disgust/shame, directed at the body. Also, within this study, they found that females were much more "apt" at being self-critical when compared to men.

What the prior discussion does highlight is how the extreme pressures of living in a twenty-four-hour media society play on the way that females feel about themselves and their bodies. There is ample evidence of how high levels of objectification of female bodies increase the proneness to experiencing marked shame/disgust towards the body, which sets the context for disordered eating patterns. Although it is unlikely that these issues directly cause EDs, they are likely to moderate any aetiological factors in their development. Moreover, there is ample research that has highlighted pervasive body dissatisfaction among females in the Western world (e.g., Striegel-Moore & Franko, 2002; Tiggemann & Slater, 2004). It will be argued that this context of population-level self-disgust of the body can become a focus when other things in the person's life are difficult, distressing, or unhappy. In other words, it does not take a great deal for a young woman to translate her negative emotions onto her body.

### *Family dynamics and childhood abuse*

As has been suggested earlier, the societal context for females experiencing their body is difficult and, at times, distressing. However, more is clearly needed for an ED to develop; otherwise, most females would have some form of ED. Within the research literature, there has been much debate over the potential role of adverse childhood events that link to EDs. Holman (2012) makes an important point about recent trends in ED research that have started to locate the basis for their understanding within the individual (e.g., biological and genetic markers) and tend to either downplay or ignore more psychological/social explanations. Often in the literature, it is discussed that EDs are the archetypal BioPsychoSocial disorder (Fox, Woodrow, & Leonard, 2012) because they clearly have all three components in their genesis (e.g., effects of starvation, distorted cognitions, objectification of female bodies). However, what has been disappointing in recent years has been the research bias towards biological factors in EDs. It continues to remain an empirical question about the influence of psychosocial factors on the developing brain in EDs, although contemporary thinking in neurology does highlight the significance of environment in shaping the brain (e.g., Roth & Sweatt, 2011).

In a recent review, Holman (2012) argues that there is sufficient evidence to suggest trauma histories are common in people with EDs, especially bulimic subtypes (e.g., Smolak & Levine, 2007). The impact of abuse on the developing self is well documented throughout the literature, and it highlights how it leaves the child with a number of overwhelming emotions, a negative view of the self, and real difficulties in maintaining interpersonal boundaries (Briere, 1996). A key emotional feature of surviving abuse is the shame and disgust that one can feel towards the body. For example, Andrews (1995) demonstrated that body shame moderates the relationship between abusive experiences (both adult and child) and depression. In a follow-up study, Andrews (1997) found that the relationship between bulimic symptomatology and childhood abuse was also moderated by bodily shame. Given some of the challenges in distinguishing between body shame and self-disgust, it is entirely possible that the emotion being described in these studies is more of a disgust emotion, rather than a shame-based emotion. The rationale for this perspective comes from the complex emotions that a person who is being abused (or has been abused) often experiences, and the emotion most often reported is disgust at how their bodies let them down (e.g., having sexual excitement resulting from the abuse) or how they feel they let themselves down (e.g., seeking abuse in order to avoid being rejected; Ainscough & Toon, 2000). These cultural transgressions are much more rooted in disgust than in shame.

However, childhood trauma can often be more complicated than just sexual and physical abuse. Holman (2012) reminds us that to achieve attachment with another is a core and essential human need; all children seek out attachments as a part of a biological drive, and it is via these attachments that the child's sense of self starts to emerge. Holman (2012) emphasises how abuse causes significant disruption/failures within attachments, and it is this that causes most of the psychological damage (in keeping with the points raised by the original attachment authors, such as Bowlby, 1969). Moreover, Kent and Waller (2000) argued that emotional abuse (e.g., criticism, neglect, and belittlement) may be stronger predictors of eating pathology than other types of trauma. Holman (2012) points out that abusers often use attachment as a means to justify the abuse and this has a "toxic" impact on the victim (e.g., "I am only doing this because you deserve it"; "you are irresistible to me"). It is through these experiences that the individual starts to internalise a very negative, critical, disgusted, attacking way of relating to the self (Greenberg et al., 1998). This problem is compounded by how trauma also disrupts the learning of emotion-regulation skills throughout childhood, which can leave the individual with a sense that their emotions are out of control and amplifies the poorly defined sense of self.

Over the last few years, the nature of these internalised "voices" has started to be explored within the literature. Dolhanty and Greenberg (2009) discussed the importance of addressing this "harsh, internal, critical voice" within treatment, and they called this the "anorexic voice". This "voice" criticises and admonishes the self for eating, and it remains an empirical question as to whether an equivalent "voice" exists within other EDs. Tierney and Fox (2010) undertook a qualitative study that looked at the "anorexic voice" by asking people to submit narratives, descriptions, and other forms of writing to describe their "voice" and their relationship with it. Following a thematic analysis of these data, the results showed that participants had a difficult relationship with their "voice", and it would berate, criticise, and emotionally hurt them. What was interesting from the data was how the participants described both positive and negative attributes of the "anorexic voice", with the former appearing to be stronger during the early stages of the ED, whilst the latter came into force once the disorder had developed. Also, despite the critical and attacking aspect of this voice, participants still felt an affiliation towards it. Interestingly, this voice did appear to induce self-disgust, but participants felt a loyalty towards it, and they often discussed how life would be empty without it. It does appear that it is better to be criticised and attacked rather than be alone and neglected.

### *Summary of self-disgust in eating disorders*

At the start of this section, it was pointed out that the relationship between shame and self-disgust is still very unclear. It may be that self-disgust is just a more severe derivative of shame, or that shame and self-disgust are complex versions of the basic emotion of disgust. We have published previously on this topic and have argued that the latter view is the correct one. There is sufficient research to suggest that there are at least five basic emotions, with disgust being one of them. Accordingly, many of the emotions that we see in everyday life may be, in fact, complex emotions that are derivatives or combinations of primary emotions (see Power & Dalgleish, 2008, for a fuller discussion).

When female body image and EDs are considered on a social level, theory and research have highlighted how females are at risk of internalising an objectification of their bodies, which focuses on both the sexual and thin-ideals of the female body. This predisposes the individual to be critical, shameful, and self-disgusted with their body. However, given that the levels of body dissatisfaction for females are generally high (e.g., Striegel-Moore & Franko, 2002; Tiggemann & Slater, 2004), there are clearly other important variables in play in the genesis of EDs. The role of abuse, in all its forms, is important in understanding EDs and has a clear link to disgust towards the self and the body. It is our clinical experience that people with EDs who have been abused often report disgust towards themselves for what has happened and how their body is seen as an object of revulsion. However, childhood negative experiences can often be more subtle in their influence, as individuals may have been criticised, humiliated, and/or neglected as a child. The internalisation of these experiences predisposes the individual to feeling unworthy, criticised, and disgusted with the self. As argued by Fox, Federici, and Power (2012), this internalisation of negative "voices" leads to the development of an internal dialogue with an ED/anorexic "voice", which continues to shame and disgust the self.

### *Multi-level models of emotion: coupling of disgust with other emotions*

So far within this chapter, disgust has been considered as a solitary emotion that is processed at a verbal level. However, this is a simplification of the emotion processes that are potentially in play within the ED. Fox and Power (2009) developed the SPAARS-ED model (see Figure 1) from the general Schematic, Propositional, Analogical, and Associative Representation Systems (SPAARS) model of emotion and emotional disorder (Power & Dalgleish, 2008). Within this model, it is argued that the ED's main function is to allow the self to avoid painful emotion (via restriction and/or bingeing/vomiting). However, somewhat ironically, this negative emotion is not completely negated by these behaviours, but subsequently becomes directed onto the body as self-disgust. This redirection of negative emotion onto the body results in a high level of revulsion towards the self and the physical body. Whilst it is, regrettably, beyond the scope of the present chapter to give a more comprehensive view of the SPAARS-ED model, we would like to recommend our

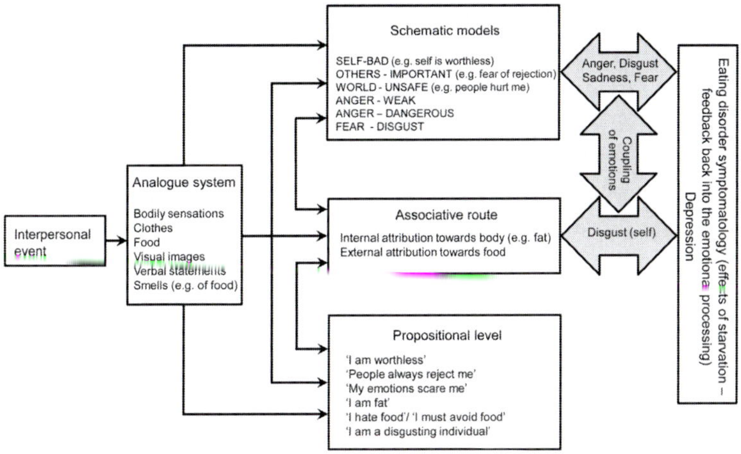


Figure 1. The SPAARS model of eating disorders (SPAARS-ED; Fox & Power, 2009).

previous chapters/papers on the subject (see Fox & Power, 2009; Fox, Federici et al., 2012).

Research has consistently highlighted that people with EDs have marked social difficulties (e.g., Treasure, Corfield, & Cardi, 2012), and these difficulties seem to be connected to beliefs about being at risk of being rejected and being worthless or bad in some way (e.g., Cooper & Hunt, 1998; Leung, Waller, & Thomas, 1999; Waller, Ohanian, Meyer, & Osman, 2000). According to the SPAARS-ED model, these beliefs are regarded as a part of a general process of cognition, which includes different forms of representations (e.g., visual, tactile, and verbal) and, therefore, above more "verbal expressible propositional concepts" (Jones, 2001). This schematic processing of information does account for the high level of complexity that is present in people with EDs, such as intellectually knowing that one is not "fat" but still "feeling fat and disgusting".

Within the SPAARS-ED model, Fox and Power (2009) argue that there are three domains of knowledge, namely about the self, others, and the world (in keeping with other cognitive authors, such as Beck et al., 1979). Across the multi-level theories of emotion, it is argued that these appraisals work on a level that is not easily translated into language (in keeping with Greenberg's theoretical notion of "emotion schemes"). However, these appraisals could be understood as

"SELF-BAD, OTHERS-IMPORTANT, and WORLD-UNSAFE", and the resulting emotions would be sadness and disgust (in keeping with the findings of Power & Tarsia, 2007; Troop et al., 2002). In other words, and as discussed throughout this chapter, the self is regarded as being "bad" or "worthless" and at high risk of being rejected by others. This places other people into an important position, where their needs are regarded as being more important, and they need to be appeased and not upset. The fear here is that the other person will find out what they are "really like" (e.g., bad/contemptible) and reject them, which leaves the world feeling unsafe and unpredictable.

Research has highlighted that the emotion of anger is a highly distressing emotion for people with an ED (e.g., Fox, 2009; Fox & Froom, 2009; Fox & Harrison, 2008; Geller, Cockell, Hewitt, Goldner, & Flett, 2000; Waller et al., 2003). From a SPAARS-ED perspective, it would be argued that anger would be appraised as being ego-dystonic and thus detached from the person's sense of self (e.g., ANGER-DANGEROUS; ANGER-THREAT-OTHERS). This ego-dystonic anger is suppressed, via restriction/bingeing–vomiting. These processes of emotion-suppression and weight loss become connected over time, which can lead to these emotions becoming "coupled". Fox and colleagues (Fox, 2009; Fox & Harrison, 2008; Fox et al., 2013) have found some experimental evidence of emotional coupling in EDs. In an initial pilot study, Fox and Harrison (2008), using a sample of female students with bulimic symptoms, demonstrated a significant increase in levels of disgust in the eating pathology group after an anger-induction task, when compared to the control group. Fox et al. (2013) undertook a similar study with a *bona fide* AN group and matched controls. Within this study, participants completed anger, disgust, and body size estimation measures. The results showed that following the anger induction, the AN participants reported significantly higher levels in disgust and body size estimations compared to controls.

Although this work is still very much in its infancy, there is a growing evidence base to suggest that disgust, self-disgust, and anger are working in tandem within EDs. Interestingly, within the Fox et al. (2013) paper, they also presented data that showed that the AN participants had significantly higher negative self-beliefs (e.g., "I am worthless", "I am bad") than controls. Furthermore, these negative self-beliefs correlated strongly ($r$ = .63) with state disgust (taken from the Basic Emotion Scale, Power, 2006a) and this is, to our best knowledge, the first time that negative beliefs have been statistically connected to the emotion of disgust. This does offer some supportive evidence for the proposal presented at the start of this chapter that negative self-beliefs may be significantly related to the emotion of disgust. What is interesting from a SPAARS-ED perspective is the relationship between disgust and self-disgust. As discussed previously, the SPAARS-ED model takes the perspective that self-disgust and shame are derivatives of the basic emotion of disgust, and it is argued that it is via self-disgust (originating from difficult childhood experiences), and the objectification of the female body, that the person starts to become disgusted with their body and, importantly, with food. In other words, pure disgust that is directed towards the body and food only comes once the ED has started.

Importantly, the SPAARS-ED model was developed on research undertaken with females, and it is unclear how it applies to males with an eating disorder. Fernandez-Aranda and colleagues (2004) discuss that male eating disorders may be the product of quite different psychological processes, and so it does remain an empirical question on how applicable the SPAARS-ED model is to males. This is in keeping with the research presented at the start of this chapter and with the shame-based models (e.g., Allan & Goss, 2012). Although it remains an empirical question, it is our contention that much of the work that is presented as shame may, in fact, be more appropriately viewed as self-disgust. It is our view that this would help explain the intensity of the emotion that is so often seen in our clients when they talk about food and their bodies.

## *Clinical implications*

### *Assessment and formulation*

One of the main weaknesses of contemporary psychological treatments of EDs is that they have an almost "folklore" approach to emotion. Emotion is regarded as a unitary concept, with very little nuance between the emotions being considered (Fox & Power, 2009). Given that attempts to understand basic emotion functioning goes back to the Ancient Greek philosophers, it is argued here that viewing emotions from a unitary perspective is a far too simplistic approach to any theoretical account of psychopathology. As has been seen throughout this chapter, each emotion has its own potential role in understanding EDs and disgust seems to be particularly important for these disorders. The SPAARS-ED model offers a possible architecture for understanding both the underlying emotion difficulties and how this manifests itself as an ED. The results from the coupled emotion studies highlight how certain emotions, such as anger, may influence how the body is viewed and create further disgust, which would have a deleterious impact upon mood. This can be an important formulatory point, because the clinician may use diaries to highlight that other emotions, such as anger, may lead to an increase in preoccupation with one's body or other ED symptoms.

Although the issue has not been fully discussed in this chapter (as it has been discussed elsewhere within this volume; see Alanazi, Powell, & Power, this volume), disgust is seen as a key emotion within depression (see Fox & Power, 2009; Overton, Markland, Taggart, Bagshaw, & Simpson, 2008). It has long been noted that depression is a key co-morbid condition with EDs with rates ranging from forty per cent to near eighty per cent (e.g., Lewinsohn, Striegel-Moore, & Seeley, 2000; Santos, Richards, & Bleckley, 2007; Zaider, Johnson, & Cockell, 2000). In the formulation of a client's difficulties, it can be valuable to describe how working with an individual on their body image problems may actually leave the individual more likely to experience shame/disgust towards the body and, via the emotion of disgust, this may lead to an increase in depression. In this situation, it may well be important to undertake some initial work in developing a compassionate approach to the self first, before attempting to unpick body image problems (as discussed by Allan & Goss, 2012). In saying this, understanding depression in EDs is a complex task, because depressed mood may also be a product of being in a starved state for those clients who are significantly underweight.

In keeping with the Robert Leahy (2003) and Steven Hayes (e.g., Hayes, Strosahl, & Wilson, 2003) perspectives, the SPAARS-ED approach acknowledges that, as human beings, we search for meaning in our lives. However, as clinicians, we often collude with our clients' search for happiness that often hides the fact that emotional responses to deeply difficult and traumatic events are healthy and normal. Key emotions within these normal responses are shame, guilt, and disgust, and the client will be extremely sensitive to the clinician inadvertently shaming them during their sessions. Equally, having a formulation that highlights the role of disgust in EDs allows for a shared formulation to be developed whereby normal emotional processes are understood.

*Intervention*

Often, our clients present with an avoidance of negative or painful emotions, and one of the most powerful interventions for the clinicians is to be compassionate, thoughtful, and "containing" of these emotions. This allows the client to accept his or her emotions, transform those that are maladaptive, and learn to experience and process emotions in a more productive manner.

In recent years, the "anorexic voice" has started to be considered more fully in psychological therapies. The interplay of different internal "voices" is often at the heart of psychological distress and, as previously argued, is driven by self-disgust. Tierney and Fox (2010) found evidence that, initially, the voice was regarded as a "critical friend", but it slowly becomes critical and attacking, leaving the individual feeling powerless and disgusted with the self. Dolhanty and Greenberg (2009) discuss that one of the most powerful ways to address this critical anorexic voice is to use two chair dialogues. Fox, Federici et al. (2012) discuss that, in this activity, the "anorexic voice" and the experiencing person are placed in opposing chairs and the client engages in a discussion with the "anorexic voice". Through this experiential task, the client is encouraged to explore the anorexic voice's perspective, including what are its "needs and wishes" for the individual. A key part of this approach is that the experiencing self is invited to respond to the "anorexic voice", and they are asked to express how the anorexic voice makes them feel. Thus, the aim is to allow the anorexic voice to soften its critical, attacking stance and thereby help the individual identify their organismic, emotional needs.

Returning to a SPAARS perspective, Power and Dalgleish (1997, 2008) discussed that there are both fast and slow change processes in therapy. According to this theoretical perspective, there are two principal routes to emotion generation, one that requires conscious cognition, whilst the other is an over-learned associative route. This second route takes longer to change than the cognitive route, because it works on a much more automatic and unconscious level. Accordingly, pure cognitive approaches will have little impact on this associative route to emotion, and it is argued that therapy will need to work directly with the emotion of disgust (e.g., as it is directed at the body). Power and Dalgleish (1997, 2008) argue that exposure and the use of "behavioural experiments" are much more useful than purely cognitive or linguistic methods for associative route change. This would enable the person to start to re-learn, via the associative route, a non-disgust emotion attached to his or her body. One such approach could be attentional training on body distortion, whereby the individual is trained to attend to parts of their body they do not dislike (by using a mirror) in order to help the person gain a more balanced perspective of their body (Jansen, Nederkoorn, & Mulkens, 2005). Within the SPAARS understanding of ED, it is argued that this would allow the individual to learn to associate alternative emotions with their bodies and, thereby, reduce the relation of disgust towards the body. Indeed, this may be an important theoretical point about why exposure work to new or banned foods may help break down the associated disgust attached to the foods. In an interesting commentary on the role of disgust in psychopathology, Meunier and Tolin (2009) argue that disgust takes longer to habituate than fear, because it involves the parasympathetic nervous system rather than the sympathetic nervous system.

## *Summary and conclusions*

The study of disgust within eating disorders has had a chequered history, as the initial results from research showed an inconsistent picture of whether general disgust played a role within their aetiology or maintenance. However, the research on self-disgust/shame in eating disorders has been a much more promising avenue of work, as it suggests a consistent pattern of self-disgust originating from abuse, neglect, and/or self-criticism. These are important findings, as it may be that understanding these self-disgust feelings leads to the development of new psychological treatments, such as emotion-focused therapies. This chapter has shown that there are a number of key empirical questions that still need to be addressed, such as the relationship between shame and self-disgust for this population. It is our hope that this chapter will inspire both further research and the development of new emotion-based treatments, as this client group remains one of the hardest to treat, with only a comparative few making a full recovery from their eating disorder.

CHAPTER TEN

# Varieties of disgust in self-harm

*Outi Benson, Zoë V. R. Boden, and Diego Vitali*

## *Introduction*[1]

Self-harm can be defined as self-administered, non-accidental injury to one's own body without suicidal intent. Whilst self-harm by overdosing on medicines, such as paracetamol, is also very common, what we go on to say in this chapter should be read as applying only to cutting, burning, scratching, punching, or otherwise damaging the skin. Overdosing, though it often co-exists with these other forms of self-harm in an individual, has a different function and phenomenology.

Self-harming is reported within both clinical and non-clinical populations (Gratz, Conrad, & Roemer, 2002), and is increasing among adolescents and young adults (Fortune & Hawton, 2005). The extant literature explores a number of reasons why individuals engage in self-harm, suggesting that it acts as a method of releasing, expressing, or regulating distress, it blocks memories/flashbacks, and/or it helps the individual manage distressing dissociative experiences (e.g., Briere & Gil, 1998; Gratz, 2003; Linehan, 1993). Self-harm appears to both down-regulate and control overwhelming feelings, and to up-regulate them, allowing the individual to "feel something" after a period of "feeling numb" (Horne & Csipke, 2009). Symbolic meanings of self-harm have also been posited, such as communicating or recording inner pain (Crowe & Bunclark, 2000; McLane, 1996; Milia, 2000; Miller, 1997).

A systematic review of quantitative empirical studies of self-harm showed that those who self-harm find identifying, understanding, and expressing their emotions more difficult than individuals who do not self-harm, and they experience higher levels of depression, anxiety, and hostility (Fliege, Lee, Grimm, & Klapp, 2009). Individuals who self-harm have been shown to have higher levels of negative emotions, including fear, hostility, guilt, and sadness, than those who have never self-harmed (Brown, Williams, & Collins, 2007). It has been shown that emotions differ before and immediately after self-harm. Chapman and Dixon-Gordon (2007) showed that anger was the most prominent reported emotion before an act of self-harm, whereas relief and other more positive emotional experiences were found after acts of self-harm. However, we have not been able to find any research studies examining explicitly the potential relationship between disgust and self-harm, and the questions of whether and how disgust and self-directed disgust are involved in self-harm remain unanswered.

Evidence does suggest that individuals who self-harm experience a higher degree of self-oriented negative emotion, for example feelings and thoughts of self-punishment, self-hatred, self-criticism, and self-loathing. Self-criticism has been shown both to motivate acts of self-harm and to distinguish those who harm themselves from those who do not. Glassman, Weierich, Hooley, Deliberto, and Nock (2007) found that self-criticism mediated between childhood abuse and self-harm, while Hooley, Ho, Slater, and Lockshin (2010) reported that individuals who self-harmed had significantly stronger self-critical beliefs than controls in a study of pain perception and self-harm. These studies measure a broad construct of self-criticism, which encompasses both a global sense of inferiority with respect to others and a persistent sense of failure with respect to subjective standards (Thompson & Zuroff, 2003). Self-directed anger and the desire to punish oneself are also known motivations for self-harm (Klonsky & Glenn, 2009; Nock & Prinstein, 2004; Zila & Kiselica, 2001). However, though self-focused hatred has been reported to accompany self-revulsion (Powell, Overton, & Simpson, 2014), it is not at all obvious that these more generally self-critical feelings and cognitions amount to self-focused disgust, in so far as this incorporates a feeling element that is qualitatively similar to the basic emotional experience of disgust (as suggested by Powell, Simpson, & Overton, this volume).

In this chapter, we propose to explore how self-disgust may manifest as part of the experience of self-harm. We will do this through analysis of first-person testimony on the experience of self-harm, combined with a focused literature review of recent work on disgust and self-disgust that seemed relevant to the reported experiences. After describing our methodology, we will start by giving an account of self-disgust drawn from existing literature. We will note that, in some senses at least, it seems rare and arguably even impossible to feel disgust immediately before an act of self-harm (though we concede the possibility that trait self-disgust influences the behaviour). We will stop short of saying that state self-disgust does not contribute to self-harm, however, and develop a notion of self-disgust that reflects what our participants experience prior to harming themselves. We will conclude by discussing experiences of self-disgust following self-harm, and close with a note on suicide and its potential relationship with self-disgust.

## *Our studies*

This chapter is based on secondary analyses of data from two studies. First, and primarily, we draw on a mixed-methods study that explored experiences of self-harm (Horne & Csipke, 2009). This study was conducted in two phases: the first was an online questionnaire (with structured and open-ended questions); the second, a series of in-depth email interviews. Participants to the questionnaire phase were 827 people with experience of self-harm. Of these, 37 consented to take part in the interview phase. The study did not ask directly about self-disgust, but did ask participants to describe their experiences before, during, and after acts of self-harm. The majority of participants in the online questionnaire phase and all participants in the email interviews referred primarily to experiences of self-cutting, although other forms of self-harm were also mentioned. Data were originally analysed using grounded theory. Second, two case studies were drawn from an ongoing interview study that explores experiences of people who have made a suicide attempt, their significant others, and those bereaved by suicide. These case studies were of individuals who had a history of self-harm and who discussed their experience of self-harm with us in some detail. All names used here are pseudonyms.

This chapter uses these studies as a springboard to explore experiences of self-disgust in self-harm. Using the original online, email, and interview data, a secondary thematic analysis was conducted following the procedure outlined in Braun and Clarke (2006). This analysis purposively searched for participants' implicit and explicit experiences of self-disgust and then analysed those occurrences inductively. Additionally, our analysis explored how participants experienced the three phases of the self-harm process; before, during, and after an act of self-harm, specifically focusing on how their emotional state shifted across the experience. We also looked at the other emotions that were experienced alongside feelings of self-disgust, and for descriptions of self-loathing, feeling repulsed, or other language that indicated a feeling of disgust was present, but not explicitly identified. Finally, we attended to how participants attributed feelings of disgust, including when they attributed those feelings to others. These findings were then interrogated in light of the existing literature on disgust, and we developed an account of how self-disgust is experienced in the context of self-harm.

## *Definitions of disgust and self-disgust: a brief review*

In its primary form, disgust implies a set of behavioural and physiological rejection responses against contamination or incorporation of contaminant material (Rozin & Fallon, 1987; Rozin, Haidt, & McCauley, 2008). It involves a sudden arousal of feelings, physiological changes, and action impulses that aim to prevent the threatening object from crossing the body boundary or from spreading within it (e.g., nausea, drop in blood pressure, vomit/gag reflexes, pulling away, and so on). We refer to this kind of disgust as "basic disgust".

Feelings of nausea and expressive behaviours related to basic disgust can sometimes also be elicited in response to morally offensive objects. We refer to this as "moral disgust". According to Rozin and colleagues (2008), moral disgust entails a sense of revulsion mixed with anger against moral violations such as stealing, harming others, betrayal, and so on. The relationship between moral disapproval and basic disgust had already been noted by Darwin (1872/1989), who wrote about spitting and its use in the expression of contempt. Though it seems to function chiefly as a culture-specific mechanism, which aims to avoid immorality and thus to maintain a certain "purity" with respect to rules, ideals, and taboos shared with others (Oaten, Stevenson, & Case, 2009), its connection with basic disgust goes beyond feelings and expressive behaviours. For example, Zhong, Strejcek, and Sivanathan (2010) observed that people who are physically clean pass more severe moral judgements than people who are dirty. Basic and moral disgust may also be directed towards the self (Power & Dalgleish, 2008), and can be both functional and dysfunctional. However, it has been hypothesised that where the part of the self that is felt to be disgusting is permanent or central to the self-concept, feelings of self-disgust are maladaptive (Powell, Simpson & Overton, 2013).

We will begin the exploration of our data in light of these concepts.

## *Self-disgust in self-harm*

### *The rarity of experiences of disgust and self-disgust in self-harm*

> By the time I started self-harming I'd already been severely depressed for a year—no self-esteem whatsoever, steadily increasing self-disgust, no sense of any kind of future, no particular enjoyment of anything, getting slowly more hung up on the idea of suicide. And the thing is … I was only fourteen/fifteen. I had no frame of reference to understand how I was feeling. (Francesca)

The above quotation from a participant to an online survey is very rare, because it refers to "self-disgust" directly. In the first-person accounts of motivation for self-harm collected for the first phase of our study, the word "disgust" is barely used at all; 25 participants (out of 827) talked about their experiences of feeling disgusting either before or after they self-harmed. Additionally, a further 33 participants described the actual or imagined responses of their family, friends, and the general public as including "disgust". Of those in the survey who described feeling disgust about themselves or their actions, only 2 label the feelings that lead to their self-harm as an experience of "self-disgust". The other 23 survey participants described feeling disgusted with themselves *after* they self-harmed. In the second-phase email interviews, explicit talk about disgust was also relatively unusual. There were just 5 interview participants (out of 37) who explicitly identified feeling self-disgust. In all these cases, the experience was part of the feelings *before* self-harming. For 1 of these 5, disgust was additionally one of the feelings that occurred in response to her self-harming.

The meaning of the word "disgust" varies depending on the context, but it appears always to incorporate the following dimensions: a sense of revulsion (Rozin et al., 2008) and the presence of a harmful, even dangerous, contaminant that is to be repelled. In this sense, then, to say "I am disgusting" would be to say: "Beware of me; you should repel me immediately". Perhaps it is no surprise, then, that participants would hesitate to use the word "disgust" of themselves, even in the anonymity of an online response. But it may also not be used because, for most, it does not capture the essence of their self-experience in the moments before acts of self-harm. The use made of the word by the 5 participants is consistent with the idea that basic and moral self-disgust, though we hypothesise that they may contribute to the emotional state that precedes self-harm in a causal way, are not directly part of it.

## Explanation of the *absence* of disgust-related expressions in descriptions of the state preceding self-harm

Reflecting on our own experience, we found it strange that the very idea of drawing a knife to open one's own skin did not make the participants "sick to their stomachs"; in other words, that it did not elicit a basic disgust response. The two case studies from our suicide research elaborated this phenomenon further for us. The first participant was surprised by her self-harm, saying:

> when I see my scars now, it's so weird to think that that's my arm because I am so squeamish, like I am the most squeamish person in the world towards blood and cutting and I'd never in a million years would have thought that I would ever do that. (Eva)

The second participant said that she doesn't feel disgust in response to wounds, corpses, vomit, and so on, and has never had to turn away from anything of this kind because she has felt she can no longer bear looking at it. She has never felt, and doesn't know what it is like to feel, disgust in the true sense; she has never felt sickened by bad news, never experienced a physical sensation of disgust. The lack of disgust response to the idea and the act of self-harm can therefore be either a more permanent feature of the experience of those who harm themselves, or associated only with the emotional state immediately preceding acts of self-harm. This absence of basic disgust, as we shall see, is derivative of a more general condition in which certain kinds of emotional response are radically diminished.

Both basic and moral disgust can be characterised as reactions with a violent start during which the feelings of revulsion "well up". This is followed by a period in which they first abate and then continue in a more subdued form, as the associated avoidance behaviours are carried through. It is just such flexible emotional reactions that seem to be impossible when people harm themselves.

> … I feel numb—physically and emotionally. I get in a state where I feel separate from everything. As if a thick piece of plexi-glass separates me from the world. Sounds are muted, I can't focus on conversations, I don't feel things I touch. I can't feel my own skin. The self-harm brings me back. I usually don't feel the initial damage, but at some point, I feel the pain. Getting myself to bleed also brings me back into the world. (Lisa)

People who self-harm are, prior to the act, either in a state of high arousal, in which overwhelming anger, anxiety, or a mixture of unidentifiable emotions is typically experienced, or they are depersonalised. The DSM-5 (American Psychiatric Association, 2013, p. 302) defines episodes of depersonalisation as "characterised by a feeling of unreality or detachment from, or unfamiliarity with, one's whole self or from aspects of the self", symptoms of which include emotional or physical numbing. Persistent or recurrent depersonalisation may merit the diagnosis of depersonalisation/derealisation disorder of which "the core complaint is a persistent and disturbing feeling that experience of oneself and the world has become empty, lifeless, and not fully real" (Medford, 2012, p. 139).

In a study by Phillips and colleagues (2001), the subjective reports of blunted disgust responses to aversive stimuli in depersonalised patients were shown to correlate with "reduced neural responses in emotion-sensitive regions, and increased responses in regions associated with emotion regulation" (p. 145). This finding has been repeated for responses to facial expressions (Sierra, Senior, Phillips, & David, 2006). In both studies, the *recognition* of the stimuli or the expression *as* disgusting or disgust was not impaired: the depersonalised participants understood what they saw but did not respond emotionally to it. Interestingly, Sierra and colleagues (2006) observed that judgements of the *intensity* of the emotional expression were also affected. The experience of disgust may also be suspended in highly aroused emotional states. A study by Borg and de Jong (2012) found that sexually aroused women showed diminished disgust responses. Emotions that are associated with life threatening situations, such as anxiety, fear, and panic are also associated with high arousal. Such emotions have been found to have a significant association with depersonalisation, though the relationship is complex (Sierra, Medford, Wyatt, & David, 2012). Anger, associated with fight rather than flight, is another such aroused emotion, and we have evidence from one of our suicide research participants, who described having to make herself angry in order to overcome a gag reflex and continue her suicide attempt. Some instances of anger towards the self before an attack on the self can therefore be what Tamir and colleagues (Tamir & Ford, 2012; Tamir, Mitchell, & Gross, 2008) describe as active manipulation of one's own emotions for instrumental benefits.

In our view, self-harm rarely takes place without at least some degree of depersonalisation being evident. Depersonalisation is known to be associated with emotional response deficits (Medford, 2012; Monde, Ketay, Giesbrecht, Braun, & Simeon, 2013). In fact, it seems plausible that the predicament in which self-harm becomes part of the person's emotion-regulation system is one where some degree of depersonalisation has become engrained, preventing tacit, non-verbal understanding of emotions or the integration of such understanding with explicit, language-based representation (Horne & Csipke, 2009). These emotional response deficits could also account for the relative absence of disgust in self-harm.

## Explanation of the *presence* of disgust-related expressions in descriptions of the state preceding self-harm

Yet it does not seem right to say categorically that self-disgust is not part of the experience before self-harm. For one thing, a few of our participants did use the word, or words that evoke the notion of disgust such as "sick", "revolting", or "messed up" to describe their experience. For another, on a closer inspection, whether such words are used or not, the phenomenology of self-harm involved experiences that are both structurally very disgust-like, and are directed towards the self. In the next section, we develop a notion of self-disgust that it is possible to experience even in the presence of the kinds of emotional deficit associated with depersonalisation. It does not rely on the person's capacity to have the kinds of feelings or responses characteristic of basic disgust but retains many features of the complex emotion of disgust nevertheless.

## *Self-disgust as a precursor of (some instances of) self-harm: "integral disgust"*

In the self-harm study, we found that there were a number of experiences we began to think of as a variety of self-disgust, which we call "integral self-disgust". Participants described these experiences as happening before they self-harmed, and as directly contributing towards their self-harm.

### *Aspects of "integral self-disgust" in self-harm: emotions (and thoughts) as "other"*

Derrida (1981) described objects of disgust as those which cannot be assimilated as part of oneself, that is, those which are "other". The disgusting thing is that which cannot be "digested", the irrepresentable that can only be "vomited" (Derrida, 1981, pp. 23–24). The participants of the self-harm study who used disgust-related words (and many participants besides) experienced a part of themselves, specifically their emotions and related thoughts, as something that could not be assimilated into the self. Their emotional experience was something that could not be reflected upon or mastered, it was unapproachable, unknowable, unrecognisable, unacknowledged, uncontained, amorphous, unidentifiable, disordered, and something that could not be articulated, or made sense of. These experiences included:

#### Overwhelming, unidentifiable emotions and thoughts

Emotions are experienced as overwhelming and intense, so much so they cannot be recognised: "the feelings were so strong they couldn't even be identified as emotions" (Joanna). Participants struggled to identify the emotions they were feeling: "I couldn't put a name to any of the emotions" (Natalie). Emotions and emotional thoughts seemed "messy" and "muddled", a mass of different, jumbled-up feelings which were difficult to separate or name: "sometimes I'd feel lots of different emotions at once, and I couldn't work out what they were. I'd want to scream and cry and shout and be angry all at the same time" (Natalie).

### Feeling out of control

Feeling out of control involves an experience of a lack of autonomy and agency over one's internal states. Emotions and thoughts are experienced as unstable and rapidly shifting: "like all the feelings/thoughts had been flying around too fast to catch or contain" (Joanna). This is experienced as very frightening: "I feel I've lost control of my mind. When I feel out of control I completely panic" (Vicki).

### Feeling uncontained or boundary-less

The self begins to feel less contained and coherent as the person experiences a loss of agency and control over her thoughts and feelings (her "mind"). The self begins to be experienced as if no longer bounded by the body, but as uncontained or boundary-less emotional turmoil: "I would begin to feel as if my mind had come adrift from the body, that the body did not even exist and I had become just this flying mass of mental turmoil" (Joanna).

## *Aspects of "integral self-disgust" in self-harm: a threat to self*

These un-assimilable feelings and thoughts about an aspect of the self are experienced as a threat to the integrity of the self as a whole: "the other" invades, contaminates, threatens to break the body or explode out of it. The felt body-border is under attack.

### Overwhelming emotions threaten the integrity of the self

The intensity and unmanageability of the emotions are experienced as a threat to the integrity of the body-self. Participants feel as though their emotions will break their bodies: "before cutting I feel as if I'm going to explode" (Carly); "The emotions I used to feel used to be so strong and somehow untameable that I felt my body was not strong enough to contain them" (Joanna).

## Feeling of fragmenting, disintegrating, or being scattered

Experiencing emotions as threatening to the integrity of the body-self leads to feelings of becoming fragmented, disintegrating, or being scattered: "I felt like I was fragmenting into nothingness" (Joanna); "I feel like my body is all 'bitty', like it's all wee [little] squares joined together" (Carly).

As already noted, a threat of harm to the organism is part of the experience of basic disgust, and arguably also moral disgust. Just as with other forms of disgust, the threat creates a need to act in order to protect the organism and/or others:

> Feeling compelled to harm was a very physical sensation for me. I'd feel really tense and overwound, like something inside me has been cracked up to breaking point and was going to explode or snap if I didn't do something to defuse it … how I was feeling was very dangerous—like carrying it around and leaving it undealt it wasn't an option because if I did I would fracture under the strain. (Francesca)

We suggest that, together, these experiences amount to a variety of disgust which we have called "integral disgust". This type of disgust is basic in the sense that it is experienced pre-reflectively, yet without being derivative of what we've called "basic disgust". Our concept of "integral disgust" bears some resemblance to Mary Douglas's analysis of dirt as "matter out of place" (1966/2002, p. 36), in so far as disgust is a reaction to dirtiness understood as a breach of proper, orderly relations between things. It also echoes Baron's (2011, p. 287) suggestion that there may be "something like disgust that is a reaction to disorder and messiness, to things not being whole or not working properly". He cites Lamb (1989), who argues that this disgust-like response is part of moral development in young children. Lamb (1993) observed that two-year-olds showed particular interest in, and became distressed about, flawed objects, like a broken toy, as they became increasingly aware of moral standards and norms. Similar descriptions of disgust can be found in the classic work *On Obsession* by the psychiatrist Straus (1968). Discussing the context of contamination obsessions, Stanghellini and Muscelli (2007) turn to Straus, who argued that disgust is the central emotion in this psychopathology. Of importance to our analysis is Straus's description of what can lead to disgust feelings. He saw disgust as a response to loss of integrity, loss of form, fragmentation, loss of unity, and loss of a neat shape. Similarly relevant is the idea of disgust as an emotion evolved to defend the body-boundary, to resist the "mixing of the self's substance with the substance of another" (Rozin et al., 2008, p. 770). The perceived dangerousness of the emotions experienced by people who self-harm relates to a felt threat to the boundary around the body-self, a threat to the very existence of it.

Within the context of self-harm, this type of integral disgust is self-oriented. The pre-reflective experience of self, as it is typically encountered in action as a "fitting" and "functioning" part of the totality of the world and others, is disrupted. In the context of obsessions, Straus was describing the breakdown of material objects—the world around the individual—but in our analysis of self-harm, the same can be said for the experience of the self, particularly in its emotional aspect. It is no longer unified, neat, and clearly formed, and so the individual responds with repulsion and disgust towards themselves. An analogy might be a reaction to seeing a broken ankle that sits at an unnatural angle, or features that are deformed and disproportionate. These cannot be encountered as part of ordinary, active, bodily engagement with the world, and a disruption is created in tacit understanding of the ankle or features, which are experienced as unrepresentable (they cannot be initially understood or communicated). Typically, one doesn't well up with nausea—although one might, and then the experience would be mixed with basic disgust—but shudders and seeks to turn away. In the experiences preceding self-harm, however, the object of disgust is a self that is "messed up", disordered, failing to function, and ill-fitting, and turning away is impossible. Taking the place of the upwelling of reactive, physiological arousal and the associated feeling that is part of basic and moral (self-)disgust is instead a stagnant sense of frustration. A sense of being stuck is part of the experience and what is sought is release.

> Sometimes, feeling so numb frustrates me, and it gets out of control. I get really irritable and upset, which sounds completely contradictive, as I just said I didn't feel anything. I don't know. It's hard to explain. … I probably sound disgusting[ly] inarticulate. (Esther)

### *"Integral self-disgust" and the function of self-harm: order, mastery, and function*

Participants described a number of ways their self-harm acted to manage the experience of integral disgust. Where integral self-disgust was a feeling of dysfunction, being out of control, and being about to explode with the pressure of unwieldy, messy emotions, self-harm brings about order, control, release, and a feeling of integrity. The outcomes of self-harm our participants described were achievements both in managing the disordered aspect of integral disgust, and the accompanying feeling of threatened integrity.

### Ordering emotions by making them visible

Self-harm acts as a transformative process that turns unidentifiable, messy, or jumbled emotions into something visible, tangible, and nameable, as wounds and scars: "[I'll] be so overwhelmed with disgust, shame, embarrassment, rage, and pure hatred so harming myself becomes a way of showing that" (Carly). The self-harm act "catches" emotions that were previously felt to be "untameable" and amorphous; the wound, scar, and/or blood becomes a representation of the experience that can be attended to, contemplated, and something that the individual can act upon. Emotions thereby become understandable to that individual and others. Of course, *how* they are understood is then a secondary issue that will be discussed below.

### Helping the self become functional

Self-harm is experienced as a way to gain clarity and order over thoughts and feelings, and thereby allow the mind to "work" properly: "there was that feeling of mental clarity and focus again" (Francesca); "it would seem to bring my mind back in focus" (Joanna). Participants report that self-harm allows them to behave normally, and to function again, where before self-harm this was impossible as they were overwhelmed with emotion: "it would … make me feel more able to function and think clearly and rationalise my thoughts" (Abbey); "if I cut, I'll start 'feeling' and 'working' again. My body will start and my brain can function" (Cat).

### Providing a feeling of being in control

Where emotions are experienced as "other" and out of control, the individual attempts to gain mastery over them: "I'm feeling things that are too strong such as anger or upset and so I cut to control those things" (Lucy). Self-harm acts as a way for some people to control those overwhelming, amorphous feelings, but also provides a behaviour that itself can be controlled. Self-harm is an exercise in agency and control that counters feelings of being out of control, messy, and disordered: "I found self-harm a comforter, something that I was in control of" (Vicki).

## *"Integral self-disgust" and the function of self-harm: releasing the threat and a sense of integrity*

### Releasing the unwanted part from the self

The feeling before the act of self-harm was often described as one of unbearable tension within the body, such that the body may explode at any point. The amorphous emotional state is understood to be dangerous and threatening to the integrity of the self (like any disgust-object), and, therefore, the appropriate response (following Derrida's 1981 analysis of disgust) is to try to purge that emotional state from the self: "The hatred that was directly inwards has now been dispelled from my body" (Carly). Through the act of self-harm, the messy emotions are acted out upon the body in order to expel them: "I'm making a mess of my body as it takes away the mess in my head" (Cat). In turn, this is experienced as a felt sense of release, and relief in the body, that comforts and pacifies: "self-harm seems to calm me down" (Vicki). Nearly half of participants from the online questionnaire ($N = 815$) reported these feelings of release or relief following an act of self-harm (46.5%; $n = 379$).

### Providing a feeling of containment and a sense of integrity

Where overwhelming feelings led to a sense of losing bodily and psychic integrity, self-harm seems to act in the opposite way. It draws the person's attention towards the surfaces of their body: "Self-harming kinda defined the edges of my body and made it clear that I was here and I had these boundaries" (Francesca). The pain, when it arrives, is experienced as a positive achievement because it offers a way to attend to and confirm the body boundary: "the pain on my skin acted as a physical reminder that there was a firm boundary, that I had, was finite, contained" (Joanna). A sense of integrity after self-harm comes from a feeling of being a defined object in space rather than a "flying mass of mental turmoil" (Joanna).

Through these ways, self-harm is understood to order, control, and master painful and overwhelming emotions, thereby allowing the self to function in a normal way, and to release those dangerous emotions from the body and provide a sense of containment, and bodily and psychic integrity. The body border feels secure once more.

In some cases, we noticed that the same overwhelming, amorphous feelings that were seen as destructive to the self could also be viewed as a threat to others. Participants spoke about harming themselves in order to not harm someone else. In these cases, self-harm comes to be seen as a "non-destructive" way to manage this threat: "I've taken it out on myself, so it no longer feels as if I'm going to explode or take it out on someone or something else" (Carly). Self-harm, therefore, is understood as a way to purge the overwhelming feelings of integral disgust: the feeling that the emotional self is disordered, dysfunctional, and dangerous to the self and to others, and must therefore be rejected.

To summarise, the internal emotional state experienced before an act of self-harm—while not disgust in a basic emotional sense—is akin to a disgusting object; it is irrepresentable, intrusive, and threatens the felt body-border, it needs to be confined, repelled, or fought off in order to avoid disintegration. The disgust experienced towards this project is of a kind that is a reaction to messiness, disorder, and dysfunction—in our terminology, "integral self-disgust". Though experienced as "other", the disgusting object is a part of the self, and cannot be easily separated off. Self-harm appears to manage this experience of self-disgust both by affecting the object of disgust (regulating the emotional state) and by transforming the emotional mess into an entity (the "cut", the "burn", the wound) that can then be understood. As a visible manifestation of hitherto intangible and uncontrollable mental turmoil, though an injury would be the kind of thing that might occasion a disgust response, a wound is typically not disgusting to the self-harming individual—at least not at the outset. However, self-disgust can be felt soon after self-harm.

## *Self-disgust after self-harm*

Self-harm appears to be a disgust response (integral self-disgust) to intense and overwhelming emotions which transforms that part of the self which is disgusting and unknowable into something tangible and visible, which can be recognised and understood by the individual and others. However, *how* the self-harm is to be understood is context dependent. During an experience of integral disgust, self-harming behaviour appears to be the only way to avoid disintegration or annihilation of the self, for example a suicide attempt: "the fear that if you don't express it in some way like self harm then it will come out in a more dangerous way, such as a serious suicide attempt" (Olivia). Harming the self is an extreme attempt to represent the irrepresentable, to objectify and control the overwhelming emotional experience. During the act of self-harm, basic and moral disgust must be "suspended", but afterwards, the capacity for feeling is returned (Horne & Csipke, 2009), and with it both again become possible.

With the renewed possibility for feeling, including feeling disgusted with the self, the individual is able to better reflect on (and articulate) her feelings, as represented by her injuries. However, sometimes the wounds do not elicit a compassionate response to her inner turmoil, but instead visually represent the disgusting, messy internal state she has been experiencing: "I can look down at myself and say 'yes, you are a shit person, and this just proves it'" (Carly). In addition, in this new post-harming state, the person who has harmed often assumes the perspective of the other, and experiences the self-conscious moral emotions; guilt, shame, and (moral) self-disgust, as well as self-directed anger. In the online questionnaire ($N = 815$), feeling hatred, anger, or disgust towards oneself after an act of self-harm was reported by 12.3% ($n = 100$) of participants, while 25% ($n = 204$) reported feelings of shame, guilt, or embarrassment: "I feel more relieved but also more guilty and sometimes disgusted with myself" (Vicki). It is unsurprising that we found feelings of self-disgust were experienced alongside other moral, self-conscious emotions, given that self-disgust has been conceptualised as a self-conscious emotion in its own right, and has been theorised to co-exist with shame, embarrassment, and guilt (Roberts & Goldenberg, 2007).

However, a lot of the talk about "disgust" in the online questionnaire was attributed to family and friends ($n = 35$). Self-harming individuals often face the real or imagined emotions of others who learn (or may learn) about their behaviour. This can include shock, fear, anger, and disgust (Gardner, 2001). In this study, disgust was either the imagined response, should the significant other find out about the self-harm, or the perceived actual response. For example: "My last boyfriend told me I disgusted him and he left me" (Participant ID: 432). When the significant other is perceived as responding with disgust to the self-harm, in this case both emotionally and in his behaviour (the boyfriend rejects her because she is disgusting), this evaluation is internalised and the self is viewed as morally disgusting. Similarly: "Sometimes I'll tell my best friend, but she was pretty disgusted when she first found out, only because she cares but it did make me feel more of a freak" (Participant ID: 496). Here, revealing her self-harm to her friend resulted in what she understood as a disgust response, which made her feel like "a freak", someone who is different and cannot be understood or assimilated into the social group. Thus, through self-harm and others' real or imagined negative response to it, integral self-disgust (a feeling that the emotional part of the self is disgusting and needs to be rejected) can be transformed into an internalised moral disgust (a feeling that the whole self is disgusting to others and should be rejected by them). These new feelings of moral self-disgust then contribute to the overwhelming negative emotional state that leads to a feeling of integral disgust, and the cycle begins again. This, we believe, accounts for much of the "addictive" quality that self-harm is reported to have.

In some cases, the perceived disgust of the other fails to materialise: "Before I told anyone, I thought they would be disgusted by me, but actually they have been really kind" (Participant ID: 260). In this case, perhaps there is the opportunity for the self to be viewed as other than disgusting, which may allow the individual to better assimilate the unbearable emotional aspects of themselves and avoid overwhelming integral disgust. This ought then in turn reduce the need to self-harm as a way to purge these feelings. When responses to self-harm are not those of disgust, this helps disrupt, or even break, the cycle.

## *The question of suicide*

Although suicidal acts and self-harm have traditionally been grouped together under the term "suicidal behaviour", both in clinical and research work, for most purposes this is, in our view, a mistake. Three factors are likely contributors to this tendency to conflate. First, there is some degree of ambivalence involved in most acts of suicide, and suicidal intent is thus difficult to establish or deny in many cases of overdose. Overdoses account for the majority of A&E visits, but acts of cutting are more common by far (Horrocks, House, & Owens, 2002). Second, there is a well-known association between completed suicide and self-harm: twenty-five to fifty per cent of adolescents completing suicide have previously either engaged in self-harm or attempted suicide (Hawton, James, & Viner, 2005), and increased suicide risk has been shown in those who self-harm repeatedly (Zahl & Hawton, 2004). Twenty per cent of more than five hundred participants to our online self-harm survey wrote that they were using self-harm as a way to combat suicidal feelings (Horne & Csipke, 2009). Third, the functions and meanings of self-harm have been insufficiently understood in the past. In the last decade, many research teams in several different countries have addressed this knowledge gap (see Klonsky, 2007, for a review), and these days it is increasingly understood that suicidal acts and acts of self-harm are, though not unrelated, still separate phenomena with quite different meanings, motivations, and functions attached.

As was the case with our self-harm data, our recently completed analysis of interviews about the suicidal process with people who had attempted suicide ($n$ = 14), who were interviewed with their family member or friend ($n$ = 15), and people bereaved by suicide ($n$ = 25), produced very few explicit references to self-disgust. However, in many narratives, the moral worth of the self was at issue, and particularly the part of self that feels was frequently rejected or hidden. This suggests a potential application of a concept of moral self-disgust to the experience of people close to attempting or completing suicide. Further analysis of these data needs to be carried out to explore this.

## *Conclusions*

An act of self-harm, seen as a transformation of an emotional state, is also a journey through varieties of disgust and self-disgust. At the start, basic and moral disgust recede, but "integral self-disgust" may be experienced strongly and motivates the act of self-harm. Through cutting, integral self-disgust is managed; first, by controlling the emotional state that is the object of disgust, and second, by transforming it into a physical entity that is now part of the social world. The post-self-harm state is characterised by a pronounced vulnerability to moral self-disgust and other related self-conscious emotions.

Understanding disgust and integral self-disgust as a motivation for self-harm highlights the importance of focusing on the acceptance of difficult feelings in therapy. It also elucidates the meaning of the wound and highlights the importance of appropriate responses to self-harm injuries at A&E departments and by the friends and family of those affected.

## Note

1. We would like to thank the participants who took part in the studies described herein for their generosity in sharing their experiences of self-harm, and the BIG Lottery Fund Research Programme and the James Wentworth-Stanley Memorial Fund for supporting our research on suicide.

*CHAPTER ELEVEN*

# Psychodynamics of self-disgust: expulsion and attack as attempts to retain integrity of the personality

*David Jones*

## *Introduction*

While shame has received much attention in the psychotherapeutic literature, far less regard has been paid to disgust. Yet self-focused disgust, an unstable phenomenon, may stimulate highly violent responses, both physical and emotional, as it threatens the integrity of the personality. In this chapter, which is primarily based on clinical practice, it is argued that prejudice and violence are often linked with self-disgust reactions, which operate both on an individual level and also on a broader social level (Hodson & Costello, 2007; Inbar, Pizarro, Iyer, & Haidt, 2012; Inbar, Pizarro, Knobe, & Bloom, 2009). This is examined using the psychoanalytic concepts of splitting, projection, and introjection, which are defences concerned with the interplay between the deepest, most primitive parts of the mind (the instinctual location of disgust) and experience of, and enactment within, the internal world. Clinical examples, including some from forensic practice, are given to illustrate these psychological processes at work. Most of these examples relate to feelings around same-sex relations (homosexuality), which has featured prominently in my own clinical work.

It is important to note that while Sigmund Freud argued that humans are universally bisexual, with a tendency to one sexual orientation or another (Freud, 1905a/1991), there remain many societies in which homosexuality is abhorred, criminalised, and even punishable by death (Mackay, 2001; Whitaker, 2006). For many young gay and lesbian people, it has been their common experience to be subjected to physical and verbal abuse from peers and adults. Such behaviours frequently cause multiple social and emotional problems, including internalised homophobia, self-harm, and substance misuse (Savin-Williams, 1994). While the same author reports that matters have shifted over the past twenty years in respect to self-regard within the gay community (Savin-Williams, 2006), there remains the problem of the social and cultural disgust that drives attacks against gay people (Doward, 2013).

Furthermore, as disgust is a powerful force which produces unease at the very least, the fear of contagion is present in psychotherapists, within the therapeutic space, and elsewhere. If unnoticed, it can produce negative therapeutic and other effects. This chapter suggests that the desired therapeutic stance of unbiased free association is not easy to achieve when deeply anxious parts of the self are approached.

## *Prelude*

In *King Lear*, Shakespeare presents us with a most painful scene that occurs when the Duke of Cornwall gouges out the eyes of the Earl of Gloucester (Act III, Scene VII). This act is calculated, steeped in cruelty and revenge, and, while the idea may fill us with disgust, it represents the pleasure to be gained from a transfer of power. By contrast, in another, real event, a man plunges a knife into the eye of a friend. He takes the knife out then repeats the action to the second eye, leaving the blade fatally embedded in the brain. This is a powerful acting out of an instinctual urge. The man has had an encounter with something within himself that filled him with self-disgust. The violent act happened immediately after a homosexual encounter. Terrified of his activated homosexual feelings, the murderer projected this onto his victim who, in his eyes, became critical and hateful. The eyes were identified, in a moment of psychotic delusion, as the concrete source of the unwanted sexuality and the route for a disapproving gaze. These examples illustrate, in the Lear case, the use of disgust as an aspect of relationship and, in the second, the genuine impulsive acting out of a dramatic emotional interaction in the internal world.

## *Disgust and psychoanalysis*

Disgust is an affect originally founded in response to bad tastes and smells, with their link to spoiled food, and over the ages has generalised to certain wider tactile experiences (e.g., sliminess), through to thoughts of something expected to be disgusting. For Darwin, the term "disgust" meant something offensive to taste. He thought that it primarily arose in connection with eating or tasting, thus the emotion often causes movements around the mouth. But it also often provokes associated annoyance in the subject, hence a frown is a frequent feature; extreme disgust makes the subject look as if he is about to vomit. Retching or vomiting may also be induced by a mere thought, particularly if it is associated with some previously disgusting object, as an impression may be retained and transferred to other similar objects. Smell is also a powerful evoker (Darwin, 1872/1989). Furthermore, disgust features notably in our interpersonal relationships, where it is experienced as a response to others; characteristically, it entails a forceful emotional or physical rejection of someone felt to be threatening an invasion of the self. It may be expressed through rejection, attacking, or nauseated tolerance (Miller, 1993). Disgust can be culturally engendered and encouraged, historically or contemporaneously, and can also occur spontaneously as a thought enters the mind.

A suggestion of why disgust has been examined relatively little in the psychoanalytic literature is that it is the fear of contamination that is central to disgust reactions. Contact with the disgusting makes one disgusting (Miller, 1993). In the clinical material arising from the cases of the patients described in this chapter, it can be seen that it can play a part in counter-transference (i.e., the unconscious relationship that develops between an analyst and patient arising from the projections from the patient and the way these interact with the emotional life of the analyst). Contamination, or the fear of it, is at the core of disgust and, over vast periods of time, this fear has become located within our mental structures. Consequently, it is no longer necessary for there to be a real contaminant; just the association or the idea is sufficient for an object to evoke an unpleasant feeling of disgust.

Freud identified disgust, shame, and morality as the forces that acted against sexual development, seeing them as arising from inhibitory factors, externally applied in the long process of the emotional development of the human race (Freud, 1905a/1991). A helpful expansion of the concept of disgust was offered by Shand from outside the field of psychoanalysis (Shand, 1914). At its primitive level, Shand saw disgust as a physical impulse rather than an emotion; indeed, when the physical sensations are strongest, they tend to dominate the attention and any subjectively felt emotion may be absent. This impulse is concerned with ejecting something from the body or withdrawing from something that repulses. The *emotion* of disgust will only develop when the bodily sensations are not so intense as to absorb attention, and the nature of the emotion allows us to turn away from its object. Another interesting point made by Shand is that disgust tends to repress sympathy, so that we are more likely to feel contempt as an adjunct to disgust. Contempt can develop into harsher feelings of dislike or hatred.

Another pertinent theme in relation to the conceptualisation of disgust is the existential anxiety about our own mortality. The determination to avoid the fact of what we know, that we will each of us die at some point, contributes to the development of complex social habits and patterns, and to the determination to avoid our own "creatureliness" (Goldenberg et al., 2001). Accordingly, certain substances and objects become disgusting depending upon their very closeness to mortality.

My suggestion/proposal in this chapter is that, for some patients, disgust is directed towards a part of themselves that can be split off from the rest of the self. If the split-off part is projected out onto, or into, some person or object, then rejection (and aggression) is thus also directed outwards, and thereby some temporary relief is gained from self-denigration and depression. However, this is bought at the cost of reduced intimacy in personal relationships, since the personality becomes truncated and rigid as a means of forestalling the re-emergence of the critical elements. Thus, as the problematic disgust is really experienced against the self, or a part of it, that it actually disappears is really an illusion, no matter how violent the projection or the attack upon the invaded object.

## *Disgust and associated emotional reactions*

Unlike disgust, shame has received a great deal of attention within the psychoanalytic literature over the past thirty years or so. While it was initially regarded as an internal barrier to the libido (Levin, 1971), a broader definition seems to be emerging. Central to this is the feeling of being exposed, of one's failure being on view to some other.

The circularity of this increases a "tormenting sense of inferiority and sinfulness" (Berke, 1986). It arises from exposure that threatens the integrity of the self, or "the self defined as a self before others" (Lansky, 1994). A number of writers have also identified a connection between the avoidance behaviour of shame and aggression (Lansky, 1991; Levin, 1971; Pines, 1995). Thomas (1995) argues that shame is a primitive physiological response to a rejection of oneself by another. It may be experienced as an intense psychological pain which stimulates anger, which in turn may be directed outwards toward another or inward against part of oneself.

Rather than just a primitive physiological response, shame can also be seen as a complex emotion, linked to the superego and operating as a dynamic, inhibiting the impulses of the id through the production of emotional pain. If the perceived failing of the self is split off and projected outwards it can contribute to disgust towards the object that is its recipient or, if split off and internalised, it may act as the focus for disgust with self. If the pain is strong, it may produce anger and aggression which, according to the status of the projections, may be directed towards self or to others. The result is highly dependent upon conditions within the mind. Projection and introjection are not in themselves unhealthy or damaging; indeed the developing mind of the human infant is shaped by such processes (Malancharuvil, 2004). However, when the structure of the personality is insufficiently robust, disintegration can occur accompanied by peaks of fear and anxiety. I have elsewhere described such experiences as shards of the unbearable, since they have a sharp damaging effect that stimulates a desire for retaliation (Jones, 2006).

Psychoanalytic psychotherapists conduct their work at the margins; they are immersed in the cognitive and emotional world of the patient and strive to avoid being sucked in. They will be aroused—physically, sensually, and emotionally—but need to be able to keep an eye on what is happening and to think about it. The activity between the psychotherapist and the patient may be a speculation upon the conscious narrative; a joint struggle to understand a dream or the detection of something unspoken, some unconscious communication. The narrative is not always linear. How does one understand a patient who describes how she licks the eyes of her two cats to clean them, or the man who explains that he listens to the sounds of his friend making love then surreptitiously collects soiled tissues, sniffs them, and masturbates? Both of these statements could be understood as the confession of something thought to be embarrassing or shameful, testing out the safety of the relationship, or a cry of pain at the awareness of a part of the self thought to be unacceptable. Both describe and put into the mind of the therapist something that might evoke the label "disgusting", crossing a boundary of what is commonly thought of as usual behaviour, though if we are marginally reflective and honest with ourselves, we would probably discover that we have done something similar or equally "disgusting".

Emotions—embarrassment, shame, humiliation, horror, and disgust—occur on a continuum, and we apply names to help us understand something of their quality. Thus, embarrassment is the emotional pain experienced when our mistakes or failings are exposed to view. Humiliation is closely allied but is normally considered to arise from exposure involving loss of status or position. Shame can be seen as a complex emotion, critical in tone, linked to the superego and operating as a dynamic inhibiting the impulses of the id, the area of raw emotion, through the production of emotional pain. If the perceived failing is split off and projected outwards, it can produce disgust towards the object which is the recipient. If it is split off from the self (ego) and internalised, it may act as the focus for self-disgust. This may also be projected and, if the pain is strong, it may produce anger and aggression which, according to the status of the projections, may be directed towards self or others.

### *Disgust and boundary violations: clinical examples*

Each of the aforementioned emotions can lead to distress, anger, or aggression, but it is disgust that has a particular explosive rejecting quality (i.e., the ability to stimulate physically vomiting), and which can operate at an unconscious level until bursting into action. The following clinical examples illustrate the different shades of the emotion and the way it can be expressed. Fundamental to each of these is an interaction and often a transaction, something passing from one mind to another or within different areas of a single mind.

A colleague had a particularly powerful experience in her therapy group:

> One of my most disturbing dreams symbolised forced penetration. In my dream I wakened to find my left arm covered in a sheath

> of composted manure with lots of little seedlings growing out of it. I could not scrape it off, felt uncomfortable, disgusted, felt sick, my skin crawled and I was confused. I was filled with dread and thought that this was a mad dream. I knew, however that there must be some meaning and that I would have to bear this madness for some reason. Within the week one man [in the therapy group] talked of his experience of being drugged and anally raped by several men as a child. The dream had been forced into me prior to the telling of his story and allowed me to get in touch with the feelings of dread, disgust, disbelief, confusion, despair, powerless, impotence, annihilation, and shame. (McLure, 2004, p. 92)

What McLure (2004) describes is the unconscious communication that took place (Hook, 2001) and how she received the projected self-disgust. Her mind was making some meaning from an experience or series of experiences in the group. Although something disgusting had been deposited—shit—there was also growth that seemed to be more positive. Such communication is not uncommon but, as in this case, the meaning is not always clear when it occurs. The psychoanalytic stance of suspended attention may be sensitive enough to pick up such micro-communications, but often it is through dreams, when the rational mind is switched off, that something emerges. Further, in this case, the therapist demonstrates the way in which her reception of the experience, and capacity to contain and try to understand it, served to ameliorate some of the pain for the group member so that he was able to share it with his peers. This can be thought of as a healthy therapeutic interaction, through which a toxic experience could be brought to the point of being at least tolerable. The following are examples of communications that are instead uncontained and unmoderated.

### *Paul*

As a young man, Paul had committed a murder. He had stalked his victim on the internet and formed a sexual relationship with him before stabbing and torturing him to death, then mutilating the body with corrosive fluid. The details of the murder are harrowing, involving extreme cruelty and calculation in the manipulation of a whole series of events relating to his relationship to the victim.

Paul was from a second-generation immigrant family that had generally adapted well to the different conditions and cultures in Britain. He attended college but got into difficulties with studies and around relationships because of the stories he made up, which initially engendered sympathy but later anger when they were uncovered as untrue. This storytelling seemed to be a pattern over a long period of his life. Following the murder, he was eventually caught and sentenced to life imprisonment. He later moved to a treatment centre to be treated for a personality disorder. He is a charming man and rather beautiful in appearance, which greatly assisted his ability to engage with people in what was invariably a superficial manner, and to convince them of his stories.

While in treatment, he several times engaged with senior medical staff and confided a history of sexual abuse. This was an extraordinary account of being sent to his ancestral home as a child and subjected to extreme abuse and practices such as I had never heard before. Of course, it was not known if there was any truth in these descriptions, but the effect upon the clinicians involved was very powerful. They were, separately, shocked, sickened, disgusted, and disturbed. Something had been placed in their minds that stained their experience of the world.

In this clinical example, we can see three quite distinct situations of disgust and its ramifications. In the first, and clearly most serious, there is the eruption of violence against the boyfriend/victim. This disturbance arises from the confusion around finding who he is and disapproving of who he feels himself to be. His previous history of making up and telling stories is indicative of a lonely man seeking sympathy for something that he could not say and perhaps could not recognise himself. The homosexual encounters that he had with his victim ran counter to his religion and his culture, both of which were strongly disapproving. However, it was his internal construction, the fusion of these external features, which turned his desires repellent to the extent that they had to be expelled.

The second situation was the experience of those friends of the victim who came across the mutilated and barely recognisable body. They received a traumatic impact from the visual experience which pushed them out of the room and flat, leaving a toxic and lasting picture in the mind and provoking the classical symptom of disgust: vomiting.

The final situation came some time after the trial and sentencing and is the forcing of extreme sexual abuse into the minds of clinicians. This, of course, is a very difficult issue since we expect mental health clinicians to be able to hear painful matters and to be understanding and sympathetic. Nevertheless, the processes that psychoanalysts describe—transference and counter-transference, projection and projective identification—occur whatever the situation and are perhaps even more likely to provoke an actual response outside of the psychotherapeutic setting. So, in this case, the images were brought forth and placed in the mind of the doctor. There, they aroused feelings of confusion and nausea. With Paul, some of this was conscious manipulation; that is, the wish to impress, make a mark on, and soften up the clinician who may also begin to feel sympathetic. It is also a behaviour that can split teams, most of whom are not caught up in these processes, and contributes to poor clinical management. At the unconscious level, the communication is about a disturbed and fragmented personality struggling to retain some shape and integrity by trying to enter and control the internal world of another.

This set of circumstances clearly illustrates the different manifestations of disgust. The murder itself was linked to the most archaic level, as the mind shattered in what must have seemed a defensive activity, responding to the encounter with the toxic mixture of sexual drive and cultural and religious disapproval. This was a catastrophic response to self-disgust. Moreover, in what was represented as an especially callous act, the murderer slept on the victim's bed before vacating the property. However, this can be seen differently: the massive decompensation and depletion of self may have left the perpetrator exhausted. The second manifestation, when friends arrive at the scene, is clearly a more straightforward disgust reaction caused by the sight of blood and bowels and the smells they encountered. The final manifestation, placing a picture into the minds of clinicians, an expunging of elements of self-disgust, produces an example of socially created disgust and, while the motivation is unclear, the end result—revulsion and disgust—is genuine, leaving a taint in the mind of the receiver that remains as a new and uncomfortable part of the self.

While official statistics give no information on numbers of homophobic murders in England and Wales (Smith, 2012), a study in New South Wales, with a population of seven million people, identified seventy-four homophobic murders over a twenty-year period (Tomsen,

2002). It is likely that there are a significant number of men in the prisons of England and Wales serving life for offences of killing other men following a sexual incident. These men are invariably less well integrated, more impulsive, and less rooted in a supportive social structure than Paul. Many of the men have lost a parent before the age of sixteen and report physical and sexual abuse (Tomsen, 2001). Even allowing for a degree of exaggeration for the purpose of gaining sympathy, rates of abuse are high, and recent court cases relating to offences committed at children's homes over a number of decades have confirmed many of these claims (BBC, 2013b). Perpetrators of homophobic murders are more likely to be young, aged seventeen to twenty-four, and killings are more often the result of unusually brutal and sustained attacks (Mouzos & Thompson, 2000). This is suggestive of high levels of anxiety about sexuality, and particularly homosexuality, which may be culturally supported but within individuals whose sexual identity is unstable.

Conditions in prisons pose particular challenges for sexuality and sexual expression. James Gilligan uses the term "homosexual panic" to describe a specific kind of emotional event. This occurs when "an inmate experiences a degree of homosexual stimulation that is intolerable to his self-esteem and his sense of his own masculinity" (Gilligan, 2000, p. 156). Curiously, and as a further illustration of "slipperiness" of internal moral boundaries, prison is a setting where two boundaries are crossed with little cost to the perpetrators in terms of stigma or social standing. Here, it is possible (for some) to have sex with another man and not be labelled a homosexual, and for that sex to be forced without being labelled as rape (Human Rights Watch, 2001). The mechanism of this requires the perpetrator to designate his (male) victim as a woman. This may be confirmed by the use of derogatory terms such as "queen", "pretty girl", or "bitch". Furthermore, the perpetrator may justify the rape by saying that the victim secretly wanted the sexual contact; a distortion commonly used following incidents of sexual offence against women (Scully & Marolla, 1985). In such situations, a perpetrator may well have his position and status enhanced and be "served" by the surrogate "woman" for many years. Both of these activities would have been considered disgusting, even within that culture, in circumstances where sexual desires had been otherwise satisfied. As one patient said to me while describing the frenetic nature and wide variety of his sexual encounters: "Fucking … it doesn't matter who, or what, it is, it's all in the mind" (Jones, 2012, p. 55).

### *Malcolm*

In such further circumstances as are described below, a common scenario is that the perpetrator knows or is friendly with the victim, may have been drinking or sharing drugs with him, and agrees to go with him. He may have sex with the man and kill him afterwards, or the murder may be triggered by some related event short of sexual contact.

In this situation, Malcolm had developed a relationship with a gay man. Eventually, this resulted in a sexual relationship. Malcolm feared that he might be exposed and blackmailed. This led to him killing the man and trying to cover his tracks. After several years of imprisonment, he discovered or imagined a different version of what he thought had happened. This was that he had been kidnapped and subject to violence by a group of men and the killing occurred when he tried to escape. Each of these explanations has escape as a theme: Malcolm wanted to escape public labelling as being gay, but also to escape the self-knowledge and the subsequent self-disgust by subscribing to an extravagant conspiracy theory. This alteration in his belief, which is not at all in his interest for progress towards release, can be understood as part of a psychotic process, disconnected from reality. The personality fragmented, causing massive anxiety and panic and disgust with that part of himself. The emotional imperative was to find an alternative explanation since a part of him had an association with those he felt would threaten and blackmail him. His attraction to men had to be denied, expelled, and attacked. Through this method, and fleetingly, a level of stasis was achieved, but at severe cost to himself in the longer term.

## *The notion of the internal world*

The thesis of this chapter is that processes deep in the mind, which can be termed "relationships", can interact in such a way as to create conscious thought, or occasionally action, which seems to circumvent the usual control mechanisms. On these occasions, the mind may seem crowded with emotions that urge the action to be completed in the speediest manner. The psychoanalytic idea that a part of the mind may be in a relationship with another part of the mind, that there may even be conflict between parts of the mind, or that parts of the mind may split off and become located with another person or object, is by no means straightforward. It differs from the imaginative world, or from Cartesian internalism or externalism (Stalnaker, 2010). Rather, it describes a place in the mind where internal objects are experienced as relating to each other within the overall self. They may be identified with by the individual and assimilated as part of the self or ego, or they may be felt as separate from, but at the same time existing within, the self. These elements of the internal world can exist on several levels. They can be more or less unconscious and more or less primitive. This internal life may be represented to the self in dreams, fantasies, and in language. Empirically based psychologists for long denied the existence of an unconscious, preferring to consider behaviours that can be observed, measured, calibrated, and manipulated (Power, 2006b). However, psychoanalytic psychotherapists also observe. They observe the behaviour of clients during therapy sessions, the nuances and changes of feeling, the presentation of material and the effect that this has upon them. They also infer a meaning from this to bring into focus the status of the client's internal world. The psychoanalyst Melanie Klein argued that these processes begin at a very early age and described it thus:

> The baby, having incorporated his parents, feels them to be live people inside his body in the concrete way in which deep unconscious phantasies are experienced … They are in his mind, "internal" or "inner" objects, as I have termed them. Thus an inner world is being built up in the child's unconscious mind, corresponding to his actual experiences and the impressions he gains from people and the external world and yet altered by his own phantasies and impulses. If it is a world of people predominantly at peace with each other and with the ego, inner harmony, security, and integration ensue. (Klein, 1940, pp. 345–346)

Klein goes on to argue that it is the totality of experiences that have been taken in (introjected) that constitute the adult personality, wherein relationships coalesce, interact, and disperse. The integrity of that personality is dependent on the quality of what is taken in and how it can bond to form a coherent whole.

More recently, there has been a degree of rapprochement within the field of psychology. Empirical psychologists have been able to devise experiments that could be argued to demonstrate the existence of an unconscious, and phenomena such as transference (e.g., Andrews & Brewin, 2000). The development of cognitive-behavioural approaches recognises the importance of feelings as well as behaviours and schema theories (Young, 1999), and illustrates the existence of structures of belief below the level of conscious thinking. However, these seem to be describing essentially static scripts that cause particular behaviours, and this is very different from the idea of a dynamic internal world wherein elements of the personality are in perpetual interaction with other elements and with the outside world.

As Klein suggests, the internal world is affected both by internal relations and the impact of the external world, and the degree of personality coherence, wellbeing, and integration is dependent upon these internal relations. A psychological defence that splits off a disagreeable or unacceptable part of the personality and locates it in the external world, or even an area of the internal world that is experienced as being separate from the central ego, can bring some relief but only at the price of a fresh discord or general impoverishment of the personality. When this splitting occurs, then the critical object, which may give rise to feelings of inadequacy, shame, or disgust, can appear to become more persecutory and so set off a cycle of violence that can lead to murder or suicide (Wilson, 1995).

## *The social being and disgust*

One of the most troubling discoveries since earliest times is that human beings as a general species are capable of anything and that (almost) anything that can be fantasised has already been done. Complex rituals of socialisation have crafted communities wherein safety may be enjoyed by many people much of the time. However, frequent outbreaks of mass violence or genocide, or individual acts of murder or mayhem, indicate that fundamental and primitive tendencies are barely contained within the social matrix. How is this to be understood? As we constantly indulge in hindsight, it is relatively easy, although unjustifiably so, to comfort ourselves that such disasters will be avoided in future, or individual acts of crime will be diminished with the correct policy or therapeutic approach. We have always looked back, though not necessarily with a degree of liberalism. Indeed, Heinrich Himmler addressed the SS Gruppenführer in 1937, contending that:

> Unfortunately we don't have it as easy as our forefathers … the homosexual was drowned in a swamp. The professorial gentlemen

> who find these corpses in the peat bogs are certainly unaware that in ninety out of a hundred cases they have before them a homosexual … That was not a punishment, but simply the extinguishing of abnormal life. (Burleigh, 1991, p. 193)

This statement from less than one hundred years ago seems shocking today, but the attitude was commonplace at the time. Following shortly after that and, as if oblivious of the persecution of gays in the period leading up to and during the Second World War, the psychoanalyst Edmund Bergler wrote:

> I have no bias against homosexuals … [they] are essentially disagreeable people, regardless of their pleasant or unpleasant manner [which] is a mixture of superciliousness, false aggression, and whimpering. [They are] subservient when confronted with a stronger person, merciless when in power, unscrupulous about trampling on a weaker person. (Bergler, 1956, p. 28)

Quite apart from the subject matter, there are similarities in these statements in that both lay claim to some kind of scientific authority which masks, though in reality hardly at all, the underlying prejudice, anxiety, and dread arising from a fear of contamination (Taylor, 2007). These are discomforting statements to read because we know that the narrow thinking of the Nazi leader Himmler, arising from prejudice with its unconscious foundations, was acted out with horrific results. Tens of thousands of homosexual men were killed in concentration camps. Himmler was a bigot; he saw only what he wished and was able to see only that which matched his own distorted framework.

It is disturbing to notice that Himmler's statements are not too different from those made by a psychoanalytic colleague. I discovered that there were actually many examples of prejudiced thinking within the psychoanalytic literature. What becomes clear when we look is that there seems to have been three phases of psychoanalytic debate concerning sexual orientation and homosexuality. This is well described in the work of Lewes (1995), Izzard (1999), and, from a postmodern or deconstructivist perspective, O'Connor (2003). The first phase is marked by Freud's tentative explorations and those of his colleagues, which were often very reflective, for example advising the British Psycho-Analytic Society to accept or reject candidates on the basis of their merit and not by their sexual orientation (Spiers & Lynch, 1977, p. 8). The second, or revisionist, period of, say, the 1930s to 1960s saw some vocal psychoanalysts adopting a more strident and critical tone, arguing for treatment, conversion, or worse (Bergler, 1956; Socarides, 1994). The third period is characterised by arguments that have developed to counter these certainties and are in tune with the new liberalism and post-modernism (Dreschler, 2007). In fact, so strong has been the reaction that homosexuality had become a fairly dangerous area for psychoanalytic exploration, where condemnation can override efforts to understand. Nevertheless, it seems important to maintain an openness and interest in all areas of sexual behaviour. The challenge for psychotherapists is to be able to discover parts of their own internal world, no matter how discomforting, and to use this in creative work with the patient (Jones, 2001). Internalised and unacknowledged homophobia can have pernicious effects on all, and likely assists in the conversion from mere distress to self and projected disgust (Williamson, 2000).

## *Prejudice*

By focusing upon clinical work, I have argued that a cycle of disgust, shame, and aggression can be discerned in a group of patients. I suspect that it has also had a place in the minds of many psychotherapists, when it may lead to punitive interpretations if it is not at least noticed. The point about this is that it is not, of course, that homosexuals are intrinsically disgusting, but that many feel that they are, either consciously or unconsciously. This phenomenon is not restricted to homosexuals. I have worked with patients who had so far split off their sexuality that I became disgusting to them should I notice it in their material. As Sabine Spielrein wrote, when commenting on the ambivalence and destructiveness surrounding the sexual drive: "These negative feelings, such as anxiety and disgust, must be overcome in order to use the drive appropriately" (Spielrein, 1994). Although the psychotherapist should be aware of this dynamic, or risk getting caught up in the sadomasochistic elements of the negative therapeutic reaction, there is a wider lesson to be learned.

Psychotherapy is not the only profession and holder of authority to be caught up in the complexity of disgust. The legal profession has been willingly involved in debates about homosexuality over the years. In 1959, Lord Devlin argued for legal sanctions against homosexuality on the grounds that there "is a general abhorrence of homosexuality" (Heilbronn, Latimer, & Nielsen, 2002). Moreover, Kass argued (in relation to human cloning specifically): "in crucial cases, repugnance is the emotional expression of deep wisdom, beyond reason's power, fully to articulate it" (Kass, 1997). This notion of the wisdom of repugnance carries pernicious undertones that have been used to justify opposition to homosexual behaviours and gay marriage on the grounds of intuitive distaste (Roache & Clarke, 2009). As I have argued, disgust has no moral quality in itself. It is a pliable emotional response, which may emerge in response to a toxic substance, but equally may form around a thought or suggestion. The anxiety around a part of the self that becomes disgusted at the self may erupt as uncontrolled violence or may subtly invade the beliefs of a psychotherapist or a political creed.

## *Conclusion*

This chapter takes the idea of common disgust and explores the shift from physical revulsion to complex emotions. Central to this is the idea of disgust with a part of the self, self-disgust, as a formation of primitive disgust potentiated with early social and cultural experiences. While the phenomenon is commonplace, it is illustrated here through examples associated with sexuality, particularly fear and anxiety about homosexuality. Disgust is shown to be a pliable emotion that is not restricted to instinctual responses to toxic substances; instead, it can emerge in response to varied physical and emotional matters. Sexuality continues to pose difficulties for people at the individual, local, social, and national political level; same-sex relations can evoke powerful negative feelings and actions associated with disgust (BBC, 2013a; Hudson, 2011). These are pervasive and, as well as playing a part in social and political life, can affect professions, particularly those that claim objectivity or neutrality such as psychoanalysis and the law. These responses can be socially and culturally constructed through a process of introjection (taking in), whereby they form part of an individual psychopathology. At a point when the internal world becomes insufferable because of threats to the self arising from conflict, the structure may break down, leading to massive projection, akin to evacuation of the unwanted parts. However, the threat is not eliminated, it is merely located elsewhere, within a person, group, or object that takes on the character of the threat. Such dynamics can even lead to persecution, murder, or genocide.

CHAPTER TWELVE

# Self-disgust, self-hatred, and compassion-focused therapy

*Paul Gilbert*

Until recently, there was general agreement that the affect of disgust had been relatively neglected in the study of social relationships and psychopathology (Davey, 2011; McNally, 2002; Phillips, Senior, Fahy, & David, 1998). This may have been partly due to the fact that it was seen as an evolved emotion designed to deal with body contamination and the prevention of disease, rather than the regulation of psychological processes (Oaten, Stevenson, & Case, 2009). Now, however, as de Jong & Borg note in their chapter (this volume), disgust can be recruited into various domains such as pathogen avoidance, sexual avoidance, and certain types of purity-linked moral violations (see also Rozin, Lowery, Imada, & Haidt, 1999). So, as this book attests, we now know that disgust can be associated with interpersonal relationships (finding other people's behaviours or presentations disgusting) and self-judgements, feeling disgusted with our bodies, fantasies, emotions, and general sense of being. Power and Dalgleish (1997; and see Alanazi, Powell, & Power, this volume) suggested, for example, that disgust is central to the emotion of shame—which is a self-conscious experience that this chapter will explore.

## *The complex emotions of disgust*

Rozin, Lowery et al. (1999) point out that the word "disgust" comes from dis-gust, meaning bad-taste, and is mainly linked to "feelings of revulsion" at touching or ingesting offensive materials. The facial expression involves closing the nose and mouth (to stop ingression). Disgust is an affect that warns of contamination, triggers movement away, and in the extreme effects a vomiting reflex, which evolved for the quick expulsion of possible noxious substances; it is an emotion of avoidance and wanting to get rid of, but can turn into a desire to cleanse and eradicate, a motive of vital importance when looked at from within the self. Disgust is not there at birth (e.g., babies are not disgusted by their own faeces), although will show a disgust-like expression to bitter tastes. Disgust is subject to cultural practices (e.g., foods that might in the West be stomach-turning, such as rotten fish or grasshoppers, are eaten quite happily in some cultures), and some people can desensitise to disgust objects (e.g., those who have to clean toilets, or gut animals and fish for a living; some people find certain sexual practices exciting, others disgusting; see Powell, Simpson, & Overton, this volume).

The experience of disgust is also significantly influenced by the quality of a person's relationship. For example, various sexual practices that might involve semen, genital, anal, or oral contact might be experienced as pleasurable in the context of sexual arousal within a loving relationship, but deeply traumatic, offensive, and disgusting in the context of a forced relationship. So whether somebody else's body is experienced as traumatically disgusting or erotic seems to depend on the voluntary nature and the affiliative quality of that relationship. This is potentially important because when it comes to compassion, part of what compassion-focused therapy does is to try to create affiliative relationships with those parts of the self that are rendered or seen as disgusting.

What also complicates this area is the recognition that disgust has a primary focus (contamination) but also a range of what Oaten et al. (2009) refer to as "complex disgusts", those that are not contamination-focused specifically but link to sexual and moral responses (see de Jong & Borg, this volume). In addition, some authors have suggested that variations in disgust sensitivity may underpin certain disorders, thus suggesting trait-like qualities (Davey, 2011; Davey, Bickerstaffe, & MacDonald, 2006). Moreover, disgust relates to other primary emotions in particular ways so that disgust "textures" them, such as contempt and anger (Rozin, Lowery et al., 1999; though see Powell, Simpson, & Overton, this volume). As discussed shortly, this combination of emotions, when directed at the self, is potentially highly pathogenic. For example, while disgust can be seen as an emotion of expelling and avoidance, contempt with anger can underpin hatred, which brings the desire to "seek out, cleanse, and eradicate". In the rhetoric of leaders who wish to stir hatred, they will commonly talk about the enemy in disease terms: "They are vermin, a disease, contaminate our way of life, infect us with their values", as was common in the rhetoric of Hitler. So here, disease concepts were used to excite hatred. Jewish people were not avoided but actively sought out for persecution and eradication, and such behaviour is common in ethnic cleansing. The psychology of cleansing can also underpin intense cruelty; for example, one of the ideas of burning people at the stake was to "cleanse them of their sin". Hence, the link between disgust and cleansing motives is complex. So while it might be relatively straightforward to link certain forms of obsessive-compulsive disorder with fears of contamination to disgust, self-disgust when relating to, say, borderline difficulties, might be quite different.

Another "emotion" for which there are few data (indeed, one could discuss whether it is an emotion in the true sense) is that of being "pathetic". To label self or others as "pathetic" would seem to be closely linked to the concept of contempt, and this is a judgement that people can make of themselves in the context of fear and lack of courage: "you pathetic worm" captures a sense of disgust and contempt as well as anger. Linked to the idea of "pathetic" is also the concept of ridicule. And, of course, derogations on self and others can involve disgust concepts such as "you piece of shit"—thus likening someone or self to an object of disgust. In this chapter, therefore, I will take a very broad sweep of the concept of disgust and consider its links to anger, contempt, and hatred, and how these become recruited into our experience of self.

## *Disgust and the self-evaluative process*

Although most theories recognise that disgust properly evolved as a reaction to potential contaminating substances that would trigger defensive behaviours of avoid, repel, and vomit—evolution is notorious for utilising established systems and putting them to new uses. For example, we have a basic threat system that works through the amygdala and hypothalamic-pituitary-adrenal axis. For animals, this is triggered by signals and stimuli in the outside world, but for humans it can be triggered by thoughts and symbolic representations. Putting my hand in my pocket and discovering my wallet has gone can produce a panic even though there is nothing like a wallet in nature; suddenly having a fantasy that is socially condemned could generate panic, as happens in certain obsessional difficulties (Baer, 2002). Indeed, when I was younger, my first obsessional client was a rather shy "prim and proper" sixty-year-old lady who was in deep distress with a sense of self-disgust. This occurred because she had read something in a newspaper and had a spontaneous fantasy of having oral sex with a baby that she then could not get out of her mind. Evolution has *not* developed different threat-processing systems for every new threat; rather, what has happened is the same basic systems can become recruited in different ways. This seems to be the case for disgust as well.

One way in which basic primary emotions can be put to new uses is through the recent evolution of human cognitive systems (Gilbert, 2009). About two million years ago, humans began to evolve extraordinary capacities for cognitive processing such as abilities to anticipate, ruminate, plan, and imagine. One of the most profound and unique consequences of this cognitive evolution was that it gave rise to an objective and symbolic sense of self (Sedikides & Skowronski, 1997). Symbolic self–other awareness is the ability to imagine the self and others as objects and to judge and give value to the self and others, to have self-esteem, pride, or shame, or allocate positive or negative values to others (good and able or worthless and useless). Also, of course, we could use symbolic representations to apply concepts like disgust to an object that perhaps in nature would not have that quality (e.g., "I'm disgusted by your idea/suggestion"). These symbolic representations focus both on self in relationship to others and self in relation to oneself; that is: 1) a sense of self as object derived from how we feel we exist in the minds of others (e.g., as loved vs. unloved); and 2) a sense of self as object that one can evaluate; that is to say, one could have feelings of like or dislike, joy or anxiety about oneself as a self, or indeed a sense of self-disgust/contempt.

Not only this, but we can have what is sometimes called "part self-relating". I can like different parts of myself and dislike other parts of myself. Tomi-Ann Roberts (e.g., Roberts & Gettman, 2004; Roberts & Goldenberg, 2007) highlights the objectification of the female body and how cultural practices can make different elements of this subject to disgust, which can become internalised. In people who have body dysmorphic disorder, there can be a focus on particular elements of the self, such as the face, the nose, or breasts, which can be singled out for high-focus feelings of disgust and shame. And, of course, bodies that become ill or diseased can be experienced with feelings of disgust and fear of negative evaluation—sometimes referred to as "body shame" (Gilbert & Miles, 2002). But it is not just bodies that are subject to disgust; people can feel a sense of disgust at their fantasies and intrusive images. Indeed, disgust is probably one of the emotions that distresses people with obsessional disorders, because they are unfamiliar with the fact that humans can generate a surprising variety of potentially frightening and disgusting fantasies and intrusions (Baer, 2002).

### *External shame: living in the mind of the other*

Animals need to evaluate social signals to enable them to respond to the intents of others and also to stimulate others intents (e.g., sexual invitations, friendly or aggressive-dominance and submissive displays). Indeed, all the senses can be used as communication channels (Maynard Smith & Harper, 2003). So systems for the detection, processing, and responding to social signals are very old. It should also be noted that disgust can be transmitted in different sensory modalities such as smell, sight, and touch. With the human "new brain", however, humans were not simply dependent upon "social signals" to evaluate others' intents; they could also generate internal representations of how the self "existed in the mind of the other" and how others might be orientated towards them. This enabled humans to predict other people's behaviours in the future. So humans are able to think "others see me, judge me, feel about me, as ...". This "imagination" allows for extraordinary capacities for creating and manipulating one's social presentation. We can work out what others might like or not like, and what they find acceptable and unacceptable. Consequently, along with our evolved new type of "thinking brain" came the abilities of objective self-awareness, and for mentalising, perspective-taking, and experiencing empathy and theory of mind.

It is also the case that how we think others relate to us, and how we think they think about us, has a significant influence on our sense of self. This, in essence, is the basis of what Cooley, a century ago, called the "looking-glass self" (Cooley, 1922/1964). He highlighted that we can make self-judgements from how others treat us and how we think we "exist for them". So I can feel good about myself, feel I'm attractive and desirable, an intelligent person, or the opposite, according to how others treat me. If others treat me as if there are things that are disgusting about me, then this may well become imbued into my self-system. There is evidence that people value qualities in themselves that they think others will value, highlighting the importance of social audiences from which we take our experiences of self (Santor & Walker, 1999). Facial expressions are important here, and the shame researcher Michael Lewis (1992) pointed out that when parents show displeasure at a child's behaviour they can show anger but also contempt and disgust, or some combination, especially, but not only, to girls. The use of the disgust face can convey to the child that there is something about them that elicits this emotion in the other, the parent.

### *External shame and the unattractive self*

Shame takes different forms with different attentional foci (Gilbert, 1998a, 2002). In the case of external shame, the attention is focused on the mind of the other rather than on oneself. Internal or internalised shame is the inward focus of attention, the judgement and feeling we have for ourselves. External shame, feeling shamed in the eyes of others, is highly linked to psychopathology, and negative self-evaluation (Gilbert, 2007; Kim, Thibodeau, & Jorgensen, 2011). Some theorists continue to believe that shame is linked to falling below standards, but there is no evidence for this, and it is problematic in understanding shame (Gilbert, 1998a). In fact, shame can be seen as related to becoming the "undesired self" (Ogilive, 1987); that is, one is vulnerable to rejection, ostracism: an object for derision, disgust, and contempt. Exploring the idea that shame emerged from a failure to live up to ideals, Lindsay-Hartz, de Rivera, and Mascolo (1995), in their qualitative study, found that:

> Most of the participants rejected this formulation. Rather, when ashamed, participants talked about being who they did not want to be. That is, they experienced themselves as embodying an anti-ideal, rather than simply not being who they wanted to be. The participants said things like, "I am fat and ugly", not "I failed to be pretty"; or "I am bad and evil", not "I am not as good as I

> want to be". This difference in emphasis is not simply semantic. Participants insisted that the distinction was important … (p. 277)

These self-judgements suggest a social value focus because, since one cannot see oneself, to rate oneself as ugly means "ugly to others". The point is therefore that *self*-disgust probably cannot be de-contextualised from a social audience. If the self is the object of disgust, then it is an object of disgust for others in the first instance, which can then become internalised to become self-disgust. This is why we cannot understand shame simply as an internal self-focused experience, because the sense of self is always fluid in relationship to how we perceive we are experienced in the minds of others. Indeed, there are good reasons to believe that self-evaluation partly evolved to enable us to orientate ourselves to the minds of others.

Based on a review of the evidence and current theory, Gilbert (1998a) suggested that shame constitutes an:

> … inner experience of self as an unattractive social agent, under pressure to limit possible damage to self via escape or appeasement … It does not matter if one is rendered unattractive by one's own or other people's actions; what matters is the sense of personal unattractiveness—being in the social world as an undesired self; a self one does not wish to be. Shame is an involuntary response to an awareness that one has lost status and is devalued. (p. 22)

The unanswered question, of course, is the degree to which attractiveness and unattractiveness are underpinned by some judgement that is emotionally textured by aspects of disgust. Indeed, the whole concept of attractiveness–unattractiveness requires further research because to feel attractive to others is to feel safe to approach them, whereas to feel unattractive is likely to activate avoidance—which, of course, is classically what the disgust affect does.

### *Internal shame: self-evaluating the self*

So the self learns about its "self" within social contexts and the judgements of others. Indeed, many neurophysiological systems, including genetic expressions, are coordinated and patterned through social relationships (Cozolino, 2007; Siegel, 2001). In this way, just as one can think of other people as attractive–unattractive, one can make the same judgement about oneself and, as we noted previously, about *parts* of oneself. However, research has shown that when it comes to self-evaluation, and particularly self-criticism, it is not really the cognitive content that is problematic; rather, it is the emotions that texture the content. In their study of self-criticism, Whelton and Greenberg (2005) confirmed that it was the aggressive-contemptuous emotions in the self-criticism, not just the content of the criticism, that was linked to psychopathology and an inability to defend oneself against self-criticism. Psychodynamic therapists have looked at this in a different way in terms of hostile superego. So there is a general agreement that it is not just content but the emotion in self-critical thinking that is important (for a review, see Gilbert & Irons, 2005).

### *Measuring self-criticism*

Self-criticism, negative self-judgement, self-blaming, and a whole range of other negative experiences of the self, have been linked to psychopathology for many years (Kannan & Levitt, 2013). Freud described two sources of self-criticism. One was linked to the superego, the other to anger turned inward. Measures of self-criticism, however, did not really start until Blatt and his colleagues (e.g., Blatt, Quinlan, Chevron, McDonald, & Zuroff, 1982) distinguished between self-critical and anaclitic depressions and developed the Depressive Experiences Questionnaire (DEQ), which measures self-criticism and dependency. This scale has generated much research on self-criticism and its strong links to psychopathology (see Zuroff, Santor, & Mongrain, 2005). However, it tends to focus on a generalised trait, rather than different types of self-criticism. Thompson and Zuroff (2004) developed the Levels of Self-Criticism Scale (LOSC) where the focus is primarily on self-criticism in relationship to other people (i.e., criticising yourself because you feel inferior).

There are also different functions of self-criticism. Some years ago, Driscoll (1989) pointed out that self-criticism took many different forms and had different functions. In a series of studies, Gilbert and colleagues explored the nature, forms, and functions of self-criticism and found that they varied considerably (e.g., Gilbert, Clarke, Kempel, Miles, & Irons, 2004; Gilbert, Durrant, & McEwan, 2006; Gilbert et al., 2010). For example, some forms of self-criticism are related to feelings of inadequacy and inferiority, whereas others are associated with feelings of self-hatred. People who feel inadequate or inferior do not necessarily hate themselves, indeed, they might feel sad about their limitations. In contrast, items in the self-hatred category included "feeling disgusted with myself" and "not liking being oneself". For the most part, self-hating tends to be associated with more severe psychopathology. These findings, along with the validity and reliability of this measure of self-criticism, have been confirmed in two large independent studies (Baião, Gilbert, McEwan, & Carvalho, 2014; Castilho, Pinto-Gouveia, & Duarte, 2013). The extent to which hatred is linked to disgust is, of course, an important research question, because it is quite possible we could hate things that we are not disgusted by. On the other hand, the desire to eradicate, shed, get rid of, cleanse, cut out, and destroy appears linked to both disgust and hatred. In the case of eating disorders, for example, Birgegard, Bjorck, Norring, Sohlberg, and Clinton (2009) link up hatred to body disgust.

In terms of the functions of self-criticism, we found that a common one was trying to force oneself to do better and avoid making mistakes. Even though the emotions can be quite aggressive, there is an underlying belief that if one could just keep going, and try hard enough, or criticise oneself enough, one will make it. This sense of self seems to reflect the thought that one is "worth investing in" and it is all a matter of effort. Individuals with this type of self-criticism tend to be perfectionistic (Kannan & Levitt, 2013). They are vulnerable to depression when they try and then begin to feel they are "not going to make it", that they are "not up to it", feel defeated, and then slip into defeat states (Taylor, Gooding, Wood, & Tarrier, 2011).

What our research also showed was another function for self-criticism that we called "self-persecution". This aspect of self-criticism allows us to: "cope with things of disgust in myself; to take revenge on myself; to get rid of parts of myself". Again, self-persecuting self-criticism is more pathogenic than self-correcting self-criticism. Therefore, although agreeing with Whelton and Greenberg (2005) about the importance of the emotions associated with self-criticism, we suggested that the functions of self-criticism are also important in understanding how the self "experiences its self".

Interestingly, I have a number of anecdotal observations that when individuals start to feel that, no matter how hard they try, they are not going to succeed (e.g., in losing weight, changing the way they look, coping with multiple roles and time demands), they feel defeated and can then become more aggressive and contemptuous with themselves. Again, we see the themes of "the pathetic, weak, useless" sense of self emerging. As one patient recently said, "I just hate myself when I get into this [depressed] state. I feel pathetic, disgusted. Useless—what's the point of being here?" These comments reflect complex textures of emotion in which disgust is a component.

One of the reasons that self-criticism can be so pathogenic is that it stimulates particular physical processes associated with threat. For example, in an fMRI study, Longe et al. (2010) compared neurophysiological responses to imagined negative life events when one was being self-critical or self-reassuring. Major differences in the dorsal lateral prefrontal cortex, the insula, and in left–right processing revealed that self-criticism and self-reassurance have very different impacts on the brain when imagining (the same) stressful events. Moreover, the higher subjects scored on a self-report measure of self-criticism, the more threat systems that were activated.

To summarise, then, self-criticism is a generic term used to describe a type of relationship with oneself, and can be similar to the way we criticise others. As there are different forms and functions of self-criticism, there are different emotions that are linked to self-criticism. Some appeared to be anger-, frustration-, and disappointment-based, and may not involve a sense of disgust *per se*. These are wishing to do (i.e., will be) better. Others do appear to be more in the domain of contempt, hatred, and self-disgust. These seem to be more associated with the desire to get rid and a wish to "not have this part of me". The degree to which self-disgust is linked to contempt and hatred is a research point, because it may be that these are quite different emotional states with different triggers and histories. When focusing specifically on self-disgust, it can be seen in terms of two main dimensions: our experiences of ourselves as social agents (objects for others) and the emotions we create in other people—especially in the dimension of attractiveness-desirability, and others being interested in being close to us vs. distant and avoidant. Second, it is the emotions that we stimulate when thinking about and experiencing ourselves. It is important then to target these two domains in therapy and, if possible, develop a far greater affiliative, accepting approach to emotions in how we focus on ourselves. The rest of this chapter will address compassion-focused therapy as a treatment for self-criticism.

## *Compassion-focused therapy*

Compassion-focused therapy (CFT) was specifically designed for people with high self-criticism and shame (Gilbert, 1998a, 2007, 2010;

Gilbert & Irons, 2005). It specifically targets the internal emotional and feeling tones of how people think and talk to themselves—basically teaching people to change from hostile, critical, and disgust-based emotions in the process of self-dialogue to kind, supportive, validating, and understanding tones. Although the content of people's thoughts, and the focus of their attention, is important in CFT, it is the emotional textures of self-referenced thinking that are particularly important.

### *Setting the context for de-shaming and depersonalising*

CFT is based on an evolutionary functional analysis of the mind (Gilbert, 1992, 2009). Therefore, one of the ways in which we help shame-prone people—and those with different types of self-criticism, including self-disgust, which can be quite prevalent in people with eating difficulties (Birgegard et al., 2009)—is to loosen the identification with their mental contents. There are various way to do this (e.g., mindfulness, perspective-taking), but one way is by contextualising the mind in an evolutionary framework. We explain to clients that our minds have evolved over many millions of years and, while they can do some amazing things, they are also quite tricky. This is partly because many of our basic emotions and motivations are millions of years old. We share basic motives with other animals, such as desires to find food, have our own territories, sexual relationships, friendships, and working hard to preserve/enhance our status. Emotions such as anger, anxiety, sadness, and disgust—as well as happiness, playfulness, and joyfulness—also operate in many other mammals. However, humans have a much more recently evolved brain in relation to cognitive competencies. A zebra that has run away from a lion will calm down quite quickly, but the human is more likely to engage in a lot of simulations and "what if" thinking about potential threatening outcomes (e.g., "what would've happened if I'd been caught?", "Can you imagine being eaten alive?", etc.). We also have a mind that can give us an objective sense of self in a way that nonhuman animals do not. So, chimpanzees do not worry about putting on weight or the shape of their nose, nor do they judge themselves—or as far as we know—to become self-critical. But of course, humans do. They can come to judge and feel things about the self, anticipate, reflect, judge, and imagine; so, some of our basic emotions can get hooked up into these ways of thinking. Through no fault of our own, our sense of self can be linked to any type of emotion, so we can see ourselves as an anxious self, angry self, happy self, or even disgusting self.

To help people recognise just how much of what goes on in our mind is not our fault; that our minds have been created for us but not by us (hence reducing a sense of shame and self-criticism for what goes on inside our minds), we also use the following example. Imagine that "if I (as therapist) had been kidnapped as a three-day-old baby into a violent drug gang, what would I be like as a person?" My felt core identity, my values, would not be these. Clients are often able to recognise that I would likely be aggressive, self-centred, and I would possibly be imprisoned or dead. We are only one version of ourselves in any moment and may have little idea what other versions or potentials lie within us. So, the question becomes: how can we begin to choose and cultivate certain versions of ourselves, including those that might have far less disgust for the self?

Sometimes we spend a few minutes silently reflecting or really thinking about the implications. For people from abusive and neglectful backgrounds, this can be very moving. For example, one lady in a group for borderline difficulties said "nobody's ever told me this. I always thought that there was something bad about me; when God made me he'd run out of the nice bits". People who have a sense of self-disgust also often have a deep sense of internal shame and, therefore, creating a framework for them to begin to stand back and recognise just how much of what goes on in our mind is not our fault can be very validating. We certainly would not introduce cognitive concepts such as "maladaptive schemas" or "cognitive distortions" at this point, because shame patients will immediately see this as "things wrong inside of them".

### *Responsibility*

So we begin to see self-disgust and hatred as an evolved defensive/protective emotion and an understandable, and indeed natural, consequence from the experiences one has had, and through no fault of one's own. Also key is to help people understand what the disgust and hatred is about; what would they be like if they did not have these elements that they felt self-disgust about? How would their lives be different? Commonly, people come to see that actually what they are wanting is to feel attractive to themselves and attractive to others so that they can have a sense of connectedness, love, ability, and being welcomed into the social world.

However, of course, many things in life are not our fault but we have to take responsibility for them. If someone crashes into your car in a car park and then drives off, leaving you to discover the damage when you return—even though that clearly is not your fault—only you can get it fixed. Having the genes for diabetes is not our fault, and being surrounded by high-fat, high-sugar, high-salt foods that are completely abnormal to our natural evolved environment, is also not our fault, and constantly having to refrain and regulate our intake is unnatural. However, if we do not do this, we run the risk of obesity and diabetes. There is no law against it, but we might not like the consequences. So the trick is to give up blaming and shaming, and dig into this deep sense of shame, whilst at the same time helping people think about the potential for creating a new version of self.

### *Working with emotions*

This brings us to: how do we take responsibility? How can we begin to create a different version of ourselves with which we are more comfortable? This is the essence of CFT. So the next element is to highlight the way in which our emotions work and can become attached to different elements of ourselves. CFT uses the very simple notion of there being different evolved types of emotion systems in our brain, and these are designed by evolution to do different things; this is outlined in detail elsewhere (Gilbert, 2009, 2010), so they are only mentioned briefly here. The three systems are:

1. those that evolved to deal with threats and are designed to help protect and defend us;
2. those that evolved to excite and inspire us to go out and achieve and seek out and acquire resources;
3. those that evolved to help us feel content and peaceful wellbeing, when we are not under any threat and not trying to achieve anything.

We can represent these as three interacting systems (Figure 1); however, although we often present them as different systems, they are more blends of different patterns in our minds.

Figure 1. Three types of affect regulation system. From Gilbert (2009), *The Compassionate Mind*, reprinted with permission from Constable & Robinson Ltd.

We explain to people that, for the most part, the threat system is often our dominant processing system because primarily it is designed to protect; that the brain has a negativity bias, therefore, it is always "on guard" ready to detect threat, so it is easy to stimulate and to then take over our minds. We also explain that there are two very different types of positive emotion, and this distinction is crucial to CFT (Gilbert, 2009, 2010). The drive system is primarily an activating-seeking system and, like the threat system, is mostly stimulated by sympathetic arousal (i.e., increased heart rate and flow of oxygen to the muscles; cf. the parasympathetic, "rest and digest" system). Sympathetic arousal is good for relatively short bursts of activity but, if it becomes overly stimulated, can cause problems. It is not uncommon that when we have a threatened sense of self (one that may be vulnerable to rejection), then we can over-stimulate the drive system because of trying to achieve things, do things, or prove ourselves worthy in the minds of others. However, the system that is really important for our feelings of connectedness and safeness is actually the affiliative-soothing contentment system. The physiology of the system is for slowing down and is particularly linked to the myelinated vagal nerve of the parasympathetic autonomic nervous system (Porges, 2007). Consequently, in essence we are trying to help people shift from living in the threat system to creating experiences that will stimulate the affiliative-soothing parasympathetic system, especially in relationship to experiences of the self.

### *Embodiment*

One of the core difficulties for people with high levels of self-disgust is the experience of their bodies. For example, one of my patients talked about wanting to cut herself because she felt her blood would be black and this would let out all the inner "nasty stuff". Helping people relate to their bodies in different ways is therefore important. There are, in fact, a number of approaches for working with "the body" such as in sensory-motor psychotherapy (Ogden, Minton, & Pain, 2006) and embodiment work (Fay, 2007). In CFT, we help people become aware of their bodies in different ways. First, we use the Tai Chi concept of "centring", whereby individuals learn to focus on the body in terms of finding stability. So, for example, in sitting or walking it is helpful to focus on the idea of standing, sitting, or moving and also feeling stable and grounded (Gilbert & Choden, 2013). For those with feelings of bodily disgust from abuse, therapists can point out that the atoms and cells of the body are constantly changing and regenerating. Therefore, there is not a single cell in the body that is the same as when the abuse occurred. One is essentially biologically renewed regularly (Jung & Steil, 2013; Powell, Simpson, & Overton, this volume).

### *Breathing*

There is increasing evidence now that we can produce physiological and psychological changes by teaching people how to breathe in different ways (Porges, 2007). In CFT, we use the concept of a soothing breathing rhythm to slow and deepen on the breath, especially down into the diaphragm. Recent research has shown that this exercise can be beneficial in terms of lowering arousal, heart rate, and activity in the sympathetic nervous system (and activating the vagus parasympathetic nervous system), bringing about feelings of calmness and soothing (Streeter, Gerbarg, Saper, Ciraulo, & Brown, 2012). Helping to activate the vagus parasympathetic nervous system is important because it is linked to affiliative processes and helps create affiliative feelings (Porges, 2007), which underpins the CFT approach to compassion (Gilbert, 2010). When this works well, training the breath influences the balance between the sympathetic and parasympathetic nervous system. Greater parasympathetic regulation is important in helping patients to experience their bodies in different ways, finding points of calmness and stillness within. The ideal rhythm is around five to six breaths per minute, but this can be difficult for some people who need time and guidance. We also have noticed that some individuals struggle to have a smooth intake of breath, or a smooth letting go of the breath, and this too can have implications for the relative balance of sympathetic and parasympathetic arousal. We combine the breathing with a focus on body posture.

We next encourage people to experiment with facial expressions and voice tones. So, for example, as we slow the breath, we focus on the feelings of slowing down with each out-breath, and the body feeling more grounded and heavier with each other breath, so that we can begin to sense a point of inner stability/stillness. Next, we spend fifteen seconds on maintaining a neutral facial expression and then fifteen seconds of friendly facial expression, in order to experience subtle differences in feeling from that deliberate change of expression. We then focus on voice tone, by saying "hello" to oneself in a neutral tone and then in as kind, friendly, and supportive a tone as one can imagine. Indeed, it was helping patients create friendly emotional tones to their internal thoughts that was one of the first practices of CFT, developed nearly twenty years ago (Gilbert, 2012).

### *Mindfulness and attention training*

There is now considerable evidence that helping people learn to "pay attention to attention" (i.e., become more mindful) is immensely helpful (Siegel, 2010). This is partly because it disrupts the distressing thinking patterns and loops, especially for individuals who are getting lost in rumination and over-identifying with feeling states. Mindfulness is also very important in enhancing compassion (Gilbert & Choden, 2013). There are two elements to the mindfulness practice that are important for self-disgust patients. First is beginning to notice the repetitive patterns in one's mind, to become an observer in the traditional way of mindfulness. However, the second element is to become mindful of where one places one's attention—that is, to become more aware that our attention can get locked into "disgust centres" in our brains (through no fault of our own), but then to deliberately move one's attention to brain systems that are beneficial or helpful by refocusing attention on a compassionate image voice tone, thought, or sense of self.

### *Building compassion*

There is increasing evidence that compassion training produces a host of changes. Fredrickson, Cohn, Coffey, Pek, and Finkel (2008) found that six weekly group sessions with home practice based on a CD of loving-kindness meditations increased positive emotions, mindfulness, feelings of purpose in life, and social support, and decreased illness symptoms. Compassion training has also been shown to produce neurophysiological changes (e.g., Klimecki, Leiberg, Lamm, & Singer, 2012), and reduce shame, depression, and anxiety for personality disorders (Gilbert & Procter, 2006). Interestingly, and in support of the theoretical distinction made earlier regarding the different forms of self-criticism, it was the self-hatred and self-persecution elements that reduced more significantly than self-correcting self-criticism. Although there are few randomised controlled trials at present, a recent meta-analysis of studies that do exist has shown that CFT has a consistent effect on these processes, often above other therapies (Leaviss & Uttley, 2014).

In CFT, compassion training is based on the idea that compassion is both something we feel for and from others as well as for ourselves. Indeed, there is increasing evidence now that focusing on compassion for others has important positive impacts on our own wellbeing. For example, Lutz, Brefczynski-Lewis, Johnstone, and Davidson (2008) found that practising compassion for others through meditation (i.e., loving-kindness), had significant effects on the frontal cortex, immune system, and wellbeing. Fredrickson et al. (2013) found that different types of positive emotion (self-centeredness vs. meaning and other-focused) influenced genetic expression in the immune system.

It is known that kindness, sympathy, caring, and helpfulness are not equally dispensed but rather are targeted (for example) on kinship relationships and others we see as similar to ourselves (e.g., Loewenstein & Small, 2007). Similarly, developing kindness and compassion to parts of oneself we like is a lot easier than to parts of our self we do not like, detest, or would rather be rid of. So, again, the issue of to whom, when, and under what conditions we extend our motives and feelings of compassion is complex.

### *Creating the compassionate self*

We help people recognise that to a large extent our self-identities simply emerge within us according to the genes we inherit and the social environment we grow up and live within. Very rarely are we taught we can stand back and start to think about the kind of self we would like to cultivate; to imagine that there are many, potentially hundreds, of possible selves and we can learn to choose what we work with. For example, there could be a piano-playing or guitar-playing self, there could be a self who becomes a parent or one who stays childless. So, we can think about possible selves within us and what kind of self would be useful to cultivate and why. For many reasons, to do with the way that compassion has organising effects on our brains (Gilbert, 2009), we help people to practise deliberately shifting into the "mindset" of "themselves at their compassionate best". The qualities the individual is asked to imagine possessing include wisdom, strength, warmth, and a focus on caring; a commitment to try to be understanding and helpful. It is important that people do not feel they have to have these qualities already, but to imagine what it might be like if they did. This is using a method of acting techniques to help the creation of alternate self experiences (Gilbert, 2010). There is evidence that practising imagining one's "best possible self" is related to emotional changes such as increased optimism (Meevissen, Peters, & Alberts, 2011; Peters, Flink, Boersma, & Linton, 2010). Similarly, practising positive-self imagery (i.e., recalling a time when one felt relaxed and positive) was found to be related to higher levels of self-esteem and reduced anxiety in response to anxiety-provoking vignettes (e.g., meeting your partner's parents for the first time; Stopa, Brown, & Hirsch, 2012).

So in essence, and stated briefly, we teach individuals how to notice negative emotions arising, particularly in relationship to the self, such as self-criticism or self-disgust; to slow down, breathe slightly deeper and slower, ground oneself in the body; and then to imagine what one's compassionate self would think and how they would deal with this experience. This noticing and switching to a compassionate ideal has proved to be very helpful to people. For example, in an early study of CFT of people with chronic mental health difficulties in a day hospital, participants reported significant drops in self-criticism, and this was associated with recognising the ability to notice when it arose and then to switch to a much more compassionate state of mind (Gilbert & Procter, 2006).

### *Compassionate image*

Not only can we give ourselves compassion, and practise developing compassion and kindness towards others (which is also a part of CFT), but we can practise imagining receiving compassion. In these exercises, we guide people through imagining creating a compassionate-other sentient mind/being outside of oneself but focused on oneself. It may take a human form but not always; for example, an ideal compassionate other might be a nonhuman animal or even a tree (Gilbert & Irons, 2004). In fact, people who have been abused often find imagining compassion from a human being tricky (as they don't trust them) and may (at first) prefer animals as their compassionate image/friend. The exercise here is to spend time just imagining what it would feel like for one's compassionate image to have wisdom for you, strength and determination, and be totally committed to your wellbeing (Gilbert, 2009; Lee, 2005). They are never judgemental, always accepting, yet always wishing for your improvement and happiness. Again, this is a complicated technique that is difficult to describe clearly in this short section. However, the underlying principles are fairly straightforward. For example, if one lies in bed and imagines a sexual partner doing erotic things, this will stimulate the pituitary to release hormones from which we obtain arousal. Indeed, the whole point of fantasy in this case is physiological stimulation. This is the same basic idea with a compassionate image—of learning how to generate images that will stimulate certain systems in our brain and to work through the various feelings and fears of doing that, of which there can be many. Indeed, we have shown that self-critical people can be quite frightened of compassion feelings. This has been shown both in self-report measures and also physiological ones (Longe et al., 2010; Rockliff et al., 2011).

## *Conclusion*

Self-disgust may be linked to other emotions such as contempt, anger, and hatred. These emotions can be focused on the whole self or parts of the self, but whenever they are focused this indicates one is in a state of conflict and hostile self-relating. Some of the motivations behind self-criticism are to try to self-improve, but others are linked to wanting to get rid of, cut out, or cleanse. These are particularly associated with self-disgust.

Compassion-focused therapy was designed specifically for patients who have very high levels of shame and self-criticism, including self-disgust. Part of the goals of the therapy is to develop a different emotional relationship with oneself, one that's based on validation, understanding, and affiliation to replace the more hostile one. In that sense we are seeking to help people cultivate a certain type of identity rooted in compassion/caring motivation. It is a multi-faceted intervention that is based upon an evolutionary understanding of motivation and emotional functional systems. It teaches people how to work with breathing, body postures, attention, imagery, and imagery practice. In addition, it focuses on generating compassionate thinking and compassionate behaviour. Obviously, while there is growing evidence of this approach (Leaviss & Uttley, 2014), far more research is necessary, especially as to how to target compassion focusing with individuals who have high levels of disgust for the self.

CHAPTER THIRTEEN

# Reflections on the revolting self: a commentary and further directions

*Philip A. Powell, Paul G. Overton, and Jane Simpson*

The present volume represents the first collection of scholarly works on a topic that, until recently, received scarce attention as a potentially discrete and important psychological phenomenon in its own right. The chapters contained herein have shed some initial light on the concept of disgust for the self, in contexts as diverse as morality, disability, interpersonal violence, physical health, and mental wellbeing. Whilst it is our expectation that self-disgust is likely to be a construct of future interest primarily in the field of mental health, including in the psychology of eating disorders (see Fox, Grange, & Power, this volume), sexual dysfunctions (see de Jong & Borg, this volume), and traumatic stress (see Badour & Adams, this volume), we have seen glimpses of how it may be extended to wider, interdisciplinary problems (see Clark; Reynolds, McCambridge, & Consedine; and Jones, this volume). Selected chapters have challenged our *a priori* assumptions that self-disgust (as a maladaptive disgust-based construct) plays a pivotal role in certain experiences, including self-harm (see Benson, Boden, & Vitali, this volume) and cases of disability (see Reeve, this volume); others have served to reinforce and extend our own initial expectations (see Alanazi, Powell, & Power; and McKay & Lo Presti, this volume).

In this concluding chapter, it is our intention to highlight and discuss what we perceive as some of the most fundamental issues surrounding the psychological phenomenon of self-disgust, and to offer up some suggestions for those considering future research into the topic. Specifically, from our vantage point as the editors of the present volume, we have earmarked three key issues that are worthy of extended discussion. Broadly, we refer to these as the conceptualisation, demarcation, and quantification of self-disgust (as a psychological construct). Appealing to particular points advanced in earlier chapters of this volume, as well as evidence contained in the wider literature, we address each of these topics sequentially, as a primer to encourage ongoing debate amongst like-minded researchers. Then, in the final section of this closing chapter, an assortment of ideas for subsequent enquiry into self-disgust is presented. These are drawn, largely, from the preceding chapters but include novel areas for investigation that have yet to be explored.

## *A commentary on the revolting self*

### *On conceptualising self-disgust*

In the foremost chapter of the current volume (see Powell, Simpson, & Overton, this volume), we presented a conceptual framework that characterised self-disgust as a dysfunctional emotion schema, but were also explicit in noting its "draft" status as a model that was likely to be refined over time. Reading through the other authors' contributions has brought to the fore a number of issues concerning the nature of self-disgust (as a theoretical construct), which are apt for discussion. The first point is whether self-disgust *per se* is necessarily maladaptive and to what extent it should be theorised in this manner. There seems to be the general feeling that a degree of disgust towards the self has the potential to be beneficial. For example, Reynolds, McCambridge, and Consedine (this volume) note that some self-disgust reactions may be adaptive in the context of physical health, as a mechanism of motivating help-seeking behaviour and encouraging more diligent self-care. Clark (this volume) further alludes to a plausibly functional quality of self-disgust; by promoting withdrawal, certain instances of self-disgust may serve to protect other ingroup members from things like infection. We agree with these authors that self-disgust is likely to be adaptive under certain circumstances, such as in promoting good hygiene (Curtis, Danquah, & Aunger, 2009). Accordingly, in our model we have outlined some particulars on the conditions under which self-disgust is likely to be maladaptive. An element we view as critical in meaningfully differentiating instances of functional and dysfunctional self-oriented disgust is whether the target is (perceived as) enduring and/or important to one's identity. In the context of physical illness, for instance, we posit that self-disgust may indeed be adaptive in promoting help-seeking if the condition is deemed as curable and temporary. Moreover, we concur that disgust-based withdrawal may be beneficial (for valued others, and thereby the self) as a short-term strategy, but detrimental if adopted as an enduring pattern of behaviour, of the kind observed in certain mental health problems (e.g., Coughtrey, Shafran, Lee, & Rachman, 2012; Powell, Overton, & Simpson, 2014).

It would be revealing to test some of the above propositions formally, exploring, for example, how illness perceptions interact with (self-)disgust reactions in the prediction of health behaviours. Though important, we acknowledge that making the distinction between a lasting and transient self-disgust elicitor is unlikely to be exhaustive as an indicator of dysfunction. Relatively short-term withdrawal as a consequence of benign self-attributes that mimic the signs of contagious disease could too be considered a maladaptive "type one" error (e.g., Aktan, Ozmen, & Sanli, 2000), and certain enduring aspects of the self that were once appraised with disgust may come to be reappraised positively over time (see Reeve, this volume).

A related discussion point involves pitting that which is adaptive for the individual against that of the group. This idea has been touched upon by Clark (this volume), who introduces the stimulating idea of an extended self (i.e., the range of abstract categories with which the "self" is identified). While our current treatment of self-disgust is intentionally restricted to the individual, we recognise the need to consider the phenomenon within the context of the wider social group. The act of seemingly protecting other ingroup members by isolating oneself when sick (and revolting), or "selflessly" opting to care for an ill relative who is (temporarily) disgusting to others, can only be understood with reference to interpersonal dynamics (e.g., Isaksen, 2002). Thus, this social component is a notable omission from our general, individual differences model. For instance, we do not consider how otherwise generic disgust-based avoidance may differ depending on the entity that is being avoided, and its perceived distance from the self. Here, we join with Clark in encouraging work on "intragroup disgust", that is, instances of disgust towards those with whom we may share our sense of "self".

We would also like to comment briefly on the comprehensiveness of our descriptive model. While we hope that it will be found useful as a framework for interpreting and studying people's experiences of revulsion for the self, it is understandably not a "catch-all". In her chapter, Reeve (this volume) does a commendable service in challenging some of the *a priori* expectations that may be associated with self-disgust. In particular, she illustrates how not everyone who may be expected to experience self-disgust (as a result of being greeted with disgust in wider society) actually does so. Further, she introduces the idea of "unmaking" (i.e., adapting or becoming resilient to) self-disgust. These are important insights. In our own work, we have only recently started to look at ways that in-the-moment experiences of self-disgust may be ameliorated (Powell, 2013), and it is not yet clear how certain people may adapt. We suspect that the answer lies primarily in an individual's cognitive (re)appraisals. Thus, in the context of our theoretical model, we would hypothesise that, for some stigmatised people, the characteristic that is attracting social stigma does not (or does no longer) feature within the repertoire of what they personally find disgusting. Instead, these aspects of the self that are appraised as "disgusting" in wider social circles become identifying and meaningful parts of individuals' self-concepts (e.g., Cooper, 1998). We can but speculate on the range of mechanisms that drive such (re)appraisals (e.g., habituation to stimuli that were previously found disgusting; Rozin, 2008), but this insight is important in illustrating how our relatively general model of self-disgust may need to be modified in the context of particular populations.

Our descriptive model was generated after researching self-disgust primarily in the context of depression, and represents but one theoretical sketch of enduring self-disgust as a dysfunctional phenomenon. Other authors have previously characterised self-disgust as a special instance of self-conscious emotion, focusing on it more as a state response (e.g., Roberts & Goldenberg, 2007; Simpson, Hillman, Crawford, & Overton, 2010). At the time of writing, at least one additional extended commentary on self-disgust has been published, based on research into individuals with anorexia nervosa (Moncrieff-Boyd, Byrne, & Nunn, 2013). Moncrieff-Boyd and her colleagues (2013) theorise self-disgust in people diagnosed with anorexia as a product of impaired self/non-self discrimination, such that self-disgust results from: a failure or ambiguity in separating the self and non-self; an appraisal of aspects of the self as non-self; and a disgust-based rejection of certain elements of the self that have been deemed non-self. Thus, in their theory, appraising an object of self as non-self is a necessary precursor to the experience of self-disgust. This idea builds on the prior comments of other authors, who have—we think correctly—argued that viewing the self as the "other" (i.e., self-vs.-self) is an essential ingredient for self-disgust (e.g., Roberts & Goldenberg, 2007). However, Moncrieff-Boyd et al. (2013) go on further to suggest that an appraisal of "non-self" (i.e., self-vs.-non-self) is also necessary. The researchers cite neurological and behavioural evidence of impaired interoceptive ability in those with anorexia nervosa in support of their position. Nevertheless, there is at present an absence of data directly linking problems with interoception (i.e., self/non-self discrimination) to self-disgust responses in people with anorexia, or any other population. Therefore, we encourage further work into identifying the precise conditions that are necessary and/or sufficient for the elicitation of self-directed revulsion.

### *On demarcating self-disgust*

While a number of researchers are beginning to converge on the idea of "self-disgust" representing a potentially discrete and powerful feeling state (e.g., Moncrieff-Boyd et al., 2013; Overton, Markland, Taggart, Bagshaw, & Simpson, 2008; Powell, 2013; Roberts & Goldenberg, 2007), much of what has largely been theoretical speculation has yet to be proven empirically. In particular, data are urgently required on the relations between self-disgust and other established psychological phenomena, in order to gauge the degree to which self-disgust can be demarcated as a unique variable of interest. One of the primary topics for debate is the extent to which self-disgust can be meaningfully separated from the otherwise concomitant self-conscious emotion of shame (Roberts & Goldenberg, 2007). This issue has received some attention in a number of chapters in the current volume. Alanazi,

Powell, and Power (this volume), for example, reference Power and Dalgleish's (2008) model of emotion, in which the basic emotion of disgust turned on the self is represented in the form of more complex emotional states, such as shame and guilt. Conversely, Fox, Grange, and Power (this volume)—while noting some of the difficulties inherent in the measurement of such constructs—propose that the emotional state that has been described in some studies as one of shame (e.g., Andrews, 1997) may be more accurately rooted in the disgust emotion (as instances of self-disgust).

While this is a debate that will be fundamentally settled empirically, we have outlined our own theoretical perspective on the issue in some detail in an earlier chapter (see Powell, Simpson, & Overton, this volume). It is our view, at present, that self-disgust represents a complex derivative of the disgust emotion that is distinct from shame, which too has both complex and more primitive variants (Clark, 2010). Nonetheless, we do think that self-disgust and shame often go hand in hand (see Powell et al., 2014). In their chapter, de Jong and Borg (this volume) cleverly structure their exploration of the concept of self-disgust around three already well-established subtypes of the disgust emotion (i.e., the pathogen, sexual, and moral disgust categories; Tybur, Lieberman, & Griskevicius, 2009). In doing so, they provide a convenient scaffold for separating instances of disgust (that happen to be focused on the self) from cases of shame; self-disgust occurs when (an aspect of) the self comes to feature as a disgust elicitor in a pre-established disgust domain (e.g., being "polluted" through contact with pathogen disgust elicitors as a rape victim). Of course, such a perspective does not rule out shame being experienced as a concomitant of disgust, but it does not necessitate it either.

Disentangling self-disgust from other highly related subjective phenomena is an important task, and one that we expect may be easier in some contexts than in others. For example, the emotions of disgust and anger may be more amenable to distinction when the subject is the physical body, rather than a more abstract topic, such as morality, or complex and volatile interpersonal relationships (see Jones, this volume). To paraphrase the emotion theorist Paul Ekman, psychologists can be separated by the degree to which they are typically "sharpeners" or "flatteners" of psychological phenomena. The sharpeners, with which we most closely identity, are those who seek to clarify, refine, and make operational distinctions. We personally would like to see self-disgust sharpened and not flattened in future work. In addition to being a means of clarifying our own empirical understanding, we have conversed with clinical colleagues previously about the benefits of providing accurate labels and explanations for specific feeling states that patients may experience. Moreover, precise affective measurement enables us to better evaluate the effectiveness of promising therapies (e.g., compassion-focused therapy; see Gilbert, this volume) on relevant emotional constructs.

### *On quantifying self-disgust*

As noted in our introductory chapter (see Powell, Simpson, & Overton, this volume), achieving reliable and valid quantitative assessment(s) of self-disgust is a pressing issue. Although, sadly, this has not been the focus of any of the chapters contained within the present volume, in addition to the Self-Disgust Scale (SDS; Overton et al., 2008), we are acutely aware of one other scale that has been designed in an attempt to capture the construct of "self-disgust". The Questionnaire for the Assessment of Self-Disgust, which has been so far published exclusively in German (QASD; Schienle, Ille, Sommer, & Arendasy, 2014), mirrors closely the structure of the SDS, featuring two subscales assessing "Personal Disgust" (i.e., one's physical appearance/character) and "Behavioural Disgust". This scale has been used to assess differential levels of self-disgust in a mixed, German clinical sample, with some interesting findings (see Ille et al., 2014). Due to our collective insufficiency in the comprehension of the German language, we are regrettably not able to comment on the scale more fully at this stage. Nonetheless, we wish to voice our immediate concern that the instrument may serve to further obscure (i.e., flatten rather than sharpen) the definition of self-disgust. The example item provided for the "Behavioural Disgust" subscale in Ille et al. (2014) is "I *regret* my behaviour", which suggests to us a scale that taps more into general self-negativity than any disgust *per se*. Accordingly, it is not yet clear how the QASD improves on the SDS or to what degree it does so.

In a concerted effort to channel research on self-directed disgust in a more specific direction (i.e., to encourage researchers to explore self-disgust as primarily a *disgust*-based construct), we are taking some steps in revising the content of the SDS. In particular, we have modified the scale in order to increase its face validity for self-directed repugnance, and to reduce its apparent overlap with other conflicting constructs such as self-dislike. In total, five questionnaire items have been revised and three new items added (derived from previous qualitative work; Powell et al., 2014), to produce three proportionate domains. In the modified measure, five items were intended to measure "physical self-disgust", five were designed to measure "behavioural self-disgust", and five were included to assess overall (i.e., "general") self-disgust. An extra filler item was also included to rebalance the content of the scale. Lastly, the Likert scale was reversed to allow for more convenient scoring. A copy of the Self-Disgust Scale-Revised (SDS-R) is included at the end of this chapter. While a full psychometric evaluation of the SDS-R is pending, we have conducted some preliminary analyses on a non-clinical sample of 293 individuals affiliated either with the University of Sheffield or of Lancaster in the UK. The age of this sample ranged from 18 to 77 years, with a median of 24 (IQR = 14). The majority were female (64.5%), undergraduate or postgraduate students (78.2%), and identified themselves as "White British" (73%). The SDS-R was found to be highly internally consistent in this group ($\alpha = .92$).

A principal components analysis was carried out on the polychoric correlation matrix of the SDS-R data (as recommended for non-normal or ordinal data; Field, Miles, & Field, 2012), with varimax rotation, and largely supported the intended factor structure of the measure (see Table 1). The Kaiser criterion, parallel analysis, and very simple structure criterion (see Basto & Pereira, 2012) all converged to indicate the optimum extraction of two factors. In total, the rotated solution explained 58% of the variance, and showed five items (numbers 8, 12, 15, 19, 21) with salient loadings (>.40) on factor one (explaining 33% of the variance), which were all related to physical self-disgust. An additional five items (numbers 3, 11, 14, 18, 22) had salient loadings on factor two (explaining 25% of the variance), and were all based on behavioural self-disgust. Lastly, five items (numbers 1, 2, 5, 7, 9) cross—loaded (having salient loadings >.40 on both factors), supporting their intended inclusion as indicators of overall disgust with the self, incorporating both physical and behavioural traits. One of these items (number 1: "I find myself repulsive") had a considerably higher loading on factor one (.73) than factor two (.42), and so can be considered more strongly allied to appearance than behavioural characteristics.

Regarding its relationship with other measures, the SDS-R has so far been found to have a significant and strong positive correlation with the Disgust Sensitivity subscale of the Disgust Propensity and Sensitivity

Table 1. Component loadings of the SDS-R.

| *Item no.* | *Item content* | *Component 1: physical self-disgust* | *Component 2: behavioural self-disgust* |
|---|---|---|---|
| 19 | It bothers me to look at myself | **.87** | .24 |
| 15 | I avoid looking at my reflection | **.82** | .06 |
| 21 | I find the way I look nauseating | **.80** | .24 |
| 8 | I consider myself attractive | **.68** | .13 |
| 12 | I do not want to be seen | **.66** | .28 |
| 1 | I find myself repulsive | **.73** | **.42** |
| 5 | I can't stand being me | **.66** | **.56** |
| 7 | I am revolting for many reasons | **.61** | **.53** |
| 2 | I am proud of who I am | **.47** | **.43** |
| 9 | People avoid me | **.43** | **.47** |
| 22 | My behaviour repels people | .21 | **.73** |
| 11 | I feel good about the way I behave | .27 | **.72** |
| 3 | I am sickened by the way I behave | .21 | **.72** |
| 14 | I often do things I find revolting | .20 | **.63** |
| 18 | I behave as well as everyone else | .05 | **.61** |

*Note*: Salient item loadings (>.40) are in bold.

Scale-Revised (DPSS-R; van Overveld, de Jong, Peters, Cavanagh, & Davey, 2006), $r_s(291) = .41$, $p < .001$, and the Depression subscale of the Depression, Anxiety and Stress Scales (DASS; Lovibond & Lovibond, 1993), $r_s(291) = .65$, $p < .001$. This can be compared to some data for the SDS, from a contemporaneously sourced, similarly sized independent student sample of 321. These participants' ages ranged from 18 to 74, with a median of 23 (IQR = 12). As with the SDS-R sample, most of the participants were female (65.1%), undergraduate or postgraduate students (77.3%), and "White British" (68.8%). In this sample, the SDS exhibited a smaller correlation with the Disgust Sensitivity subscale of the DPSS-R, $r_s(319) = .30$, $p < .001$, and a slightly smaller association with the DASS-DEP, $r_s(319) = .60$, $p < .001$, than that recorded for the SDS-R. While the results of this, admittedly limited, analysis suggest that associations with disgust sensitivity and depressive symptoms appear to be slightly stronger for the SDS-R than the SDS, clearly more formal psychometric testing and development is a necessary venture. Additional comparisons between the SDS and SDS-R are essential to gauge whether the SDS-R represents a definitive and worthwhile improvement.

## *Further directions*

As we reach the close of the present volume, it is our intention to summarise here what we see as the most promising next steps for research into self-disgust. A few ideas for subsequent work have been hinted at previously, both in our earlier writings and in the present chapter, and were nested predominantly in suggestions for further refinement on the theory and measurement of self-disgust (as a psychological construct). Such comments have included the need to pursue and ensure the discriminant validity of self-directed revulsion, and to complement self-report instruments with more objective behavioural, neurological, and psychophysiological indices. This is a psychometric problem that will require continual attention, likely to be undertaken as part of more specified research aims that address complementary questions. Here we present some suggestions for such investigations.

An area that we anticipate will receive the most immediate research attention—at least initially—is the role that self-disgust may have across different mental health problems. These include disorders that have been addressed directly in the present volume and others, which otherwise intuitively appear as potentially fitting candidates for self-revulsion. To date, the studies that have looked at self-disgust explicitly have been situated within the context of depression (e.g., Overton et al., 2008; Powell, Simpson, & Overton, 2013), yet some attempt has been made to expand this focus recently (Ille et al., 2014). Taking as a first step the mental health issues that have been the topics of chapters in the current work, there is scope to further elucidate the role of self-disgust in psychological problems such as post-traumatic stress (see Badour & Adams, this volume), sexual dysfunction (see de Jong & Borg, this volume), and eating disorders (see Fox, Grange, & Power, this volume), amongst others. In some cases, specific frameworks have been advocated as a means for pursuing this. For example, de Jong and Borg (this volume) present a heuristic model of the relationship between self-disgust (plus general disgust) and sexual arousal that is conductive to empirical investigation. Moreover, given their promising exploratory non-clinical data, there is an opportunity to extend this model to a sample exhibiting sexual problems of a clinical nature. Elsewhere, general trends have been noted that are open to more formal empirical testing and verification. For instance, Benson and colleagues (this volume) hypothesise a general absence of any disgust feelings immediately prior to incidents of self-harm. This is especially interesting in the context of other findings that note diminished disgust as a function of sexual arousal (Borg & de Jong, 2012), and it would be useful to know whether this effect extends to (non-specific) arousal (e.g., prior to harming) more generally.

In addition to the mental health problems featured herein, we encourage researchers to engage with additional psychological issues that have not been addressed directly in the current volume. For instance, one could sample individuals who experience overt problems with their physical and/or psychological identity, such as in gender identity disorder and body integrity identity disorder. Intuitively, these seem like phenomena that would involve a sense of self-disgust, as they inherently involve the physical body (and certain bodily products) being appraised as foreign. We think this is likely to be fertile ground, and cannot surmise a more explicit test of Moncrieff-Boyd and colleague's (2013) hypothesis of the link between self-disgust and impaired self/non-self discrimination. Further, dissociations in personality, such as in borderline personality disorder, too could be of prime interest (Rusch et al., 2011). Of relevance here is Benson et al.'s (this volume) idea of "integral self-disgust" as an experience involving depersonalisation and losing the integral boundaries of the "self".

Many of the chapter authors in this book have emphasised the importance of considering self-oriented revulsion from a therapeutic perspective, and we would agree with that. Fox et al. (this volume) would like to see some attention afforded to self-disgust as part of more emotion-based treatments for individuals with eating disorders, as these represent a difficult group to treat successfully. Gilbert's (e.g., this volume) compassion-focused therapy would benefit from the development of a formal evidence base, exploring its utility across a number of mental health issues. Other authors (e.g., Reynolds, McCambridge, & Consedine, this volume) make a case for efforts to "normalise" self-disgust (or the stimuli that elicit self-disgust), through techniques such as mindfulness, in order to improve outcomes for affected individuals. Indeed, induced mindfulness has been shown to influence disgust-based responses in an experimental health context (Reynolds, Consedine, & McCambridge, 2013), and it would be curious to observe its effect on participants' *self-directed* disgust reactions.

Beyond the focus of psychopathology, we can think of a number of other research questions that have clear utility. First, it is of theoretical interest how self-focused disgust relates to disgust responding more generally (i.e., towards external stimuli). The disgust response is heterogeneous, and future studies could assess the relations between self-disgust and the full range of established disgust elicitors (see de Jong & Borg, this volume). One paper that did investigate the relationship between self- and sociomoral disgust reported that individuals higher in trait behavioural self-disgust produced significantly higher disgust and punishment ratings of non-moral offences, but significantly lower disgust and punishment ratings of severe sociomoral transgressions (Olatunji, David, & Ciesielski, 2012). It would be useful to explore these findings further, and discover how self-focused disgust is associated with other disgust domains. Second, the "positive" role of (state) self-disgust reactions in areas such as morality and physical health should be investigated further (see Reynolds, McCambridge, & Consedine, this volume). Third, self-referent disgust could be explored through the lens of established theoretical perspectives. For example, McKay and Lo Presti (this volume) advocate terror-management theory as a tool for this, clarifying self-disgust as a function of mortality salience. Cross-disciplinary approaches too may be particularly valuable in this regard.

## Conclusion

As the first ever volume dedicated to the psychological concept of self-disgust, we hope that the current work has raised (nearly) as many questions as it has answered. Through putting together the chapters of this book, it was our aspiration to both clarify and draw attention to this particularly noxious feeling state as a specific, disgust-based cognitive-affective phenomenon. In so doing, we have become acutely aware that—in the wake of a wide range of fascinating and novel insights into disgust for the self—we have but scratched the surface. Thus, while the present selection of papers have served, both informatively and meaningfully, to ground self-disgust as a topic for psychological enquiry, it is evident that there is still much to learn of the revolting self.

* * *

### *Self-Disgust Scale Revised (SDS-R)*

This questionnaire is concerned with how you feel about yourself. When responding to the statements below, please circle the appropriate number according to the following definitions: 1 = Strongly disagree; 2 = Very much disagree; 3 = Slightly disagree; 4 = Neither agree nor disagree; 5 = Slightly agree; 6 = Very much agree; 7 = Strongly agree.

| | *Strongly disagree* | | | | | *Strongly agree* | |
|---|---|---|---|---|---|---|---|
| 1. I find myself repulsive | 1 | 2 | 3 | 4 | 5 | 6 | 7 |
| 2. I am proud of who I am | 1 | 2 | 3 | 4 | 5 | 6 | 7 |
| 3. I am sickened by the way I behave* | 1 | 2 | 3 | 4 | 5 | 6 | 7 |
| 4. Sometimes I feel tired† | 1 | 2 | 3 | 4 | 5 | 6 | 7 |
| 5. I can't stand being me* | 1 | 2 | 3 | 4 | 5 | 6 | 7 |
| 6. I enjoy the company of others | 1 | 2 | 3 | 4 | 5 | 6 | 7 |
| 7. I am revolting for many reasons† | 1 | 2 | 3 | 4 | 5 | 6 | 7 |
| 8. I consider myself attractive* | 1 | 2 | 3 | 4 | 5 | 6 | 7 |
| 9. People avoid me* | 1 | 2 | 3 | 4 | 5 | 6 | 7 |
| 10. I enjoy being outdoors | 1 | 2 | 3 | 4 | 5 | 6 | 7 |
| 11. I feel good about the way I behave | 1 | 2 | 3 | 4 | 5 | 6 | 7 |
| 12. I do not want to be seen | 1 | 2 | 3 | 4 | 5 | 6 | 7 |
| 13. I am a sociable person | 1 | 2 | 3 | 4 | 5 | 6 | 7 |
| 14. I often do things I find revolting | 1 | 2 | 3 | 4 | 5 | 6 | 7 |
| 15. I avoid looking at my reflection† | 1 | 2 | 3 | 4 | 5 | 6 | 7 |
| 16. Sometimes I feel happy | 1 | 2 | 3 | 4 | 5 | 6 | 7 |
| 17. I am an optimistic person | 1 | 2 | 3 | 4 | 5 | 6 | 7 |
| 18. I behave as well as everyone else† | 1 | 2 | 3 | 4 | 5 | 6 | 7 |
| 19. It bothers me to look at myself | 1 | 2 | 3 | 4 | 5 | 6 | 7 |
| 20. Sometimes I feel sad | 1 | 2 | 3 | 4 | 5 | 6 | 7 |
| 21. I find the way I look nauseating† | 1 | 2 | 3 | 4 | 5 | 6 | 7 |
| 22. My behaviour repels people | 1 | 2 | 3 | 4 | 5 | 6 | 7 |

*Note*: * = Revised item; † = New item (from the original SDS).

# REFERENCES


aan het Rot, M., Hogenelst, K., & Schoevers, R. A. (2012). Mood disorders in everyday life: a systematic review of experience sampling and ecological momentary assessment studies. *Clinical Psychology Review, 32*: 510–523.

Abela, J. R. Z., & D'Alessandro, D. U. (2002). Beck's cognitive theory of depression: a test of the diathesis-stress and causal mediation components. *British Journal of Clinical Psychology, 41*: 111–128.

Ablon, J. (2012). Social stigma in Neurofibromatosis 1. In: M. Upadhyaya & D. N. Cooper (Eds.), *Neurofibromatosis Type 1* (pp. 673–682). Berlin Heidelberg: Springer.

Adams, T. G. J., Badour, C. L., Cisler, J. M., & Feldner, M. T. (2014). Contamination aversion and posttraumatic stress symptom severity following sexual trauma. *Cognitive Therapy and Research, 38*: 449–457.

Adams, T. G. J., Cisler, J. M., Brady, R. E., & Lohr, J. M. (2012). The effects of cognitive and affective priming on law of contagion appraisals. *Journal of Experimental Psychopathology, 3*: 470–478.

Adams, T. G. J., Cisler, J. M., Brady, R. E., Lohr, J. M., & Olatunji, B. O. (2013). Preliminary psychometric evidence for distinct affective and cognitive mechanisms mediating contamination aversion. *Journal of Psychopathology and Behavioral Assessment, 35*: 375–388.

Adams, T. G. J., & Lohr, J. M. (2012). Disgust mediates the relation between attentional shifting and contamination aversion. *Journal of Behavior Therapy and Experimental Psychiatry, 43*: 975–980.

Adams, T. G. J., Willems, J. L., & Bridges, A. J. (2011). Contamination aversion and repeated exposure to disgusting stimuli. *Anxiety, Stress and Coping: An International Journal, 24*: 157–165.

Agamben, G. (1998). *Homo Sacer: Sovereign Power and Bare Life*. D. Heller-Roazen (Trans.). Stanford, CA: Stanford University Press.

Aharoni, R., & Hertz, M. M. (2012). Disgust sensitivity and anorexia nervosa. *European Eating Disorders Review, 20*: 106–110.

Ahmed, K., & Bhugra, D. (2007). The role of culture in sexual dysfunction. *Psychiatry, 6*: 115–120.

Ahmed, S. (2004). *The Cultural Politics of Emotion*. Edinburgh: Edinburgh University Press.

Ainscough, C., & Toon, K. (2000). *Breaking Free: Help for Survivors of Child Sexual Abuse*. London: Sheldon Press.

Aktan, S., Ozmen, E., & Sanli, B. (2000). Anxiety, depression, and nature of acne vulgaris in adolescents. *International Journal of Dermatology, 39*: 354–357.

Akute, O. O. (2000). Colorectal carcinoma in Ibadan, Nigeria: a 20-year survey—1971 to 1990. *Hepato-Gastroenterology, 47*: 709–713.

Allan, S., Gilbert, P., & Goss, K. (1994). An exploration of shame measures, II: psychopathology. *Personality and Individual Differences, 17*: 719–727.

Allan, S., & Goss, K. (2012). Shame and pride in eating disorders. In: J. R. E. Fox & K. Goss (Eds.), *Eating and Its Disorders* (pp. 154–167). Chichester: Wiley-Blackwell.

Alloy, L. B., Abramson, L. Y., Keyser, J., Gerstein, R. K., & Sylvia, L. G. (2008). Negative cognitive style. In: K. S. Dobson & D. Dozois (Eds.), *Risk Factors for Depression* (pp. 237–262). New York: Academic Press.

Altamura, A. C., Dell'Osso, B., Mundo, E., & Dell'Osso, L. (2007). Duration of untreated illness in major depressive disorder: a naturalistic study. *International Journal of Clinical Practice, 61*: 1697–1700.

American Psychiatric Association (APA) (1994). *Diagnostic and Statistical Manual of Mental Disorders* (4th edn.). Washington, DC: APA Press.

American Psychiatric Association (APA) (2013). *Diagnostic and Statistical Manual of Mental Disorders* (5th edn.). Washington, DC: APA Press.

Amir, N., Klumpp, H., Elias, J., Bedwell, J. S., Yanasak, N., & Miller, L. S. (2005). Increased activation of the anterior cingulate cortex during processing of disgust faces in individuals with social phobia. *Biological Psychiatry, 57*: 975–981.

Amir, N., Najimi, S., Bomyea, J., & Burns, M. (2010). Disgust and anger in social anxiety. *International Journal of Cognitive Therapy, 3*: 3–10.

Amodio, D. M., & Frith, C. D. (2006). Meeting of minds: the medial frontal cortex and social cognition. *Nature Reviews Neuroscience, 7*: 268–277.

Andersen, B. L., & Anderson, B. (1989). Controlled prospective longitudinal study of women with cancer: II. Psychological outcomes. *Journal of Consulting and Clinical Psychology, 57*: 692–697.

Andrews, B. (1995). Bodily shame as a mediator between abusive experiences and depression. *Journal of Abnormal Psychology, 104*: 227–285.

Andrews, B. (1997). Bodily shame in relation to abuse in childhood and bulimia: a preliminary investigation. *British Journal of Clinical Psychology, 36*: 41–49.

Andrews, B., & Brewin, C. R. (2000). What did Freud get right? *The Psychologist, 13*: 605–607.

Andrews, B., Brewin, C. R., Rose, S., & Kirk, M. (2000). Predicting PTSD symptoms in victims of violent crime: the role of shame, anger, and child abuse. *Journal of Abnormal Psychology, 109*: 69–73.

Andrews, B., & Hunter, E. (1997). Shame, early abuse, and course of depression in a clinical sample: a preliminary study. *Cognition and Emotion, 11*: 373–381.

Andrews, B., Qian, M., & Valentine, J. D. (2002). Predicting depressive symptoms with a new measure of shame: the experience of shame scale. *British Journal of Clinical Psychology, 41*: 29–42.

Angyal, A. (1941). Disgust and related aversions. *Journal of Abnormal and Social Psychology, 36*: 393–412.

Archer, T., Sjoden, P. O., & Nilsson, L. G. (1985). Contextual control of taste-aversion conditioning and extinction. In: P. D. Balsam & A. Tomie (Eds.), *Context and Learning* (pp. 225–271). Hillsdale, NJ: Lawrence Erlbaum Associates.

Ariely, D., & Loewenstein, G. (2006). The heat of the moment: the effect of sexual arousal on sexual decision-making. *Journal of Behavioral Decision Making, 19*: 87–98.

Arocho, J., Brand, J., Weiner, E., & McKay, D. (2011). Examining the relationship between moral disgust and PTSD. In: D. Maack (Chair), *Exploring Disgust and Its Role in the Pathogenesis of Clinical Disorders*. Symposium presented at the annual meeting of the Association for Behavioral and Cognitive Therapies, Toronto, ONT.

Arocho, J., McKay, D., Adams, T., & Lohr, J. (2014). The moral disgust scale: development, reliability, validity, and relation with measures of psychopathology. Manuscript submitted for publication.

Badour, C. L., Bown, S., Adams, T. G., Bunaciu, L., & Feldner, M. T. (2012). Specificity of fear and disgust experienced during traumatic interpersonal victimization in predicting posttraumatic stress and contamination-based obsessive-compulsive symptoms. *Journal of Anxiety Disorders, 26*: 590–598.

Badour, C. L., Feldner, M. T., Babson, K. A., Blumenthal, H., & Dutton, C. E. (2013). Disgust, mental contamination, and posttraumatic stress: unique relations following sexual versus non-sexual assault. *Journal of Anxiety Disorders, 27*: 155–162.

Badour, C. L., Feldner, M. T., Babson, K. A., Smith, R. C., Blumenthal, H., Trainor, C. D., Bunaciu, L., & Olatunji, B. O. (2011). Differential emotional responding to ideographic cues of traumatic interpersonal violence compared to non-interpersonal traumatic experiences. *Journal of Experimental Psychopathology, 2*: 400–417.

Badour, C. L., Feldner, M. T., Blumenthal, H., & Bujarski, S. J. (2013). Examination of increased mental contamination as a potential mechanism in the association between disgust sensitivity and sexual assault-related posttraumatic stress. *Cognitive Therapy and Research, 37*: 697–703.

Badour, C. L., Feldner, M. T., Blumenthal, H., & Knapp, A. (2013). Preliminary evidence for a unique role of disgust-based conditioning in posttraumatic stress. *Journal of Traumatic Stress, 26*: 280–287.

Badour, C. L., Ojserkis, R., McKay, D., & Feldner, M. T. (2014). Disgust as a unique affective predictor of mental contamination following sexual trauma. *Journal of Anxiety Disorders, 28*: 704–711.

Baer, L. (2002). *The Imp of the Mind: Exploring the Silent Epidemic of Obsessional Bad Thoughts*. London: Plume.

Baer, R. A., Walsh, E., & Lykins, E. L. B. (2009). Assessment of mindfulness. In: F. Didonna (Ed.), *Clinical Handbook of Mindfulness* (pp. 153–168). New York: Springer.

Baião, R., Gilbert, P., McEwan, K., & Carvalho, S. (2014). Forms of Self-Criticising/Attacking & Self-Reassuring Scale: Psychometric properties and normative study. *Psychology and Psychotherapy: Theory, Research and Practice*. doi:10.1111/papt.12049.

Bancroft, J., & Janssen, E. (2000). The dual control model of male sexual response: a theoretical approach to centrally mediated erectile dysfunction. *Neuroscience and Biobehavioral Reviews, 24*: 571–579.

Bargh, J. A., Schwader, K. L., Hailey, S. E., Dyer, R. L., & Boothby, E. J. (2012). Automaticity in social-cognitive processes. *Trends in Cognitive Sciences, 16*: 593–605.

Barker, K., & Davey, G. C. L. (1997). Categories of disgust: a factor analysis study. *Cognitive Science Research Paper 471*. University of Sussex, ISSN 1350–3162.

Barnes, C. D., Brown, R. P., & Osterman, L. L. (2009). Protection, payback, or both? Emotional and motivational mechanisms underlying avoidance by victims of transgressions. *Motivation and Emotion, 33*: 400–411.

Baron, J. (2011). Utilitarian emotions: suggestions from introspection. *Emotion Review, 3*: 286–287.

Bastian, B., & Haslam, N. (2010). Excluded from humanity: the dehumanizing effects of social ostracism. *Journal of Experimental Social Psychology, 46*: 107–113.

Bastian, B., & Haslam, N. (2011). Experiencing dehumanization: cognitive and emotional effects of everyday dehumanization. *Basic and Applied Social Psychology, 33*: 295–303.

Basto, M., & Pereira, J. M. (2012). An SPSS R-menu for ordinal factor analysis. *Journal of Statistical Software, 46*: 1–29.

Beck, A. T. (1967). *The Diagnosis and Management of Depression*. Philadelphia: University of Pennsylvania Press.

Beck, A. T. (1976). *Cognitive Therapy and the Emotional Disorders*. New York: Meridian.

Beck, A. T., Rush, A. J., Shaw, B. F., & Emery, G. (1979). *Cognitive Therapy of Depression*. New York: Guilford.

Becker, D., & Mester, R. (1996). Further insights into transsexualism. *Psychopathology, 29*: 1–6.

Bediou, B., Krolak-Salmon, P., Saoud, M., Henaff, M., Burt, M., Dalery, J., & D'Amato, T. (2005). Facial expression and sex recognition in schizophrenia and depression. *Canadian Journal of Psychiatry, 50*: 525–533.

Bekkers, M. J. T. M., van Knippenberg, F. C. E., van Dulmen, A. M., van den Borne, H. W., & van Berge Henegouwen, G. P. (1997). Survival and psychosocial adjustment to stoma surgery and nonstoma bowel resection: a 4-year follow-up. *Journal of Psychosomatic Research, 42*: 235–244.

Bergler, E. (1956). *Homosexuality: Disease or Way of Life*. New York: Hill and Wang.

Berke, J. H. (1986). Shame and envy. *British Journal of Psychotherapy, 2*: 262–270.

Berle, D., & Phillips, E. S. (2006). Disgust and obsessive-compulsive disorder: an update. *Psychiatry, 69*: 228–238.

Berlins, M. (2008). Emotions run high over right-to-die case. *The Guardian*. Retrieved from http://www.guardian.co.uk/commentisfree/2008/mar/24/law.

Berman, N. C., Wheaton, M. G., Fabricant, L. E., & Abramowitz, J. S. (2012). Predicting mental pollution: the contribution of religion, parenting strategies, and childhood trauma. *Journal of Obsessive-Compulsive and Related Disorders, 1*: 143–158.

Biby, E. L. (1998). The relation between body dysmorphic disorder and depression, self-esteem, somatization, and obsessive-compulsive disorder. *Journal of Clinical Psychology, 54*: 489–499.

Birgegard, A., Bjorck, C., Norring, C., Sohlberg, S., & Clinton, D. (2009). Anorexic self-control and bulimic self-hate: differential outcome prediction from initial self-image. *International Journal of Eating Disorders, 42*: 522–530.

Blair, R. J. R., & Cipolotti, L. (2000). Impaired social response reversal: a case of "acquired sociopathy". *Brain, 123*: 1122–1141.

Blanchard, E. B., & Hickling, E. J. (2004). *After the Crash*. Washington, DC: American Psychological Association.

Blatt, S. J., Quinlan, D. M., Chevron, E. S., McDonald, C., & Zuroff, D. (1982). Dependency and self-criticism: psychological dimensions of depression. *Journal of Consulting and Clinical Psychology, 50*: 113–124.

Bloom, P. (2013). *Just Babies: The Origins of Good and Evil.* New York: Random House.

Borg, C. (2013). *Sex, Disgust, and Penetration Disorders.* Unpublished doctoral dissertation. Groningen, the Netherlands: University of Groningen.

Borg, C., & de Jong, P. J. (2012). Feelings of disgust and disgust-induced avoidance weaken following induced sexual arousal in women. *PloS one, 7*: e44111.

Borg, C., de Jong, P. J., & Weijmar-Schultz, W. (2011). Vaginismus and dyspareunia: relationship with general and sex-related moral standards. *Journal of Sexual Medicine, 8*: 223–231.

Bovin, M., & Marx, B. P. (2011). The importance of the peritraumatic experience in defining traumatic stress. *Psychological Bulletin, 137*: 47–67.

Bowlby, J. (1969). *Attachment and Loss.* London: Pimilico.

Braun, V., & Clarke, V. (2006). Using thematic analysis in psychology. *Qualitative Research in Psychology, 3*: 77–101.

Brewin, C. R., Andrews, B., & Rose, S. (2000). Fear, helplessness, and horror in posttraumatic stress disorder: investigating DSM-IV criterion A2 in victims of violent crime. *Journal of Traumatic Stress, 13*: 499–509.

Briant, E., Watson, N., & Philo, G. (2011). *Bad News for Disabled People: How the Newspapers Are Reporting Disability.* Glasgow: Strathclyde Centre for Disability Research and Glasgow Media Unit.

Briere, J. (1996). A self-trauma model for treating adult survivors of severe child abuse. In: J. Briere, L. Berliner, J. A. Bulkley, C. Jenny, & T. Reid (Eds.), *The APSAC Handbook on Child Maltreatment* (pp. 140–157). California: Sage Publications.

Briere, J., & Gil, E. (1998). Self-mutilation in clinical and general population samples: prevalence, correlates, and functions. *American Journal of Orthopsychiatry, 68*: 609–620.

British Broadcasting Corporation (BBC) (2013a). Q&A: Gay Rights in Russia. *BBC.* Retrieved from http://www.bbc.co.uk/news/world-europe-23604142.

British Broadcasting Corporation (BBC) (2013b). Jillings Report: the main points. *BBC.* Retrieved from http://www.bbc.co.uk/news/uk-wales-23225368.

Brittain, K. R., & Shaw, C. (2007). The social consequences of living with and dealing with incontinence: a carer's perspective. *Social Science and Medicine, 65*: 1274–1283.

Brouse, C. H., Basch, C. E., Wolf, R. L., & Shmukler, C. (2004). Barriers to colorectal cancer screening: an educational diagnosis. *Journal of Cancer Education, 19*: 170–173.

Brown, G. W., & Harris, T. (1978). *The Social Origins of Depression*. London: Tavistock.

Brown, S. A., Williams, K., & Collins, A. (2007). Past and recent deliberate self-harm: emotion and coping strategy differences. *Journal of Clinical Psychology, 63*: 791–803.

Bruch, H. (1978). *The Golden Cage: The Enigma of Anorexia Nervosa*. Cambridge, MA: Harvard University Press.

Buckels, E. E., & Trapnell, P. D. (2013). Disgust facilitates outgroup dehumanization. *Group Processes and Intergroup Relations, 16*: 771–780.

Burleigh, M. (1991). *The Racial State: Germany 1933–1945*. Cambridge: Cambridge University Press.

Bush, G., Luu, P., & Posner, M. I. (2000). Cognitive and emotional influences in anterior cingulate cortex. *Trends in Cognitive Sciences, 4*: 215–222.

Calder, A. J., Beaver, J. D., Davis, M. H., van Ditzhuijzen, J., Keane, J., & Lawrence, A. D. (2007). Disgust sensitivity predicts the insula and pallidal response to pictures of disgusting foods. *European Journal of Neuroscience, 25*: 3422–3428.

Calder, A. J., Lawrence, A. D., & Young, A. W. (2001). Neuropsychology of fear and loathing. *Nature Reviews Neuroscience, 2*: 352–363.

Campbell, F. A. K. (2005). Legislating disability: negative ontologies and the government of legal identities. In: S. Tremain (Ed.), *Foucault and the Government of Disability* (pp. 108–130). Ann Arbor, MI: University of Michigan Press.

Campbell, F. A. K. (2009). *Contours of Ableism: The Production of Disability and Abledness*. Basingstoke: Palgrave Macmillan.

Carey, C. L., & Harris, L. M. (2005). The origins of blood-injection fear/phobia in cancer patients undergoing intravenous chemotherapy. *Behaviour Change, 22*: 212–219.

Carolan, L. A., & Power, M. J. (2011). What basic emotions are experienced in bipolar disorder? *Clinical Psychology and Psychotherapy, 18*: 366–378.

Caruana, F., Jezzini, A., Sbriscia-Fioretti, B., Rizzolatti, G., & Gallese, V. (2011). Emotional and social behaviors elicited by electrical stimulation of the insula in the macaque monkey. *Current Biology, 21*: 195–199.

Castle, D. J., & Phillips, K. A. (2002). Disordered body image in psychiatric disorders. In: D. J. Castle & K. A. Phillips (Eds.), *Disorders of Body Image* (pp. 55–66). Petersfield, Hampshire: Wrightson Biomedical Publishing.

Castilho, P., Pinto-Gouveia, J., & Duarte, J. (2013). Exploring self-criticism: Confirmatory factor analysis of the FSCRS in clinical and nonclinical samples. *Clinical Psychology and Psychotherapy*. doi:10.1002/cpp.1881.

Champion, L. A., & Power, M. J. (1995). Social and cognitive approaches to depression: towards a new synthesis. *British Journal of Clinical Psychology, 34*: 485–503.

Chapkis, W. (1988). *Beauty Secrets: Women and the Politics of Appearance*. London: The Women's Press.

Chapman, A. L., & Dixon-Gordon, K. L. (2007). Emotional antecedents and consequences of deliberate self-harm and suicide attempts. *Suicide and Life-Threatening Behavior, 37*: 543–552.

Chapman, G. B., & Coups, E. J. (2006). Emotions and preventive behavior: worry, regret, and influenza vaccination. *Health Psychology, 25*: 82–90.

Chapman, H. A., & Anderson, A. K. (2012). Understanding disgust. *Annals of the New York Academy of Sciences, 1251*: 62–76.

Chapman, H. A., & Anderson, A. K. (2013). Things rank and gross in nature: a review and synthesis of moral disgust. *Psychological Bulletin, 139*: 300–327.

Chapman, H. A., Kim, D. A., Susskind, J. M., & Anderson, A. K. (2009). In bad taste: evidence for the oral origins of moral disgust. *Science, 323*: 1222–1226.

Chapple, A., Ziebland, S., Hewitson, P., & McPherson, A. (2008). What affects the uptake of screening for bowel cancer using a faecal occult blood test (FOBt): a qualitative study. *Social Science and Medicine, 66*: 2425–2435.

Christensen, J. F., & Gomila, A. (2012). Moral dilemmas in cognitive neuroscience of moral decision-making: a principled review. *Neuroscience and Biobehavioral Reviews, 36*: 1249–1264.

Ciaramelli, E., Braghittoni, D., & di Pellegrino, G. (2012). It is the outcome that counts! Damage to the ventromedial prefrontal cortex disrupts the integration of outcome and belief information for moral judgment. *Journal of the International Neuropsychological Society, 18*: 962–971.

Ciaramelli, E., Muccioli, M., Làdavas, E., & di Pellegrino, G. (2007). Selective deficit in personal moral judgment following damage to ventromedial prefrontal cortex. *Social Cognitive and Affective Neuroscience, 2*: 84–92.

Ciaramelli, E., Sperotto, R. G., Mattioli, F., & di Pellegrino, G. (2013). Damage to the ventromedial prefrontal cortex reduces interpersonal disgust. *Social Cognitive and Affective Neuroscience, 8*: 171–180.

Cisler, J. M., Adams, T. G., Brady, R. E., Bridges, A. J., Lohr, J. M., & Olatunji, B. O. (2011). Unique affective and cognitive processes in contamination appraisals: implications for contamination fear. *Journal of Anxiety Disorders, 25*: 28–35.

Cisler, J. M., Olatunji, B. O., Feldner, M. T., & Forsyth, J. P. (2010). Emotion regulation and the anxiety disorders: an integrative review. *Journal of Psychopathology and Behavioral Assessment, 32*: 68–82.

Cisler, J. M., Olatunji, B. O., & Lohr, J. M. (2009). Disgust, fear, and the anxiety disorders: a critical review. *Clinical Psychology Review, 29*: 34–46.

Clark, D. A., & Beck, A. T. (2010). Cognitive theory and therapy of anxiety and depression: convergence with neurobiological findings. *Trends in Cognitive Sciences, 14*: 418–424.

Clark, J. A. (2010). Relations of homology between higher cognitive emotions and basic emotions. *Biology and Philosophy, 25*: 75–94.

Clark, J. A., & Fessler, D. M. T. (2011). The role of disgust in norms, and the role of norms in disgust research: why liberals shouldn't be morally disgusted by moral disgust. *Topoi: An International Review of Philosophy*. doi:10.1007/s11245-014-9240-0.

Coggins, J., & Fox, J. R. E. (2009). A qualitative exploration of emotional inhibition: a basic emotions and developmental perspective. *Clinical Psychology and Psychotherapy, 16*: 55–76.

Consedine, N. S. (2008). The health-promoting and health-damaging effects of emotions: the view from developmental functionalism. In: M. Lewis, J. Haviland-Jones, & L. F. Barrett (Eds.), *Handbook of Emotions* (3rd edn.; pp. 676–690). New York: Guilford.

Consedine, N. S., & Moscowitz, J. T. (2007). The role of discrete emotions in health outcomes: a critical review. *Applied and Preventive Psychology, 12*: 59–75.

Cooley, M. (1922/1964). *Human Nature and Conduct*. New York: Schocken Books.

Cooper, C. (1998). *Fat and Proud: The Politics of Size*. London: The Women's Press.

Cooper, M. J., & Hunt, J. (1998). Core beliefs and underlying assumptions in bulimia nervosa and depression. *Behaviour Research and Therapy, 36*: 895–898.

Cooper, M. J., Todd, G., & Wells, A. (1998). Content, origins and consequences of dysfunctional beliefs in anorexia nervosa and bulimia nervosa. *Journal of Cognitive Psychotherapy: An International Quarterly, 12*: 213–230.

Coughtrey, A. E., Shafran, R., Lee, M., & Rachman, S. J. (2012). It's the feeling inside my head: a qualitative analysis of mental contamination in obsessive-compulsive disorder. *Behavioural and Cognitive Psychotherapy, 40*: 163–173.

Coughtrey, A. E., Shafran, R., Lee, M., & Rachman, S. J. (2013). The treatment of mental contamination: a case series. *Cognitive and Behavioral Practice, 20*: 221–231.

Cougle, J. R., Lee, H., Horowitz, J. D., Wolitzky-Taylor, K., & Telch, M. J. (2008). An exploration of the relationship between mental pollution and

OCD symptoms. *Journal of Behavior Therapy and Experimental Psychiatry, 39*: 340–353.

Cox, C. R., Goldenberg, J. L., Pyszczynski, T., & Weise, D. (2007). Disgust, creatureliness, and the accessibility of death-related thoughts. *European Journal of Social Psychology, 37*: 494–507.

Cozolino, L. (2007). *The Neuroscience of Human Relationships: Attachment and the Developing Brain*. New York: Norton.

Craig, A. D. (2002). How do you feel? Interoception: the sense of the physiological condition of the body. *Nature Reviews Neuroscience, 3*: 655–666.

Craig, A. D. (2003). Interoception: the sense of the physiological condition of the body. *Current Opinion in Neurobiology, 13*: 500–505.

Craig, A. D. (2009). How do you feel—now? The anterior insula and human awareness. *Nature Reviews Neuroscience, 10*: 59–70.

Craig, A. D. (2011). Significance of the insula for the evolution of human awareness of feelings from the body. *Annals of the New York Academy of Sciences, 1225*: 72–82.

Crowe, M., & Bunclark, J. (2000). Repeated self-injury and its management. *International Review of Psychiatry, 12*: 48–53.

Curtis, V., Aunger, R., & Rabie, T. (2004). Evidence that disgust evolved to protect from risk of disease. *Proceedings of the Royal Society B: Biological Sciences, 271*: S131–S133.

Curtis, V., & Biran, A. (2001). Dirt, disgust, and disease: is hygiene in our genes? *Perspectives in Biology and Medicine, 44*: 17–31.

Curtis, V., Danquah, L. O., & Aunger, R. (2009). Planned, motivated and habitual hygiene behaviour: an eleven-country review. *Health Education Research, 24*: 655–673.

Curtis, V., de Barra, M., & Aunger, R. (2011). Disgust as an adaptive system for disease avoidance behaviour. *Philosophical Transactions of the Royal Society B: Biological Sciences, 366*: 389–401.

Dalgleish, T., & Power, M. J. (2004). Emotion-specific and emotion-non-specific components of posttraumatic stress disorder (PTSD): implications for a taxonomy of related psychopathology. *Behaviour Research and Therapy, 42*: 1069–1088.

Damasio, A. (1994). *Descartes's Error: Emotion, Reason and the Human Brain*. New York: Grosset and Putnam.

Damasio, A., Grabowski, T. J., Bechara, A., Damasio, H., Ponto, L. L. B., Parvizi, J., & Hichwa, R. D. (2000). Subcortical and cortical brain activity during the feeling of self-generated emotions. *Nature Neuroscience, 3*: 1049–1056.

Damasio, H. (2005). Disorders of social conduct following damage to prefrontal cortices. In: J. -P. P. Changeux, A. Damasio, & W. Singer (Eds.), *Neurobiology of Human Values* (pp. 37–46). Berlin: Springer Verlag.

Damasio, H., Grabowski, T., Frank, R., Galaburda, A. M., & Damasio, A. (1994). The return of Phineas Gage: clues about the brain from the skull of a famous patient. *Science, 264*: 1102–1105.

Darwin, C. (1872/1989). *The Expression of the Emotions in Man and Animals*. New York: New York University Press.

Davey, G. C. L. (1994a). Self-reported fears to common indigenous animals in an adult UK population: the role of disgust sensitivity. *British Journal of Psychology, 85*: 541–554.

Davey, G. C. L. (1994b). Disgust. In: V. S. Ramachandran (Ed.), *Encyclopedia of Human Behavior* (pp. 135–143). San Diego, CA: San Diego Press.

Davey, G. C. L. (2011). Disgust: the disease-avoidance emotion and its dysfunctions. *Philosophical Transactions of the Royal Society B: Biological Sciences, 366*: 3453–3465.

Davey, G. C. L., Bickerstaffe, S., & MacDonald, B. A. (2006). Experienced disgust causes a negative interpretation bias: a causal role for disgust in anxious psychopathology. *Behaviour Research and Therapy, 44*: 1375–1384.

Davey, G. C. L., & Bond, N. (2006). Using controlled comparisons in disgust psychopathology research: the case of disgust, hypochondriasis and health anxiety. *Journal of Behavior Therapy and Experimental Psychiatry, 37*: 4–15.

Davey, G. C. L., Buckland, G., Tantow, B., & Dallos, R. (1998). Disgust and eating disorders. *European Eating Disorders Review, 6*: 201–211.

Davey, G. C. L., & Chapman, L. (2009). Disgust and eating disorder symptomatology in a non-clinical population: the role of trait anxiety and anxiety sensitivity. *Clinical Psychology and Psychotherapy, 16*: 268–275.

Davey, G. C. L., MacDonald, B. A., & Brierley, L. (2008). The effect of disgust on anxiety ratings to fear-relevant, disgust-relevant and fear-irrelevant stimuli. *Journal of Anxiety Disorders, 22*: 1347–1354.

Davey, G. C. L., & Marzillier, S. (2009). Disgust and animal phobias. In: B. O. Olatunji & D. McKay (Eds.), *Disgust and Its Disorders: Theory, Assessment, and Treatment Implications* (pp. 169–190). Washington, DC: APA.

David, B., & Olatunji, B. O. (2011). The effect of disgust conditioning and disgust sensitivity on appraisals of moral transgressions. *Personality and Individual Differences, 50*: 1142–1146.

Davidson, J., Foa, E. B., Blank, A. S., Brett, E. A., Fairbank, J., Green, B. L., Herman, J. L., Keane, T. M., Kilpatrick, D. L., March, J. S., McNally, R. J., Pitman, R. K., Resnick, H. S., & Rothbaum, B. O. (1996). Posttraumatic stress disorder. In: T. A. Widiger, A. J. Frances, H. A. Pincus, R. Ross, M. B. First, & W. Wakefield-Davis (Eds.), *DSM-IV Sourcebook. Vol. 2* (pp. 557–605). Washington, DC: American Psychiatric Association.

de Jong, P. J., & Merckelbach, H. (1998). Blood-injection-injury phobia and fear of spiders: domain-specific individual differences in disgust sensitivity. *Personality and Individual Differences, 24*: 153–158.

de Jong, P. J., & Muris, P. (2002). Spider phobia: intersection of disgust and perceived likelihood of involuntary physical contact. *Journal of Anxiety Disorders, 16*: 51–65.

de Jong, P. J., & Peters, M. L. (2009). Sex and the sexual dysfunctions: the role of disgust and contamination sensitivity. In: B. Olatunji & D. McKay (Eds.), *Disgust and Its Disorders: Theory, Assessment, and Treatment* (pp. 253–270). Washington, DC: American Psychological Association.

de Jong, P. J., van Overveld, M., & Borg, C. (2013). Giving in to arousal or staying stuck in disgust? Disgust-based mechanisms in sex and sexual dysfunction. *Annual Review of Sex Research, 50*: 247–262.

de Silva, P., & Marks, M. (1999). The role of traumatic experiences in the genesis of obsessive-compulsive disorder. *Behaviour Research and Therapy, 37*: 941–951.

Deacon, B., & Olatunji, B. O. (2007). Specificity of disgust sensitivity in the prediction of behavioral avoidance in contamination fear. *Behaviour Research and Therapy, 45*: 2110–2120.

Deal, M. (2003). Disabled people's attitudes toward other impairment groups: a hierarchy of impairments. *Disability and Society, 18*: 897–910.

Decety, J., Chen, C., Harenski, C., & Kiehl, K. A. (2013). An fMRI study of affective perspective-taking in individuals with psychopathy: imagining another in pain does not evoke empathy. *Frontiers in Human Neuroscience, 7*: 489.

Denburg, N. L., Cole, C. A., Hernandez, M., Yamada, T. H., Tranel, D., Bechara, A., & Wallace, R. B. (2007). The orbitofrontal cortex, real-world decision-making, and normal aging. *Annals of the New York Academy of Sciences, 1121*: 480–498.

Deonna, J. A., Rodogno, R., & Teroni, F. (2011). *In Defense of Shame: The Faces of an Emotion*. New York: Oxford University Press.

Derrida, J. (1981). Economimesis. *Diacritics, 11*: 3–25.

DeSteno, D., Dasgupta, N., Bartlett, M. Y., & Cajdric, A. (2004). Prejudice from thin air: the effect of emotion on automatic intergroup attitudes. *Psychological Science, 15*: 319–324.

Dolhanty, J., & Greenberg, L. S. (2009). Emotion-focused therapy in a case of anorexia nervosa. *Clinical Psychology and Psychotherapy, 16*: 336–382.

Doubeni, C. A., Weinmann, S., Adams, K., Kamineni, A., Buist, D. M., Ash, A. S., Rutter, C. M., Doria-Rose, V. P., Corley, D. A., Greenlee, R. T., Chubak, J., Williams, A., Kroll-Desrosiers, A. R., Johnson, E., Webster, J., Richert-Boe, K., Levin, T. R., Fletcher, R. H., & Weiss, N. S. (2013). Screening colonoscopy and risk for incident late-stage colorectal cancer diagnosis in average-risk adults. *Annals of Internal Medicine, 158*: 312–320.

Douglas, K. M., & Porter, R. J. (2010). Recognition of disgusted facial expressions in severe depression. *The British Journal of Psychiatry, 197*: 156–157.

Douglas, M. (1966/2002). *Purity and Danger: An Analysis of the Concepts of Pollution and Taboo*. London: Routledge.

Doward, J. (2013). Homophobia still rife in UK, survey claims. *The Observer*. Retrieved from http://www.theguardian.com/world/2013/aug/25/homophobia-uk-survey.

Drellich, M. G., & Bieber, I. (1958). The psychologic importance of the uterus and its functions: some psychoanalytic implications of hysterectomy. *The Journal of Nervous and Mental Disease, 126*: 322–336.

Dreschler, J. (2007). From bisexuality to intersexuality: rethinking gender categories. *Contemporary Psychoanalysis, 43*: 204–228.

Driscoll, R. (1989). Self-condemnation: a comprehensive framework for assessment and treatment. *Psychotherapy: Theory, Research, Practice, Training, 26*: 104–111.

Dunmore, E., Clark, D. M., & Ehlers, A. (2001). A prospective investigation of the role of cognitive factors in persistent posttraumatic stress disorder (PTSD) after physical or sexual assault. *Behaviour Research and Therapy, 39*: 1063–1084.

Ehlers, A., & Clark, D. M. (2000). A cognitive model of posttraumatic stress disorder. *Behaviour Research and Therapy, 38*: 319–345.

Ekman, P. (1992). An argument for basic emotions. *Cognition and Emotion, 6*: 169–200.

Ekman, P. (1999). Basic emotions. In: T. Dalgleish, & M. J. Power (Eds.), *Handbook of Cognition and Emotion* (pp. 45–60). Chichester: John Wiley.

Ekman, P., & Cordaro, D. (2011). What is meant by calling emotions basic. *Emotion Review, 3*: 364–370.

Ekman, P., Friesen, W. V., & Ellsworth, P. (1982). What emotion categories or dimensions can observers judge from facial behaviour? In: P. Ekman (Ed.), *Emotion in the Human Face* (pp. 39–55). New York: Cambridge University Press.

Elfenbein, H. A., & Ambady, N. (2002). On the universality and cultural specificity of emotion recognition: a meta-analysis. *Psychological Bulletin, 128*: 203–235.

Elias, N. (2000). *The Civilizing Process* (revised edn.; E. Jephcott (Trans.)). Oxford: Blackwell.

Elliott, C. M., & Radomsky, A. S. (2009). Analyses of mental contamination: Part I, experimental manipulations of morality. *Behaviour Research and Therapy, 47*: 995–1003.

Elliott, C. M., & Radomsky, A. S. (2012). Mental contamination: the effects of imagined physical dirt and immoral behaviour. *Behaviour Research and Therapy, 50*: 422–427.

Elliott, C. M., & Radomsky, A. S. (2013). Meaning and mental contamination: focus on appraisals. *Clinical Psychologist, 17*: 17–25.

Elwood, L. S., & Olatunji, B. O. (2009). A cross-cultural perspective on disgust. In: B. O. Olatunji & D. Mckay (Eds.), *Disgust and Its Disorders: Theory, Assessment, and Treatment Implications* (pp. 99–122). Washington, DC: APA.

Engelhard, I. M., Olatunji, B. O., & de Jong, P. J. (2011). Disgust and the development of posttraumatic stress disorder among soldiers deployed to Afghanistan. *Journal of Anxiety Disorders, 25*: 58–63.

Erskine, R. G. (2011). Attachment, relational needs, and psychotherapeutic presence. *International Journal of Integrative Psychotherapy, 2*: 10–18.

Eskine, K. J., Novreske, A., & Richards, M. (2013). Moral contagion effects in everyday interpersonal encounters. *Journal of Experimental Social Psychology, 49*: 947–950.

Espeset, E. M. S., Gulliksen, K. S., Nordbo, R. H. S., Skarderud, F., & Holte, A. (2012). The link between negative emotions and eating disorder behaviour in patients with anorexia nervosa. *European Eating Disorders Review, 20*: 451–460.

Etkin, A., Egner, T., & Kalisch, R. (2011). Emotional processing in anterior cingulate and medial prefrontal cortex. *Trends in Cognitive Sciences, 15*: 85–93.

Fairbrother, N., Newth, S. J., & Rachman, S. (2005). Mental pollution: feelings of dirtiness without physical contact. *Behaviour Research and Therapy, 43*: 121–130.

Fairbrother, N. & Rachman, S. (2004). Feelings of mental pollution subsequent to sexual assault. *Behaviour Research and Therapy, 42*: 173–189.

Fairburn, C. G., Cooper, Z., & Shafran, R. (2003). Cognitive behaviour therapy for eating disorders: a "transdiagnostic" theory and treatment. *Behaviour Research and Therapy, 41*: 509–528.

Fay, D. (2007). *Becoming Safely Embodied: A Skills-Based Approach to Working with Trauma and Dissociation*. Somerville, MA: Heart for Life Publishing.

Feiring, C., Taska, L., & Lewis, M. (1996). A process model for understanding adaptation to sexual abuse: the role of shame in defining stigmatization. *Child Abuse and Neglect, 8*: 767–782.

Feiring, C., Taska, L., & Lewis, M. (1998). The role of shame and attributional style in children's and adolescents' adaptation to sexual abuse. *Child Maltreatment, 3*: 129–142.

Feldner, M. T., Frala, J., Badour, C., Leen-Feldner, E. W., & Olatunji, B. O. (2010). An empirical test of the association between disgust and sexual assault. *International Journal of Cognitive Therapy, 3*: 11–22.

Ferdenzi, C., Roberts, S. C., Schirmer, A., Delplanque, S., Cekic, S., Porcherot, C., Sander, D., & Grandjean, D. (2013). Variability of affective responses to odors: culture, gender, and olfactory knowledge. *Chemical Senses, 38*: 175–186.

Ferguson, T. J., & Stegge, H. (1995). Emotional states and traits in children: the case of guilt and shame. In: J. P. Tangney & K. W. Fischer (Eds.), *Self-Conscious Emotions: Shame, Guilt, Embarrassment and Pride* (pp. 174–197). New York: Guilford Press.

Fernandez-Aranda, F., Aitken, A., Badia, A., Gimenez, L., Solano, R., Collier, D., Treasure, J., & Vallejo, J. (2004). Personality and psychopathological traits of males with an eating disorder. *European Eating Disorders Review, 12*: 367–374.

Fessler, D. M. T. (2007). From appeasement to conformity: evolutionary and cultural perspectives on shame, competition, and cooperation. In: J. L. Tracy, R. W. Robins, & J. P. Tangney (Eds.), *The Self-Conscious Emotions: Theory and Research* (pp. 174–193). New York: Guilford Press.

Fessler, D. M. T., Eng, S. J., & Navarrete, C. D. (2005). Elevated disgust sensitivity in the first trimester of pregnancy: evidence supporting prophylaxis the compensatory hypothesis. *Evolution and Human Behavior, 26*: 344–351.

Fessler, D. M. T., & Haley, K. J. (2006). Guarding the perimeter: the outside–inside dichotomy in disgust and bodily experience. *Cognition and Emotion, 20*: 3–19.

Fessler, D. M. T., & Navarrete, C. D. (2003). Domain-specific variation in disgust sensitivity across the menstrual cycle. *Evolution and Human Behavior, 24*: 406–417.

Fessler, D. M. T., & Navarrete, C. D. (2004). Third-party attitudes toward sibling incest: evidence for Westermarck's hypotheses. *Evolution and Human Behavior, 25*: 277–294.

Fessler, D. M. T., Pillsworth, E. G., & Flamson, T. J. (2004). Angry men and disgusted women: an evolutionary approach to the influence of emotions on risk-taking. *Organizational Behavior and Human Decision Processes, 95*: 107–123.

Field, A., Miles, J., & Field, Z. (2012). *Discovering Statistics Using R*. London: Sage.

Finucane, A. M., Dima, A., Ferreira, N., & Halvorsen, M. (2012). Basic emotion profiles in healthy, chronic pain, depressed, and PTSD individuals. *Clinical Psychology and Psychotherapy, 19*: 14–24.

Fischer, A. H., & Roseman, I. J. (2007). Beat them or ban them: the characteristics and social functions of anger and contempt. *Journal of Personality and Social Psychology, 93*: 103–115.

Fisher, A. D., Bandini, E., Ricca, V., Ferruccio, N., Corona, G., Meriggiola, M. C., Jannini, E. A., Manieri, C., Ristori, J., Forti, G., Mannucci, E., & Maggi, M. (2010). Dimensional profiles of male to female gender identity disorder: an exploratory research. *Journal of Sexual Medicine, 7*: 2487–2498.

Fleischman, D. S., & Fessler, D. M. T. (2011). Progesterone's effects on the psychology of disease avoidance: support for the compensatory behavioral prophylaxis hypothesis. *Hormones and Behavior, 59*: 271–275.

Fleischman, D. S., Hamilton, L. D., Fessler, D. M. T., & Meston, C. M. (2014). Disgust versus lust: exploring the reciprocal interaction of disgust and fear on sexual arousal in women. Manuscript submitted for publication.

Fliege, H., Lee, J. -R., Grimm, A., & Klapp, B. F. (2009). Risk factors and correlates of deliberate self-harm behaviour: a systematic review. *Journal of Psychosomatic Research, 66*: 477–493.

Foa, E. B., & Kozak, M. J. (1995). DSM-IV field trial: obsessive-compulsive disorder. *American Journal of Psychiatry, 152*: 90–96.

Foa, E. B., Kozak, M. J., Goodman, W. K., Hollander, E., Jenike, M. A., & Rasmussen, S. A. (1995). DSM-IV field trial: obsessive-compulsive disorder: correction. *American Journal of Psychiatry, 152*: 654.

Foa, E. B., Kozak, M. J., Salkovskis, P., Coles, M. E., & Amir, N. (1998). The validation of a new Obsessive-Compulsive Disorder Scale: the Obsessive-Compulsive Inventory. *Psychological Assessment, 10*: 206–214.

Foa, E. B., & Rauch, S. A. M. (2004). Cognitive changes during prolonged exposure versus prolonged exposure plus cognitive restructuring in female survivors with posttraumatic stress disorder. *Journal of Consulting and Clinical Psychology, 72*: 879–884.

Foa, E. B., & Rothbaum, B. O. (1998). *Treating the Trauma of Rape: Cognitive Behavioral Therapy for PTSD*. New York: Guilford Press.

Fortune, S. A., & Hawton, K. (2005). Deliberate self-harm in children and adolescents: a research update. *Current Opinion in Psychiatry, 18*: 401–406.

Fostick, L., Nacasch, N., & Zohar, J. (2012). Acute obsessive compulsive disorder (OCD) in veterans with posttraumatic stress disorder (PTSD). *The World Journal of Biological Psychiatry, 13*: 312–315.

Fox, J. R. E. (2009). A qualitative exploration of the perception of emotions in anorexia nervosa: a basic emotion and developmental perspective. *Clinical Psychology and Psychotherapy, 16*: 276–302.

Fox, J. R. E., Federici, A., & Power, M. J. (2012). Emotions and eating disorders. In: J. R. E. Fox & K. Goss (Eds.), *Eating and Its Disorders* (pp. 167–184). Chichester: Wiley-Blackwell.

Fox, J. R. E., & Froom, K. (2009). Eating disorders: a basic emotion perspective. *Clinical Psychology and Psychotherapy, 16*: 328–335.

Fox, J. R. E., & Harrison, A. (2008). The relation of anger to disgust: the potential role of coupled emotions within eating pathology. *Clinical Psychology and Psychotherapy, 15*: 86–95.

Fox, J. R. E., & Power, M. J. (2009). Eating disorders and multi-level models of emotion: an integrated model. *Clinical Psychology and Psychotherapy, 16*: 240–267.

Fox, J. R. E., Smithson, E., Kellett, S., Ferreira, N., Mayr, I., & Power, M. J. (2013). Emotion coupling and regulation in anorexia nervosa. *Clinical Psychology and Psychotherapy, 20*: 319–333.

Fox, J. R. E., Woodrow, C., & Leonard, K. (2012). Working with anorexia nervosa on an eating disorders inpatient unit: consideration of the issues. In: J. R. E. Fox & K. Goss (Eds.), *Eating and Its Disorders* (pp. 344–360). Chichester: Wiley-Blackwell.

Foy, D. W., Sipprelle, R. C., Rueger, D. B., & Carroll, E. M. (1984). Etiology of posttraumatic stress disorder in Vietnam veterans: analysis of premilitary, military, and combat exposure influences. *Journal of Consulting and Clinical Psychology, 52*: 79–87.

Frank, E. S. (1991). Shame and guilt in eating disorders. *American Journal of Orthopsychiatry, 61*: 303–306.

Franklin, M. E., & Foa, E. B. (2011). Treatment of obsessive compulsive disorder. *Annual Review of Clinical Psychology, 7*: 229–243.

Fredman, S. J., Monson, C. M., Schumm, J. A., Adair, K. C., Taft, C. T., & Resick, P. A. (2010). Associations among disaster exposure, intimate relationship adjustment, and PTSD symptoms: can disaster exposure enhance a relationship? *Journal of Traumatic Stress, 23*: 446–451.

Fredrickson, B. L., Cohn, M. A., Coffey, K. A., Pek, J., & Finkel, S. M. (2008). Open hearts build lives: positive emotions, induced through loving-kindness meditation, build consequential personal resources. *Journal of Personality and Social Psychology, 95*: 1045–1062.

Fredrickson, B. L., Grewen, K. M., Coffey, K. A., Algoe, S. B., Firestine, A. M., Arevalo J. M. G., Ma, J., & Cole, S. W. (2013). A functional genomic perspective on human well-being. *Proceedings of the National Academy of Sciences of the United States of America, 110*: 13684–13689.

Fredrickson, B. L., & Roberts, T. (1997). Objectification theory: toward understanding women's lived experiences and mental health risks. *Psychology of Women Quarterly, 21*: 173–206.

Freud, S. (1905a/1991). *On Sexuality: Three Essays on the Theory of Sexuality and Other Works* (Penguin Freud Library). London: Penguin Books.

Freud, S. (1938). *The Basic Writings of Sigmund Freud* (A. A. Brill, Trans.). New York: Random House.

Frith, C. D., & Frith, U. (2006). The neural basis of mentalizing. *Neuron, 50*: 531–534.

Gardner, F. (2001). *Self-Harm: A Psychotherapeutic Approach*. Hove: Brunner-Routledge.

Garner, D. M., Olmsted, M. P., Bohr, Y., & Garfinkel, P. E. (1982). The Eating Attitudes Test: psychometric features and clinical correlates. *Psychological Medicine, 12*: 871–878.

Garthwaite, K. (2011). "The language of shirkers and scroungers?" Talking about illness, disability and coalition welfare reform. *Disability and Society, 26*: 369–372.

Gee, A., & Troop, N. A. (2003). Shame, depressive symptoms and eating, weight and shape concerns in a non-clinical sample. *Eating and Weight Disorders, 8*: 72–75.

Geller, J., Cockell, S. J., Hewitt, P. L., Goldner, E. M., & Flett, G. L. (2000). Inhibited expression of negative emotions and interpersonal orientation in anorexia nervosa. *International Journal of Eating Disorders, 28*: 8–19.

Gershuny, B. S., Baer, L., Radomsky, A. S., Wilson, K. A., & Jenike, M. A. (2003). Connections among symptoms of obsessive-compulsive disorder and posttraumatic stress disorder: a case series. *Behaviour Research and Therapy, 41*: 1029–1041.

Ghatavi, K., Nicolson, R., MacDonald, C., Osher, S., & Levitt, A. (2002). Defining guilt in depression: a comparison of subjects with major depression, chronic medical illness and healthy controls. *Journal of Affective Disorders, 68*: 307–315.

Gilbert, P. (1992). *Depression: The Evolution of Powerlessness*. Hove: Lawrence Erlbaum; New York: Guilford Press.

Gilbert, P. (1997). The evolution of social attractiveness and its role in shame, humiliation, guilt and therapy. *British Journal of Medical Psychology, 70*: 113–147.

Gilbert, P. (1998a). What is shame? Some core issues and controversies. In: P. Gilbert & B. Andrews (Eds.), *Shame: Interpersonal Behaviour, Psychopathology and Culture* (pp. 3–38). New York: Oxford University Press.

Gilbert, P. (1998b). Shame and humiliation in the treatment of complex cases. In: N. Tarrier, G. Haddock, & A. Wells (Eds.), *Complex Cases: The Cognitive Behavioural Approach* (pp. 241–271). Chichester: Wiley.

Gilbert, P. (2000). The relationship of shame, social anxiety and depression: the role of the evaluation of social rank. *Clinical Psychology and Psychotherapy, 7*: 174–187.

Gilbert, P. (2007). The evolution of shame as a marker for relationship security. In: J. L. Tracy, R. W. Robins, & J. P. Tangney (Eds.), *The Self-Conscious Emotions: Theory and Research* (pp. 283–309). New York: Guilford Press.

Gilbert, P. (2009). *The Compassionate Mind: A New Approach to the Challenge of Life*. London: Constable & Robinson.

Gilbert, P. (2010). *Compassion-Focused Therapy: The CBT Distinctive Features Series*. London: Routledge.

Gilbert, P., & Choden, K. (2013). *Mindful Compassion*. London: Constable & Robinson.

Gilbert, P., Clarke, M., Hempel, S., Miles, J. N. V., & Irons, C. (2004). Criticising and reassuring oneself: an exploration of forms, styles and reasons in female students. *British Journal of Clinical Psychology, 43*: 31–50.

Gilbert, P., Durrant, R., & McEwan, K. (2006). Investigating the relationship between perfectionism, forms and functions of self-criticism and sensitivity to put-down. *Personality and Individual Differences, 41*: 1299–1308.

Gilbert, P., & Irons, C. (2004). A pilot exploration of the use of compassionate images in a group of self-critical people. *Memory, 12*: 507–516.

Gilbert, P., & Irons, C. (2005). Focused therapies and compassionate mind training for shame and self-attacking. In: P. Gilbert (Ed.), *Compassion: Conceptualisations, Research and Use in Psychotherapy* (pp. 263–325). London: Routledge.

Gilbert, P., Irons, C., McEwan, K., Bhundia, R., Christie, R., & Broomhead, C. (2010). Self-harm in a mixed clinical population: the roles of shame, forms and functions of self-criticism and social rank. *British Journal of Clinical Psychology, 49*: 563–576.

Gilbert, P., & Miles, J. (2002). *Body Shame: Conceptualisations, Research and Treatment*. London: Brunner-Routledge.

Gilbert, P., & Procter, S. (2006). Compassionate mind training for people with high shame and self-criticism: overview and pilot study of a group therapy approach. *Clinical Psychology and Psychotherapy, 13*: 353–379.

Gilboa-Schechtman, E., & Foa, E. B. (2001). Patterns of recovery from trauma: the use of intraindividual analysis. *Journal of Abnormal Psychology, 11*: 392–400.

Gilligan, J. (2000). *Violence: Reflections on Our Deadliest Epidemic*. London: Jessica Kingsley.

Giner-Sorolla, R., Bosson, J. K., Caswell, T. A., & Hettinger, V. E. (2012). Emotions in sexual morality: testing the separate elicitors of anger and disgust. *Cognition and Emotion, 26*: 1208–1222.

Giner-Sorolla, R., & Espinosa, P. (2011). Social cuing of guilt by anger and of shame by disgust. *Psychological Science, 22*: 49–53.

Giner-Sorolla, R., & Russell, P. S. (2009). Anger, disgust and sexual crimes. In: M. Horvath, & J. Brown (Eds.), *Rape: Challenging Contemporary Thinking* (pp. 46–73). Devon: Willan.

Giner-Sorolla, R., & Russell, P. S. (2014). Not just disgust: fear and anger attitudes also predict intergroup dehumanization. Manuscript submitted for publication.

Glassman, L. H., Weierich, M. R., Hooley, J. M., Deliberto, T. L., & Nock, M. K. (2007). Child maltreatment, non-suicidal self-injury, and the mediating role of self-criticism. *Behaviour Research and Therapy, 45*: 2483–2490.

Goldberg, J. H., Lerner, J. S., & Tetlock, P. E. (1999). Rage and reason: the psychology of the intuitive prosecutor. *European Journal of Social Psychology, 29*: 781–795.

Goldenberg, J. L., Arndt, J., Hart, J., & Routledge, C. (2008). Uncovering an existential barrier to breast self-exam behavior. *Journal of Experimental Social Psychology, 44*: 260–274.

Goldenberg, J. L., Pyszczynski, T., Greenberg, J., Solomon, S., Kluck, B., & Cornwell, R. (2001). I am not an animal: mortality salience, disgust, and the denial of human creatureliness. *Journal of Experimental Psychology, General, 130*: 427–435.

Goldsmith, S. K., Pellmar, T. C., Kleinman, A. M., & Bunney, W. E. (Eds.) (2002). *Reducing Suicide: A National Imperative*. Washington, DC: National Academies Press.

Goode, M. L. (2004). Psychological needs of patients when dressing a fungating wound: a literature review. *Journal of Wound Care, 13*: 380–382.

Gratz, K. L. (2003). Risk factors for and functions of deliberate self-harm: an empirical and conceptual review. *Clinical Psychology: Science and Practice, 10*: 192–205.

Gratz, K. L., Conrad, S. D., & Roemer, L. (2002). Risk factors for deliberate self-harm among college students. *American Journal of Orthopsychiatry, 72*: 128–140.

Green, S., Moll, J., Deakin, J. F. W., Hulleman, J., & Zahn, R. (2013). Proneness to decreased negative emotions in major depressive disorder when blaming others rather than oneself. *Psychopathology, 46*: 34–44.

Greenberg, L. S. (2008). Emotion and cognition in psychotherapy: the transforming power of affect. *Canadian Psychology, 49*: 49–59.

Greenberg, L. S., Watson, J. C., & Goldman, R. (1998). Process-experiential therapy of depression. In: L. S. Greenberg, J. C. Watson, & G. Lietaer (Eds.), *Handbook of Experiential Psychotherapy* (pp. 227–248). New York: Guilford Press.

Greene, J. D., Nystrom, L. E., Engell, A. D., Darley, J. M., & Cohen, J. D. (2004). The neural bases of cognitive conflict and control in moral judgment. *Neuron, 44*: 389–400.

Greene, J. D., Sommerville, R. B., Nystrom, L. E., Darley, J. M., & Cohen, J. D. (2001). An fMRI investigation of emotional engagement in moral judgment. *Science, 293*: 2105–2108.

Griffiths, J., & Troop, N. A. (2006). Disgust and fear ratings of eating disorder-relevant stimuli: associations with dieting concerns and fat intake. *Anxiety, Stress and Coping: An International Journal, 19*: 421–433.

Griffiths, L. J., & Page, A. S. (2008). The impact of weight-related victimization on peer relationships: the female adolescent perspective. *Obesity, 16*: 39–45.

Gross, J. J., & Levenson, R. W. (1993). Emotional suppression: physiology, self-report, and expressive behavior. *Journal of Personality and Social Psychology, 64*: 970–986.

Grozier, W. R. (1998). Self-consciousness in shame: the role of the "other". *Journal for the Theory of Social Behaviour, 28*: 273–286.

Grunert, B. K., Devine, C., Matloub, H. S., Sanger, J. R., Yousif, N. J., Anderson, R. C., & Roell, S. M. (1992). Psychological adjustment following work-related hand injury: 18-month follow-up. *Annals of Plastic Surgery, 29*: 537–542.

Grunert, B. K., Smucker, M. R., Weis, J. M., & Rusch, M. D. (2003). When prolonged exposure fails: adding an imagery-based cognitive restructuring component in the treatment of industrial accident victims suffering from PTSD. *Cognitive and Behavioral Practice, 10*: 333–346.

Guimon, J., Las Hayas, C., Guillen, V., Boyra, A., & Gonzalez-Pinto, A. (2007). Shame, sensitivity to punishment and psychiatric disorders. *European Journal of Psychiatry, 21*: 124–133.

Gusnard, D. A., Akbudak, E., Shulman, G. L., & Raichle, M. E. (2001). Medial prefrontal cortex and self-referential mental activity: relation to a default mode of brain function. *Proceedings of the National Academy of Sciences, 98*: 4259–4264.

Gutierrez, R., & Giner-Sorolla, R. (2007). Anger, disgust, and presumption of harm as reactions to taboo-breaking behaviours. *Emotion, 7*: 853–868.

Gutierrez, R., Giner-Sorolla, R., & Vasiljevic, M. (2012). Just an anger synonym? Moral context influences predictors of disgust word use. *Cognition and Emotion, 26*: 53–64.

Haidt, J., McCauley, C., & Rozin, P. (1994). Individual differences in sensitivity to disgust: a scale sampling seven domains of disgust elicitors. *Personality and Individual Differences, 16*: 701–713.

Haidt, J., Rozin, P., Mccauley, C., & Imada, S. (1997). Body, psyche, and culture: the relationship between disgust and morality. *Psychology and Developing Societies, 9*: 107–131.

Hamilton, W. D. (1964). The genetical evolution of social behaviour. I. *Journal of Theoretical Biology, 7*: 1–16.

Hanson, J., Bichard, J. -A., & Greed, C. (2007). *The Accessible Toilet Design Resource*. London: University College London.

Hardy, D. (2010). *When We Dare Not Speak Its Name: Anal Taboo, Anal Health, and Affect Theory*. Ed.D. dissertation, Widener University, Pennsylvania. Retrieved from http://proquest.umi.com/pqdweb?id=2206480111&Fmt=7&clientId=13395&RQT=309&VName=PQD. (last accessed 17 September 2014).

Harris, L. M., Jones, M. K., & Carey, C. L. (2009). Characteristics of blood-injection-injury fears in people receiving intravenous chemotherapy. *Current Psychology, 28*: 124–132.

Harris, L. T., & Fiske, S. T. (2006). Dehumanizing the lowest of the low: neuroimaging responses to extreme out-groups. *Psychological Science, 17*: 847–853.

Harris, L. T., & Fiske, S. T. (2007). Social groups that elicit disgust are differentially processed in mPFC. *Social Cognitive and Affective Neuroscience, 2*: 45–51.

Harris, L. T., & Fiske, S. T. (2009). Social neuroscience evidence for dehumanised perception. *European Review of Social Psychology, 20*: 192–231.

Harris, L. T., & Fiske, S. T. (2011). Dehumanized perception: a psychological means to facilitate atrocities, torture, and genocide? *Zeitschrift für Psychologie/Journal of Psychology, 219*: 175–181.

Harris, L. T., McClure, S. M., van den Bos, W., Cohen, J. D., & Fiske, S. T. (2007). Regions of the MPFC differentially tuned to social and nonsocial affective evaluation. *Cognitive, Affective, and Behavioral Neuroscience, 7*: 309–316.

Hart, B. L. (1990). Behavioral adaptations to pathogens and parasites: five strategies. *Neuroscience and Biobehavioral Reviews, 14*: 273–294.

Harvey, T., Troop, N. A., Treasure, J. L., & Murphy, T. (2002). Fear, disgust, and abnormal eating attitudes: a preliminary study. *International Journal of Eating Disorders, 32*: 213–218.

Hawkesworth, M. (2001). Disabling spatialities and the regulation of a visible secret. *Urban Studies, 38*: 299–318.

Hawton, K., James, A., & Viner, R. (2005). Suicide and deliberate self-harm in young people. *British Medical Journal, 330*: 891–894.

Hayes, J., Schimel, J., Arndt, J., & Faucher, E. H. (2010). A theoretical and empirical review of the death-thought accessibility concept in terror management research. *Psychological Bulletin, 136*: 699–739.

Hayes, S. C., Strosahl, K. D., & Wilson, K. G. (2003). *Acceptance and Commitment Therapy: An Experiential Approach to Behavior Change*. New York: Guilford Press.

Heilbronn, G. N., Latimer, P., & Nielsen, J. M. (2002). *Introducing the Law* (6th edn.). CCH Australia, North Ryde, NSW.

Help the Aged (2008). *Incontinence: Help the Aged Policy Statement 2008*. London: Help the Aged.

Herba, J. K., & Rachman, S. (2007). Vulnerability to mental contamination. *Behaviour Research and Therapy, 45*: 2804–2812.

Herz, R. S. (2003). The effect of verbal context on olfactory perception. *Journal of Experimental Psychology: General, 132*: 595–606.

Hickey, M., Neziroglu, F., & McKay, D. (2010). Psychophysiological and self-report components of disgust in body dysmorphic disorder: the effects of repeated exposure. *International Journal of Cognitive Therapy, 3*: 40–51.

Hickey, M., Neziroglu, F., & McKay, D. (2013). Behavioral avoidance tests for disgust in body dysmorphic disorder. Paper presented at the annual meeting of the Association for Behavioral and Cognitive Therapies, Nashville, TN.

Highfield, J., Markham, D., Skinner, M., & Neal, A. (2010). An investigation into the experience of self-conscious emotions in individuals with bipolar disorder, unipolar depression and non-psychiatric controls. *Clinical Psychology and Psychotherapy, 17*: 395–405.

Hodgson, R. J., & Rachman, S. J. (1972). The effects of contamination and washing in obsessional patients. *Behaviour Research and Therapy, 10*: 111–117.

Hodgson, R. J., & Rachman, S. J. (1977). Obsessional-compulsive complaints. *Behaviour Research and Therapy, 15*: 389–395.

Hodson, G., & Costello, K. (2007). Interpersonal disgust, ideological orientations, and dehumanization as predictors of intergroup attitudes. *Psychological Science, 18*: 691–698.

Hoek, H. W. (2006). Incidence, prevalence and mortality of anorexia nervosa and other eating disorders. *Current Opinion in Psychiatry, 19*: 389–394.

Hoek, H. W., & van Hoeken, D. (2003). Review of the prevalence and incidence of eating disorders. *International Journal of Eating Disorders, 34*: 383–396.

Holman, C. (2012). Trauma and eating disorders. In: J. R. E. Fox & K. Goss (Eds.), *Eating and Its Disorders* (pp. 167–184). Chichester: Wiley-Blackwell.

Hook, J. K. (2001). Beyond the surface. *Psychoanalytic Social Work, 7*: 1–48.

Hooley, J. M., Ho, D. T., Slater, J., & Lockshin, A. (2010). Pain perception and nonsuicidal self-injury: a laboratory investigation. *Personality Disorders: Theory, Research, and Treatment, 1*: 170–179.

Horberg, E. J., Oveis, C., Keltner, D., & Cohen, A. B. (2009). Disgust and the moralization of purity. *Journal of Personality and Social Psychology, 97*: 963–976.

Horne, O., & Csipke, E. (2009). From feeling too little and too much, to feeling more and less? A nonparadoxical theory of the functions of self-harm. *Qualitative Health Research, 19*: 655–667.

Hornsveld, R. H., Kraaimaat, F. W., & Van Dam-Baggen, R. M. (1979). Anxiety/discomfort and handwashing in obsessive-compulsive and psychiatric control patients. *Behaviour Research and Therapy, 17*: 223–228.

Horrocks, J., House, A., & Owens, D. (2002). *Attendances in the Accident and Emergency Department Following Self-Harm: A Descriptive Study*. Leeds: University of Leeds.

Houben, K., & Havermans, R. C. (2012). A delicious fly in the soup: the relationship between disgust, obesity, and restraint. *Appetite, 58*: 827–830.

Hudson, J. (2011). The world reacts to Clinton's gay rights speech. *The Atlantic Wire*. Retrieved from http://www.the atlanticwire.com/global/2011/12/world-reacts-clintons-gay-rights-speech/45883/.

Hughes, B. (2012). Civilizing modernity and the ontological invalidation of disabled people. In: D. Goodley, B. Hughes, & L. J. Davis (Eds.), *Disability and Social Theory: New Developments and Directions* (pp. 17–32). London: Palgrave Macmillan.

Human Rights Watch (2001). *No Escape: Male Rape in US Prisons*. New York: Human Rights Watch.

Hyman, S., Chisholm, R., Kessler, V., Patel, H., & Whiteford, H. (2006). Mental disorders. In: D. Jamison, J. Breman, A. Measham, G. Alleyne, M. Claeson, & D. Evans (Eds.), *Disease Control Priorities in Developing Countries* (pp. 605–626). Washington, DC: World Bank.

Ille, R., Schoggl, H., Kapfhammer, H. -P., Arendasy, M., Sommer, M., & Schienle, A. (2014). Self-disgust in mental disorders: symptom-related or disorder-specific? *Comprehensive Psychiatry*. doi:10.1016/j.comppsych.2013.12.020.

Ille, R., Schony, M., Kapfhammer, H., & Schienle, A. (2010). Elevated disgust proneness in schizophrenia. *Journal of Clinical Psychology, 66*: 1090–1100.

Inbar, Y., & Pizarro, D. A. (2014). Pollution and purity in moral and political judgment. In: J. C. Wright & H. Sarkissian (Eds.), *Advances in Experimental Moral Psychology: Affect, Character, and Commitments*. New York: Continuum Press.

Inbar, Y., Pizarro, D. A., & Bloom, P. (2012). Disgusting smells cause decreased liking of gay men. *Emotion, 12*: 23–27.

Inbar, Y., Pizarro, D. A., Iyer, R., & Haidt, J. (2012). Disgust sensitivity, political conservatism, and voting. *Social Psychological and Personality Science, 3*: 537–544.

Inbar, Y., Pizarro, D. A., Knobe, J., & Bloom, P. (2009). Disgust sensitivity predicts intuitive disapproval of gays. *Emotion, 9*: 435–439.

Iris Marion, Y. (1980). Throwing like a girl: a phenomenology of feminine body comportment motility and spatiality. *Human Studies, 3*: 137–156.

Isaksen, L. W. (2002). Towards a sociology of (gendered) disgust: images of bodily decay and the social organization of care work. *Journal of Family Issues, 23*: 791–811.

Izard, C. E. (1971). *The Face of Emotion*. New York: Appleton-Century Crofts.

Izard, C. E. (1977). *Human Emotions*. New York: Plenum Press.

Izard, C. E. (1993). Organizational and motivational functions of discrete emotions. In: M. Lewis & J. Haviland (Eds.), *The Handbook of Emotions* (pp. 631–641). New York: Guilford.

Izard, C. E. (2007). Basic emotions, natural kinds, emotion schemas, and a new paradigm. *Perspectives on Psychological Science, 2*: 260–280.

Izard, C. E. (2009). Emotion theory and research: highlights, unanswered questions, and emerging issues. *Annual Review of Psychology, 60*: 1–25.

Izard, C. E. (2011). Forms and functions of emotions: matters of emotion-cognition interactions. *Emotion Review, 3*: 371–378.

Izard, C. E., Youngstrom, E. A., Fine, S. E., Mostow, A. J., & Trentacosta, C. J. (2006). Emotions and developmental psychopathology. In: D. Cicchetti & D. J. Cohen (Eds.), *Developmental Psychology: Theory and Method* (2nd edn., Vol. 1, pp. 244–292). New York: John Wiley.

Izzard, S. (1999). Oedipus: baby or bathwater? A review of psychoanalytic theories of homosexual development. *British Journal of Psychotherapy, 16*: 43–55.

Jackson, P. L., Meltzoff, A. N., & Decety, J. (2005). How do we perceive the pain of others? A window into the neural processes involved in empathy. *Neuroimage, 24*: 771–779.

Jansen, A., Nederkoorn, C., & Mulkens, S. (2005). Selective visual attention for ugly and beautiful body parts in eating disorders. *Behaviour Research and Therapy, 43*: 183–196.

Johnson-Laird, P. N., & Oatley, K. (1989). The language of emotions: an analysis of a semantic field. *Cognition and Emotion, 3*: 81–123.

Johnson-Laird, P. N., & Oatley, K. (1992). Basic emotions, rationality, and folk theory. *Cognition and Emotion, 6*: 201–223.

Jones, D. (2001). Shame, disgust, anger and revenge: homosexuality and countertransference. *British Journal of Psychotherapy, 17*: 493–504.

Jones, D. (2006). Special section: the malign transference. Dealing with the unbearable in the internal world of the murderer. *Group Analysis, 39*: 51–58.

Jones, D. (2012). Therapy in perversity: seduction, destruction and keeping balance. In: A. Aiyegbusi & G. Kelly (Eds.), *Professional and Therapeutic Boundaries in Forensic Mental Health Practice* (pp. 53–62). London: Jessica Kingsley.

Jones, S. H. (2001). Circadian rhythms, multilevel models of emotion and bipolar disorder—an initial step towards integration? *Clinical Psychology Review, 21*: 1193–1209.

Jung, K., & Steil, R. (2012). The feeling of being contaminated in adult survivors of childhood sexual abuse and its treatment via a two-session program of cognitive restructuring and imagery modification: a case study. *Behaviour Modification, 36*: 67–86.

Jung, K., & Steil, R. (2013). A randomized controlled trial of cognitive restructuring and imagery modification to reduce the feeling of being contaminated in adult survivors of childhood sexual abuse suffering from posttraumatic stress disorder. *Psychotherapy and Psychosomatics, 82*: 213–220.

Kannan, D., & Levitt, H. M. (2013). A review of client self-criticism in psychotherapy. *Journal of Psychotherapy Integration, 23*: 166–178.

Kass, L. R. (1997). Wisdom of repugnance: why we should ban the cloning of humans. *New Republic, 216*: 17–26.

Katon, W. J., Rutter, C., Simon, G., Lin, E. H. B., Ludman, E., Ciechanowski, P., Kinder, L., Young, B., & Von Korff, M. (2005). The association of comorbid depression with mortality in patients with type 2 diabetes. *Diabetes Care, 28*: 2668–2672.

Kawada, C. L. K., Oettingen, G., Gollwitzer, P. M., & Bargh, J. A. (2004). The projection of implicit and explicit goals. *Journal of Personality and Social Psychology, 86*: 545–559.

Keane, T. M., Zimering, R. T., & Caddell, J. M. (1985). A behavioral formulation of posttraumatic stress disorder in Vietnam veterans. *The Behavior Therapist, 8*: 9–12.

Keith, L. (1996). Encounters with strangers: the public's responses to disabled women and how this affects our sense of self. In: J. Morris (Ed.), *Encounters With Strangers: Feminism and Disability* (pp. 69–88). London: Women's Press.

Kelley, W. M., Macrae, C. N., Wyland, C. L., Caglar, S., Inati, S., & Heatherton, T. F. (2002). Finding the self? An event-related fMRI study. *Journal of Cognitive Neuroscience, 14*: 785–794.

Kelly, D. R. (2011). *Yuck!: The Nature and Moral Significance of Disgust*. Massachusetts: The MIT Press.

Kelly, J. B. (2002). *Incontinence*. Ragged Edge Online. Retrieved from http://www.raggededgemagazine.com/0102/0102ft3.htm.

Keltner, D. (1995). Signs of appeasement: evidence for the distinct displays of embarrassment, amusement, and shame. *Journal of Personality and Social Psychology, 68*: 441–454.

Keltner, D., & Harker, L. A. (1998). The forms and functions of the nonverbal display of shame. In: P. Gilbert & B. Andrews (Eds.), *Interpersonal Approaches to Shame* (pp. 78–98). Oxford: Oxford University Press.

Kemeny, M. E., Gruenewald, T. L., & Dickerson, S. S. (2004). Shame as the emotional response to the social self: implications for physiology and health. *Psychological Inquiry, 15*: 153–160.

Kendler, K. S., & Prescott, C. A. (1999). A population-based twin study of lifetime major depression in men and women. *Archives of General Psychiatry, 56*: 39–44.

Kent, A., & Waller, G. (2000). Childhood emotional abuse and eating psychopathology. *Clinical Psychology Review, 20*: 887–903.

Kessler, R. C., Berglund, P., Demler, O., Jin, R., Merikangas, K. R., & Walters, E. E. (2005). Lifetime prevalence and age of onset distributions of DSM-IV disorders in the national comorbidity survey replication. *Archives of General Psychiatry, 62*: 593–602.

Kessler, R. C., Bimbaum, H., Bromet, E., Hwang, I., Sampson, N., & Shahly, V. (2010). Age differences in major depression: results from the national comorbidity survey replication (NCS-R). *Psychological Medicine, 40*: 225–237.

Kessler, R., Sonnega, A., Bromet, E., Hughes, M., & Nelson, C. (1995). Posttraumatic stress disorder in the National Comorbidity Survey. *Archives of General Psychiatry, 52*: 1048–1060.

Kiecolt-Glaser, J. K., McGuire, L., Robles, T. F., & Glaser, R. (2002). Emotions, morbidity, and mortality: new perspectives from psychoneuroimmunology. *Annual Review of Psychology, 53*: 83–107.

Kikyo, H., Ohki, K., & Miyashita, Y. (2002). Neural correlates for feeling-of-knowing: an fMRI parametric analysis. *Neuron, 36*: 177–186.

Kim, S., Thibodeau, R., & Jorgensen, R. S. (2011). Shame, guilt, and depressive symptoms: a meta-analytic review. *Psychological Bulletin, 137*: 68–96.

Klein, M. (1940). Mourning and its relation to manic-depressive states. *The International Journal of Psychoanalysis, 21*: 125–153.

Klimecki, O. M., Leiberg, S., Lamm, C., & Singer, T. (2012). Functional neural plasticity and associated changes in positive affect after compassion training. *Cerebral Cortex, 23*: 1552–1561.

Klonsky, E. D. (2007). The functions of deliberate self-injury: a review of the evidence. *Clinical Psychology Review, 27*: 226–239.

Klonsky, E. D., & Glenn, C. R. (2009). Assessing the functions of non-suicidal self-injury: psychometric properties of the Inventory of Statements About Self-injury (ISAS). *Journal of Psychopathology and Behavioral Assessment, 31*: 215–219.

Klonsky, E. D., & Muehlenkamp, J. J. (2007). Self-injury: a research review for the practitioner. *Journal of Clinical Psychology: In Session, 63*: 1045–1056.

Kluger, J. (2013). The Angelina effect: TIME's new cover image revealed. *TIME*. Retrieved from http://healthland.time.com/2013/05/15/the-angelina-effect-times-new-cover-image-revealed/.

Koenigs, M., Young, L., Adolphs, R., Tranel, D., Cushman, F., Hauser, M., & Damasio, A. (2007). Damage to the prefrontal cortex increases utilitarian moral judgments. *Nature, 446*: 908–911.

Kollei, I., Brunhoeber, S., Rauh, E., de Zwaan, M., & Martin, A. (2012). Body image, emotions and thought-control strategies in body dysmorphic disorder compared to eating disorders and healthy controls. *Journal of Psychosomatic Research, 72*: 321–327.

Koster-Hale, J., & Saxe, R. (2013). Functional neuroimaging of theory of mind. In: S. Baron-Cohen, M. Lombardo, & H. Tager-Flusberg (Eds.), *Understanding Other Minds: Perspectives From Developmental Social Neuroscience* (3rd edn., pp. 132–163). Oxford: Oxford University Press.

Koukounas, E., & McCabe, M. (1997). Sexual and emotional variables influencing sexual response to erotica. *Behaviour Research and Therapy, 35*: 221–231.

Krendl, A. C., Moran, J. M., & Ambady, N. (2013). Does context matter in evaluations of stigmatized individuals? An fMRI study. *Social Cognitive and Affective Neuroscience, 8*: 602–608.

Krienen, F. M., Tu, P. C., & Buckner, R. L. (2010). Clan mentality: evidence that the medial prefrontal cortex responds to close others. *Journal of Neuroscience, 30*: 13906–13915.

LaGrange, B., Cole, D. A., Jacquez, F., Ciesla, J., Dallaire, D., Pineda, A., Truss, A., Weitlauf, A., Tilghman-Osborne, C., & Felton, J. (2011). Disentangling the prospective relations between maladaptive cognitions and depressive symptoms. *Journal of Abnormal Psychology, 120*: 511–527.

Lam, W. W. T., Shing, Y. T., Bonanno, G. A., Mancini, A. D., & Fielding, R. (2012). Distress trajectories at the first year diagnosis of breast cancer in relation to six years' survivorship. *Psycho-Oncology, 21*: 90–99.

Lamb, S. (1989). *The Emergence of Morality in the Second Year of Life*. Article presented at the Biennial Meeting of the Society for Research in Child Development, Kansas City, KS.

Lamb, S. (1993). First moral sense: an examination of the appearance of morally related behaviours in the second year of life. *Journal of Moral Education, 22*: 97–109.

Lambrou, C., Veale, D., & Wilson, G. (2011). The role of aesthetic sensitivity in body dysmorphic disorder. *Journal of Abnormal Psychology, 120*: 443–453.

Lansky, M. (1991). Shame and the problem of suicide: a family systems perspective. *British Journal of Psychotherapy, 7*: 230–242.

Lansky, M. (1994). Shame: contemporary psychoanalytic perspectives. *The Journal of the American Academy of Psychoanalysis, 22*: 433–441.

Leahy, R. L. (2003). *Roadblocks in Cognitive-Behavioral Therapy: Transforming Challenges into Opportunities for Change*. New York: Guilford Press.

Leahy, R. L., & Tirch, D. (2011). *Emotion Regulation in Psychotherapy: A Practitioner's Guide*. New York: Guilford Press.

Leaviss, J., & Uttley, L. (2014). Psychotherapeutic benefits of compassion-focused therapy: An early systematic review. *Psychological Medicine*. doi:10.1017/S0033291714002141.

Lee, D. A. (2005). The perfect nurturer: a model to develop a compassionate mind within the context of cognitive therapy. In: P. Gilbert (Ed.), *Compassion: Conceptualisations, Research and Use in Psychotherapy* (pp. 326–351). London: Brunner-Routledge.

Lee, D. A., Scragg, P., & Turner, S. (2001). The role of shame and guilt in traumatic events: a clinical model of shame-based and guilt-based PTSD. *British Journal of Medical Psychology, 74*: 451–466.

Leskela, J., Dieperink, M., & Thuras, P. (2002). Shame and posttraumatic stress disorder. *Journal of Traumatic Stress, 15*: 223–226.

Leung, N., Waller, G., & Thomas, G. (1999). Core beliefs in anorexic and bulimic women. *The Journal of Nervous and Mental Disease, 187*: 736–741.

Levenson, R. W. (1999). The intrapersonal functions of emotion. *Cognition and Emotion, 13*: 481–504.

Levenson, R. W. (2011). Basic emotion questions. *Emotion Review, 3*: 379–386.

Levin, R. J., & van Berlo, W. (2004). Sexual arousal and orgasm in subjects who experience forced or non-consensual sexual stimulation: a review. *Journal of Clinical Forensic Medicine, 11*: 82–88.

Levin, S. (1971). The psychoanalysis of shame. *The International Journal of Psychoanalysis, 52*: 355–362.

Lewes, K. (1995). *Psychoanalysis and Male Homosexuality*. New York: Jason Aronson.

Lewinsohn, P. M., Striegel-Moore, R. H., & Seeley, J. R. (2000). Epidemiology and natural course of eating disorders in young women from adolescence to young adulthood. *Journal of the American Academy of Child and Adolescent Psychiatry, 39*: 1284–1292.

Lewis, M. (1992). *Shame: The Exposed Self*. New York: The Free Press.

Lewis, M. (1993). The emergence of human emotions. In: M. Lewis & J. M. Haviland (Eds.), *Handbook of Emotions* (pp. 304–319). New York: Guilford Press.

Lewis, M. (1999). The role of the self in cognition and emotion. In: T. Dalgleish & M. J. Power (Eds.), *Handbook of Cognition and Emotion* (pp. 125–142). Chichester: John Wiley.

Lewis, M., Alessandri, S. M., & Sullivan, M. W. (1992). Differences in shame and pride as a function of children's gender and task difficulty. *Child Development, 63*: 630–638.

Libeton, M., Dixon, J. B., Laurie, C., & O'Brien, P. E. (2004). Patient motivation for bariatric surgery: characteristics and impact on outcomes. *Obesity Surgery, 14*: 392–398.

Lieberman, D., Tooby, J., & Cosmides, L. (2007). The architecture of human kin detection. *Nature, 44*: 727–731.

Lindsay-Hartz, J., de Rivera, J., & Mascolo, M. F. (1995). Differentiating guilt and shame and their effects on motivations. In: J. P. Tangney & K. W. Fischer (Eds.), *Self-Conscious Emotions: The Psychology of Shame, Guilt, Embarrassment and Pride* (pp. 274–300). New York: Guilford Press.

Linehan, M. M. (1993). *Cognitive-Behavioral Treatment for Borderline Personality Disorder*. New York: Guilford Press.

Loewenstein, G., & Small, D. (2007). The scarecrow and the tin man: the vicissitudes of human sympathy and caring. *Review of General Psychology, 11*: 112–126.

Longe, O., Maratos, F. A., Gilbert, P., Evans, G., Volker, F., Rockliffe, H., & Rippon, G. (2010). Having a word with yourself: neural correlates of self-criticism and self-reassurance. *NeuroImage, 49*: 1849–1856.

Lovibond, S. H., & Lovibond, P. F. (1993). *Manual for the Depression, Anxiety and Stress Scales* (*DASS*). Toronto, Canada: Psychology Foundation of Canada (Psychology Foundation Monograph).

Lutz, A., Brefczynski-Lewis, J., Johnstone, T., & Davidson, R. J. (2008). Regulation of the neural circuitry of emotion by compassion meditation: effects of the meditative expertise. *Public Library of Science, 3*: 1–5.

MacDonald, L. D., & Anderson, H. R. (1984). Stigma in patients with rectal cancer: a community study. *Journal of Epidemiology and Community Health, 38*: 284–290.

Mackay, J. (2001). Global sex: sexuality and sexual practices around the world. *Sexual and Relationship Therapy, 16*: 71–82.

Majdandži , J., Bauer, H., Windischberger, C., Moser, E., Engl, E., & Lamm, C. (2012). The human factor: behavioral and neural correlates of humanized perception in moral decision-making. *PloS one, 7*: e47698.

Malancharuvil, J. M. (2004). Projection, introjection, and projective identification: a reformulation. *The American Journal of Psychoanalysis, 64*: 375–382.

Mancini, R., Gragnani, A., & D'Olimpio, F. (2001). The connection between disgust and obsession and compulsions in a non-clinical sample. *Personality and Individual Differences, 31*: 1173–1180.

Manderson, L. (2005). Boundary breaches: the body, sex and sexuality after stoma surgery. *Social Science and Medicine, 61*: 405–415.

Maner, J. K., Kenrick, D. T., Becker, D. V., Robertson, T. E., Hofer, B., Neuberg, S. L., Delton, A. W., Butner, J., & Schaller, M. (2005). Functional projection: how fundamental social motives can bias interpersonal perception. *Journal of Personality and Social Psychology, 88*: 63–78.

Marks, D. (1999). Dimensions of oppression: theorising the embodied subject. *Disability and Society, 14*: 611–626.

Marschall, D. E., Saftner, J., & Tangney, J. P. (1994). *The State Shame and Guilt Scale*. Fairfax, VA: George Mason University.

Martens, J. P., Tracy, J. L., & Shariff, A. F. (2012). Status signals: adaptive benefits of displaying and observing the nonverbal expressions of pride and shame. *Cognition and Emotion, 26*: 390–406.

Marzillier, S. L., & Davey, G. C. L. (2004). The emotional profiling of disgust-eliciting stimuli: evidence for primary and complex disgusts. *Cognition and Emotion, 18*: 313–336.

Mason, E. C., & Richardson, R. (2010). Looking beyond fear: the extinction of other emotions implicated in anxiety disorders. *Journal of Anxiety Disorders, 24*: 63–70.

Matchett, G., & Davey, G. C. L. (1991). A test of a disease-avoidance model of animal phobias. *Behavior Research and Therapy, 29*: 91–94.

Mayer, B., Bos, A. E. R., Muris, P., Huijding, J., & Vlielander, M. (2008). Does disgust enhance eating disorder symptoms? *Eating Behaviors, 9*: 124–127.

Mayer, B., Muris, P., Bos, A. E. R., & Sujkerbuijk, C. (2008). Disgust sensitivity and eating disorder symptoms in a non-clinical population. *Journal of Behavior Therapy and Experimental Psychiatry, 39*: 504–514.

Mayer, B., Muris, P., Busser, K., & Bergamin, J. (2009). A disgust mood state causes a negative interpretation bias, but not in the specific domain of body-related concerns. *Behavior Research and Therapy, 47*: 876–881.

Mayer, B., Muris, P., & Wilschut, M. (2011). Fear- and disgust-related covariation bias and eating disorders symptoms in healthy young women. *Journal of Behavior Therapy and Experimental Psychiatry, 42*: 19–25.

Maynard Smith, J., & Harper, D. (2003). *Animal Signals*. Oxford: Oxford University Press.

McCambridge, S. A., & Consedine, N. S. (2014a). For whom the bell tolls: experimentally manipulated disgust and embarrassment may cause anticipated sexual healthcare avoidance among some people. *Emotion, 14*: 407–415.

McCambridge, S. A., & Consedine, N. S. (2014b). Which physician and what to tell them? An experimental study of embarrassment and disgust in physician preferences and communication. Manuscript submitted for publication.

McDougall, W. (1926). *An Introduction to Social Psychology*. Boston: Luce.

McKay, D. (2006). Treating disgust reactions in contamination-based obsessive-compulsive disorder. *Journal of Behavior Therapy and Experimental Psychiatry, 37*: 53–59.

McKay, D., Abramowitz, J., Calamari, J., Kyrios, M., Radomsky, A., Sookman, D., Taylor, S., & Wilhelm, S. (2004). A critical evaluation of obsessive-compulsive disorder subtypes: symptoms versus mechanism. *Clinical Psychology Review, 24*: 283–313.

McKay, D., Gosselin, J. T., & Gupta, S. (2008). Body dysmorphic disorder. In: J. S. Abramowitz, D. McKay, & S. Taylor (Eds.), *Obsessive-Compulsive Disorder: Subtypes and Spectrum Conditions* (pp. 177–195). Oxford: Elsevier.

McLane, J. (1996). The voice on the skin: self-mutilation and Merleau-Ponty's theory of language. *Hypatia, 11*: 107–118.

McLure, L. (2004). Working with the unbearable. In: D. Jones (Ed.), *Working with Dangerous People: The Psychotherapy of Violence* (pp. 81–98). Abingdon, Oxon: Radcliffe Publishing.

McMillen, J. C., North, C. S., & Smith, E. M. (2000). What parts of PTSD are normal: intrusion, avoidance, or arousal? Data from the Northridge, California earthquake. *Journal of Traumatic Stress, 13*: 57–75.

McNally, R. J. (2002). Disgust has arrived. *Journal of Anxiety Disorders, 16*: 561–566.

McNamara, C., Chur-Hansen, A., & Hay, P. (2008). Emotional responses to food in adults with an eating disorder: a qualitative exploration. *European Eating Disorders Review, 16*: 115–123.

Medford, N. (2012). Emotion and the unreal self: depersonalisation disorder and de-affectualization. *Emotion Review, 4*: 139–144.

Meevissen, Y. M. C., Peters, M. L., & Alberts, H. J. E. M. (2011). Become more optimistic by imagining a best possible self: effects of a two-week intervention. *Journal of Behavior Therapy and Experimental Psychiatry, 42*: 371–378.

Menninghaus, W. (2003). *Disgust: The Theory and History of a Strong Sensation*. H. Eiland & J. Golb (Trans.). New York: State University of New York Press.

Merens, W., Booij, L., Haffmans, P. M. J., & Van der Does, A. J. W. (2008). The effects of experimentally lowered serotonin function on emotional information processing and memory in remitted depressed patients. *Journal of Psychopharmacology, 22*: 653–662.

Meunier, S. A., & Tolin, D. F. (2009). The treatment of disgust. In: B. O. Olatunji & D. McKay (Eds.), *Disgust and Its Disorders: Theory, Assessment, and Treatment Implications* (pp. 271–284). Washington, DC: American Psychological Association.

Milia, D. (2000). *Self-Mutilation and Art Therapy*. London: Jessica Kingsley.

Miller, S. B. (1993). Disgust reactions: their determinants and manifestations in treatment. *Contemporary Psychoanalysis, 29*: 711–735.

Miller, W. I. (1997). *The Anatomy of Disgust*. London: Harvard University Press.

Mitchell, J. P., Banaji, M. R., & Macrae, C. N. (2005). General and specific contributions of the medial prefrontal cortex to knowledge about mental states. *Neuroimage, 28*: 757–762.

Mitchell, J. P., Macrae, C. N., & Banaji, M. R. (2006). Dissociable medial prefrontal contributions to judgments of similar and dissimilar others. *Neuron, 50*: 655–663.

Mobbs, D., Yu, R., Meyer, M., Passamonti, L., Seymour, B., Calder, A. J., Schweizer, S., Frith, C. D., & Dalgleish, T. (2009). A key role for similarity in vicarious reward. *Science, 324*: 900.

Moll, J., de Oliveira-Souza, R., Moll, F. T., Ignácio, F. A., Bramati, I., Caparelli-Dáquer, E., & Eslinger, P. (2005). The moral affiliations of disgust: a functional MRI study. *Cognitive and Behavioral Neurology, 18*: 68–78.

Moll, J., & Schulkin, J. (2009). Social attachment and aversion in human moral cognition. *Neuroscience and Biobehavioral Reviews, 33*: 456–465.

Moncrieff-Boyd, J., Byrne, S., & Nunn, K. (2013). Disgust and anorexia nervosa: confusion between self and non-self. *Advances in Eating Disorders: Theory, Research and Practice*, doi:10.1080/21662630.2013.820376.

Monde, K. M., Ketay, S., Giesbrecht, T., Braun, A., & Simeon, D. (2013). Preliminary physiological evidence for impaired emotion regulation in depersonalization disorder. *Psychiatry Research*, doi: http://dx.doi.org/10.1016/j.psychres.2013.02.020.

Moore, R., Brodsgaard, I., & Rosenberg, N. (2004). The contributions of embarrassment to phobic dental anxiety: a qualitative research study. *BMC Psychiatry, 4*: 10.

Moretz, M. W., & McKay, D. (2008). Disgust sensitivity as a predictor of obsessive-compulsive contamination symptoms and associated cognitions. *Journal of Anxiety Disorders, 22*: 707–715.

Morris, E. J. A., Whitehouse, L. E., Farrell, T., Nickerson, C., Thomas, J. D., Quirke, P., Rutter, M. D., Rees, C., Finan, P. J., Wilkinson, J. R., & Patnick, J. (2012). A retrospective observational study examining the characteristics and outcomes of tumours diagnosed within and without of the English NHS Bowel Cancer Screening Programme. *British Journal of Cancer, 107*: 757–764.

Moussavi, S., Chatterji, S., Verdes, E., Tandon, A., Patel, V., & Ustun, B. (2007). Depression, chronic diseases, and decrements in health: results from the World Health Surveys. *Lancet, 370*: 851–858.

Mouzos, J., & Thompson, S. (2000). Gay-hate related homicides: an overview of major findings in New South Wales. *Trends and Issues in Crime and Criminal Justice*, paper #155. Canberra: Australian Institute of Criminology.

Mulkens, S. A. N., de Jong, P. J., & Merckelbach, H. (1996). Disgust and spider phobia. *Journal of Abnormal Psychology, 105*: 464–468.

Muris, P. (2006). The pathogenesis of childhood anxiety disorders: consideration from a developmental psychopathology perspective. *International Journal of Behavioral Development, 30*: 5–11.

Muris, P., Merckelbach, H., Nederkoom, S., Rassin, E., Chandel, I., & Horselenberg, R. (2000). Disgust and psychopathological symptoms in a nonclinical sample. *Personality and Individual Differences, 29*: 1163–1167.

Muris, P., Merckelbach, H., Schmidt, H., & Tierney, S. (1999). Disgust sensitivity, trait anxiety and anxiety disorders symptoms in normal children. *Behaviour Research and Therapy, 37*: 953–961.

Muris, P., van der Heiden, S., & Rassin, E. (2008). Disgust sensitivity and psychopathological symptoms in non-clinical children. *Journal of Behavior Therapy and Experimental Psychiatry, 39*: 133–146.

Murphy, R. (1987). *The Body Silent*. London: Phoenix House.

Murray, C. J., & Lopez, A. D. (1997). Global mortality, disability, and the contribution of risk factors: global burden of disease study. *Lancet, 17*: 1436–1442.

Nabi, R. L. (2002). The theoretical versus the lay meaning of disgust: implications for emotion research. *Cognition and Emotion, 16*: 695–703.

National Institute for Health and Clinical Excellence (NICE) (2010). *Depression: The Treatment and Management of Depression in Adults (update)*. Clinical Guideline 90. London: NICE.

Navarrete, C. D., & Fessler, D. M. (2006). Disease avoidance and ethnocentrism: the effects of disease vulnerability and disgust sensitivity on intergroup attitudes. *Evolution and Human Behavior, 27*: 270–282.

Nemeroff, C., & Cavanaugh, C. J. (1999). The ethics of emaciation: moral connotations of the body, self, and diet. In: M. Siegal & C. C. Peterson (Eds.), *Children's Understanding of Biology and Health* (pp. 183–206). New York: Cambridge University Press.

Nemeroff, C. B., & Rozin, P. (1994). The contagion concept in adult thinking in the United States: transmission of germs and of interpersonal influence. *Ethos, 22*: 158–186.

Neuberg, S. L., Kenrick, D. T., & Schaller, M. (2011). Human threat management systems: self-protection and disease avoidance. *Neuroscience and Biobehavioral Reviews, 35*: 1042–1051.

Neziroglu, F., Hickey, M., & Mckay, D. (2010). Psychophysiological and self-report components of disgust in body-dysmorphic disorder: the effects of repeated exposure. *International Journal of Cognitive Therapy, 3*: 40–51.

Nicholson, E., & Barnes-Holmes, D. (2012). Developing an implicit measure of disgust propensity and disgust sensitivity: examining the role of implicit disgust propensity and sensitivity in obsessive-compulsive tendencies. *Journal of Behavior Therapy and Experimental Psychiatry, 43*: 922–930.

Niedenthal, P., & Halberstadt, J. (2003). Top-down influences in social perception. *European Review of Social Psychology, 14*: 49–76.

Nisbett, R. (2004). *The Geography of Thought: How Asians and Westerners Think Differently … and Why*. New York: Free Press.

Nock, M., & Prinstein, M. (2004). A functional approach to the assessment of self-mutilative behavior. *Journal of Consulting and Clinical Psychology, 72*: 885–890.

Noonan, M. P., Sallet, J., Rudebeck, P. H., Buckley, M. J., & Rushworth, M. F. (2010). Does the medial orbitofrontal cortex have a role in social valuation? *European Journal of Neuroscience, 31*: 2341–2351.

Norris, F. (1992). Epidemiology of trauma: frequency and impact of different potentially traumatic events on different demographic groups. *Journal of Consulting and Clinical Psychology, 60*: 409–418.

Nussbaum, M. C. (2004). *Hiding From Humanity: Disgust, Shame, and the Law*. New Jersey: Princeton University Press.

Nussbaum, M. C. (2010). *From Disgust to Humanity: Sexual Orientation and Constitutional Law*. New York: Oxford University Press.

O'Carroll, R. E., Foster, C., McGeechan, G., Sandford, K., & Ferguson, E. (2011). The "ick" factor, anticipated regret, and willingness to become an organ donor. *Health Psychology, 30*: 236–245.

O'Connor, N. (2003). *Wild Desires and Mistaken Identities: Lesbianism and Psychoanalysis*. London: Karnac.

O'Donnell, M. L., Elliott, P., Wolfgang, B. J., & Creamer, M. (2007). Posttraumatic appraisals in the development and persistence of posttraumatic stress symptoms. *Journal of Traumatic Stress, 20*: 173–182.

Oaten, M., Stevenson, R. J., & Case, T. I. (2009). Disgust as a disease-avoidance mechanism. *Psychological Bulletin, 135*: 303–321.

Oaten, M., Stevenson, R. J., & Case, T. I. (2011). Disease avoidance as a functional basis for stigmatization. *Philosophical Transactions of the Royal Society B: Biological Sciences, 366*: 3433–3452.

Oatley, K., & Duncan, E. (1992). Incidents of emotion in daily life. In: K. T. Strongman (Ed.), *International Review of Studies on Emotion, Vol. 2* (pp. 249–293). Chichester: Wiley.

Oatley K., & Johnson-Laird, P. N. (1987). Towards a cognitive theory of emotions. *Cognition and Emotion, 1*: 29–50.

Ochsner, K. N., Knierim, K., Ludlow, D. H., Hanelin, J., Ramachandran, T., Glover, G., & Mackey, S. C. (2004). Reflecting upon feelings: an fMRI study of neural systems supporting the attribution of emotion to self and other. *Journal of Cognitive Neuroscience, 16*: 1746–1772.

Ogden, P., Minton, K., & Pain, C. (2006). *Trauma and the Body: A Sensorimotor Approach to Psychotherapy*. New York: Norton.

Ogilive, D. M. (1987). The undesired self: a neglected variable in personality research. *Journal of Personality and Social Psychology, 52*: 379–388.

Ojserkis, R., Arocho, J., & McKay, D. (2012). Does the relationship between disgust and posttraumatic stress vary by type of stressor? Paper presented at the annual meeting of the Association for Behavioral and Cognitive Therapies, Washington, DC, 15–18 November.

Olatunji, B. O. (2008). Disgust, scrupulosity and conservative attitudes about sex: evidence for a mediational model of homophobia. *Journal of Research in Personality, 42*: 1364–1369.

Olatunji, B. O., Adams, T., Ciesielski, B., David, B., Sarawgi, S., & Broman-Fulks, J. (2012). The Three Domains of Disgust Scale: factor structure, psychometric properties, and conceptual limitations. *Assessment, 19*: 205–225.

Olatunji, B. O., Armstrong, T., Fan, Q., & Zhao, M. (2014). Risk and resiliency in posttraumatic stress disorder: distinct roles of anxiety and disgust sensitivity. *Psychological Trauma: Theory, Research, Practice, and Policy, 6*: 50–55.

Olatunji, B. O., Arrindell, W. A., & Lohr, J. M. (2005). Can the sex differences in disgust sensitivity account for the sex differences in blood-injection-injury fears? *Personality and Individual Differences, 39*: 61–71.

Olatunji, B. O., Babson, K. A., Smith, R. C., Feldner, M. T., & Connolly, K. M. (2009). Gender as a moderator of the relation between PTSD and disgust: a laboratory test employing individualized script-driven imagery. *Journal of Anxiety Disorders, 23*: 1091–1097.

Olatunji, B. O., & Broman-Fulks, J. J. (2009). Latent structure of aversion: taxometric exploration. *Journal of Anxiety Disorders, 23*: 87–92.

Olatunji, B. O., & Cisler, J. M. (2009). Disgust sensitivity: psychometric overview and operational definition. In: B. O. Olatunji & D. McKay (Eds.), *Disgust and Its Disorders: Theory, Assessment, and Treatment Implications* (pp. 31–56). Washington, DC: American Psychological Association.

Olatunji, B. O., Cisler, J., McKay, D., & Phillips, M. L. (2010). Is disgust associated with psychopathology? Emerging research in the anxiety disorders. *Psychiatry Research, 175*: 1–10.

Olatunji, B. O., Connolly, K. M., & David, B. (2008). Behavioral avoidance and self-reported fainting symptoms in blood/injury fearful individuals: an experimental test of disgust domain specificity. *Journal of Anxiety Disorders, 22*: 837–848.

Olatunji, B. O., David, B., & Ciesielski, B. G. (2012). Who am I to judge? Self-disgust predicts less punishment of severe transgressions. *Emotion, 12*: 169–173.

Olatunji, B. O., Elwood, L., Williams, N., & Lohr, J. M. (2008). Feelings of mental pollution and PTSD symptoms in victims of sexual assault: the mediating role of trauma-related cognitions. *Journal of Cognitive Psychotherapy, 22*: 37–47.

Olatunji, B. O., Forsyth, J. P., & Cherian, A. (2007). Evaluative differential conditioning of disgust: a sticky form of relational learning that is resistant to extinction. *Journal of Anxiety Disorders, 21*: 820–834.

Olatunji, B. O., & Mckay, D. (2007). Disgust and psychiatric illness: have we remembered? *British Journal of Psychiatry, 190*: 457–459.

Olatunji, B. O., & McKay, D. (2009). Introduction: the emerging importance of disgust in psychopathology. In: B. O. Olatunji & D. McKay (Eds.), *Disgust and Its Disorders: Theory, Assessment, and Treatment Implications* (pp. 3–6). Washington, DC: American Psychological Association.

Olatunji, B. O., Moretz, M. W., Wolitzky-Taylor, K. B., McGrath, P. B., & Ciesielski, B. G. (2010). Disgust vulnerability and symptoms of contamination-based OCD: descriptive tests of incremental specificity. *Behavior Therapy, 41*: 475–490.

Olatunji, B. O., & Sawchuk, C. N. (2005). Disgust: characteristic features, social manifestations, and clinical implications. *Journal of Social and Clinical Psychology, 24*: 932–962.

Olatunji, B. O., Sawchuk, C. N., de Jong, P. J., & Lohr, J. M. (2006). The structural relation between disgust sensitivity and blood-injection-injury fears: a cross-cultural comparison of US and Dutch data. *Journal of Behavior Therapy and Experimental Psychiatry, 37*: 16–29.

Olatunji, B. O., Sawchuk, C. N., Lohr, J. M., & de Jong, P. J. (2004). Disgust domains in the prediction of contamination fear. *Behaviour Research and Therapy, 42*: 93–104.

Olatunji, B. O., Smits, J. A., Connolly, K. M., Willems, J., & Lohr, J. M. (2007). Examination of the rate of decline in fear and disgust during exposure to threat-relevant stimuli in blood-injection-injury phobia. *Journal of Anxiety Disorders, 21*: 445–455.

Olatunji, B. O., Unoka, Z. S., Beran, E., David, B., & Armstrong, T. (2009). Disgust sensitivity and psychopathological symptoms: distinctions from harm avoidance. *Journal of Psychopathology and Behavioral Assessment, 31*: 137–142.

Olatunji, B. O., Williams, N., Lohr, J. M., Connolly, K., Cisler, J., & Meunier, S. (2007). Structural differentiation of disgust from trait anxiety in the prediction of specific anxiety disorder symptoms. *Behaviour Research and Therapy, 45*: 3002–3017.

Olatunji, B. O., Williams, N. L., Tolin, D. F., Abramowitz, J. S., Sawchuk, C. N., Lohr, J. M., & Elwood, L. S. (2007). The disgust scale: item analysis, factor structure, and suggestions for refinement. *Psychological Assessment, 19*: 281–297.

Olatunji, B. O., Wolitzky-Taylor, K. B., Ciesielski, B. G., Armstrong, T., Etzel, E. N., & David, B. (2009). Fear and disgust processing during repeated exposure to threat-relevant stimuli in spider phobia. *Behaviour Research and Therapy, 47*: 671–679.

Onden-Lim, M., Wu, R., & Grisham, J. R. (2012). Intrusive imagery experiences in a high dysmorphic concern population. *Journal of Psychopathology and Behavioral Assessment, 35*: 99–105.

Orbach, S. (2006). *Fat is a Feminist Issue*. London: Arrow Books.

Orth, U., Berking, M., & Burkhardt, S. (2006). Self-conscious emotions and depression: rumination explains why shame but not guilt is maladaptive. *Personality and Social Psychology Bulletin, 32*: 1608–1619.

Orth, U., & Maercker, A. (2009). Posttraumatic anger in crime victims: directed at the perpetrator and at the self. *Journal of Traumatic Stress, 22*: 158–161.

Ortony, A., Clore, G. L., & Collins, A. (1988). *The Cognitive Structure of Emotions*. New York: Cambridge University Press.

Otto, M. W., Teachman, B. A., Cohen, L. S., Soares, C. N., Vitonis, A. F., & Harlow, B. L. (2007). Dysfunctional attitudes and episodes of major depression: predictive validity and temporal stability in never-depressed, depressed, and recovered women. *Journal of Abnormal Psychology, 116*: 475–483.

Overton, P. G., Markland, F. E., Taggart, H. S., Bagshaw, G. L., & Simpson, J. (2008). Self-disgust mediates the relationship between dysfunctional cognitions and depressive symptomatology. *Emotion, 8*: 379–385.

Page, A. C., & Tan, B. J. (2009). Disgust and blood-injury-injection phobia. In: B. O. Olatunji & D. McKay (Eds.), *Disgust and Its Disorders: Theory, Assessment, and Treatment Implications* (pp. 191–209). Washington, DC: American Psychological Association.

Park, J. H., Faulkner, J., & Schaller, M. (2003). Evolved disease-avoidance processes and contemporary anti-social behavior: prejudicial attitudes and avoidance of people with physical disabilities. *Journal of Nonverbal Behavior, 27*: 65–87.

Park, J. H., van Leeuwen, F., & Stephen, I. D. (2012). Homeliness is in the disgust sensitivity of the beholder: relatively unattractive faces appear especially unattractive to individuals higher in pathogen disgust. *Evolution and Human Behaviour, 33*: 569–577.

Parker, L. A. (2003). Taste avoidance and taste aversion: evidence for two different processes. *Learning and Behavior, 312*: 165–172.

Parker, L. A., Limebeer, C. L., & Rana, S. A. (2009). Conditioned disgust, but not conditioned taste avoidance, may reflect conditioned nausea in rats. In: S. Reilly & T. R. Schachtman (Eds.), *Conditioned Taste Aversion: Behavioral and Neural Processes* (pp. 92–113). New York: Oxford University Press.

Payne, E. (2013). Angelina Jolie undergoes double mastectomy. *CNN*. Retrieved from CNN website: http://edition.cnn.com/2013/05/14/showbiz/angelina-jolie-double-mastectomy.

Penley, J. A., & Tomaka, J. (2002). Associations among the big five, emotional responses, and coping with acute stress. *Personality and Individual Differences, 32*: 1215–1228.

Persson, E., & Hellström, A. -L. (2002). Experiences of Swedish men and women 6 to 12 weeks after ostomy surgery. *Journal of Wound Ostomy and Continence Nursing, 29*: 103–108.

Peters, M. L., Flink, I. K., Boersma, K., & Linton, S. J. (2010). Manipulating optimism: can imagining a best possible self be used to increase positive future expectancies? *The Journal of Positive Psychology, 5*: 204–211.

Petrak, J., Doyle, A. -M., Williams, L., Buchan, L., & Forster, G. (1997). The psychological impact of sexual assault: a study of female attenders of a sexual health psychology service. *Sexual and Marital Therapy, 12*: 339–345.

Pettit, J. W., Lewinsohn, P. M., Roberts, R. E., Seeley, J. R., & Monteith, L. L. (2009). The long-term course of depression: development of an empirical index and identification of early adult outcomes. *Psychological Medicine, 39*: 403–412.

Phillips, K. A., Pinto, A., & Jain, S. (2004). Self-esteem in body dysmorphic disorder. *Body Image, 14*: 385–390.

Phillips, M., Medford, N., Senior, C., Bullmore, E., Suckling, J., Brammer, M., Andrew, C., Sierra, M., Stephen, C. R., & David, A. S. (2001). Depersonalization disorder: thinking without feeling. *Psychiatry Research: Neuroimaging, 108*: 145–160.

Phillips, M. L., Senior, C., Fahy, S. T., & David, A. S. (1998). Disgust: the forgotten emotion of psychiatry. *British Journal of Psychiatry, 172*: 373–375.

Pietrzak, R. H., Goldstein, R. B., Southwick, S. M., & Grant, B. F. (2011). Prevalence and Axis I comorbidity of full and partial posttraumatic stress disorder in the United States: results from Wave 2 of the National Epidemiologic Survey on Alcohol and Related Conditions. *Journal of Anxiety Disorders, 25*: 456–465.

Piggott, L., & Grover, C. (2009). Retrenching Incapacity Benefit: Employment Support Allowance and paid work. *Social Policy and Society, 8*: 159–170.

Pines, M. (1995). The universality of shame: a psychoanalytic approach. *British Journal of Psychotherapy, 11*: 346–357.

Pinquart, M., & Duberstein, P. R. (2010). Depression and cancer mortality: a meta-analysis. *Psychological Medicine, 40*: 1797–1810.

Pizarro, D., Inbar, Y., & Helion, C. (2011). On disgust and moral judgment. *Emotion Review, 3*: 267–268.

Plutchik, R. (1980). A general psychoevolutionary theory of emotion. In: R. Plutchik & H. Kellerman (Eds.), *Emotion: Theory, Research, and Experience: Vol. 1. Theories of Emotion* (pp. 3–31). New York: Academic Press.

Pond, Jr., R. S., DeWall, C. N., Lambert, N. M., Deckman, T., Bonser, I. M., & Fincham, F. D. (2012). Repulsed by violence: disgust sensitivity buffers trait, behavioral, and daily aggression. *Journal of Personality and Social Psychology, 102*: 175–188.

Porges, S. W. (2007). The polyvagal perspective. *Biological Psychology, 74*: 116–143.

Powell, P. A. (2013). *Sickened by the Self: Elucidating Self-Disgust in the Context of Depression*. Unpublished doctoral thesis. Sheffield University. Available (by request) at http://etheses.whiterose.ac.uk/5198/.

Powell, P. A., Overton, P. G., & Simpson, J. (2014). The revolting self: an interpretative phenomenological analysis of the experience of self-disgust in females with depressive symptoms. *Journal of Clinical Psychology, 70*: 562–578.

Powell, P. A., Simpson, J., & Overton, P. G. (2013). When disgust leads to dysphoria: a three-wave longitudinal study assessing the temporal relationship between self-disgust and depressive symptoms. *Cognition and Emotion, 27*: 900–913.

Power, M. J. (1999). Sadness and its disorders. In: T. Dalgleish & M. J. Power (Eds.), *Handbook of Cognition and Emotion* (pp. 497–519). Chichester: John Wiley.

Power, M. J. (2006a). The structure of emotion: an empirical comparison of six models. *Cognition and Emotion, 20*: 694–713.

Power, M. J. (2006b). A life in the unconscious. *The Psychologist, 19*: 546–547.

Power, M. J. (2010). *Emotion-Focused Cognitive Therapy*. Chichester: John Wiley.

Power, M. J., & Dalgleish, T. (1997). *Cognition and Emotion: From Order to Disorder*. Hove: Psychology Press.

Power, M. J., & Dalgleish, T. (2008). *Cognition and Emotion: From Order to Disorder* (2nd edn.). Hove: Psychology Press.

Power, M. J., & Fyvie, C. (2013). The role of emotion in PTSD: two preliminary studies. *Behavioural and Cognitive Psychotherapy, 41*: 162–172.

Power, M. J., & Tarsia, M. (2007). Basic and complex emotions in depression and anxiety. *Clinical Psychology and Psychotherapy, 14*: 19–31.

Prokop, P., & Fančovičová, J. (2013). Self-protection versus disease avoidance: the perceived physical condition is associated with fear of predators in humans. *Journal of Individual Differences, 34*: 15–23.

Prokop, P., Fančovičová, J., & Fedor, P. (2010). Health is associated with antiparasite behavior and fear of disease-relevant animals in humans. *Ecological Psychology, 22*: 222–237.

Pyszczynski, T., Greenberg, J., & Solomon, S. (1999). A dual process model of defense against conscious and unconscious death-related thoughts: an extension of terror-management theory. *Psychological Review, 106*: 835–845.

Quarmby, K. (2008). *Getting Away With Murder: Disabled People's Experiences of Hate Crime in the UK*. London: Scope.

Rachman, S. (1994). Pollution of the mind. *Behaviour Research and Therapy, 32*: 311–314.

Rachman, S. (2004). Fear of contamination. *Behaviour Research and Therapy, 42*: 1227–1255.

Rachman, S. (2005). Vancouver Obsessional Compulsive Inventory—Mental Contamination (VOCI-MC). Rachman Lab, University of British Columbia.

Rachman, S. (2006). *Fear of Contamination: Assessment and Treatment*. Oxford: Oxford University Press.

Rachman, S. (2010). Betrayal: a psychological analysis. *Behaviour Research and Therapy, 48*: 304–311.

Rachman, S., Radomsky, A. S., Elliott, C. M., & Zysk, E. (2012). Mental contamination: the perpetrator effect. *Journal of Behavior Therapy and Experimental Psychiatry, 43*: 587–593.

Radomsky, A. S., & Elliott, C. M. (2009). Analyses of mental contamination: Part II, individual differences. *Behaviour Research and Therapy, 47*: 1004–1011.

Rait, G., Walters, K., Griffin, M., Buszewicz, M., Petersen, I., & Nazareth, I. (2009). Recent trends in the incidence of recorded depression in primary care. *British Journal of Psychiatry, 195*: 520–524.

Raman, L., & Gelman, S. A. (2008). Do children endorse psychosocial factors in the transmission of illness and disgust? *Developmental Psychology, 44*: 801–813.

Reeve, D. (2008). *Negotiating Disability in Everyday Life: The Experience of Psycho-Emotional Disablism*. Unpublished doctoral dissertation. Lancaster University, Lancaster, UK.

Reilly, S., & Schachtman, T. R. (2008). *Conditioned Taste Aversion: Neural and Behavioral Processes*. New York: Oxford University Press.

Reiss, S., Peterson, R. A., Gursky, D. M., & McNally, R. J. (1986). Anxiety sensitivity, anxiety frequency and the prediction of fearfulness. *Behaviour Research and Therapy, 24*: 1–8.

Resick, P. A., & Miller, M. W. (2009). Posttraumatic stress disorder: anxiety or traumatic stress disorder? *Journal of Traumatic Stress, 22*: 384–390.

Resick, P. A., & Schnicke, M. K. (1992). Cognitive processing therapy for sexual assault survivors. *Journal of Consulting and Clinical Psychology, 60*: 748–756.

Resnick, H. S., Kilpatrick, D. G., Dansky, B. S., Saunders, B. E., & Best, C. L. (1993). Prevalence of civilian trauma and posttraumatic stress disorder in a representative national sample of women. *Journal of Consulting and Clinical Psychology, 61*: 984–991.

Reuven, O., Liberman, N., & Dar, R. (2013). The effect of physical cleansing on threatened morality in individuals with obsessive-compulsive disorder. *Clinical Psychological Science*. doi:10.1177/2167702613485565.

Reynolds, L. M., Consedine, N. S., & McCambridge, S. A. (2014). Mindfulness and disgust in colorectal cancer scenarios: non-judging and non-reacting components predict avoidance when it makes sense. *Mindfulness, 5*: 442–452.

Reynolds, L. M., Consedine, N. S., Pizarro, D. A., & Bissett, I. P. (2013). Disgust and behavioral avoidance in colorectal cancer screening and treatment: a systematic review and research agenda. *Cancer Nursing, 36*: 122–130.

Reynolds, L. M., McCambridge, S. A., Bissett, I. P., & Consedine, N. S. (2014). Trait and state disgust: an experimental investigation of disgust and avoidance in colorectal cancer decision scenarios. *Health Psychology, 33*: 1495–1506.

Riggs, D. S., Rothbaum, B. O., & Foa, E. B. (1995). A prospective examination of symptoms of posttraumatic stress disorder in victims of nonsexual assault. *Journal of Interpersonal Violence, 10*: 210–214.

Riskind, J. H. (1997). Looming vulnerability to threat: a cognitive paradigm for anxiety. *Behaviour Research and Therapy, 35*: 386–404.

Rivers, W. H. R. (1920). *Instinct and the Unconscious: A Contribution to a Biological Theory of the Psycho-Neuroses*. Cambridge: Cambridge University Press.

Roache, R., & Clarke, S. (2009). Bioconservatism, bioliberalism, and the wisdom of reflecting on repugnance. *Monash Bioethics Review, 28*: 1–21.

Roberts, J. E., & Monroe, S. M. (1994). A multidimensional model of self-esteem in depression. *Clinical Psychology Review, 14*: 161–181.

Roberts, R. O., Rhodes, T., Panser, L. A., Girman, C. J., Chute, C. G., Oesterling, J. E., Lieber, M. M., & Jacobsen, S. J. (1994). Natural history of prostatism: worry and embarrassment from urinary symptoms and health care-seeking behavior. *Adult Urology, 43*: 621–628.

Roberts, T. A., & Gettman, J. Y. (2004). Mere exposure: gender differences in the effects of priming a state of self-objectification. *Sex Roles, 51*: 17–27.

Roberts, T. A., & Goldenberg, J. L. (2007). Wrestling with nature: an existential perspective on the body and gender in self-conscious emotions. In: J. L. Tracy, R. W. Robins, & J. P. Tangney (Eds.), *The Self-Conscious Emotions: Theory and Research* (pp. 389–406). New York: Guilford Press.

Robertson, D., Snarey, J., Ousley, O., Harenski, K., Bowman, F. D., Gilkey, R., & Kilts, C. (2007). The neural processing of moral sensitivity to issues of justice and care. *Neuropsychologia, 45*: 755–766.

Robertson, S. (2004). Men and disability. In: J. Swain, S. French, C. Barnes, & C. Thomas (Eds.), *Disabling Barriers, Enabling Environments* (2nd edn., pp. 75–80). London: Sage.

Rockliff, H., Karl, A., McEwan, K., Gilbert, J., Matos, M., & Gilbert, P. (2011). Effects of intranasal oxytocin on compassion-focused imagery. *Emotion, 11*: 1388–1396.

Rohrmann, S., Hopp, H., & Quirin, M. (2008). Gender differences in psychophysiological responses to disgust. *Journal of Psychophysiology, 22*: 65–75.

Roseman, I. J. (1984). Cognitive determinants of emotion: a structural theory. *Review of Personality and Social Psychology, 5*: 11–36.

Rosen, J. C., & Ramirez, E. (1998). A comparison of eating disorders and body dysmorphic disorder on body image and psychological adjustment. *Journal of Psychosomatic Research, 44*: 441–449.

Rosen, R., Brown, C., Heiman, J., Leiblum, S., Meston, C., Shabsigh, R., Ferguson, D., & D'Agostino, R. Jr. (2000). The Female Sexual Function Index (FSFI): a multidimensional self-report instrument for the assessment of female sexual function. *Journal of Sex and Marital Therapy, 26*: 191–208.

Rosenstein, D., & Oster, H. (1988). Differential facial responses to four basic tastes in newborns. *Child Development, 59*: 1555–1568.

Rosman, S. (2004). Cancer and stigma: experience of patients with chemotherapy-induced alopecia. *Patient Education and Counseling, 52*: 333–339.

Roth, T. L., & Sweatt, J. D. (2011). Annual research review: epigenetic mechanisms and environmental shaping of the brain during sensitive periods of development. *Journal of Child Psychology and Psychiatry, 52*: 398–408.

Rothbaum, B. O., Foa, E. D., Riggs, D. S., & Murdock, T. (1992). A prospective examination of post-traumatic stress disorder in rape victims. *Journal of Traumatic Stress, 5*: 455–475.

Rozin, P. (2008). Hedonic "adaptation": specific habituation to disgust/death elicitors as a result of dissecting a cadaver. *Judgement and Decision Making, 3*: 191–194.

Rozin, P., & Fallon, A. E. (1987). A perspective on disgust. *Psychological Review, 94*: 23–41.

Rozin, P., Fallon, A., & Mandell, R. (1984). Family resemblance in attitudes to foods. *Developmental Psychology, 20*: 309–314.

Rozin, P., Haidt, J., & Fincher, K. (2009). From oral to moral: is moral disgust an elaboration of a food-rejection system? *Science, 323*: 1179–1180.

Rozin, P., Haidt, J., & McCauley, C. R. (1999). Disgust: the body and soul emotion. In: T. Dalgleish & M. J. Power (Eds.), *Handbook of Cognition and Emotion* (pp. 430–445). Chichester: John Wiley.

Rozin, P., Haidt, J., & McCauley, C. R. (2000). Disgust. In: M. Lewis & J. Haviland-Jones (Eds.), *Handbook of Emotions* (2nd edn., pp. 637–653). New York: Guilford Press.

Rozin, P., Haidt, J., & McCauley, C. R. (2008). Disgust. In: M. Lewis, J. M. Haviland-Jones, & L. F. Barrett (Eds.), *Handbook of Emotions* (3rd edn., pp. 757–766). New York: Guilford Press.

Rozin, P., Haidt, J., & McCauley, C. R. (2009). Disgust: the body and soul emotion in the 21st century. In: B. O. Olatunji & D. McKay (Eds.), *Disgust and Its Disorders: Theory, Assessment and Treatment Implications* (pp. 9–29). Washington, DC: American Psychological Association.

Rozin, P., Haidt, J., McCauley, C. R., Dunlop, L., & Ashmore, M. (1999). Individual differences in disgust sensitivity: comparisons and evaluations of paper-and-pencil versus behavioral measures. *Journal of Research in Personality, 33*: 330–351.

Rozin, P., Lowery, L., Imada, S., & Haidt, J. (1999). The CAD triad hypothesis: a mapping between three moral emotions (contempt, anger, disgust) and three moral ethics (community, autonomy, divinity). *Journal of Personality and Social Psychology, 76*: 574–586.

Rozin, P., Markwith, M., & McCauley, C. (1994). Sensitivity to indirect contacts with other persons: AIDS aversion as a composite of aversion to strangers, infection, moral taint, and misfortune. *Journal of Abnormal Psychology, 103*: 495–505.

Rozin, P., Markwith, M., & Nemeroff, C. (1992). Magical contagion beliefs and fear of AIDS. *Journal of Applied Social Psychology, 22*: 1081–1092.

Rozin, P., Millman, L., & Nemeroff, C. (1986). Operation of the laws of sympathetic magic in disgust and other domains. *Journal of Personality and Social Psychology, 50*: 703–712.

Rozin, P., & Nemeroff, C. (1990). The laws of sympathetic magic: a psychological analysis of similarity and contagion. In: J. W. Stigler, R. A. Schweder, & H. Gilbert (Eds.), *Cultural Psychology: Essays on Comparative Human Development* (pp. 205–232). New York: Cambridge University Press.

Rozin, P., Taylor, C., Ross, L., Bennett, G., & Hejmadi, A. (2005). General and specific emotion recognition abilities: relations among individual differences in recognition of disgust and other emotional expressions in facial and bodily representations, obsessive-compulsive tendencies, and disgust sensitivity. *Cognition and Emotion, 19*: 397–412.

Rudebeck, P. H. (2006). A role for the macaque anterior cingulate gyrus in social valuation. *Science, 313*: 1310–1312.

Rusch, N., Schulz, D., Valerius, G., Steil, R., Bohus, M., & Schmahl, C. (2011). Disgust and implicit self-concept in women with borderline personality disorder and posttraumatic stress disorder. *European Archives of Psychiatry and Clinical Neuroscience, 261*: 369–376.

Russell, P. S., & Giner-Sorolla, R. (2011a). Social justifications for moral emotions: when reasons for disgust are less elaborated than for anger. *Emotion, 11*: 637–646.

Russell, P. S., & Giner-Sorolla, R. (2011b). Moral anger, but not moral disgust, responds to intentionality. *Emotion, 11*: 233–240.

Russell, P. S., & Giner-Sorolla, R. (2011c). Moral anger is more flexible than moral disgust. *Social Psychological and Personality Science, 2*: 360–364.

Russell, P. S., & Giner-Sorolla, R. (2013). Bodily moral disgust: what it is, how it is different from anger, and why it is an unreasoned emotion. *Psychological Bulletin, 139*: 328–351.

Rust, J., & Golombok, S. (1986). The GRISS: a psychometric instrument for the assessment of sexual dysfunction. *Archives of Sexual Behavior, 15*: 157–165.

Ryan, S., Oaten, M., Stevenson, R. J., & Case, T. I. (2012). Facial disfigurement is treated like an infectious disease. *Evolution and Human Behavior, 33*: 639–646.

Salerno, J. M., & Peter-Hagene, L. C. (2013). The interactive effect of anger and disgust on moral outrage and judgments. *Psychological Science, 24*: 2069–2078.

Sanders, B., & Becker-Lausen, E. (1995). The measurement of psychological maltreatment: early data on the Child Abuse and Trauma Scale. *Child Abuse and Neglect, 19*: 315–323.

Santor, D., & Walker, J. (1999). Garnering the interests of others: mediating the effects among physical attractiveness, self-worth and dominance. *British Journal of Social Psychology, 38*: 461–477.

Santos, M., Richards, C. S., & Bleckley, K. (2007). Comorbidity between depression and disordered eating in adolescents. *Eating Behaviors, 8*: 440–449.

Sasson, Y., Dekel, S., Nacasch, N., Chopra, M., Zinger, Y., Amital, D., & Zohar, J. (2005). Posttraumatic obsessive-compulsive disorder: a case series. *Psychiatric Research, 135*: 145–152.

Saver, J. L., & Damasio, A. R. (1991). Preserved access and processing of social knowledge in a patient with acquired sociopathy due to ventromedial frontal damage. *Neuropsychologia, 29*: 1241–1249.

Savin-Williams, R. C. (1994). Verbal and physical abuse as stressors in the lives of lesbian, gay male, and bisexual youths: associations with school problems, running away, substance abuse, prostitution, and suicide. *Journal of Consulting and Clinical Psychology, 62*: 261–269.

Savin-Williams, R. C. (2006). *The New Gay Teenager*. London: Harvard University Press.

Sawchuk, C. N. (2009). Acquisition and maintenance of disgust: developmental and learning perspectives. In: B. O. Olatunji & D. Mckay (Eds.), *Disgust and Its Disorders: Theory, Assessment, and Treatment Implications* (pp. 77–97). Washington, DC: APA.

Sawchuk, C. N., Lohr, J. M., Lee, T. C., & Tolin, D. F. (1999). Exposure to disgust-evoking imagery and information-processing biases in blood-injection-injury phobia. *Behaviour Research and Therapy, 37*: 249–257.

Sawchuk, C. N., Lohr, J. M., Westendorf, D. H., Meunier, S. A., & Tolin, D. F. (2002). Emotional responding to fearful and disgusting stimuli in specific phobics. *Behaviour Research and Therapy, 40*: 1031–1046.

Saxe, R., Moran, J. M., Scholz, J., & Gabrieli, J. (2006). Overlapping and non-overlapping brain regions for theory of mind and self reflection in individual subjects. *Social Cognitive and Affective Neuroscience, 1*: 229–234.

Schaich Borg, J., Lieberman, D., & Kiehl, K. A. (2008). Infection, incest, and iniquity: investigating the neural correlates of disgust and morality. *Journal of Cognitive Neuroscience, 20*: 1529–1546.

Scherer, K. R., & Wallbott, H. G. (1994). Evidence for universality and cultural variation of differential emotion response patterning. *Journal of Personality and Social Psychology, 66*: 310–328.

Schienle, A., Ille, R., Sommer, M., & Arendasy, M. (2014). Diagnostik von Selbstekel im Rahmen der Depression. *Verhaltenstherapie, 24*: 15–20.

Schienle, A., Schafer, A., Stark, R., Walter, B., Franz, M., & Vaitl, D. (2003). Disgust sensitivity in psychiatric disorders: a questionnaire study. *Journal of Nervous and Mental Disease, 191*: 831–834.

Schienle, A., Stark, R., Walter, B., & Vaitl, D. (2003). The connection between disgust sensitivity and blood-related fears, faintness symptoms, and obsessive-compulsiveness in a non-clinical sample. *Anxiety, Stress, and Coping, 16*: 185–193.

Schlosser, T., Dunning, D., & Fetchenhauer, D. (2013). What a feeling: the role of immediate and anticipated emotions in risky decisions. *Journal of Behavioral Decision Making, 26*: 13–30.

Schmitz, T. W., Kawahara-Baccus, T. N., & Johnson, S. C. (2004). Metacognitive evaluation, self-relevance, and the right prefrontal cortex. *Neuroimage, 22*: 941–947.

Schnall, S., Haidt, J., Clore, G. L., & Jordan, A. H. (2008). Disgust as embodied moral judgment. *Pesonality and Social Psychology Bulletin, 34*: 1096–1109.

Schweik, S. M. (2009). *The Ugly Laws: Disability in Public*. New York: New York University Press.

Scully, D., & Marolla, J. (1985). Riding the bull at Gilley's: convicted rapists describe the rewards of rape. *Social Problems, 32*: 251–263.

Sedikides, C., & Skowronski, J. J. (1997). The symbolic self in evolutionary context. *Personality and Social Psychology Review, 1*: 80–102.

Seymour, W. (1998). *Remaking the Body: Rehabilitation and Change*. London: Routledge.

Shakespeare, T., Gillespie-Sells, K., & Davies, D. (1996). *The Sexual Politics of Disability: Untold Desires*. London: Cassell.

Shand, A. F. (1914). *The Foundations of Character: Being a Study of the Tendencies of the Emotions and Sentiments*. London: Macmillian.

Shanmugarajah, K., Gaind, S., Clarke, A., & Butler, P. E. M. (2012). The role of disgust emotions in the observer response to facial disfigurement. *Body Image, 9*: 455–461.

Sherry, M. (2010). *Disability Hate Crimes: Does Anyone Really Hate Disabled People?* Farnham: Ashgate.

Shin, L. M., McNally, R. J., Kosslyn, S. M., Thompson, W. L., Rauch, S. L., Alpert, N. M., Metzger, L. J., Lasko, N. B., Orr, S. P., & Pitman, R. K. (1999). Regional cerebral blood flow during script-driven imagery in childhood sexual abuse-related PTSD: a PET investigation. *American Journal of Psychiatry, 156*: 575–584.

Siebers, T. (2012). A sexual culture for disabled people. In: R. McRuer & A. Mollow (Eds.), *Sex and Disability* (pp. 37–53). Durham, NC: Duke University Press.

Sieg, J., & Scholz, O. B. (2001). Subjective emotional and physical experience during compulsive washing and checking. *Verhaltenstherapie, 11*: 288–296.

Siegal, M., Fadda, R., & Overton, P. G. (2011). Contamination sensitivity and the development of disease-avoidant behaviour. *Philosophical Transactions of the Royal Society B: Biological Sciences, 366*: 3427–3432.

Siegel, D. J. (2001). Toward an interpersonal neurobiology of the developing mind: attachment relationships, "mindsight", and neural integration. *Infant Mental Health Journal, 22*: 67–94.

Siegel, D. J. (2010). *Mindsight: Transform Your Brain with the New Science of Kindness*. New York: Bantam.

Sierra, M., Medford, N., Wyatt, G., & David, A. S. (2012). Depersonalization disorder and anxiety: a special relationship. *Psychiatry Research, 197*: 123–127.

Sierra, M., Senior, C., Phillips, M. L., & David, A. S. (2006). Autonomic response in the perception of disgust and happiness in depersonalization disorder. *Psychiatry Research, 145*: 225–231.

Simpson, J., Carter, S., Anthony, S. H., & Overton, P. G. (2006). Is disgust a homogeneous emotion? *Motivation and Emotion, 30*: 31–41.

Simpson, J., Hillman, R., Crawford, T., & Overton, P. G. (2010). Self-esteem and self-disgust both mediate the relationship between dysfunctional cognitions and depressive symptoms. *Motivation and Emotion, 34*: 399–406.

Singer, T., Critchley, H. D., & Preuschoff, K. (2009). A common role of insula in feelings, empathy and uncertainty. *Trends in Cognitive Sciences, 13*: 334–340.

Singer, T., Seymour, B., O'Doherty, J., Kaube, H., Dolan, R. J., & Frith, C. D. (2004). Empathy for pain involves the affective but not sensory components of pain. *Science, 303*: 1157–1162.

Singleton, N., Bumpstead, R., O'Brien, M., Lee, A., & Meltzer, H. (2001). *Psychiatric Morbidity among Adults Living in Private Households, 2000*. London: The Stationery Office.

Smith, D. M., Loewenstein, G., Rozin, P., Sherriff, R. L., & Ubel, P. A. (2007). Sensitivity to disgust, stigma, and adjustment to life with a colostomy. *Journal of Research in Personality, 41*: 787–803.

Smith, K. (2012). *Homicides, Firearm Offences and Intimate Violence 2010/11, Supplementary Volume 2 to Crime in England and Wales 2010/11*. London: Home Office.

Smith, K. S., Tindell, A. J., Aldridge, J. W., & Berridge, K. C. (2009). Ventral pallidum roles in reward and motivation. *Behavioural Brain Research, 196*: 155–167.

Smits, J. A., Telch, M. J., & Randall, P. K. (2002). An examination of the decline in fear and disgust during exposure-based treatment. *Behaviour Research and Therapy, 40*: 1243–1253.

Smolak, L., & Levine, M. P. (2007). Trauma, eating problems and eating disorders. In: S. Wonderlich, J. E. Mitchell, M. de Zwann, & H. Steiger (Eds.), *Annual Review of Eating Disorders—Part 1* (pp. 113–124). Oxford: Radcliffe Publishing.

Socarides, C. (1994). The erosion of heterosexuality. *Washington Post*, 5 July.

Soldatic, K., & Meekosha, H. (2012). The place of disgust: disability, class and gender in spaces of workfare. *Societies, 2*: 139–156.

Soldatic, K., & Pini, B. (2009). The three Ds of welfare reform: disability, disgust and deservingness. *Australian Journal of Human Rights, 15*: 77–96.

Spielrein, S. (1994). Destruction as the cause of coming into being. *Journal of Analytical Psychology, 39*: 155–186.

Spijker, J., de Graaf, R., Bijl, R. V., Beekman, A. T. F., Ormel, J., & Nolen, W. A. (2002). Duration of major depressive episodes in the general population:

results from the Netherlands Mental Health Survey and Incidence Study (NEMESIS). *British Journal of Psychiatry, 181*: 208–213.

Stalnaker, R. (2010). *Our Knowledge of the Internal World*. Oxford: Oxford University Press.

Stanghellini, G., & Muscelli, C. (2007). Real person's experience of contamination obsessions: hypotheses from a Strausian analysis (Editorial). *South African Journal of Psychiatry, 13*: 79–82.

Stark, R., Walter, B., Schienle, A., & Vaitl, D. (2005). Psychophysiological correlates of disgust and disgust sensitivity. *Journal of Psychophysiology, 19*: 50–60.

Steele, J. D., & Lawrie, S. M. (2004). Segregation of cognitive and emotional function in the prefrontal cortex: a stereotactic meta-analysis. *Neuroimage, 21*: 868–875.

Steil, R., Jung, K., & Stangier, U. (2011). Efficacy of a two-session program of cognitive restructuring and imagery modification to reduce the feeling of being contaminated in adult survivors of childhood sexual abuse: a pilot study. *Journal of Behavior Therapy and Experimental Psychiatry, 42*: 325–329.

Steiner, J. E., Glaser, D., Hawilo, M. E., & Berridge, K. C. (2001). Comparative expression of hedonic impact: affective reactions to taste by human infants and other primates. *Neuroscience and Biobehavioral Reviews, 25*: 53–74.

Stellman, R. E., Goodwin, J. D., Robinson, J., Dansak, D., & Hilgers, R. D. (1984). Psychological effects of vulvectomy. *Psychosomatics, 25*: 779–783.

Stevenson, R. J., Case, T. I., & Oaten, M. (2011). Effect of self-reported sexual arousal on responses to sex-related and non-sex-related disgust cues. *Archives of Sexual Behavior, 40*: 79–85.

Stipek, D. (1998). Differences between Americans and Chinese in the circumstances evoking pride, shame, and guilt. *Journal of Cross-Cultural Psychology, 29*: 616–629.

Stone, A. M. (1992). The role of shame in post-traumatic stress disorder. *American Journal of Orthopsychiatry, 62*: 131–136.

Stopa, L., Brown, M. A., & Hirsch, C. R. (2012). The effects of repeated imagery practice on self-concept, anxiety and performance in socially anxious participants. *Journal of Experimental Psychopathology, 3*: 223–242.

Straus, E. (1968). On obsession: a clinical and methodological study. *Nervous and Mental Disease Monographs, no. 73*. London: Johnson Reprint.

Streeter, C. C., Gerbarg, P. L., Saper, R. B., Ciraulo, D. A., & Brown, R. P. (2012). Effects of yoga on the autonomic nervous system, gamma-aminobutyric acid, and allostasis in epilepsy, depression, and post-traumatic stress disorder. *Medical Hypotheses, 78*: 571–579.

Striegel-Moore, R., & Franko, D. (2002). Body image issues among girls and women. In: T. F. Cash & T. Pruzinsky (Eds.), *Body Image: A Handbook of Theory, Research, and Clinical Practice* (pp. 183–191). New York: Guilford Press.

Stuewig, J., & McCloskey, L. A. (2005). The relation of child maltreatment to shame and guilt among adolescents: psychological routes to depression and delinquency. *Child Maltreatment, 10*: 324–336.

Sullivan, M., Levy, W. C., Russo, J. E., & Spertus, J. A. (2004). Depression and health status in patients with advanced heart failure: a prospective study in tertiary care. *Journal of Cardiac Failure, 10*: 390–396.

Surguladze, S. A., El-Hage, W., Dalgleish, T., Radua, J., Gohier, B., & Phillips, M. L. (2010). Depression is associated with increased sensitivity to signals of disgust: a functional magnetic resonance imaging study. *Journal of Psychiatric Research, 44*: 894–902.

Sussner, K. M., Thompson, H. S., Jandorf, L., Edwards, T. A., Forman, A., Brown, K., Kapil-Pair, N., Bovbjerg, D. H., Schwartz, M. D., & Valdimarsdottir, H. B. (2009). The influence of acculturation and breast cancer-specific distress on perceived barriers to genetic testing for breast cancer among women of African descent. *Psycho-Oncology, 18*: 945–955.

Swain, J., & Cameron, C. (1999). Unless otherwise stated: discourses of labelling and identity in coming out. In: M. Corker & S. French (Eds.), *Disability Discourse* (pp. 68–78). Buckingham: Open University Press.

Talbot, E. S., & Ellis, H. (1896). A case of developmental degenerative insanity, with sexual inversion, melancholia following removal of testicles, attempted murder and suicide. *British Journal of Psychiatry, 42*: 340–346.

Tamir, M. & Ford, B. Q. (2012). When feeling bad is expected to be good: emotion regulation and outcome expectancies in social conflicts. *Emotion, 12*: 807–816.

Tamir, M., Mitchell, C., & Gross, J. J. (2008). Hedonic and instrumental motives in anger regulation. *Psychological Science, 19*: 324–328.

Tangney, J. P. (1999). The self-conscious emotions: shame, guilt, embarrassment and pride. In: T. Dalgleish & M. J. Power (Eds.), *Handbook of Cognition and Emotion* (pp. 541–568). Chichester: Wiley.

Tangney, J. P., Burggraf, S. A., & Wagner, P. E. (1995). Shame-proneness, guilt-proneness, and psychological symptoms. In: J. P. Tangney & K. W. Fischer (Eds.), *Self-Conscious Emotions: The Psychology of Shame, Guilt, Embarrassment, and Pride* (pp. 343–367). London: Guildford Press.

Tangney, J. P., & Dearing, R. L. (2003). *Shame and Guilt*. New York: Guilford Press.

Tangney, J. P., Miller, R. S., Flicker, L., & Barlow, D. H. (1996). Are shame, guilt, and embarrassment distinct emotions? *Journal of Personality and Social Psychology, 70*: 1256–1269.

Tangney, J. P., Stuewig, J., & Mashek, D. J. (2007). Moral emotions and moral behaviour. *Annual Review of Psychology, 58*: 345–372.

Tangney, J. P., Wagner, P., & Gramzow, R. (1992). Proneness to shame, proneness to guilt, and psychopathology. *Journal of Abnormal Psychology, 101*: 469–478.

Tanner, J. L., Dechert, M. P., & Frieden, I. J. (1998). Growing up with a facial hemangioma: parents and child coping and adaptation. *Pediatrics, 3*: 446–452.

Taylor, K. (2007). Disgust is a factor in extreme prejudice. *The British Journal of Social Psychology, 46*: 597–617.

Taylor, P., Gooding, P., Wood, A. N., & Tarrier, N. (2011). The role of defeat and entrapment in depression, anxiety and suicide. *Psychological Bulletin, 137*: 391–420.

Taylor, S., McKay, D., & Abramowitz, J. S. (2005). Is obsessive-compulsive disorder a disturbance of security motivation? Comment on Woody and Szechtman (2004). *Psychological Review, 112*: 650–657.

Teachman, B. A. (2006). Pathological disgust: in the thoughts, not the eye, of the beholder. *Anxiety, Stress and Coping, 19*: 335–351.

ter Kuile, M. M., Brauer, M., & Laan, E. (2006). The Female Sexual Function Index (FSFI) and the Female Sexual Distress Scale (FSDS): psychometric properties within a Dutch population. *Journal of Sex and Marital Therapy, 32*: 289–304.

Thomas, C. (2002). Best dissertation section: a literature review of the problems of delayed presentation for treatment and non-completion of treatment for tuberculosis in less developed countries and ways of addressing these problems using particular implementations of the DOTS strategy. *Journal of Management in Medicine, 16*: 371–400.

Thomas, C. (2007). *Sociologies of Disability and Illness: Contested Ideas in Disability Studies and Medical Sociology*. Basingstoke: Palgrave Macmillan.

Thomas, C. M., & Morris, S. (2003). Cost of depression among adults in England in 2000. *British Journal of Psychiatry, 183*: 514–519.

Thompson, R., & Zuroff, D. C. (2003). Dependent and self-critical mothers' responses to adolescent autonomy and competence. *Personality and Individual Differences, 24*: 311–324.

Thompson, R., & Zuroff, D. C. (2004). The Levels of Self-Criticism Scale: comparative self-criticism and internalized self-criticism. *Personality and Individual Differences, 36*: 419–430.

Thompson, R. J., & Berenbaum, H. (2006). Shame reactions to everyday dilemmas are associated with depressive disorder. *Cognitive Therapy and Research, 30*: 415–425.

Thomson, R. G. (1996). Introduction: from wonder to errot—a geneology of freak discourse in modernity. In: R. G. Thomson (Ed.), *Freakery: Cultural Spectacles of the Extraordinary Body* (pp. 1–19). New York: New York University Press.

Thornhill, R., & Gangestad, S. W. (2006). Facial sexual dimorphism, developmental stability, and susceptibility to disease in men and women. *Evolution and Human Behavior, 27*: 131–144.

Thorpe, S. J., Patel, S. P., & Simonds, L. M. (2003). The relationship between disgust sensitivity, anxiety, and obsessions. *Behaviour Research and Therapy, 41*: 1397–1409.

Tierney, S., & Fox, J. R. E. (2010). Living with the "anorexic voice": a thematic analysis. *Psychology and Psychotherapy: Theory, Research and Practice, 83*: 243–254.

Tiggemann, M., & Slater, A. (2004). Thin ideals in music television: a source of social comparison and body dissatisfaction. *International Journal of Eating Disorders, 35*: 48–58.

Tindell, A. J., Smith, K. S., Peciña, S., Berridge, K. C., & Aldridge, J. W. (2006). Ventral pallidum firing codes hedonic reward: when a bad taste turns good. *Journal of Neurophysiology, 96*: 2399–2409.

Tolin, D. F., Lohr, J. M., Sawchuk, C. N., & Lee, T. C. (1997). Disgust and disgust sensitivity in blood-injection-injury and spider phobia. *Behaviour Research and Therapy, 35*: 949–953.

Tolin, D. F., Woods, C. M., & Abramowitz, J. S. (2006). Disgust sensitivity and obsessive-compulsive symptoms in a non-clinical sample. *Journal of Behavior Therapy and Experimental Psychiatry, 37*: 30–40.

Tolin, D. F., Worhunsky, P., & Maltby, N. (2004). Sympathetic magic in contamination-related OCD. *Journal of Behavior Therapy and Experimental Psychiatry, 35*: 193–205.

Tomkins, S. S. (1984). Affect theory. In: K. R. Scherer & P. Ekman (Eds.), *Approaches to Emotion* (pp. 163–195). Hillsdale, NJ: Erlbaum.

Tomsen, S. (2001). Hate crimes and masculinity: new crimes, new responses and some familiar patterns. Paper presented at the 4th National Outlook Symposium on Crime in Australia, New Crimes or New Responses. Canberra: Australian Institute of Criminology.

Tomsen, S. (2002). *Hatred, Murder and Male Honour: Anti-Homosexual Homicides in New South Wales, 1980–2000*. Canberra: Australian Institute of Criminology.

Toronchuk, J. A., & Ellis, G. F. (2007). Disgust: sensory affect or primary emotional system? *Cognition and Emotion, 21*: 1799–1818.

Tracy, J. L., & Matsumoto, D. (2008). The spontaneous display of pride and shame: evidence for biologically innate nonverbal displays. *Proceedings of the National Academy of Sciences, 105*: 11655–11660.

Tracy, J. L., & Robins, R. W. (2004). Putting the self into self-conscious emotions: a theoretical model. *Psychological Inquiry, 15*: 103–125.

Tracy, J. L., Robins, R. W., & Schriber, R. A. (2009). Development of a FACS-verified set of basic and self-conscious emotion expressions. *Emotion, 9*: 554–559.

Treasure, J., Corfield, F., & Cardi, V. (2012). A three-phase model of the social emotional functioning in eating disorders. *European Eating Disorders Review, 20*: 431–438.

Troop, N. A., & Baker, A. (2009). Food, body and soul: the role of disgust in eating disorders. In: B. O. Olatunji & D. Mckay (Eds.), *Disgust and Its Disorders: Theory, Assessment, and Treatment Implications* (pp. 229–251). Washington, DC: APA.

Troop, N. A., Murphy, F., Bramon, E., & Treasure, J. L. (2000). Disgust sensitivity in eating disorders: a preliminary investigation. *International Journal of Eating Disorders, 27*: 446–451.

Troop, N. A., Serpell, L., Allan, S., & Treasure, J. L. (2008). Shame in women with a past or current eating disorder. *European Eating Disorders Review, 16*: 480–488.

Troop, N. A., Treasure, J., & Serpell, L. (2002). A further exploration of disgust in eating disorders. *European Eating Disorders Review, 10*: 218–226.

Tsao, S. D., & McKay, D. (2004). Behavioral avoidance tests and disgust in contamination fears: distinctions from trait anxiety. *Behaviour Research and Therapy, 42*: 207–216.

Tucker, M., & Bond, N. W. (1997). The roles of gender, sex role, and disgust in fear of animals. *Personality and Individual Differences, 22*: 135–138.

Tybur, J. M., Bryan, A. D., Magnan, R. E., & Hooper, A. E. C. (2011). Smells like safe sex: olfactory pathogen primes increase intentions to use condoms. *Psychological Science, 22*: 478–480.

Tybur, J. M., Lieberman, D., & Griskevicius, V. (2009). Microbes, mating, and morality: individual differences in three functional domains of disgust. *Journal of Personality and Social Psychology, 97*: 103–122.

Tybur, J. M., Lieberman, D., Kurzban, R., & DeScioli, P. (2013). Disgust: evolved function and structure. *Psychological Review, 120*: 65–84.

Ubel, P. A., Loewenstein, G., Schwarz, N., & Smith, D. (2005). Misimagining the unimaginable: the disability paradox and health care decision-making. *Health Psychology, 24*: S57–S62.

Vail, K. E., Juhl, J., Arndt, J., Vess, M., Routledge, C., & Rutjens, B. T. (2012). When death is good for life: considering the positive trajectories of terror management. *Personality and Social Psychology Review, 16*: 303–329.

van Lankveld, J. J. D. M., & ter Kuile, M. M. (1999). The Golombok Rust Inventory of Sexual Satisfaction (GRISS): predictive validity and construct validity in a Dutch population. *Personality and Individual Differences, 26*: 1005–1023.

van Overveld, M., de Jong, P. J., & Peters, M. L. (2006). Differential UCS expectancy bias in spider-fearful individuals: evidence toward an association between spiders and disgust relevant outcomes. *Journal of Behavior Therapy and Experimental Psychiatry, 37*: 60–72.

van Overveld, M., de Jong, P. J., & Peters, M. L. (2010). The disgust propensity and sensitivity scale—revised: its predictive value for avoidance behaviour. *Personality and Individual Differences, 49*: 706–711.

van Overveld, M., de Jong, P. J., Peters, M. L., Cavanagh, K., & Davey, G. C. L. (2006). Disgust propensity and disgust sensitivity: separate constructs that are differentially related to specific fears. *Personality and Individual Differences, 41*: 1241–1252.

van Overveld, M., de Jong, P. J., Peters, M., van Lankveld, J., Melles, R., & ter Kuile, M. M. (2013). The Sexual Disgust Questionnaire: a psychometric study and a first exploration in patients with sexual dysfunctions. *Journal of Sexual Medicine, 10*: 396–407.

Verwoerd, J., de Jong, P. J., Wessel, I., & van Hout, W. J. P. J. (2013). "If I feel disgusted, I must be getting ill": emotional reasoning in the context of contamination fear. *Behaviour Research and Therapy, 51*: 122–127.

Volz, K. G., Kessler, T., & von Cramon, D. Y. (2009). In-group as part of the self: in-group favoritism is mediated by medial prefrontal cortex activation. *Social Neuroscience, 4*: 244–260.

Von Wagner, C., Knight, K., Halligan, S., Atkin, W., Lilford, R., Morton, D., & Wardle, J. (2009). Patient experiences of colonoscopy, barium enema and CT colonography: a qualitative study. *British Journal of Radiology, 82*: 13–19.

Vrana, S. R. (1993). The psychophysiology of disgust: differentiating negative emotional contexts with facial EMG. *Psychophysiology, 30*: 279–286.

Vugt, M., & Kameda, T. (2014). Evolution of the social brain: psychological adaptation for group living. In: M. Mikulincer & P. R. Shaver (Eds.), *Mechanisms of Social Connection: From Brain to Group* (pp. 335–355). Washington, DC: American Psychological Association.

Waller, G., Babbs, M., Milligan, R. J., Meyer, C., Ohanian, V., & Leung, N. (2003). Anger and core beliefs in the eating disorders. *International Journal of Eating Disorders, 34*: 118–124.

Waller, G., Ohanian, V., Meyer, C., & Osman, S. (2000). Cognitive content among bulimic women: the role of core beliefs. *International Journal of Eating Disorders, 28*: 235–241.

Walls, M. M., & Kleinknecht, R. A. (1996). Disgust factors as predictors of blood-injury fear and fainting. Paper presented at the annual meeting of the Western Psychological Association, San Jose, CA.

Waraich, P., Goldner, E. M., Somers, J. M., & Hsu, L. (2004). Prevalence and incidence studies of mood disorders: a systematic review of the literature. *Canadian Journal of Psychiatry, 49*: 124–138.

Ware, J., Jain, K., Burgess, I., & Davey, G. C. L. (1994). Disease-avoidance model: factor analysis of common animal fears. *Behaviour Research and Therapy, 32*: 57–63.

Warin, M. (2003). Miasmatic calories and saturating fats: fear of contamination in anorexia. *Culture, Medicine and Psychiatry, 27*: 77–93.

Warnock-Parkes, E., Salkovskis, P. M., & Rachman, J. (2012). When the problem is beneath the surface in OCD: the cognitive treatment of a case of pure mental contamination. *Behavioural and Cognitive Psychotherapy, 40*: 383–399.

Watson, N. (2003). Daily denials: the routinisation of oppression and resistance. In: S. Riddell & N. Watson (Eds.), *Disability, Culture and Identity* (pp. 34–52). London: Longman.

Weber, H. (2004). Explorations in the social construction of anger. *Motivation and Emotion, 28*: 197–219.

Wegner, D. M. (1994). Ironic processes of mental control. *Psychological Review, 101*: 34–52.

Wheatley, T., & Haidt, J. (2005). Hypnotic disgust makes moral judgments more severe. *Psychological Science, 16*: 780–784.

Whelton, W. J., & Greenberg, L. S. (2005). Emotion in self-criticism. *Personality and Individual Differences, 38*: 1583–1595.

Whitaker, B. (2006). Unspeakable love. *Jewish Quarterly, 53*: 21–22.

Wicker, B., Keysers, C., Plailly, J., Royet, J., Gallese, V., & Rizzolatti, G. (2003). Both of us disgusted in my insula: the common neural basis of seeing and feeling disgust. *Neuron, 40*: 655–664.

Williamson, I. R. (2000). Internalized homophobia and health issues affecting lesbians and gay men. *Health Education Research, 15*: 97–107.

Wilson, S. (1995). *The Cradle of Violence: Essays on Psychiatry, Psychoanalysis, and Literature*. London: Jessica Kingsley.

Winston, J. S., Strange, B. A., O'Doherty, J., & Dolan, R. J. (2002). Automatic and intentional brain responses during evaluation of trustworthiness in faces. *Nature Neuroscience, 5*: 277–283.

Wong, M. R., & Cook, D. (1992). Shame and its contribution to PTSD. *Journal of Traumatic Stress, 4*: 557–562.

Woody, S. R., McLean, C., & Klassen, T. (2005). Disgust as a motivator of avoidance of spiders. *Journal of Anxiety Disorders, 19*: 461–475.

Woody, S. R., & Teachman, B. (2000). Intersection of disgust and fear: normative and pathological views. *Clinical Psychology, Science and Practice, 7*: 291–311.

Woody, S. R., & Tolin, D. F. (2002). The relationship between disgust sensitivity and avoidant behavior: studies of clinical and nonclinical samples. *Journal of Anxiety Disorders, 16*: 543–559.

World Health Organization (1992). *The ICD-10 Classification of Mental and Behavioural Disorders: Clinical Descriptions and Diagnostic Guidelines*. Geneva: WHO.

Worthley, D. L., Cole, S. R., Esterman, A., Mehaffey, S., Roosa, N. M., Smith, A., Turnbull, D., & Young, G. P. (2006). Screening for colorectal cancer by faecal occult blood test: why people choose to refuse. *Internal Medicine Journal, 36*: 607–610.

Wright, P., He, G., Shapira, N. A., Goodman, W. K., & Liu, Y. (2004). Disgust and the insula: fMRI responses to pictures of mutilation and contamination. *NeuroReport, 15*: 2347–2351.

Yarkoni, T., Poldrack, R. A., Nichols, T. E., Van Essen, D. C., & Wager, T. D. (2011). Large-scale automated synthesis of human functional neuroimaging data. *Nature Methods, 8*: 665–670.

Yartz, A. R., & Hawk, L. W., Jr. (2002). Addressing the specificity of affective startle modulation: fear versus disgust. *Biological Psychology, 59*: 55–68.

Yehuda, R., & Ledoux, J. (2007). Response variation following trauma: a translational neuroscience approach to understanding PTSD. *Neuron, 56*: 19–32.

Young, I. M. (1990). *Justice and the Politics of Difference*. Princeton, NJ: Princeton University Press.

Young, J. E. (1999). *Cognitive Therapy for Personality Disorders: A Schema-Focused Approach*. Sarasota: Professional Resource Press.

Young, L., Bechara, A., Tranel, D., Damasio, H., Hauser, M., & Damasio, A. (2010). Damage to ventromedial prefrontal cortex impairs judgment of harmful intent. *Neuron, 65*: 845–851.

Zahl, D. L., & Hawton, K. (2004). Repetition of self-harm and subsequent suicide risk: long-term follow-up of 11,583 patients. *British Journal of Psychiatry, 185*: 70–75.

Zaider, T. I., Johnson, J. G., & Cockell, S. J. (2000). Psychiatric comorbidity associated with eating disorder symptomatology among adolescents in the community. *International Journal of Eating Disorders, 28*: 58–67.

Zeeck, A., Stelzer, N., Linster, H. W., Joos, A., & Hartmann, A. (2011). Emotion and eating in binge-eating disorder and obesity. *European Eating Disorders Review, 19*: 426–437.

Zhong, C. -B., & Liljenquist, K. (2006). Washing away your sins: threatened morality and physical cleaning. *Science, 313*: 1451–1452.

Zhong, C. -B., Strejcek, B., & Sivanathan, N. (2010). A clean self can render harsh moral judgment. *Journal of Experimental Social Psychology, 46*: 859–862.

Zila, L. M., & Kiselica, M. S. (2001). Understanding and counselling self-mutilation in female adolescents and young adults. *Journal of Counseling and Development, 79*: 46–52.

Zuroff, D. C., Santor, D., & Mongrain, M. (2005). Dependency, self-criticism, and maladjustment. In: J. S. Auerbach, K. N. Levy, & C. E. Schaffer (Eds.), *Relatedness, Self-Definition and Mental Representation: Essays in Honour of Sidney J. Blatt* (pp. 75–90). London: Taylor & Francis.

# INDEX